FAKED IN CHINA

GLOBAL RESEARCH STUDIES

The Global Research Studies series is part of the Framing
the Global project, an initiative of Indiana University Press
and the Indiana University Center for the Study of Global
Change, funded by the Andrew W. Mellon Foundation.

Advisory Committee

This book is a publication of

INDIANA UNIVERSITY PRESS
Office of Scholarly Publishing
Herman B Wells Library 350
1320 East 10th Street
Bloomington, Indiana 47405 USA

iupress.indiana.edu

The paper used in this publication
meets the minimum requirements
of the American National Standard for
Information Sciences–Permanence
of Paper for Printed Library Materials,
ANSI Z39.48–1992.

*Manufactured in the
United States of America*

*Cataloging information is available
from the Library of Congress.*

ISBN 978-0-253-01839-7 (cloth)
ISBN 978-0-253-01846-5 (paperback)
ISBN 978-0-253-01852-6 (ebook)

1 2 3 4 5 21 20 19 18 17 16 15 16

Faked in China

Nation Branding,
Counterfeit Culture,
and Globalization

Fan Yang

INDIANA UNIVERSITY PRESS

Bloomington & Indianapolis

For Marc, and my parents
Yu Pin and Yang Renshan

Contents

Acknowledgments

THIS WORK BEGAN AT GEORGE MASON UNIVERSITY, WHERE I received funding from a High Potential Fellowship. I am deeply indebted to Paul Smith, who opened my eyes to the dynamic field of cultural studies and pushed me to think about the national question in a more critical light. I am equally grateful to Michael Chang, who first oriented me to the historical and theoretical debates surrounding nations and nationalisms in the Chinese context and beyond. Their continuous encouragement and guidance over the years have undoubtedly helped shape how I think and write about contemporary China and/in globalization.

At GMU, I am most fortunate to have learned from Debra Bergoffen, Jean-Paul Dumont, Dina Copelman, Cindy Fuchs, Rosemary Jann, Mark Sample, Ted Kinnaman, Amal Amireh, and Peter Mandaville, among others. I have also enjoyed and benefited from conversations with Tim Gibson, Roger Lancaster, Denise Albanese, Alok Yadav, Alison Landsberg, John O'Connor, Michelle Carr, Tim Kaposy, Lisa Breglia, J. P. Singh, and many more. I am thankful for the opportunity to have taught in the Honors College and the New Century College, which allowed me to co-design such interdisciplinary courses as Global Networks and Communities; I have learned a great deal from my fellow instructors and students, who have made this experience most enriching.

I owe special thanks to my wonderful colleagues in the Department of Media and Communication Studies (MCS) at the University of Maryland, Baltimore County (UMBC). Jason Loviglio, the chair of the department, is the most supportive mentor that a junior faculty member could wish for. I simply cannot thank him enough for his enthusiasm, his unending insights, and his constructive comments on numerous drafts of my work. Rebecca Adelman has been a role model of excellence. I thank her for generously sharing her (always beautifully written) work with me and giving me such illuminating feedback on my own writing. I have learned about (new) media and technology from Donald Snyder in more ways than I can keep track of, and I appreciated the opportunity to discuss my research with the students in his Senior Capstone Seminar in Fall 2011. Etoy Hamlin and Abigail Granger have set new standards for professionalism; their skillful administrative support has been indispensible.

The completion of the manuscript has benefited from a Summer Faculty Fellowship, an Undergraduate Research Assistantship Support award, and a Dresher Center Summer Faculty Research Fellowship at UMBC. I have enjoyed talking about research and other fun stuff with an amazing group of scholars at various gatherings on and off campus, especially Constantine Vaporis, Anna Shields, Nicole King, Edward Larkey, Amy Bhatt, Viviana MacManus, Kate Drabinski, Ana Oskoz, Rebecca Boehling, Craig Saper, Christine Mallinson, Kimberly Moffitt, Christine Mair, Kara Hunt, Meredith Oyen, Jessica Berman, Beverly Bickel, Scott Casper, Tamara Bhalla, Theodore Gonzalves, and Bill Shewbridge. Many thanks to Rebecca Boehling and Jessica Berman for the opportunity to present my work in progress at the Dresher Center for the Humanities, where the exchanges are always thoughtful and engaging.

My students at UMBC have been a constant source of inspiration. Their willingness to ask hard questions and unwillingness to settle for easy answers have continuously challenged and energized me in the classroom and in my scholarly work. I thank them for sharing their ideas and stories with me. More than a few of them have offered fresh perspectives on the objects I examine, and I particularly appreciated the input of Gabriel Fishbein, Ela Locke, Gina Gribbin, and Robbin Lee.

At the many events and conferences where I presented my research, I have gained valuable insights from Cara Wallis, Wendy Chun, Lisa Nakamura, John Durham Peters, Michael Keane, Henry Siling Li, Xiaoming Wang, Catalina Cortes Severino, Nitin Govil, Radha Hegde, Sumita Chakravarty, Geetha Ganapathy-Doré, Jinying Li, Jiayan Mi, Philip Rosen, Lynne Joyrich, Yew Kong Leong, Richard White, Andrew Ross,

Laikwan Pang, Nick Couldry, Toby Miller, Nitin Govil, Ken Wissoker, Marcella Szablewicz, Jack Linchuan Qiu, Silvia Lindtner, Gil Rodman, Wen Jin, Yu-Fang Cho, Martin Fredriksson, Stephen C. K. Chan, Jia Tan, and Xu Miaomiao, among many others. Thanks especially to Rob Gehl, who invited me to the 2011 Frontiers of New Media Symposium at the University of Utah. The time I spent with the participants of the symposium has been most memorable.

I cannot express enough gratitude for the long-time friendship, support, and intellectual stimulation provided by Katy Razzano, Lia Uy-Tioco, Xiang (Ellen) He, Rob Gehl, Pia Møller, Loubna Skalli, Leah Perry, Ludy Grandas, Olga Herrera, Sean Andrews, Jaafar Aksikas, Mika'il Petin, Vicki Watts, Lisa Andion, Tara Sheoran, Win Malaiwong, Young A Jung, Daniel Anderson, Gavin Mueller, Rachel Martin, Michael Lecker, Dai Dun, Helen Margiotti, and Daniel Hanna, among others. Special thanks to Ellen for making it possible for me to interview Liu Wanyong and Jiang Xinjie, the two investigative journalists at *China Youth Daily*. I am grateful to Liu and Jiang for sharing their keen observations of the changing landscape of Chinese media in general and their experience covering the demolition of the Silk Street Market in particular.

As I finalize the manuscript, I have come to the realization that many URLs of once existing web pages are no longer available. While this fleeting status of the online "archive" certainly points to the challenges ahead for those of us who aspire to continuously historicize the present, it also seems to make the study of contemporary culture all the more important. After all, the rate of disappearance in media contents is arguably dwarfed by the speed at which Chinese reality is changing on the ground, as the Silk Street case quite powerfully illustrates. Because of this, I would very much like to thank those (oftentimes anonymous) individuals who have partaken in the meaning-making practices that have become the focus of this book. I feel fortunate to have had the opportunity to document and engage (some of) their voices in rethinking what culture means, and what it can be, in contemporary China.

A portion of the introduction appeared in my article, "China's 'Fake' Apple Store: Branded Space, Intellectual Property and the Global Culture Industry," *Theory, Culture & Society* 31, no. 4 (July 2014): 71–96. An earlier version of chapter 2 is scheduled to be published in *positions: asia critique* 24 (2016) as "From 'Bandit Cell Phones' to Branding the Nation: Three Moments of *Shanzhai* in WTO-era China." I thank the publishers (SAGE and Duke University Press) for permission to reproduce the material here.

I have learned much from all of the anonymous reviewers who have read my work and offered helpful suggestions at various stages of the revision process. I thank Rebecca Tolen, my editor at Indiana University Press, for having faith in this project and for electing to include it in the exciting new series Global Research Studies, funded by the Andrew W. Mellon Foundation. I am also grateful to Mollie Ables, Rhonda Vander Dussen, Michelle Sybert, and Sarah Jacobi for their excellent editorial support. Thanks especially to my copyeditor James Cappio for his remarkable attention to detail. I am, of course, responsible for all of the mistakes that remain.

Lastly, and most importantly, I wish to thank my husband Marc and my parents for their unfailing love, patience, and generosity. To them I dedicate this book.

List of Frequently Used Translations and Transliterations

American Dreams in China	*Zhongguo Hehuoren* (film title)
Chinese Dream	Zhongguomeng
Crazy Stone	*Fengkuang de Shitou* (film title)
Shanzhai	"Mountain fortress," connoting Robin Hood–like banditry and often used to describe copycat products and cultural practices
Shanzhaiji	Shanzhai cell phones, or "fake brand" cell phones
Silk Street	Xiushui Jie
Silk Alley	*Xiushui Jie* (film title)

The spelling of Chinese words follows the *pinyin* system.

List of Abbreviations

ADIC	*American Dreams in China* (the film)
AIC	Administration of Industry and Commerce
CCIA	Creative China Industrial Alliance
CCTV	China Central Television
CNN	Cable News Network
COOL	country-of-origin labels
EES	Educational Exams Services (a fictional representation of ETS)
ETS	Educational Testing Services
FDI	foreign direct investment
ICT	information communication technology
IPR	intellectual property rights
KFC	Kentucky Fried Chicken
MNC	multi-national corporation
MTK	MediaTek (Taiwan)
NASDAQ	National Association of Securities Dealers Automated Quotations System
PRC	People's Republic of China
PNTR	Permanent Normal Trading Relations
RMB	Renminbi (Chinese yuan)
R&D	research and development
ROO	Rules of Origin

SEZ	special economic zone
SOE	state-owned enterprise
SSAM	Silk Street Apparel Market Ltd.
TOEFL	Test of English as a Foreign Language
TRIPS	Trade-Related Aspects of Intellectual Property Rights
USTR	Office of the United States Trade Representative
VCD	video compact disc
WIPO	World Intellectual Property Organization
WTO	World Trade Organization

FAKED IN CHINA

Introduction

AT THE GRAND OPENING CEREMONY OF THE 2008 BEIJING Olympics, two fakes entered the global media spotlight more dramatically than the spectacle itself. Lin Miaoke, the young girl who performed the song that accompanied the entry of the Chinese national flag, turned out to be lip-synching to the voice of Yang Peiyi, another girl whose look was deemed less photogenic. The firework display that brought the twenty-nine Olympic "footprints" to the stadium – a collaboration between the famed artist Cai Guoqiang and filmmaker Zhang Yimou – was also found to be pre-recorded footage rather than live projection. Four years later, at the London Olympics, "faked in China" dramas continued to unfold when the BBC confirmed that an Egyptian Olympian's workout bags, which bore the Nike trademark in front and an Adidas logo on the zippers, were counterfeits of Chinese origin.

While these "faking" events appear to be quite distinct at first sight, they share more commonalities than one might think. In Beijing, the gaze of global news media rendered it difficult for the Chinese state to retain full control over the representation of the nation's image. In London, the counterfeit objects found outside China's sovereign borders were identified as Chinese, even though the state had little direct input into their production and circulation. In both cases, objects faked in China emerged in a global context; they generated meanings about the Chinese nation not as an immediate result of state actions, but in spite of them. Between the nation and the state, then, there exists a schism of sorts. Yet what produces this schism is not easily discerned. If the Beijing Olympics as a global media spectacle naturally undermines the

1

state's representational authority over a unified national self, the Egyptian team's faked-in-China accessories also lay claim to the nation under conditions not entirely of the state's own choosing. How do these global conditions present cultural challenges for twenty-first-century China? This is the question that motivates this investigation.

The first decade of the second millennium has seen no shortage of accounts in mass media and academia alike about a so-called rising China. Dominant within this discourse is a narrative of economic ascent. Oftentimes, the story is invoked in close relation to a country-of-origin label, "Made in China." Since China's accession to the World Trade Organization (WTO) in 2001, "Made in China" has become nothing less than an emblem of job loss and capital flight for a great number of people in the West. At the tenth anniversary of the September 11 attacks, the same year that China overtook Japan to become the world's second largest economy, the *Financial Times* even headlined the "end of U.S. hegemony," pronouncing that "the three most important words in the past decade were not 'war on terror' but 'made in China.'"[1] To be sure, more recent reports in the United States suggest that China's rising labor costs, along with other factors, herald the mythical return of American manufacturing jobs. Even Apple, now the world's most valuable company, whose products are assembled in gigantic factories located in China, is touting that its new Mac Pros are "made in America."[2] If these accounts indicate that the danger of "Made in China" is waning, the endless news outbursts about Chinese counterfeits seem to suggest that the hazard of "faked in China" is on the rise. The 2011 media sensation surrounding an American expat's discovery of a fake Apple Store in China serves as a case in point. The incident even made its way into the second nationally televised debate of the 2012 presidential election, as part of Mitt Romney's accusation that China had stolen American intellectual property. What the Republican candidate did not seem to realize, though, was that the fake store actually displayed and sold genuine Apple products originally assembled in China.

While "China fakes" stories may well be operating as a kind of framing device for Euro-America to cope with the perceived threat of China, the cultural framework from which they emerge is decidedly more complex. Why, one may ask, should an unauthorized distributor of Apple products be judged to be selling fakes when the gadgets sold there were as real as those sold in authorized stores? Here, the place of production – as suggested by the "Made in China" label on the Apple products sold in the real and fake stores alike – appears to be less relevant in authenticating the goods than the embodiment of the Apple brand in the store design, the illicit imitation of which is immediately chastised as an act of fakery. Much like the "fake" accusations at the Beijing Olympics, incidents like this pose some limits on the extent to which claims about China's rise can be authenticated. After all, it is not China the manufacturer but the globalizing intellectual property rights (IPR) regime that provides the criteria for distinguishing what is real and what is not. China's economic prowess, however daunting, is seemingly offset by the state's inability to control and shape meanings in the realm of culture. Despite the government's continuous attempts to crack down on IPR offenses, the nation's global reputation remains that of a thief, one that routinely steals ideas, especially from those nation-states long secured at the higher end of the value-adding chain.

This global reputation as a "making and faking" nation has indeed triggered a state response in WTO-era China. A policy mandate supported by multiple state institutions, "From Made in China to Created in China," surfaced around 2001 when China was set to become an Olympics host as well as a WTO member. This national policy has a pronounced intent to upgrade the nation's profile from a producer of global goods to a creator of its own IPR-eligible brands. On the surface, the blueprint could not be more suitably chosen; not only does it allow the Chinese state to ratify its new status within the WTO, it also enables the government to project a hopeful national future for its domestic citizenry. However, as I will argue in this book, the cultural conditions that gave rise to this policy, as well as the ideological contestations it underwent during the first decade of the twenty-first century, epitomize China's cultural predicament within its intensified global integration.

Faked in China, then, is an attempt at an alternative account of China's rise in contemporary globalization. It places a distinct emphasis on the cultural – that is, the realm of meaning making – not to move away from the economic but instead to consider the two spheres as mutually constitutive and only separable for analytical purposes.[3] To be sure, IPR-

related issues by no means encompass all dimensions of the social transformations that China has undergone recently. Other aspects of China's
economic restructuring after entering the WTO, such as the downsizing
of state-owned enterprises and the opening of agricultural and finance
sectors to foreign competition, likely exert greater impact on the national
economy in GDP-related terms.[4] However, questions of IPR are more
closely tied to questions about _culture_ and _power,_ which by convention
are associated with nation and state, respectively. As I will demonstrate,
IPR presents a privileged site for investigating globalization's uneven
cultural effects on the Chinese nation-state precisely because it is a globalizing cultural regime. The operation of this regime, which has given
rise to myriad artifacts "faked in China," therefore reflects a condition
under which the links between nation and culture, as well as those between state and power, are increasingly destabilized. If the hyphen that
links state to nation, as Arjun Appadurai points out, "is now less an icon
of conjuncture than an index of disjuncture,"[5] what these objects bring
into view are precisely the profound discordances between the Chinese
nation and the Chinese state after 2001.

In the chapters that follow, I will trace the journeys of several cultural artifacts "faked in China." These objects are chosen because they
animate the dynamic interactions between two cultural manifestations
of IPR's global impact. The first is what I call a "nation-branding" project, which is captured by the slogan "From Made in China to Created
in China." If this discourse of "national upgrade" is in large part a
state-sponsored policy formation under the influence of IPR, it clashes
in multiple ways with another, more diffused, cultural practice that I
call "counterfeit culture." Traversing multiple geographical and media
sites, counterfeit culture encompasses the transnational making, selling, copying, imitating and buying of unauthorized brand name and
audiovisual products. It interacts with WTO-era China's nation branding
to produce wide-ranging artifacts, from knockoff mobile phones to online video spoofs, from pirate filmmaking to urban counterfeit bazaars.
Given the complexity of these cultural formations, I have no intent to
fully document the project of nation branding,[6] nor do I wish to offer an
exhaustive account of counterfeit culture.[7] Rather, I think of the interactions between the two as generative of resources for discerning the con-

tradictory impact of IPR on the Chinese nation-state. "Faked in China" artifacts are therefore treated as symptoms of IPR's cultural operations. The discursive and material conditions that give shape and meaning to these objects, then, constitute the focal points of my analysis, which in turn serve to illuminate the nation-state disjuncture of WTO-era China.

Thus, this book is simultaneously an analysis of China's cultural transformation following its WTO entry through the specific lens of IPR, and an examination of the cultural work that IPR has carried out in the Chinese context. Much exciting work has been done to document IPR's economic and legal ascent on the global stage, including its propagation of a "new global common sense."[8] Less explored, however, is the question of IPR's *cultural impact* on the nation-state, particularly in the context of the developing world. This question, of course, must be situated within broader engagement with globalization's uneven cultural workings in various (not exclusively but especially) non-Western settings – a central concern for those long immersed in the "cultural imperialism" debate. While *Faked in China* is in part motivated by the urge to revitalize the critical legacy of this debate, it also adopts a more rigorous approach to the notions of culture and nation in globalization. I will delineate this approach in the next section so as to clarify a central claim of the book, that IPR's contradictory impact manifests itself as WTO-era China's cultural dilemma.

CULTURE AND NATION IN GLOBALIZATION

The concept of culture has undergone continuous, reflexive unpacking in interdisciplinary fields like cultural studies, which have usefully incorporated anthropological and literary perspectives to encompass the multifarious ways in which people make sense of their lives. Yet for many the "national" remains a commonly used category for identifying cultural differences. This is especially the case in the vast literature on cultural imperialism since the 1960s. In much of this literature, the term "cultural imperialism" implies the "domination of one national culture by another."[9] This way of characterizing domination, however, relies on a problematic conception of the nation as state defined and territorially bound, and therefore as something that can be "invaded" by cultural as well as military means. The emphasis on "invasion," of course, has roots in the genealogy of imperialism, the critical examination of which often focuses on the unequal relations of power *between* nation-states. For instance, in Vladimir Lenin's analysis of imperialism as "the highest stage of capitalism," he maintains that it entails "the exploitation of an increasing number of small or weak nations by a handful of the richest or most powerful nations."[10] While the economic relations of domination between many developed and developing nation-states no doubt continue to exist, a more in-depth study of contemporary globalization's uneven cultural impact – a hallmark of the "cultural imperialism" discourse – necessarily entails a re-consideration of the nation-state as a unified framework for cultural and social analysis.

The reasons for this rethinking are two-pronged: not only are nations themselves cultural artifacts imagined into being, as the rich and expansive scholarship since Benedict Anderson has come to demonstrate,[11] contemporary globalization has also rendered the cultural conditions for imagining a national community ever more shifting and amorphous. In addition to long-standing local, regional, ethnic, and other differences in cultural practices that do not always align with the nation's geopolitical grid, today's global media landscape, shaped powerfully by the transnationalized operation of multinational media conglomerates, is also arguably distinct from the era of print capitalism in Anderson's account. While eighteenth-century reading publics primarily based their imagining of a national space on a linguistically conjured simultaneity,[12] media globalization and its localizing counterpart have expanded the possibilities for "imagined communities" to assume supra- or subnational forms. The emergence of these supranational or subnational types of imagined communities, rather than displacing national ties, often coexists with the national one. For instance, global sporting events like the Olympics and the World Cup, when transmitted live across the world, are moments of global simultaneity that enable viewers to imagine a community bigger than the national one. But watching the Olympics hardly weakens audience members' sense of national belonging; more often than not, it produces moments of both nationalistic feelings and cosmopolitan dreams, as demonstrated by the continued enthusiasm toward these Games in different parts of the world. Alternatively, subnational communities of belonging are just as imaginable. Viewers who choose to watch news on a local television channel rather than a national one, for example, do not necessarily forego their national sense of belonging the minute they turn to local issues that demand their more immediate attention.

The co-existence of these imagined supra- and subnational communities with the national one is complicated by another configuration: the imagining of the national community itself is no longer limited to state-defined territories. The trope of transnational "Chineseness" serves as a case in point. As Aihwa Ong argues, the "overseas Chinese" communities have become the target for the academic revival of Confucianism in post-Mao China. The idea was to construct an ethnically and culturally deterritorialized China so as to incorporate successful Chinese business people, especially those in the Pacific Rim, into the state's vision for a "flexible citizenship."[13] Conversely, as Appadurai points out, migrants moving within and across nation-states have come to inhabit "imagined worlds" – built upon a set of "*scapes*" rather than territories – that "contest and sometimes even subvert" those state-initiated and instrumentally organized communities.[14] Such "deterritorialized groupings," from Hindus to Basques and Sikhs to Quebecois, often "seek to create states of their own or carve pieces out of existing states."[15]

The eruption of these imaginable communities or worlds speaks to John Tomlinson's claim that globalization, rather than erasing identity, indeed proliferates it. By spreading its institutional makeup (the nation-state, the separation between production and consumption, urbanization, and so on), the globalization of Western modernity "produces 'identity' where none existed – where before there were perhaps more particular, more inchoate, less socially policed belongings."[16] For Tomlinson, the production of these cultural identities below and beyond the national one is "mixed in its blessings."[17] At the very least, they do not always conform to, and sometimes even challenge, the formal affiliations defined by the state. In this sense, the pluralization of identities does present a kind of threat – not to a unified national identity per se but to the state's routine efforts in solidifying that identity. This tension between the state project of nation building and the proliferating resources for identity formation in globalization is indeed fully expressed in the "faking" incident at the Beijing Games.[18] The global news media, as extensions of the institutional makeup of Western modernity and an integral part of the global market economy, have quite explicitly competed with the state in this case to produce cultural meanings about the nation – meanings that did not emanate from the state's propaganda machine but challenged the state's ability to secure its cultural tie with the nation.

This diminished "state privilege"[19] in laying claim to a unified national culture within a globalized, market-driven media landscape provides a more promising opening to re-examine the uneven cultural effects of globalization. Once the category of the nation-state is problematized as a natural unit of culture, it becomes difficult to substantiate the claim that globalization encroaches upon "national cultures" through a set of "imperialistic" mechanisms. The challenge, then, is to venture a critique of unequal relations of power while remaining sensitive to the complex forces that give rise to the nation as a cultural form and to the national as one of the many ways of conjuring senses of belonging. If a crucial question remains for Tomlinson as to "how nimble and reflexively attuned state apparatuses are capable of becoming" under the changing conditions of globalization,[20] it would appear that the category of the state should be subject to a cultural analysis of a more rigorous kind. Indeed, the attempt at a critical upgrade of cultural imperialism requires that we not only recognize the "embattled" relationship between the nation and the state,[21] but also look deeper into the ways in which the state is itself a cultural formation subject to global forces not entirely of its own choosing.

In this sense, I pick up where Tomlinson left off to explore how globalization exerts cultural impact on the nation and the state simultaneously but differently. A key methodological move I undertake is to locate "China" in a number of entangled local, national, and global situations prompted by struggles with IPR. These situations enact the tensions and contradictions that underlie the cultural transformation of WTO-era China, both as a nation and as a state. IPR, then, serves as a lens through which the otherwise abstract impact of the global on the national may be scrutinized in specific locales, amid the production, circulation, and consumption of myriad artifacts and practices. This

is not to presume that IPR encompasses all dimensions of globalization's cultural impact. Rather, what is emphasized is IPR's operation as
a globalizing cultural system, a conception that serves to explain why
IPR constitutes an apt prism through which to more critically discern
the workings of globalization as cultural imperialism, particularly in a
non-Western setting like China.

IPR AND CULTURAL IMPERIALISM

While the historical emergence of IPR can be traced back to the multifarious development of trademark, patent, and copyright since the
Middle Ages, the evolution of IPR is closely intertwined with the development of modern capitalism and its global expansion.[22] The inclusion
of the Agreement on Trade Related Aspects of Intellectual Property
Rights (TRIPs) as a "founding component" of the WTO (which replaced
the General Agreement on Tariffs and Trade in 1995) signaled the rise
of IPR "to the forefront of global policymaking."[23] In this sense, to speak
of IPR as a globalizing system is to recognize that it involves a wide range
of governmental and nongovernmental "stakeholders" whose activities
extend beyond the "legal institution of the state."[24]

Yet to characterize this system as a cultural one is to reckon a shift
in perspective on culture triggered by contemporary globalization that
is, culture is increasingly deterritorialized from a nation-specific and
state-defined context and needs to be re-conceptualized as such. There
is, in Tomlinson's words, a "reciprocal relationship" between culture
and globalization: as a set of symbols and practices that enable the sense
making of everyday life, culture provides the key "conceptual vocabulary" to understanding globalization, much as globalization shapes the
"fabric of cultural experience" and "affect[s] our sense of what culture
is in the modern world."[25] The American blogger's discovery of the fake
Apple store in Kunming, China, helps to explain the cultural work of the
IPR regime by illustrating this reciprocal relationship quite vividly. For
one thing, the event invokes a number of material conditions that "globalization" has come to signify. The American expat's presence in China
is an obvious instance of the migration of people across national borders. Her blog utilizes the internet, a global communication network

that deploys an intricate mode of transmission and control to allow the instantaneous transfer of information across vast distances. The manufacturing of Apple products in China conforms to the logic of the global movement of capital in search of cheaper labor and materials. The making of the fake Apple Store into a media event was enabled by several transnational flows, from goods and people – migrant workers, bloggers, and journalists, among others – to advertising imageries and branded signs. All of these conditions point to the presence of extensive global networks and intensive transnational, border-crossing activities.

How do these processes promote a deterritorialized notion of culture? For the American blogger to recognize the Kunming store as an Apple branch at all, she would need to draw from her knowledge of the authentic Apple stores in America or elsewhere. To identify the store as a fake, she would have to operate within a specific symbolic system consisting of the legal lexicon of IPR. After all, it is this system that lends legitimacy to the distinction between the real (that is, the authorized "proper" copy) and the fake (that is, the unauthorized "improper" copy). She then took up the media tool of the blog to communicate this experience to an English-speaking audience, most of whom do not reside in China. The circulation of her blog post gave rise to follow-up coverage in multiple international news media outlets, which added the news story to the entertainment mix for more people who had perhaps never set foot in Kunming. Most significantly, the international coverage of the store led to a series of local investigations; the municipal authorities eventually ordered the shop's closure, ostensibly because it operated without a business license. In all of these moments, the local phenomenon of the Kunming Apple Store is lifted out of its physical surroundings through a multiplicity of representational systems. Its fame and fate allow us to observe "the simultaneous penetration of local worlds by distant forces, and the dislodging of everyday meanings from their 'anchors' in the local environment."[26] To the extent that the Kunming Apple Store emerged in a Chinese city, its global visibility was no doubt enmeshed in a dense collection of transnational circuits. In this sense, the globalizing system of IPR has altered the context of meaning making – that is, culture – in the particular locale of Kunming. On the other hand, the global spread of news stories about the store, which helped shape the actions of local authorities, exemplifies the fact that culture as a meaning-making system not only serves to represent but also to inform actions. It is precisely in these terms that globalization and culture enter a reciprocal relation: while culture allows us to discern the local-global dynamics that characterize globalization, globalization promotes an understanding of culture not as fixed and bounded but as constantly shifting and exerting impact on the social world.

What this example brings to light is a conceptual framework better suited for delineating IPR's (and indeed globalization's) cultural impact. Among the many paradoxes that one may discern in the fake Apple Store event, one stands out perhaps more prominently than others. As the official accounts from the provincial Administration of Industry and Commerce indicate, the investigation of Kunming's fake stores was carried out in response to the global news coverage of the event.[27] Why did a state entity see the need to take action only when the global exposure of a local artifact is re circulated back into the nation?

Questions like this prompt a closer examination of the cultural work of the IPR regime in shaping the WTO-era Chinese state. To be sure, the state plays a role in directing, promoting, and regulating the flows of the global economy. The reason that an Apple product is made in China in the first place has to do with post-Mao China's Reform and Opening Up state policies, which began in 1978 and welcomed an influx of finance capital in the form of foreign direct investment. At the same time, Apple products are sold at a higher price in China because of the state imposition of tariffs on imports, in part to nurture a nascent national industry of information technologies (chapter 2). The state, then, serves as an institutional actor in the global economic system, simultaneously aiding the flows of capital and checking the movement of goods across borders. On the other hand, the state investigated and eventually closed the store only after foreign media reported the incident. In this case, the state engaged in more of a *reaction*, as is arguably true for many state crackdowns on counterfeits over the years, including those that preceded the Beijing Games (chapter 4). While the IPR regime appears to be the structure that informs this state reaction, *how* this system exerts its cultural impact is not as easy to discern. The latter is precisely what I seek to unpack by conceptualizing the state – and not just the

I.1. Kunming's "fake" Apple Store stays open as "Smart Store" in 2014.

nation – as a problematic that is itself constituted within a set of global forces embodied by IPR.

Once the state is re-conceptualized as being in flux, IPR's uneven cultural impact on the nation-state becomes a productive way to re-open the question of power in contemporary globalization. Indeed, this re-conceptualization corresponds to Tomlinson's proposal to move from a "spatial, synchronic perspective" to a historical one in order to better delineate the workings of cultural imperialism. Central to his articulation of the unequal power relations of globalization is the category of the "imaginary," a concept borrowed from the seminal work on the "social imaginary" by Cornelius Castoriadis. Defined as a pre-rational, pre-symbolic order that shapes the particular forms of institutions in a society, the social imaginary offers a way to explain why certain institutional forms are chosen over others in a specific place and time. Often these choices cannot be explained from a functionalist perspective, because even when institutions across different societies serve similar structural purposes, they still take different cultural forms.[28] The nation state is one such institutional entity, and the notion of the imaginary allows us to rethink its constitution under the cultural influence of global modernity. Rather than considering this influence as a cultural imposition upon already constituted nation-states, the imaginary is better seen as conditioning the kinds of nation states that are imaginable at particular historical conjunctures.

The question of unequal relations of power reemerges precisely at the level of the production of the imaginary, a subtle force that privileges certain visions for the nation-state over others. As I argue in this book, the IPR regime, legally imposed upon Third World countries through global structures like the WTO, proffers an "imaginary of the brand" that influences the cultural formation of the Chinese state in the WTO era. Like other imaginaries stemming from Western modernity, such as "development," the imaginary of the brand works to "enforce a new set of moral norms,"[29] from naturalized notions of ownership and property rights to legally demarcated criteria for distinguishing "proper" from "illicit" (or pirate) copies. In doing so, it has become an important ideological state apparatus that participates in the reification of global capitalism.[30] A key inflection of this reification on the level of the nation-states is the WTO's establishment of a formal equivalence between members based on an Enlightenment-inspired ideology of equality. This is evidenced perhaps most distinctly by the WTO's insistence that "All countries, big or small, weak or powerful, have to follow broadly the same rules," despite the immense differences in size, population, resources, and so on between actual nations.[31] In other words, it is through masking the unevenness of power among member states that IPR is conjured as a "quasi-objective social totality," if not a governing cultural network that operates through a performative acceptance of the "social contract."[32] China's joining of the WTO, which required it to upgrade its intellectual property laws "to be virtually consistent with TRIPs,"[33] can be seen as part of the process by which it is obliged to "become the same as the West."[34] This movement toward "general equivalence" is part and parcel of what Dan Vukovich calls a kind of "new orientalism" – "not just the production of knowledge about an 'area' but the would-be management and administration of the area for economic, political and cultural-symbolic benefit."[35]

At the same time, the impact of IPR's imaginary of the brand in homogenizing the state is only part of the story. In this study I turn to the interactions between nation branding and counterfeit culture – two objects that are informed and shaped by the globalizing IPR regime that in turn give rise to competing visions for the nation and the state. While the nation-branding project manifests IPR's work in constructing the state as a "global type,"[36] the nation also emerges as a marker of cultural difference among the various publics of counterfeit culture. The contestations between these visions as they are manifested within the nation-state disjuncture present a historically specific challenge faced by China after its WTO entry. This challenge is what I call a cultural dilemma. In other words, this book aims to revisit globalization not in terms of what it destroys but what it produces – sameness and difference at once. Brands and counterfeits, two cultural forms produced in the IPR regime, stand out perhaps most prominently as embodiments of IPR's cultural work in promoting homogenization and heterogenization simultaneously. Our task, then, is to examine how IPR's imaginary of the brand works to prevent or contain the production of alternative national visions to those prescribed by Western modernity, as WTO-era China continues to participate in "the struggle over the means of production of multiple modernities."[37]

It is in this sense that this book seeks to revive a critique of cultural imperialism. It goes beyond debunking a territorially bound notion of national culture and related critiques of the power imbalance between states, instead seeking to articulate the cultural impact of IPR as a global structure. If a global system has "its own processes and mechanisms" that are different from the "the national form of integration,"[38] the workings of the cultural forms that IPR produces demand a different analytical lens than the one provided by a nation-based framework. In other words, to engage IPR's uneven effects on the nation-state more seriously, we need a more sophisticated model of how brands and counterfeits operate as "cultures of circulation."[39]

THE BRAND AND THE COUNTERFEIT

Brands permeate our common vocabulary and everyday life. They make visible aspects of global production, distribution, and consumption perhaps more powerfully than any other cultural forms. Stories of globalization are often told to a mass audience through the biographies of global brands like Nike and Apple, in part because of their immense visibility.[40] The making of brands emblematizes the increased media convergence since the advent of digital technologies, a process characterized by the interaction and migration of industries, users, and content across multiple media platforms.[41] The most recognized logos, like Coca-Cola and McDonald's, enjoy an almost ubiquitous global presence, thanks to continuously staged multi- or transmedia campaigns that encompass print, electronic, and digital forms.

It comes as no surprise that when conceptualizing their account of the "global culture industry," Scott Lash and Celia Lury suggest that the brand is the archetype of a "thingified" culture. By "global," they imply two dimensions, one extensive and the other intensive. The extensive dimension refers to the expansion of global operations on the part of Euro-American brand owners after 1975, a period that coincides with the onset of contemporary globalization. The intensive dimension refers to the collapse of the cultural into the economic and vice versa.

It launched a new mode of capitalist accumulation that is distinct from the Frankfurt School's version of the classical (or national) culture industry. In Lash and Lury's global culture industry, culture is no longer representation but the "mediation of things"; cultural forms like the brand are performative objects that emerge from a meaning-generative process. They are produced in circulation, not just transmitted by it.[42] For example, the Apple brand cult in China and around the world is as attributable to word-of-mouth marketing as to the company's advertising efforts. Apple fans actively circulate Apple-related news and updates, both online and offline. In doing so, they help to produce meanings about the brand and collectively contribute to the brand's name recognition in the process.

The brand, therefore, is a cultural object "created by the interactions between specific types of circulating forms and the interpretive communities built around them."[43] The same can be said about the counterfeit. The *New Oxford American Dictionary* defines a counterfeit object as a product "made in exact imitation of something valuable or important with the intention to deceive or defraud."[44] In the more specialized IPR literature, the act of counterfeiting is "the knowing duplication of a product by a party who wishes to usurp the brand or trademark of another."[45] It is a violation in the realm of "industrial property," which encompasses patents, industrial designs, trademarks, service marks, and geographical destinations. As such, it is distinguishable from "piracy," which refers to the infringement of copyright and is reserved for the reproduction of "artistic creations" or "technology-based works."[46] However, in common English usage as well as journalistic and management accounts, the distinction between counterfeiting and piracy is often blurred. "Counterfeit" is used interchangeably with "fake," "knockoff," "bootleg," and "pirate copy," among others. In a growing body of journalistic accounts all of these carry a derogatory meaning that is associated with acts of "stealing," "illicit trade," and in the worst-case scenario, complicity with terrorist acts and networks.[47]

These accounts suggest that just like the brand, the counterfeit's objecthood emerges in a process of circulation. Its formation depends upon a community of meaning makers who are cognizant of the institutional arrangement that authorizes the brand's "original" status. While derivative of the brand, the counterfeit remains metonymically as well as materially linked to it; both operate to signify "the dynamic interactions between part (the commodity) and whole (brand)."[48] From the standpoint of production, it is worth noting that word "counterfeit" contains the Latin roots *contra-* (in opposition) and *facere* (make).[49] A counterfeit is therefore "counter-made." It implies an oppositional relation to what is simply "made" – that is, produced under normal, if not normalized, conditions. From the standpoint of consumption, a counterfeit is recognized based on this relation to the real. Without some kind of reference to the brand, the "legit," the authentic, the genuine, the counterfeit cannot constitute itself as such. Its identity only comes into being through exchange, which depends on the recognition of counterfeit as relational to the IPR-protected, authorized branded commodity. This recognition is achieved by a conception of the object as a less valuable copy (or as valuable, as when "the fake" is taken to be "the real"). In other words, a counterfeit object assumes a referential identity when it is interpreted and evaluated in the act of exchange.

In this sense, the counterfeit matches the brand in emblematizing an "intensive economy" predicated upon information.[50] The "crime" of counterfeiting broadly defined also suggests a global-extensive mode of operation. The "second-oldest profession" according to intellectual property lawyers,[51] the production of counterfeits is "no longer a localized industry" but "a sophisticated global business" specializing in wide-ranging goods.[52] According to the Organization for Economic Cooperation and Development, the market value of internationally traded counterfeit goods is estimated at $250 billion in 2007.[53] These counterfeiting activities are also noted to be on the rise thanks to the expansion of global communication networks and deregulated commodity flows, among other things.

Meanwhile, the consumption of counterfeit goods has long been a transnational practice. Kuala Lumpur's Petaling Street, Canal Street in New York, and the K Street corridor in Washington, DC, among many others, are famous markets for counterfeit bargains. In post-Communist Lithuania, market traders travel to places as far as the United Arab Emirates and Turkey to import falsified brand-name products before putting fake labels of origin on them to convey a sense of "Western" authenticity.[54] The Silk Street Market in Beijing (chapter 4) is listed in numerous English-language guidebooks as a must-visit site for international tourists, who arrive daily in large buses and are greeted by sales staff fluent in multi-lingual haggling terms.

The transnational character of counterfeit practice, however, is dwarfed by China's presence in the American public imagination as the nation "who makes and fakes."[55] Since at least the 1990s, the "faking" nation has been the location of a great number of counterfeit factories and markets. As a brochure from the Anti-Counterfeiting Group points out, it "is cited by every Western country as the largest single source of counterfeit products today."[56] The Office of the United States Trade Representative (USTR) and the European Commission both report that the total number of seized counterfeit goods of Chinese origin far exceeds those of other countries. Global counterfeiting networks emanating from China sell consumer items, health products, drugs, and even defense-related computer chips through online channels or underground border-crossing trade routes.[57] Understandably, the nation beats forty-five other countries to be No. 1 on USTR's Priority Watch List.[58]

The spectacular rise of China as a faking nation is often mystified in ahistorical, essentialist claims about China's "cultural" tendency to violate intellectual property rights. For instance, in *Poorly Made in China,* a "first hand" account that claims to unveil the dark side of China's manufacturing industry, Paul Midler, a business consultant, cites a story of Qing-dynasty Emperor Qianlong, who praised a craftsman's talent to have perfectly counterfeited a Ming-dynasty jade piece. For Midler, this kind of "reverence" for the fake serves as evidence for "the cultural origins" of the nation's counterfeit culture in the present.[59] Midler's definition of China's "counterfeit culture," although not without empirical support, is certainly questionable, considering that China is not the only country in history that has had to bear the notoriety of being called "the counterfeit nation." The "Made in Germany" label in late nineteenth-century Britain and "Made in Japan" in the United States in the 1980s are two well-known precedents. The United States itself, in its first decades, relied on "theft of foreign-owned technology" to expand its industries.[60] Contemporary China also does not monopolize all market segments of the counterfeit trade. For instance, South Korea is known as the world capital of "supercopies" – that is, "meticulous imitations of luxury goods,"[61] whereas Italy specializes in "quality counterfeits" that boast genuine leather and craftsmanship.[62]

If these instances help to discredit the cultural-essentialist view, they also prompt us to examine the "faked in China" discourse as a historical formation.[63] As Kavita Philip has argued, the rise of "China" as a prime figure of (Asian) piracy in the twenty-first century is best situated within "the emerging forms of global informational capitalism," when a "confluence" of forces at once technological, economic, and cultural have produced a crisis of "bourgeois legalities," especially with regard to "the postcolonial margin."[64] A critical unpacking of "faked in China" artifacts and narratives, then, demands that we recognize simultaneously the "cultural specificity"[65] of the IPR regime and its historically specific role in perpetuating the power relations that embed the global culture industry. It is in this vein that I analyze the rise of nation branding as an ideological project in WTO-era China in chapter 1. I trace the formation of "Made in China" as a brand amid transnational circulation of goods and media discourses. The image crisis of the brand, generated largely by global news media's reportage of quality threats, prompted the state to take matters into its own hands. Not only did it seek to rebrand "Made in China" as a trustworthy and affordable brand for the global consumer, it also worked to project a developmentalist vision, "From Made in China to Created in China," to assure its citizens of the nation's future and the role of the state in shaping that future. The state, in other words, has repositioned itself not only as an agent to manage the crisis of "Made in China" but also as the leader to direct the nation's progress – toward a branded future – in global modernity.

The ideological formation of nation branding in WTO-era China, then, manifests the role of IPR in reshaping the cultural constitution of the state. If this re-configuration of the state speaks to the ways in which brands and counterfeits, as cultural products of the IPR regime, exert an impact on the nation-state, the question remains: how is the contemporary Chinese situation attributable more distinctly to globalization's uneven workings of power? After all, ideological productions of the nation for purposes of shoring up state legitimacy, even in such historically powerful nation-states as Britain or the United States, can also be said to be subject to the influence of these transnational cultural forms. What do we gain, then, from situating the challenges faced by WTO-era China in the context of unequal global relations of power? This question cannot be fully answered without a more in-depth understanding of the distinct mode of ideological state apparatus known as "Chinese postsocialism," a discussion of which will prepare us to address the question of WTO-era China's cultural dilemma under the influence of IPR.

POSTSOCIALIST CHINA AND DECOLONIALITY

It has been over two decades since Arif Dirlik first put forth the notion of "postsocialism" in a deconstructive analysis of Deng Xiaoping's 1982 coinage, "socialism with Chinese characteristics."[66] For Dirlik, the "post-" here is not to be understood as "end of," but rather the simultaneous remaking of socialism's utopian principle into an ideology of the present and the liberation of its form from a teleological immanence.[67] This theoretical reorientation has spurred numerous attempts to debunk conventional binaries such as "socialism versus capitalism," "state versus civil society," or "state versus market," none of which can be easily applied to the Chinese situation, itself currently changing at dramatic speed.

Specifically, a few turning points should be noted with regard to the relation between ideology and the post-Mao Chinese state. The first decade after Deng Xiaoping's launching of the Reform and Opening Up policy in 1978 saw a retreat of the Party from various spheres of social life. However, this ostensible withdrawal of state influence over everyday life has led the leadership to retain its status through more, not less, ideological work (*sixiang gongzuo*). As Ann Anagnost suggests, the post-Mao state's ideological practice reversed Maoist "superstructural determinism"; instead of providing "subjective will" to overcome "an underdeveloped material base," ideology now appeared as a "stabilizing force in the face of the profound dislocations of the economic reforms."[68] There is, in other words, a contradiction between the state's mandate to retreat from civil society (especially its economic subset) and its ideological need to re-insert itself as a leading agent of nation building. On the one hand, the state is under the pressure to reduce its overly large presence in the market and everyday social spheres so as to substantiate its claim in promoting the market economy; on the other hand, the state also has to exert itself more prominently in legal and economic matters in order to avoid potential chaos in the market, regulate the nascent national industries, and structure new modes of private and public life.

This contradiction has deepened after 1989, particularly since the symbolic event of Deng's 1992 "Southern Tour" to the special economic zones in coastal China's Guangdong province. David Harvey, among others, has marked this moment as the beginning of the Chinese state's "neoliberal turn."[69] Yet the legacies of the Chinese revolution as they are experienced in the present have made the application of the term more difficult. The experiences of the Maoist past still "serve as reminders of an earlier challenge to the capitalist world-system," and claims of socialism remain an integral part of the Party-state's self-legitimizing discourse – even if they manifest themselves in the capacity to be "more successful at capitalism than capitalist societies."[70]

Despite reconciling attempts of the economic kind, such as maintaining a stunning GDP growth, China's postrevolutionary and post-socialist conditions have combined to produce a crisis of legitimacy for the Chinese state: people may draw on state-promoted market principles to critique the state's ideological rule while invoking the state's socialist roots to critique the reform policy of the postsocialist state.[71] While the affirmation of market mechanisms indeed accelerated economic growth, it also intensified social problems such as the inertia of state-owned enterprises, lagging agricultural growth, structural corruption, and massive class polarization.[72] More importantly, the state's promotion of the so-called socialist market economy separated the political from the social sphere; in allowing "more balance and flexibility within the organs of state power and more economic, social and personal freedom outside it," it also evaded "the socialist commitment to the people as a whole as well as the will to create a new kind of democracy, freedom, and equality that supersedes the bourgeois model."[73] The 1997 Southeast and East Asian financial crisis arguably brought this paradox of the state to the fore, signaling another turning point in the ideological state apparatus. Among other things, the crisis prompted discussions about the state's protective role in isolating China from the whims of foreign capital. But the reality of economic globalization, affirmed through the interdependence of China and the affected nations, ultimately allowed the state to justify a more aggressive agenda in joining the WTO.[74] In this sense, neoliberalism, a globally hegemonic ideological force associated with "the market and development," was mobilized as a means to shore up state legitimacy, one that co-exists with continuous claims to the socialist tradition, however tenuous the latter might appear.[75]

The transformation of the postsocialist ideological state apparatus after China's WTO entry is the focus of this book. A premise for the project is that the need to distinguish "the postsocialist state" from "China," the imagined national community, is more important than ever, now that the state is formally integrated into a global institutional apparatus. The WTO accession, above all, "signaled China's willingness to play by international trade rules," which entails shaping its "governmental apparatus" to fit in the demands of "a world order."[76] This global context urges us to disentangle the simultaneous and mutually constitutive transformations of the state and the nation. For this reason, I use the descriptor "WTO-era China"[77] to signify the nexus that brings the globally implicated postsocialist state and the transnational narrative production of the Chinese nation into a dynamic unity.

As Jing Wang notes, the postsocialist state in the 1990s has reshaped and solidified its hegemony through cultural means, rendering its rule more diffused and regulatory in nature.[78] This book continues this line of inquiry and probes further into the cultural influence of globalization on the state apparatus. As I argue in chapter 1, the state not only interpellates its citizen-subjects by way of laying claim to the nation but also is itself subject to the interpellation of a globally hegemonic structure – a structure that exerts its cultural power primarily through the IPR regime. The global-national ideological formation that is nation branding, then, epitomizes the contradictory effects of globalization because it undermines the state's legitimacy while prescribing how that legitimacy is to be regained.

These contradictory effects of globalization are most vividly embodied by the "faked in China" artifacts that I examine in chapters 2, 3, and 4. The making of these cultural objects, taken together, speaks to the complex hegemonic struggles between the state and the global system represented by IPR. For one thing, the producers of counterfeit cultural artifacts often conjure up social visions that simultaneously challenge the globalizing IPR regime and the state's attempt to conform to that regime. Whether it is through the making of fake cell phone brands, the engagement in the piracy-inflicted networks of film production and distribution, or the (re-)claiming of an urban space famous for selling counterfeit goods, these participants present cultural visions that diverge from the IPR doctrine in important ways. Emerging from their discourses and practices is an understanding of culture as a symbolic system for meaning making rather than value making. This cultural vision not only departs from the state vision of "Created in China" but also presents an alterative approach to counter the cultural workings of the IPR regime. Operating within the IPR-sanctioned imaginary of the brand, the state is blinded by its desire to produce culturally valuable nation brands that can compete more successfully with global brands. In doing so, the state fails to consider the alternative visions of the national, presented by the makers and participants of counterfeit culture, as a site of counterhegemonic struggle. What ensues is a cultural dilemma exemplifying the paradoxical situation noted by Fredric Jameson: the state's cultural production of the nation (that is, nation branding), while meant to counter the encroachment of global forces (that is, brands owned by multinational corporations), itself encounters resistance within its sovereign borders (that is, counterfeit practices); this resistance, however, appropriates the "transnational mass culture" (that is, global brands), which is the source of the very "external hegemony" that the state intends to resist.[79]

Notably, what presents political challenges in counterfeit cultural practices is not so much a local appropriation of global brands and logos, often touted in studies of IPR offenses as resistance toward the dominant regime; rather, the alternative visions these practices bring forth stem from a defiance of IPR's cultural logic. As Lawrence Liang argues, the political potentiality of piracy (and by extension, counterfeit culture) lies in what it "does," not what it "is."[80] While IPR legitimizes the distinction between the real and the fake, between the pure and the hybrid, counterfeit cultural artifacts conjure up communities and publics that engage in the production of culture itself – that is, as practices of meaning making. Together, these communities of meaning makers present visions for the social that are distinguishable from the individuated subjectivity proffered by IPR institutions – the same institutions that, by proffering a branded imaginary, shape the manner in which the state consolidates itself ideologically. As I will argue, the ideological practice of nation branding privileges the national over the social, to the point of excluding alternative modes of national membership (chapter 3) and state-citizen relationship (chapter 4). In failing to recognize and engage with the cultural forces that have erupted in counterfeit culture, the state's ideological maneuvering works to sustain rather than disrupt the unequal power relations of globalization, despite its ostensible intent to strengthen the nation vis-à-vis intensified global competition.

WTO-era China's cultural dilemma, then, can be described as the struggle between a countercultural production and a counterproduction of culture. By "countercultural production" I refer to the kinds of meaning-making practices that emerge in the circulation of counterfeit artifacts. They produce culture by affirming its aim as existential meaning making rather than instrumental value creation. In doing so, the participants in counterfeit culture point to alternative ways of imagining the national as a site of hegemonic contestation over and against the global system. Counterfeit culture is countercultural in the sense that it presents a cultural challenge not only for the globalizing IPR regime, but also for the state ideological formation of nation branding. The state project "From Made in China to Created in China" is on the surface a production of culture; it understands culture as a source of value, one that generates profit by means of a conversion into so-called cultural goods. But it is indeed culturally counterproductive in that it prevents an affirmation of national difference vis-à-vis the global culture industry. Instead, by conforming to the cultural logic of the IPR regime, it steers the nation further into a cultural crisis brought on by globalization and forecloses the possibilities of imagining an alternative modernity.

The story of *Faked in China* is thus as much about China as about the cultural potentialities that are yet to be realized within what was formerly known as the Third World. As postcolonial theorists like Partha Chatterjee and Radhika Desai have argued, anti-imperialist or decolonizing national formations in these locales are often more creative and imaginative than what Benedict Anderson and other (Eurocentric) theorists have accounted for.[81] This in part has to do with Anderson's overemphasis on "empty, homogeneous time" as a precondition for imagining the national community.[82] As my analysis will show, the heterogeneous temporalities in which counterfeit cultural producers find themselves provide abundant resources for affirming the national as a site of difference making. Among other things, they remind us that China's "revolutionary past" is not to be forgotten as "an earlier challenge to the capitalist world-system."[83] By portraying the distinct social visions conjured up by the cultural publics of counterfeiting, I also join anthropologists like Cori Hayden (who works on pharmaceutical copying in Latin America) in bringing into view alternative "political languages and imaginations"[84] that lie outside the limiting liberal framework often deployed by First World anti-IPR activists.[85] In so doing, I move beyond a process of "debunking" to engage in a project of "assembling," one that does not jettison the faith of "naïve believers" but instead "offers the participants arenas in which to gather."[86] The cultural dilemma faced by WTO-era China, one that manifests itself in the nation-state disjuncture, may not be unique after all. But the recognition of its historically specific conditions of production certainly prompts further inquiries into the latent political solidarities that exist in the Global South. The value of this alternative account of China's rise, then, ultimately lies in this repositioning of China – not as an ascending global hegemon en route to replace the United States, nor as a revived imperialist power now penetrating Africa more rapidly than old European empires, but as a nation-state whose struggles for an alternative modernity are caught in intense global contradictions. If China's nation-branding project fails to contest the culturally imperialistic forces of IPR, this failure is more attributable to the latter's global operation – through the hegemonic imaginary of the brand – than to the lack of cultural resources for conjuring new horizons of state and citizenship. These resources therefore must continue to be assembled – in part by way of documenting the unsuccessful cultural struggles that they enable – so as to pave the way for re-imagining alternative (trans)national alliances that would present more concrete challenges for the postcolonial world order increasingly masked as the global culture industry.

CHAPTER OUTLINE

In chapter 1, I begin with an account of WTO-era China's nation branding as a formation in a global-national imaginary. This imaginary stems
from "Made in China," a globally constructed and circulated nation
brand. To be sure, there is a definitive difference between trademark-
protected brands and the discursive construction of "Made in China"
as a brand. But the formation of this nation brand calls attention to the
complex operation of the postsocialist state; it is at once an institutional
actor from which policy directives emanate and a configuration that
arises from globally circulated images and discourses. The global media
coverage of "Made in China" as a nation brand in crisis afforded the state
the opportunity to consolidate its transnational consumer-based constituency. It also enabled the state to take on a new mission to regulate
as well as to upgrade the nation's brand name. The emergence of the slogan "From Made in China to Created in China" after China's 2001 WTO
entry speaks precisely to this hegemonizing move on the part of the
state. The manner in which this discourse takes shape, I argue, is emblematic of the global encroachment of the IPR regime, which operates
through the imaginary of the brand and its presumed "intangible value."
This nation-branding project presents a national vision that privileges
the subject position of the national bourgeoisie, now interpellated as
nation-brand builders, while marginalizing the working-class labor that
contributed to the nation brand "Made in China."

In chapter 2, I examine the cultural formation of Shanzhai, a new
name for wide-ranging knockoff products and copycat media forms that
took the Chinese mediascape by storm in 2008. Literally referring to a
"mountain fortress" occupied by anti-official bandits and often invoking Robin Hood–like populism, the "Shanzhai" brand connotes a sense
of defiance against the globalizing IPR regime. Tracing Shanzhai's rise
from the informal mobile phone sector in southern China to its proliferation on the internet and its representation on state-run television, I
argue that its discursive formation makes visible an imaginary of collectivity, one that disrupts the state's continuous claim to "the nation"
as a signifier for "the people." To re-align the national interest with that
of "the people," state media have reshaped the Shanzhai discourse by

separating "Shanzhai economy" from "Shanzhai culture." While the fixation of the former as "illicit" and "fake" allows the state to re-establish itself as a protector of the people, the acknowledgment of the latter re-inserts the state as a leader that can direct the energy of "the people" toward national progress. The meaning-making capacity of Shanzhai is thus reworked to fit with a value-making notion of creativity. As such, it is channeled into a developmental force suitable for building the nation's own brands.

If the story of Shanzhai points to the ideological challenge confronted by the Chinese state, in chapter 3 I discuss how a low-budget film came to enact a temporal heterogeneity that disrupts the imagined modern temporality on which nation branding depends. I situate the film *Crazy Stone* (Ning Hao, 2006) in WTO-era China's counterfeit film culture. Supported by a transnational network, this culture thrives on the unauthorized reproduction and distribution of copyrighted audiovisual products. It has created complex conditions of film consumption and production, within which the question of national cinema must be re-thought. Despite the film's non-star cast and low-profile marketing, *Crazy Stone* achieved cult popularity in China and overseas Chinese communities. It depicts a series of thefts that revolve around a precious jade stone found in a run-down state-owned factory. The director, a self-proclaimed avid consumer of pirate DVDs, calls the film a "dark comedy." Importantly, the film brought many former addicts of pirated DVDs into the theater. While academics and critics celebrated its exploitation of locally specific entertaining contents to compete with imported Hollywood blockbusters, large numbers of bloggers and online forum discussants came to recognize the film's style as copied from British director Guy Ritchie's *Snatch* (2000). Considering that *Snatch* was never released in China, it was the pirate film network that helped to spread the knowledge of the so-called original among many of the self-identified Chinese viewers. This accusation of copying contrasted with the celebration of the film's "realist" portrayal of a city and nation in flux. The interplay between the "realist" claims and "copying" charges, I argue, creates a temporal disjuncture. It probes questions of the modern – that is, the present – in ways that reveal the possibility of a historical agency predicated on a performative mode of being in the nation.

While chapters 2 and 3 highlight the competing visions of national membership presented in nation branding and counterfeit culture, chapter 4 examines the contradictory workings of the globalizing IPR regime more directly through the case of the Silk Street Market (also known as Xiushui Street or Silk Alley) in Beijing. Located in the diplomatic quarter of the capital city, the market first emerged in the 1980s (the beginning years of the Dengist Reform and Opening Up) as an open-air bazaar famous for counterfeit global brand-name products and local souvenirs. It had since established itself as a key urban landmark frequented mostly by foreign tourists. I trace the market's spatial history, particularly its entanglement in WTO-era China's nation branding project, through a series of property disputes surrounding the brand of Silk Street and the fake luxury brands sold at the market. I suggest that it is the conception of Silk Street as an intangible asset for the city and nation that legitimized the government's move to privatize the site in the name of protecting a "public" interest. This state-sponsored privatization literally deterritorialized its original tenants, who were the early participants in the production of its meaning. While the state's nation-branding policy aims to compensate for the nation's "lack" of IPR knowledge by penalizing the sales of counterfeit goods, the local constituents' defense of their rights to the place affirms this "lack" of IPR consciousness as a source of national-cultural distinction. In their protests, they sought to re-claim their spatial presence in the city and in the nation by invoking a collectivized notion of property. The ongoing protests at Silk Street thus point to an embodied vision of citizenship, one that the state has failed to recognize as it continues to engage in the production of the nation as an abstracted, brandable property for global tourist consumption.

In the concluding chapter, I recast the contestations between nation branding and counterfeit culture in WTO-era China through the lens of cultural imperialism and argue that it operates through a set of culturally productive mechanisms that exert contradictory impacts on the Chinese nation-state. These impacts manifest themselves not so much through the invasion of a self-contained national culture or the diminishing of state power per se, but rather in creating disjunctive tensions within the "hyphen" that links the nation to the state. It is precisely these tensions that create the chasm between the cultural counterproduction of nation branding and the countercultural production of counterfeit culture. The continuing relevancy of the cultural imperialism framework, therefore, lies precisely in its emphasis on the unequal power relations that persist in privileging certain cultural visions for the nation as more desirable and "natural" than others. In other words, the cultural struggle at the site of the national, which encompasses the state's continuous production of "national cultures" but also the state's own cultural formation in globalization, is where a critical perspective informed by cultural imperialism can become most productive.

In order to illustrate this in the context of contemporary globalization, wherein America remains a hegemonic figure, I engage with a more recent discursive formation, that of the "Chinese Dream." The term, first invoked by the newly inaugurated Chinese president Xi Jinping as a hallmark of his administration in 2012, now permeates the Chinese mediascape and has generated much international attention, in part because of its close resemblance to the globally circulated signifier of the "American Dream." I suggest that the Chinese Dream may be seen as a new episode of WTO-era China's nation branding in that it not only shares a developmental vision with the discourse "From Made in China to Created in China," but also manifests the effects of another cultural imaginary on the Chinese state, that of the American Dream. Therefore, it brings into sharper relief the historical specificity of U.S. imperialism, particularly its cultural operation, in the contemporary era.

The cultural workings of IPR and "America" indeed converge in a 2013 popular film, *Chinese Partners* (*Zhongguo Hehuoren*), a domestic hit that not only features an IPR dispute at its climax but also has a telling English name, *American Dreams in China*. Through an analysis of this cultural artifact, which emerges from and participates in the discourse of the "Chinese Dream," I argue that the film is best seen as an allegory of WTO-era China's cultural dilemma, one that symptomatically reveals the global cultural constraints that continue to delimit how the nation's future is to be imagined. By way of this example, which enacts the unequal power relation that exerts a cultural impact on WTO-era China, I ultimately suggest that a cultural studies approach to the nation-state question can contribute to studies of globalization, particularly concerning the non-West or the Global South. While this approach remains critical of the culturally imperialistic forces at work in the postcolonial world order, it also highlights the centrality of human agency in shaping social institutions, a task that is achievable by nothing other than re-imagining the possibilities of culture.

ONE

"From Made in China to Created in China": Nation Branding and the Global-National Imaginary

In 2004, two days after Christmas, a writer-journalist from Louisiana named Sara Bongiorni launched her family into a yearlong experiment to boycott goods made in China. That night, upon noticing that most of the presents in the house bore the label, Bongiorni decided to "kick China out of the house," simply to see whether it was possible.[1] She quickly discovered that the idea was not as original as she had thought; Peggy and Dave Smedley, a magazine-publishing couple, had banned Chinese-made presents and bought only American that very Christmas. After calling Mrs. Smedley for advice, Bongiorni learned about the challenge ahead: not only is it difficult to track down goods without the label, some ostensibly non-China-made goods might also have China-made contents. Weighing the difficulties in the year to come, Bongiorni decided to "avoid one thing only: labels bearing the words *Made in China*."[2]

Bongiorni documented the experience in a book, *A Year without Made in China: One Family's True Life Adventure in the Global Economy*. Its publication in 2007 perfectly coincided with China's run-up to the Olympic Games. As the global media spotlight zoomed in more intensely on the nation,[3] a series of China-made consumer product scandals grabbed national headlines: tainted pet foods exported to America, followed by the recall of a million lead-painted Thomas & Friends toy trains in the U.S. and U.K., and finally, the withdrawal of July 4 fireworks due to a "dangerously unpredictable sense of direction."[4] As "Made in China" came to pose threats to American lives, Bongiorni's book enjoyed extensive media coverage in U.S. and international news outlets, from CBS News, the *Christian Science Monitor,* and National Public Radio to newspapers in the Middle East.

To be sure, the idea of boycotting China was not new. After all, global media have made it a routine to report that nation's suppression of political dissidents, abuses of human rights, and internet censorship, among other standard Communist or "authoritarian" practices. In the pre-Olympics media craze of 2008, these reports culminated in the infamous Olympics torch relay, when violent protests erupted in London, Paris, and elsewhere aiming to stop the Chinese delegates from passing through. While spectacles of this kind may be reflective of anti-China sentiments among large numbers of media consumers in the West, the idea or place called "China" they invoke remains distant enough to exert little or no impact on the spectators' everyday life. As fleeting moments on media screens, they at best serve to remind the viewers of their fortunate situation in the "free world" and are capable of moving no more than a handful of activists into action.

However, the threat of "Made in China" in 2007 appeared to be much more imminent and closer to home. In addition to the danger of consuming unsafe products, the label also conjured up the specter of a looming economic downturn, a trend often attributed to the shift of production from America to China. "As many as 2 million Americans have lost their jobs to Chinese competition," notes Bongiorni, "but we still can't get enough of what China is selling."[5] This predicament was compounded by the fact that many Americans who had "lost their jobs to Chinese competition" could now only afford to buy cheap goods made in China, as opposed to more expensive ones made by unionized, higher-paid American labor. One may argue that more than any other China-related news, the media stories surrounding "Made in China" had taken center stage to become a dominant framework for the American public to process the United States' growing connections with that "rising power."

Upon the publication of her book, Bongiorni became the source of "China-free" advice for numerous Americans seeking to de-link from China, sometimes to protect their families from hazardous products while at other times to inject some personal stimulus into the American economy. Like Bongiorni, these consumers felt a "real" and "personal" connection with "China's place in the world."[6] In some sense, the often-times "negative" connection between the American consumer and the "Made in China" label continues the age-old "Buy American" movement motivated by economic nationalism.[7] But the historical forces that gave rise to this new manifestation, the medium via which it was communicated, and the state-citizen relation it came to promote on both sides of the Pacific are indeed telling a new story about China, the United States, and their relationship in globalization.

In this chapter, I will suggest that what distinguishes the 2007 spectacle of "Made in China" from other China-related news events is the emergence of the label as shorthand for a *nation brand*. Not only was "Made in China" cross-promoted on multiple global media platforms as a brand for a nation, it was also portrayed by both U.S. and Chinese news media as a brand in crisis, the ramifications of which transcended geopolitical boundaries. The formation of this nation brand calls attention to the globally imbricated operation of the postsocialist state – as at once an institutional actor from whom policy directives emanate and a subject continuously imagined into being amid globally circulated images and discourses. The formation of this state-subject, I argue, is emblematic of the entrenchment of the IPR regime, which operates through the global imaginary of the brand. The cultural effect of this regime has manifested itself most powerfully in China's WTO era national policy, "From Made in China to Created in China," or what I call a "nation branding" project. While not exclusively a product of the transnational discursive circulation of "Made in China," this project nonetheless presents a national vision that corresponds to the same ideological forces and material conditions that gave rise to the brand name itself. The formation of this nation brand in crisis is where I shall begin.

"MADE IN CHINA": A TRANSNATIONAL PRODUCTION

What is "Made in China?" On a very basic level, it is a country-of-origin label. First introduced in the U.S. by the Tariff Act of 1890, the labeling requirement based on rules of origin (ROO) has never been favored by the proponents of free trade.[8] This is because the labeling requirements are often perceived as "non-tariff trade barriers" offsetting the free flow of capital and goods. For instance, the World Trade Organization (WTO) ruled in November 2011 that the U.S. requirement for meat products to be stamped with country-of-origin labels (COOL) was a case of "technical barriers to trade."[9] The U.S. law came into effect in March 2009 in part as a response to domestic food safety concerns. But it was later said to have affected major multinational food companies, whose cost to import livestock from Canada and Mexico had increased due to the added process of labeling. The complaint, filed by Canada and Mexico at the WTO, faced an appeal by the United States in defense of its own citizens' right to know.[10] Incidents like this point to a paradox of economic globalization qua trade liberalization embodied by the country-of-origin label. On the one hand, capital's global move in search of low-cost labor and raw materials shows no regard for national boundaries, except when governments offer tax, anti-union, or other incentives to attract foreign capital. On the other hand, the state's mandate to protect "national interests" or promote the "national economy" calls for particularized trade policies, such as the stamping of imported goods with a nation-specific mark. These measures are sometimes meant to protect specific domestic enterprises from being trampled by the influx of foreign goods and at other times to inform citizen-consumers about the geopolitical origins of their goods when making purchasing decisions.

The institutionalization of the country-of-origin label complicates Marx's notion of the commodity fetish in some sense. For Marx, a commodity stands in for the social relations behind its own production. Commodity fetishism refers to a condition whereby the product of human labor appears as an objective entity completely devoid of the labor that produced it.[11] The country-of-origin label seemingly disrupts this fetish by placing a location stamp on a commodity, thus bringing into view the place-specific presence of assembling labor. However, by presenting the assembling nation itself as a stand-in for the "globally dispersed forces that actually drive the production process," the label also creates a new kind of fetish – what Appadurai has called "production fetishism."[12] While the labeling requirement ostensibly seeks to capture the locality of production in one nation's name, it participates in the masking of the voluminous border-crossing transactions most often engendered by transnational or multinational corporations (MNCs).

Precisely this fetish was at work in the "Made in China" discourse that garnered such attention circa 2008 in the American context. For Sara Bongiorni as well as the candidates in the 2008 (and 2012) presidential race, "Made in China" signifies the transfer of employment opportunities from the United States to China on the one hand, and the growing trade deficit that America holds with respect to China on the other. This rhetoric portrays China as the winner of the game, as the "Made in China" process brings more jobs and a bigger trade surplus to that country. To be sure, these charges are not without material grounding. But more than representing the nation of China, the label embodies a set of transnational processes. The seeming ubiquity of the label in the United States is the result of the massive shift of production from America to mainland China after the congressional granting of Permanent Normal Trading Relations (PNTR) status to China – a "prelude" to the latter's 2001 accession to the WTO.[13] This process, of course, was first set in motion by China's Reform and Opening Up policy since 1978. To attract foreign direct investment (FDI), Deng Xiaoping set up export processing zones in China's coastal cities, many of which became the destination of production plants originally located in Southeast Asia. In 2002, the leading consulting firm A. T. Kearney announced that China had surpassed the United States to become the "most attractive" destination for FDI.[14] Actual numbers soon caught up with this indicator of confidence, when China replaced the United States as the largest recipient of FDI in 2003, before repeating the act for a second time in 2012.[15]

In this light, the label "Made in China" can be seen as a material manifestation of the border-crossing mobility specific to finance capital. While state policies and decisions in America and China play a definitive role in aiding and facilitating capital movement, it is the transborder character of that capital, as well as the transborder commodities it engenders, that are expressed by the country-of-origin label. After all, there is no legal requirement in China or elsewhere to indicate a commodity's place of origin if it is produced and consumed within the national borders. The labeling practice only becomes an issue that concerns the state (specifically, the American state) when there is a geopolitical separation between a commodity's place of production and its place of consumption. "Made in China," then, is a physical expression of the transnational movement of capital and goods.

At the same time, country-of-origin labels of this kind by no means capture the extensive outsourcing and subcontracting activities spread by MNCs throughout increasingly divergent geographical locales. The growth of these activities in the past few decades has no doubt made the determination of the "national" origins of products more difficult. As a response, U.S. Customs and Border Protection (part of the Department of Homeland Security) now designates "the last country in which (a product) has been substantially transformed" as the official mark to be stamped on an imported item.[16] Since China has become a chief locale that provides an abundance of cheap assembling labor, "Made in China" has become an almost ubiquitous label in the United States, despite the fact that various components and parts for goods thus labeled are often made from materials produced in other nations.[17] Even as the "Made in China" label reveals the transnational condition of its own making to some degree, it also conceals the more complex, multi-directional flows that characterize the contemporary global economic system.

Recognizing the complex processes that "Made in China" simultaneously reveals and conceals, however, does not provide the answer to another crucial question: How has "Made in China," a quintessentially *transnational* label, come to be politicized as to shape China's *national* politics at this particular moment? In some ways, the rejection of "Made in China" is a new development in the union-organized "Buy American" movements, which have been instrumental in mobilizing economic nationalism in the United States throughout the twentieth century.[18] Often fused with anti-Asian racism (toward Japan in the '50s–'60s and China in the present), the union-motivated call for consumers to purchase products "Made in America" operates on an anti-foreign, "us versus them" logic.[19] What this logic hides, of course, is that the profit generated in this global system of production is seldom if ever retained by the workers who produce the surplus value. More often than not, it flows back to where capital originates. As a 2007 study of iPod's "value capturing" chain suggests, when an iPod leaves the Chinese factory to enter the United States, the factory price of $150 is the figure recorded as America's import from China. However, when the iPod is later sold at the price of $300 in the United States, the largest portion of its profit goes to the American company (Apple), whereas the assembling country of China only "captures" a few dollars.[20] Rather than displaying competition between the nations of America and China, this disparity manifests an exploitative relationship between transnational classes. As such, the casting of "Made in China" as a marker of *inter*-national job transfers and trade imbalance, much like the "Buy American" movements in the past, obscures the *trans*-national flow from labor to capital, from surplus value to profit earnings. By obfuscating corporate capital's state-sanctioned border-crossing mobility, the protest against China precludes the possibility for transnational worker solidarity.

What remains puzzling, however, is the ability of "Made in China" to galvanize *national* feelings despite its own production in the "in-between" spaces of the transnational, be it trade, capital, earnings, or commodities stamped with the country-of-origin label. Arguably, the "Made in China" boycott is a new manifestation of Appadurai's notion of the "fetishism of the consumer."[21] Here, consumer action is constructed as a prime site for an individual to imagine and exercise his or her national citizenship vis-à-vis a globalized economic system. While Appadurai emphasizes global advertising – another set of "flows" – as the main productive force of the consumer's make-believe agency, there is no meticulously designed, large-scale corporate marketing campaign to deliver the intended message of "Made in China." Nor are the transnational conditions of its production and representation sufficiently captured by the imagery of "global flows." If anything, what the country-of-origin label makes visible is that nation-states and transnational corporations are engaged in more complex tensions than may have been indicated in the rhetoric of "flows." It is indeed more illuminating to consider the label another way, in which self-proclaimed "multinational" corporations retain multiple ties to specific nation-states, legally, institutionally, and culturally.[22]

Given the complexities brought on by the country-of-origin labeling practice in general and the "Made in China" discourse in particular, it behooves us to ask harder questions about the reconfiguration of nation-states in globalization. As I will demonstrate below, the rise of "Made in China" in the American public discourse is better grasped as the formation of a nation brand. What makes this branding distinct is that its agent of representation is not the Chinese government's propaganda branch or the marketing department of any particular MNC, but the global communication networks exemplified by CNN and the like. These channels of communication, by linking the nation with a country-of-origin label, also consolidate what may first appear to be an amorphous constituency for China's postsocialist state. What enables this consolidation is a shared sense of temporality between two cultural formations: the nation and the brand.

THE MAKING OF A NATION BRAND

A two-part television special called "Made in China," aired on CNN International in 2007, begins with the following introduction:

> What's in a brand? Ideally, the guarantee of safety and quality. But what happens when poisonous pet food, toxic toothpaste and dangerous drugs share a common label? Those are only some of the hazardous products that carry the label – "Made in China."[23]

The host goes on to recap several recent scandals regarding Chinese imports to the United States. The show depicts Beijing's response as "silence" at first, "damage control" second, and finally "turning the tables to protect the brand name." The 2008 Beijing Olympics is noted verbally and visually as an opportunity for the Chinese government to enhance its "global profile." The reporter cites the 2006 trade deficit between the United States and China ($232.5 billion), stating that "60% of recalls of consumer products in the US have come from China." He also makes reference to the earlier "cheap and unreliable" signifier "Made in Japan" but cautions that "China's challenge is much greater."

Noting that "Made in China" now "reads like a consumer warning," another correspondent interviews several shoppers, experts, and pedestrians in New York and other cities. While some express their preference for items not made in China, others remain oblivious of the location of the production of their goods. One young woman preparing for her prom expresses her concern that the merchandise she is about to pay for "was made in sort of a sweatshop there (in China)." (Her friend standing behind her, upon hearing this comment, shrugs and says: "Everything is.") However, because "the other ones are much more expensive," the young woman decides to make the purchase regardless.

Beijing's brand protection measures are reported to have taken various forms. Among them are organized tours of safety inspection facilities and death sentences for corrupt officials in the Chinese equivalent of the Food and Drug Administration. A government spokesperson, appearing in a press conference, blames the Western media for hyping the story. Scott Kronick, the head of the leading advertising agency Ogilvy's Beijing branch, subsequently dismisses this "West-bashing" tactic as "a mistake." Instead, he advises Chinese officials not to lay blame on others. This is followed by an appearance by Mike Leavitt, President George W. Bush's Health and Human Services secretary, who informs the audience that in his talks "with the ministers of the various parts of their government," "the 'Made in China' brand" is something "they are taking very seriously."[24]

The second part of the CNN program features two "human stories," one in China and the other in Panama, of families who suffered the death of loved ones from taking substandard drugs. The correspondent then poses the question: "What responsibilities do importing countries have for protecting their citizens?" President Bush, speaking at a cabinet-level panel he has organized to tackle the food safety issue, also affirms that this issue is "very serious" for consumers. Citing critics' view that America's "food safety laws are out of date and not designed to meet the modern day challenges . . . like imports and bio-terrorism," the reporter states that "food safety is now an issue of national security." He concludes by urging U.S. consumers "to educate and protect themselves, while Beijing tries to restore the world's confidence in that label, Made in China."[25]

Although this might not be the first time that the "Made in China" label was referred to as a brand for the Chinese nation, the use of the omnipresent "branding" language to signify an equally ubiquitous country-of-origin label is far from coincidental. While the production of "Made in China" certainly differs from that of corporate brands, the identification of the label as a brand for a nation is predicated upon a commonality between the nation and the brand – as cultural artifacts, both are produced in relation to time. The idea of one's belonging to a national community, as Benedict Anderson reminds us, is grounded in an understanding of the self in relation to others in time. The same can be said about a consumer's association of various commodities with a particular brand name. It is because of this shared sense of temporality that the two converged so seamlessly in the formation of "Made in China" as a nation brand.

For Anderson, the development of print capitalism provided the condition for a wider public to imagine the nation "as a solid community moving steadily down (or up) history."[26] If this account overemphasizes a modern conception of time – as "homogeneous and empty" – as the basis for national imagination, it is complicated by Homi Bhabha's notion of a "double time," which emphasizes the contingency of the national formation.[27] For Bhabha, the temporality of the nation is simultaneously fixed and destabilized. On the one hand, the hegemony of the national elite depends upon, and is reinforced by, the unquestionable unity of a national past and a linear temporality of progress. In this case, the time of the nation is presumed to be homogeneous and empty. On the other hand, those in lesser positions of power are also engaged in the constant making and renewal of the nation. In doing so, they perform a different national present by becoming historical agents themselves, rather than being the mere objects of the elites' nationalist pedagogy. In this latter scenario, the time of the nation is heterogeneous and disjunctive.

This characteristic of the nation's "double time" is arguably shared by brands as well. On the one hand, brands constitute the chief means through which capital accumulation takes place in the age of the "global culture industry."[28] They are different from commodities in that they "do not typically exchange" but "are only for sale on capital markets, where their value is a function of the expected future profits above those contributed by all other assets."[29] The IPR regime, most specifically its branch of trademark law, plays a crucial role in legitimizing and sustaining the value of the brand. The ideological principle of "intangible assets" that underlies IPR works to homogenize the temporality of the brand, such that the future realization of the brand value is continuous and can be accumulated from its present form. In this sense, brands can be seen as corresponding to what Randy Martin calls "the financialization of daily life" – a process that "reorients our sense of time to beckon the future in the present."[30]

On the other hand, the brand can also be understood as a performative object, a "dynamic unity" built upon "a set of relations between products in time."[31] These relations in time refer to the built-in feedback loop that engages brand owners and consumers in a series of accommodation, contestation, and co-optation. Much like the national subalterns who continuously contest the national-elitist pedagogy, consumers constantly participate in the production of the brand's meanings either by repeating or advocating purchases of the branded products – as in the case of brand loyalists – or by rejecting or reworking the brand, as in the case of cultural jammers, adbusters, and counterfeiters (chapter 2).[32] In other words, the brand also operates within a heterogeneous temporality; its signification is more contingent and disjunctive than what may be prescribed by trademark law. The brand's subjection to heterogeneous meaning-making practices, from imitations and fakes to playful appropriations, indeed challenges the attempt on the part of the IPR regime to homogenize brand values based on the intangibility of intellectual property.

This comparison between the nation and the brand and their respective temporalities helps us explain why "Made in China" came to be invoked as a brand for a nation. Despite the fact that goods stamped with that label are transnational objects circulating between nations rather than within them, the CNN special and other media accounts of its kind have effectively obscured the transnational spaces these objects traverse and the multi-directional processes they embody. Instead, what these accounts do is to consolidate the various commodities into a singular brand name – a unified country-of-origin label – thereby turning "Made in China" into a representative marker for a particular nation. This consolidation would not have appeared to be so natural if not for the temporality on which "Made in China" narratives are based. Bongiorni's "year without China" adventure, for instance, is narrated through a temporal flow organized by important dates on the calendar: the birthdays of family members, the summer beach season, July 4, Halloween, and the grand finale of Christmas. All of these occasions, of course, are associated with very particular types of products that are deemed seasonal necessities, from Halloween costumes to beach toys, from summer pool supplies to Christmas gifts. The family's movement through the calendar, however, is met with the struggle to avoid the omnipresent "Made in China" sign. The difficulty of the task often results in a series of mini-meltdowns and crises, manifested as temporal disruptions in the homogeneous, calendrically organized national time.

These disruptions of national time culminate in programs like the CNN special, which further condense time in the form of a televisual crisis and pave the way for the solidification of the "Made in China" brand. In these spectacles, items stamped with the label are presented as low-price objects of inferior quality that fail to meet safety standards. When brought to the American public in overabundance, they threaten immense danger. Combining qualitative lack and quantitative excess, this crisis mode of representing "Made in China" is heightened by a sense of urgency. As the word's Greek origin – "*krisis,* or decision" – suggests, crisis is "a time when decisions have to be made."[33] It calls particular (political) agents into action. The intrusion of "Made in China" into the daily life of American consumers is constructed in such a way as to position the states – both the Chinese and the American ones – as subjects of intervention to ameliorate the effects of a crisis. Whereas the American state is held up as a protector of the nation's citizen-consumers, the Chinese state is assigned the role of a brand manager, now responsible for the quality of life of consumers in America and worldwide.

To be sure, the fixation of "Made in China" as a nation brand differs from an increasingly widespread practice dubbed "nation branding," which refers to the adoption of marketing principles and means of mass communication by national governments "to maintain and perpetuate the nation through time and across space."[34] The key difference between the two lies in the role of the state, or more specifically, how the state can be conceptualized. In the case of nation-branding campaigns that are directly organized by governmental units, the state assumes the position of an institutional subject, one who interpellates its national citizenry through marketing practices intended to promote the nation's image. In the case of "Made in China," even though the Chinese government played a role in creating the material conditions for its making, the linking of the label with the nation itself has more to do with how the label is circulated, by way of commodities and media discourses, beyond the confines of the state. Insofar as this transnational circulation comes to project meanings about the nation, these meanings do not directly emanate from the institutional entity of the state. Rather, the state is itself interpellated, as it were, by global media representatives like CNN, as a subject responsible for the brand crisis of "Made in China." In turn, the media spectacle of "Made in China" consolidates what may first appear to be an amorphous constituency for China's postsocialist state. Replacing a conventional notion of the state-defined citizen is the figure of the global – read "foreign" – consumer.

The formation of the consumer-citizen subjectivity in time is crucial in naturalizing the conception of "Made in China" as a nation brand. For one thing, the production of this consumer-citizen depends on the disjunctive temporality of "Made in China" as a transnationally circulated "brand," albeit one to be avoided, not embraced. The label's "disruption" of the American nation's calendrical time positions Bongiorni and her fellow China boycotters as consumer subjects through the act of negation. Both Bongiorni and the consumers interviewed by CNN showed an awareness of, if not distaste for, "American consumerism," as well as the various injustices (such as "sweatshop labor") it often entails. However, just as Bongiorni would usually return to her "normal" state of being an "American consumer again,"[35] the young women buying prom merchandise on CNN still chose to make the purchase because of the cheap price. Bongiorni herself, at the end of her year-long experiment, concluded that "I may miss the boycott *from time to time* but I don't know that I'd try it again. In some ways I'd rather not know how much harder life without Chinese goods might be *a decade from now*" (my emphasis).[36] Here, the difficulty of imagining a life without products "made in China" is projected onto a future. This imagined temporality, rather than conjuring up a national community of belonging, instead evokes a deterritorialized notion of membership – based on the subject's relationship to a particular "nationality" of goods rather than a specific nation-state.

Certainly the relationship between the consumer-citizen and the "Made in China" nation brand is marked by a sense of contingency. While boycotting acts invoke a form of "inverse" consumer agency, it often contradicts the "self-interested rationality" on which a "subject of value" ultimately depends.[37] This contradiction is not unlike the simultaneously affective and rational processes through which consumers associate (or disassociate) themselves with (or from) corporate brands. Brand campaigns work to infuse specific meanings into logos that appeal to various market segments and target customers, but there is no guarantee that these affective processes would trump the consumer subject's rational choice to minimize the cost of living by resorting to the cheapest product available. Similarly, while a negation of "Made in China" feeds into a nation-based structure of feeling, it ultimately contradicts the subject's recognition of "its fundamental needs" and its capacity in "calculating the best way to attain those needs."[38] Yet it is precisely this ambiguous consumer-citizen subject position that presents an opportunity, if not a mandate, for China's postsocialist state apparatus to engage in the production and negotiation of meanings for the nation. The disjunctive time of the crisis, from which "Made in China" emerged, calls for a state-subject to intervene, to re-unify the now deterritorialized national image by offering a homogeneous time frame – one akin to that of the brand – in which the national community can be re-imagined. But the state's pedagogical "object" – the people – is to be found not only within but also outside of its sovereign borders. This consumption-based (as opposed to, say, residency-based) citizenry also helps to shape the cultural production of the state, since the ideological formation to which it corresponds is now simultaneously national and global.

REBRANDING "MADE IN CHINA"

Well before Bongiorni's adventurous year ended, the Chinese press started contacting her for interviews. The first telephone call from a Chinese journalist lead to an article that contained passages never voiced by Bongiorni herself – "The children had no toys . . . Gone were their laughing, smiling faces."[39] Later, a Chinese television crew came to her house. Having spent three hours there amiably making friends with the family, they left them a vase as a gift. When Bongiorni's neighbor warned her about the looming threat of "red China" and reminded her to examine the vase for microphones, she waved it off. As someone "raised by peaceniks in California," Bongiorni distances herself from those in the "Bible Belt," who would more willingly subscribe to an outdated rhetoric of China scares.[40] However, another reporter soon followed up with an interview that chiefly focused on the negative outcomes of the boycott.[41] Only then did Bongiorni realize that she had "inadvertently become an instrument of propaganda for the Chinese government."[42] Her book was quickly translated into Chinese, with the title *"Likai Zhongguo Zhizao de Yinian."* While it still literally reads as "A Year without 'Made in China,'" it conveys just a bit more sense of passivity – "away from" (*likai*) – than activity – "boycott" (*dizhi*). An article she wrote for the *Christian Science Monitor* was also translated and published in *Global Times*, a state-run newspaper, almost immediately. As displayed on the "Foreign Telegraph Reference" section of the *People's Net*, the central government's official online news outlet, the title for the article now appears as "American Family Sighed: Days without Chinese Products Became Difficult," with the original English heading subtly displayed at the end of the page.

The television footage, it turned out, was featured on none other than China Central Television (CCTV), long considered the party-state's mouthpiece. It was a centerpiece in a weeklong special campaign called "Believe in Made in China."[43] Aired on the Finance Channel during its peak hours, the show consisted of three parts: "Believing in Made in China," "Tracing Made in China," and "Experiencing Made in China."[44] In this and other similar programs (such as one that appeared two months later on Shanghai's equally prestigious Oriental Satellite TV), Bongiorni's story was cited as an example to demonstrate global consumers' dependence on Chinese-made products. Numerous officials in charge of quality control took the platform to assure the domestic audience as well as invited foreign nationals that they could trust Chinese products.[45] These actions, in the eyes of Russell Leigh Moses, a professor of political science at People's University in Beijing, reflect "an attempt by the government to convince people that they are on the job" and well aware that the negative image of Chinese products has seeped into the nation through the internet.[46]

Moses's comment is illustrative of the fact that the "Made in China" label entered the Chinese government's brand consciousness through transnational channels (such as CNN and the internet). A late 2007 episode of the *World Weekly* program on CCTV News, for instance, devoted almost one-third of its thirty-minute segment to Bongiorni's "economic experiment," including a brief visual sequence from CNN's "Made in China" program.[47] The CNN images come in after Bongiorni's voice-over comments, attributing her book's popularity to the fact that it is "about a family, life, and about how this (made in China) has affected us."[48] A CNN logo appears on the upper-left-hand corner to remind the viewer of the clip's origin. A few seconds of somewhat blurred shots of the tainted drugs, the Chinese mother of the victim, toothpaste, and toys are accompanied by the narrator's voiceover:

> Not only so, after this year-long experiment, Bongiorni also modified some of her previous opinions on Made in China. When she continuously found the "Made in China" sign on the labels of Chanel clothing and brand-name computers, she realized that Made in China has long surpassed the realm of "cheap commodities."[49]

Clearly, the producers of the CCTV program were not only aware of the CNN reportage but saw it necessary to deploy its imagery to convey new meanings. The intertextual reference to CNN may not come as a surprise, especially considering that CCTV, the long-time representative of state-run media, has in recent years moved toward a "China's CNN" model in preparation for its WTO-era competition with transnational communications conglomerates.[50] In this program, CCTV continues its tradition of reporting "good" news to its viewers (chapter 2). Predictably, its tone differs from that of the CNN original, which warns American consumers of the questionable quality of the "Made in China" brand. While the CNN narrative calls upon the U.S. and Chinese governments to take political responsibility in managing the crisis for the citizen-consumer, the CCTV version emphasizes the world's desire for and reliance on goods made in China. Citing Bongiorni and her readers, the program highlights the label's increased presence in "expensive, high quality" products, in addition to playing a key role in the lives of common American consumers.[51] As if to reinforce this finding, the prominent Beijing newspaper *China Youth Daily* points out that "'Made in China' is no longer just an illustration of a place of origin, but has become a way of life deeply influencing a large number of foreigners."[52] Headlines from "Without 'Made in China,' American(s) cannot survive" to "Without 'Made in China,' Life is a Mess" likewise portray Ms. Bongiorni's experiment as having produced no less than a family disaster.

What characterizes this reworking, one may argue, is the appropriation of a global discourse in constructing a national imaginary. To be sure, nationalist movements that arise out of issues related to international trade are not without historical precedent in China. One such precedent is the "National Products Movement" in the early twentieth century. At the time, the Nationalist state was in too weak a position to establish trade barriers, and the imposition of unequal, imperialist treaties resulted in an influx of foreign products into the Chinese market. In response, the movement called for wide-ranging institutional and individual actions to promote consumer preferences for "Chinese" (read "national") products over "foreign" (*yang*) ones. There are distinct differences between this consumer-citizen movement in Republican China (1911–1937) and the more recent Chinese media appropriation of the "Made in China" discourse. A century ago, the categorization of product nationality was based on "raw materials, labor, management and capital."[53] In the twenty-first century, by contrast, it is "brand name" that has emerged as the category most strongly associated with a nation's name.[54] Certainly the branding of Chinese products through nationalist symbols and myths remains a common practice among Chinese companies today.[55] Increasingly, however, there has emerged a new mode of branding, intending to promote a "new China" through the "convergence of multiple initiatives" on the part of the government and global advertising firms alike.[56] As Jing Wang points out, part of the challenge for nation branding is that the "global" audience for the nation is much more difficult to pin down than it is for product branding.[57] This challenge is in some sense met by Chinese media's immediate appropriation of the globally circulated "Made in China" discourse.

Central to this immediate appropriation is the figure of the global consumer, constructed as not only an important witness for China's global rise but also a significant target audience to be courted by the Chinese state. The foreign consumers' reliance on and endorsement of the "Made in China" brand would ultimately boost the nation's profile among its citizenry proper and vis-à-vis foreign governments' unequal trade policies. In this sense, the WTO-era Chinese "Made in China" discourse has a more distinct focus on the global image of the Chinese nation. This image is to be conveyed by the global reach of products "made in China," whose customer base is conceived as consisting of a great many "foreign" buyers of Chinese exports. Compared with the National Products Movement of the last century, this re-branding of "Made in China" has a decidedly more global outlook. And it is this global outlook that works to solidify an otherwise elusive constituency for the nation brand.

For this reason, I suggest "global-national imaginary" as an analytical term that captures the ideological practice of nation branding in WTO-era China. Following Cornelius Castoriadis, I understand "imaginary" as a pre-rational, pre-symbolic cultural order that informs the decisions and actions of a specific group of people.[58] It is within an imaginary that a collective subject is called upon to engage in particular actions. While the imaginary itself may not be immediately present in the language adopted by social actors, it nonetheless helps to shape the form of actions taken and the choice of language used to initiate or describe them. WTO-era China's nation branding is precisely such a project of collective agent making, of calling into being a citizen-subject who is to imagine the nation in a manner that conforms to a particular cultural order. Central to the symbolic matrix that makes up this cultural order is the brand, a construct supported by a set of IPR lexicons, from trademarks to intangible values. The conjuring up of the nation in terms of the brand informs the actions of the citizen-subjects in ways that are often unconscious to those implicated in the process, whether the news crews that interviewed Bongiorni or the producers who repurposed the CNN footage for the CCTV program.

What makes the term "global-national imaginary" particularly useful is that it captures the simultaneously transnational and national cultural production of the state. For one thing, the transnational formation of the "Made in China" brand construes "China" as a globalized object of consumption. It is, to be sure, an object of both desire and fear. The making of this complex object in global media also creates the condition for the self-insertion of the Chinese state, as may be observed from the state media's appropriation of the CNN/Bongiorni discourse. At the same time, the production of the state's subject position depends on the nation's global visibility, embodied in the transnationally produced object "Made in China." The global-national imaginary, by capturing this dynamic, attunes us to the simultaneous production of the nation as an "imagined community" à la Benedict Anderson and a "global type" à la Craig Calhoun (see introduction). It describes a global-national ideological formation, one that enables the production of the state as a primary agent of the nation's global ascendency. It does so through the protection and promotion of the "Made in China" brand as a globally circulated nation brand. It also manifests the self-repositioning of the party-state as a subject of history that will ensure the nation's progress along the "homogeneous, empty time" of global modernity (as will be made more visible in the move toward "Created in China.")

Perhaps no other example speaks to the workings of this global-national imaginary better than a thirty-second commercial aired on CNN after Thanksgiving 2009, "Made in China, Made with the World (*Zhongguo Zhizao, Shijie Hezuo*)." The sponsorship for the ad (created by a private public relations firm) came from China's Ministry of Commerce and the Advertising Association of Commerce, as well as chambers of commerce for three industries: the Import and Export of Machinery and Electronic Products, Light Industrial Products and Arts-Crafts, and Textiles. These industries ostensibly represent the pillars of China's export sector, which suggests a "globally" minded branding scheme. The ad showcases several sequences of visibly "foreign" (read "Caucasian") consumers using Chinese-made products, including running shoes, a refrigerator, an MP3 player, a fashion model's garment, and an airplane. In every sequence, a close-up shot of the label reveals their "connections" with the world – "with American sports technology," "with European style," "with software from Silicon Valley," "with French designers," and "with engineers from all over the world."[59]

Some commentators speculated that the ad was supposed to be broadcast earlier but "was delayed as a result of the melamine-tainted milk scandal,"[60] which broke out in October 2008.[61] However, at a press conference Liu Libin, the deputy director of general affairs of China's Advertising Association of Commerce, denied that there was a delay and revealed that the whole production process took a year and a half. After numerous meetings between government officials and ad professionals, the theme for the commercial also evolved from "Made in China is Right Next To You" to "Enjoy Made in China," before finally turning into "Made with the World."[62] The final choice manifests at once the alliance between "the world" and the nation of China, as well as the desire to connect more intimately with the "world's" spectators – in this case, the audience of CNN. The entire spot contains very few typical symbols of "Chineseness." The only nation-specific touch comes at the end, when a miniature red traditional seal-style four-character set, *zhong guo zhi zao* ("Made in China"), appears to the right of the English characters "Made with the World." Even the choice of music – a light-hearted guitar tune – may be more easily identified as the hip "global" type of indie rock than anything more typically associated with "traditional Chineseness."

State-affiliated researchers favorably interpreted this ad as a display of the "Made in China" brand, one that reflects the national strategy of "soft power."[63] Proposed by the Harvard political scientist Joseph Nye in 1990, the concept of "soft power" (*ruan shili*, or *ruan quanli*) was introduced into China's policy discourse in 1993 by Fudan University professor Wang Huning, who later became the central government's top consultant on international politics. The term made its way into official strategy in President Hu Jintao's address at the Chinese Communist Party's Seventeenth National Congress in 2007.[64] Under the section "Promoting the Great Development and Great Enrichment of Socialist Culture," Hu calls for "enhancing the nation's cultural soft power," as culture "has increasingly become an important source for national cohesion and creativity, a key factor in the competition of comprehensive national power."[65] The "Made with the World" ad, in this sense, can be seen as a strategic move in presenting the national image to the world through cultural means. At the same time, this "culture" is more accurately understood as a soft powered (if not "American-styled") industrially produced culture (witness the ad's use of "indie" music) that is at once globally communicable and nationally specific. It is precisely this global-national imaginary that prompted the Chinese government and relevant industrial alliances to take up the mission of producing the CNN ad.

More significantly, the state's subject position inculcated in the global-national imaginary is dependent on the object status of the nation brand. After all, the "Made in China" brand emerged as an object in crisis. Its crisis-ridden characteristics afford the state the opportunity to present itself as a subject that can not only lead the nation out of crisis but also direct it toward a future – a future that is to be prescribed by the global imaginary of the brand. The state, in essence, appears as a split subject.[66] The interpellation of the citizen-subjects is itself subject to globally implicated contestations.

This establishment of the state's subjectivity takes two primary forms. On the one hand, the state establishes itself as an arbiter of international trade relations. The ad happened to appear on CNN a few months after several major Sino-U.S. trade disputes that resulted in penalties for China's exporters. Among them, President Obama's use of the product-specific safeguard provision to raise tariffs on tires imported from China – a response to the United Steelworkers union's complaint – generated the most criticism of America's "protectionism" in Chinese media. Journalistic accounts repeatedly cited this and other foreign "technical trade barriers" as the reason for the major loss of revenue among China's export industries.[67] The head of the National Quality Inspection Bureau even denounced "the 'Chinese Product Threat' discourse itself" as "a form of trade protection" and a defensive response on the part of foreigners to "the increasing share of Chinese products in the international market."[68] These narratives of China's "subjection" to international trade disputes equate the low cost of the "Made in China" brand with its perceived global market competitiveness. This attribution at once elevates "Made in China" to a marker of national success and re-casts it as a victim of the unequal power relations in the international trade system. It not only affirms the state policy of Reform and Opening Up but recycles the long-standing anti-imperialist sentiment more closely associated with the Maoist era. The idea, then, is that even as China has become a much more powerful nation – thanks to the correctness of state policies – it still demands stronger state voices in representing the nation in such international arenas as the WTO.

On the other hand, the state is also positioned as a regulator of the "Made in China" brand. This involves not only ensuring its global consumers' satisfaction but also protecting it from being tarnished by deviant behavior, such as counterfeiting. As some commentators on the "Made with the World" ad point out, "the nurturing of brand loyalty is

a long process,"[69] one that requires "the 'hard power' of product quality."[70] What is implied is that this "hard power" is in need of the state's
tightened quality control and institutional as well as procedural oversight. In the words of the National Quality Inspection Bureau official,
the brand-nurturing process entails more severe criminalization of those
producers who "make or sell fake" products.[71] This differentiation of the
"good" (and "real") "Made in China" from the "bad" "Faked in China"
does the job of transferring the consumer's ability to discern fakes to
the (quality) control of the state. In assuming the role of a protector,
the state's interest is realigned with that of the "global" consumer, both
domestic and foreign.

    These narrative deployments of "Made in China," championed by
CCTV (the emblem of state media), have been pervasive in the nation's
media discourse. However, part of my task here is to resist their simpli-
fication as so-called state propaganda. For one thing, CCTV itself has
undergone profound changes over the Reform years. Formerly Beijing
Television, founded in 1958, the station was officially re-established in
1978.[72] It was meant to "unify the country through presentation of official news and information, culturally-appropriate entertainment," and
the promotion of Mandarin (or Putonghua) as the national language.[73]
In and after the 1990s, the "iron rice bowl" system that guaranteed
lifelong employment, typical of labor conditions in the cultural sector,
largely began giving way to a more "flexible" contract-based model.[74]
One of the most significant outcomes of this shift was the rise of a "new
breed" of "cultural workers" hired independently by producers. They
occupy a "new space" that is capable of destabilizing the totalizing state
voices in significant ways.[75] In addition, with "global capital" rather than
the state constituting its "main source of funding," the station had to
adjust the programming to "ensure high ratings" and attract "advertising
and sponsorship dollars."[76] This commercialization has certainly shifted
the orientation of the station from a concern chiefly with the delivery
of political messages to a concentration on profit making – what Yuezhi
Zhao calls the internalization of "the discourses of transnational capitalism" by "a national media system."[77]

    At the same time, CCTV's monopoly status means that it retains
a powerful presence in the national psyche, even as it has increasingly

become the target of online parody and mockery (chapter 2). The "Believe in Made in China" program, like many other CCTV productions, generated a significant round of blogger responses. One post titled itself "Made in China, I Don't Believe." The blogger, named "Agent of Delusion," collected a series of diatribes against the program and CCTV in general. While some of these comments display a distrust of the typical "fooling" rhetoric of the state's mouthpiece, others link the attitude presented in this program to the famous character depicted in the modernist author Lu Xun's novel, Ah Q.[78] The idea is that much like Ah Q, a character known for his ability to construct self-satisfying narratives through the so-called "method of psychological victory" (*Jingshen Shenglifa*), CCTV always comes up with stories to make China feel good about itself. A more sarcastic note states that "whoever CCTV supports (*ting*) would die. 'Made in China' is being supported, [and that's how] I know that 'Made in China' is about done." Others invoke a slogan imitating the rhetoric of an antidrug campaign, "Cherish your life, keep CCTV far away (*zhenxi shengming, yuanli* CCTV), which has become a widely circulated tag line online.[79]

A more elaborate response came from the outspoken Wharton-trained economist Lang Xianping. Lang, a professor in Hong Kong, became famous for stimulating a media debate on the legitimacy of neoliberalism in 2003.[80] While continuing to publicize his criticism of the exploitative nature of globalized industrial production chains, Lang now appears twice a week on a late-night talk show featuring his views on finance and economics. This show is aired on the Guangdong Satellite TV station and made immediately available on his online fan site. On December 13, 2009, the theme for discussion was "Made in China overseas," and the host opened with a plotline from the Hollywood blockbuster 2012. "Just as in the Bible, Noah is the trusted producer for God," he states, "in the movie, China is the trusted producer for America, as Noah's Ark is made in China." However, "in reality," he goes on, "America's colored lenses have never been taken off," implying that the United States has been biased toward China in handling trade disputes.

After reviewing the "Made in China, Made with the World" ad, Lang claims that the ad producers "got it all wrong." For him, the message of the ad is this:

> The design belongs to others. The core technologies belong to others. We are
> only in charge of manufacture. It's clearly telling other people that we are just
> workers, peasant migrants (*nongmin gong*). Everything is controlled by you.
> High-value-added components are controlled by you. [Since] we already serve
> as such low-value-added laborers, why are you treating us so badly? Please give
> us a break.... [81]

Lang's reading of the ad excavates a subject-object relationship that is
quite different from that of its "official" interpreters. Rather than understanding "Made in China" as enunciated by the speaking subject
of the (abstracted) Chinese nation, he locates "we" in the bodies of the
migrant peasants-turned-workers. This reading then complicates the
emergent subjectivity of the nation in the world; it reveals the objectifying process – the commodification of "the people" – that materially
underlies the making of the nation brand. Instead of reading "the world"
as China's collaborator, he interprets "you" (the "world" for whom the
ad is made) as owners of "design" and "core technologies," that is, intellectual property. The agency of control, then, remains safely in the
hands of global capital, which ultimately owns the means of production
in the so-called information/knowledge economy. The inherent contradictions of the global-national imaginary masked by the CCTV ad are
thus made visible; what provides the foundation for the nation's global
ascendency and the state's self-imagination as a subject in the world is
the objectification of "the people."[82]

Wang Mudi, the talk-show host, then brings up a recent formulation
in the media – "From Made in China to Created in China." Amid the
"Made in China" brand crisis, this slogan has been taking on a discursive
momentum unmatched by the media's earlier "Made in China" rebranding efforts. What mobilizes this reconfiguration, which projects a movement from the present model of "Made in China" to a future of "Created in China?" How does this discourse contribute to the ideological
production of the global-national imaginary? These questions warrant
further investigation into the production of the rhetoric itself. As I will
demonstrate through a mapping of the "Created in China" discourse, the
adoption of this slogan as a national policy directive is indicative of the
effect of the IPR regime on WTO-era China's global-national imaginary,
an effect that is manifested most visibly through the distinct temporality
of the brand.

"CREATED IN CHINA" AS NATIONAL POLICY

The making of the slogan "From Made in China to Created in China" may be attributed to the biggest global-national branding event of the decade – the 2008 Beijing Olympics. In 1999, as part of the preparation for the bid to host the Games, a state-level symposium was held to promote the idea expressed as "New Beijing, New Olympics." Its organizers went on to form a non-profit organization called Creative China Industrial Alliance (CCIA, or *Chuangyi Zhongguo*).[83] As its director Su Tong explained, the goal of the organization is to "take a global outlook" in urban planning, "responsive to local contexts" while "reaching out to the world" through "a comprehensive branding strategy."[84] The invocation of "branding" here is indicative of the rising brand consciousness on the part of China's cultural policymakers. Not only did Su address the need to "allow China to refresh its understanding of the world and allow the world to rediscover a new China," he also emphasized that "creativity is not just about big cities and the middle classes; it needs to be distributed to become *people-centred*" (my emphasis).[85] This emphasis on "the people" is significant, as it reflects a default status of "the people" as other than the urban middle class – that is, the rural (and migrant) population that constitutes the majority of the citizenry.[86] Implicitly acknowledged is the highly unequal distribution of "creativity" within China's vast geographical differences and widening class gaps.

However, this suggested focus on the "people" is seemingly elided in the subsequent policy formation of "Created in China" (*zhongguo chuangzao*). The term began appearing in publications like *Chinese Business* and *Modern Enterprise Education* in 2003.[87] Before long, Liu Shifa, an official from the Ministry of Culture, put forth the idea "From Made in China to Created in China" (*cong Zhongguo zhizao dao Zhongguo chuangzao*). The slogan was first publically displayed at the Seventh Beijing Science Expo in May 2004. Subsequently, a national policy that promotes "creative industries" (*chuangyi chanye*) began to take hold, replacing the language of developing "culture industries" (*wenhua chanye*) formally adopted in the Tenth Five-Year Plan.[88] This did not reflect a motivation to cultivate rural creativity, however; those who infused the policies with the new vocabulary of the "creative economy" were none

other than businesses and officials in megacities like Beijing and Shanghai.[89] As the "From Made in China to Created in China" slogan has
evolved from a CCIA coinage into a branding strategy, it has increasingly
moved away from the ostensible claim to serve the people and closer to
a mandate to serve the nation.

How then does the state justify the political legitimacy of this policy
initiative at this particular historical moment, given that the Maoist
principle to "Serve the People" has been one of the founding ideologies of the party-state?[90] Certainly, what distinguished the WTO era
from the past was the pressure to present a perfected national image
for the Olympics, a global media event that called for a comprehensive
branding strategy for the entire nation. The concern for the global media
gaze has no doubt helped shape the language and imagery of "Created
in China." For one thing, the "green idea" of creativity as a seemingly
"unlimited" resource is appealing for "a country where the 'Made in
China' model had turned skies a brownish grey."[91] These associations
between creativity and national development reasonably lured the municipal, township, and county officials into lending their consent to the
"Created in China" notion. Having discarded environmental and labor
standards in favor of manufacturing capacity for three decades, Chinese
leaders are now presumably able to discern the "limits of growth" and
the risk of losing manufacturing contracts to "less-expensive locations"
due to the rising costs of production.[92] The idea of the "*long* economy
(*changjiu jingji*)" (*long* as both the pinyin spelling/pronunciation for
the Chinese symbol of the dragon and the signifier for long-term, sustainable growth), put forth by Su himself, is illustrative of this anxiety
and the wish to overcome it.[93] Still, these linkages between the nation's
global outlook and national policymaking practices do not explain how
and why this particular formation of "Created in China" came to be
solidified as the national vision, accumulating such discursive power as
to preclude other ways of imagining the nation's future. To get a glimpse
into its workings in prescribing a specific kind of temporality for the nation, it is worthwhile to analyze the media discourse surrounding "From
Made in China to Created in China" in light of the global imaginary
of the brand.

"FROM MADE IN CHINA TO CREATED IN CHINA": A CULTURAL PRODUCTION

In 2009, CCTV aired a five-part series with the English title *Across Made in China*. ("Across" here appears to be a mistranslation of the Chinese term *kua yue*, which literally refers to "surpassing" or "overcoming.") A highly sophisticated production that took two years to complete, the program reiterates China's competitiveness in manufacturing before telling several stories of domestic brands going global, with a finale called "Upgrading Made in China."[94] It features several Chinese entrepreneurs who have succeeded in creating their own brand-name products, even bringing them into overseas markets. Business experts from Japan, America, and elsewhere are also invited to comment on China's situation vis-à-vis those previously faced by more "advanced" nations.

Early on, the program invokes two key markers of the "global" present: the 2008 Beijing Olympics and the subsequent global financial meltdown. The first sets the Beijing Games in a comparative light along with the only other two former Olympics staged in Asia in history: the 1964 Tokyo Games and the 1988 Olympics in Seoul. The second heightens the downfall of numerous "global giants" at the onset of the economic crisis, implying that "Made in China" is both a foundation and a precursor to a new era of development for China. Strategically blending the two, the narrator asks: "Can Lenovo be like Sony and Panasonic after the Tokyo Olympics?" or "Samsung after Seoul's?" This narrative mirrors a pervasive discourse in print media in the wake of the 2008 global financial meltdown, a crisis that forced many export processing companies in China into downsizing if not bankruptcy.[95] Numerous observers have come to attribute this consequence of the crisis to China's lack of IPR-protected values.[96] To avoid future disasters of this kind, they argue, it is imperative for Chinese enterprises to establish their own brands.[97] Taking this rhetoric one step further, the CCTV program carefully merges a diagnosis of the present – signaled by Sara Bongiorni's proved-to-be-challenging "year without" experiment – with an image of the future. It implies that the post-Olympics success of Japanese and Korean brands can be replicated by brands created in China, if one recognizes the present as an opportunity to "reshuffle the cards for the game." "History is in our own hands," states the voice-over, "and it requires every single Chinese to share our individual responsibility."[98]

The ostensible alignment of "every single Chinese" with the subject position as the maker of the nation's history is hardly a new interpellating strategy. One may argue that this way of mobilizing a mass subjectivity harks back to Mao's Great Leap Forward, whereby the nation was set on a path to overtake the Western imperialist powers through high-speed industrialization.[99] However, the protagonists featured in the CCTV program are the creators of globally significant domestic brands – that is, the entrepreneur-capitalists. Indeed, they are endowed with the mission of reinventing the nation's future. In the words of one business leader: "An enterprise is the unit in the nation. Only when each enterprise is big can the country be strong, the nation be strong."[100] The linking of the interests of capitalists with that of the nation not only portrays them as the prime movers who are to realize the "Created in China" vision; it also serves to marginalize the subject status of those who are the "mere manufacturers" of foreign brands – the migrant workers as the producers of items "made in China."

This "re-shuffling" of subject positions signals a deeper transformation in the ideological state apparatus. For one thing, the state appears to be operating within a global branding imaginary. This imaginary not only specifies a "branded" – that is, IPR-friendly – vision for the nation but also prescribes the set of actors and actions that are indispensible for realizing that vision. If the "Made in China" brand emerged in a transnational crisis of product quality, this crisis is now more tangibly linked with the global financial crisis in 2008, when signs of global capital's movement from China to lower-cost regions like Vietnam began to develop.[101] The former emphasis on the competitiveness of "Made in China" began to seem a less effective means to boost citizens' confidence in this nation brand. As a result, the abundant "human resource" that contributes to price competitiveness is itself no longer as attractive a feature to highlight when describing the "Made in China" nation brand. What is called for, instead, is a set of actors that would lift the nation out of its present state toward a future whose landscape is clearly laid out – in the imaginary of the Chinese-created global brand. These historical actors are the "creative" class of entrepreneurs, not the workers engaged in manual labor; if anything, the latter are now positioned as "the people," an a priori object for national pedagogy.[102]

The production of the "Created in China" vision thus speaks to the hegemonic formation of the national bourgeoisie – that is, knowledge- or information capitalists expected to create products eligible for IPR protection. What makes this particular "narration" of the nation unique is that it no longer portrays the nation through representation, as is often the case in a literary culture based on a national language. Rather, the national vision is conjured up through the brand, a construct inscribed with intangible value, sanctioned by the IPR discourse. The citizen-subject is thus sutured into a branded temporality to which China must conform in order to fulfill the vision of development toward a predetermined future. This particular way of imagining the nation in a global time of "progress" ascribes historical agency to subjects in a particular class – that of the so-called creative entrepreneurs who are capable of producing intangible value. Those precluded from these subject positions are then reduced to objects for the "nation branding" pedagogy of the elites.

A speech made by Fred Hu Zuliu, the director of Tsinghua University's Chinese Economics Research Center and the managing director for Goldman Sachs (Asia), helps to illustrate this IPR-informed suturing process. When speaking to a group of government officials and business executives, Hu situates China in a low-end position in the global supply chain, arguing that the "labor-intensive" model upon which China has depended for the past couple of decades is now faced with worsening trade and environmental conditions. In order to ensure the nation's "future development of a comprehensive economy," Hu calls upon Chinese manufacturing industries to transform themselves "from low-end manufacturing to mid- or high-end segments of the value chain."[103] Noting that "a key marker to distinguish 'Made' from 'Created' is the amount of holdings in intellectual property," Hu invokes the "Made" to "Created" paths taken previously by Europe, America, Japan, Taiwan, and Korea. He emphatically singles out the example of the United States: "Nowadays not many products can be found 'made in USA,' with the exception of software, medicine, airplanes, and Hollywood movies, but no one would doubt that those products 'made in China' or 'made in

Mexico' contain elements 'created in USA.' [*sic*]" Linking this U.S. example back to the need for China to embark on a more sustainable path of "scientific development," Hu suggests that "a fundamental change needs to take shape from the tangible 'Made in China' to the intangible 'Created in China,'" which entails boosts in educational and human resources, greater research and development investment, and "intellectual property protection and capital market development."[104]

Hu's characterization of the "Created in China" national vision as an intangible value places China on a global developmentalist trajectory. In this and other commentaries, such as those championed by CCTV, the future value of brands "created in China" is guaranteed if the "Made in China" present can be overcome in the same way as its predecessors, such as "Made in Germany" in the nineteenth century, "Made in Japan" in the 1950s, and "Made in Korea" in the 1980s.[105] Once China is positioned in a global time frame of development by way of comparison, the eventual global success of these formerly tainted domestic brands serves to instill a sense of confidence that "Created in China" will be the next to overcome the pitfalls of "Made in China." China's future is thus envisioned as one of "virtual capitalism," distinguishable from the "actual capitalism" that characterized the earlier "national manufacturing order." This is a mode of capital accumulation that depends "less on the abstract, homogenous labour of actuals, and more on the generative and invention-based potential of virtual objects."[106] In other words, the nation of the future is to extract its value from brands created in China rather than products made in China. This movement depends on the conversion of the nation's participation in making actual products into a capacity for generating intangible value in "virtual" brands. The success of this conversion is itself predicated on the idea that brand values are to be realized in the future. In this way, the campaign "From Made in China to Created in China" not only entrenches the nation deeper in the teleology of development and modernization, but has also more aggressively naturalized the "higher time" of advanced capitalism.[107]

The pervasiveness of the "Created in China" discourse is also evidenced by wide-ranging cultural productions and events. Among them was a song performed by the famous Western-style opera singer Liao Changyong to celebrate the launching of the Shenzhou No. 7 space shuttle. CCTV's 2009 *Annual Economic Figures* included two groups of business executives under the categories "Made in China" and "Created in China."[108] The two labels also made their way into an award-winning high-school student essay, entitled "How Far is it from Made in China to Created in China?" The author, a ninth-grader from Rudong County, Jiangsu Province, points out that the "China price" comes at the expense of the workers' harsh conditions, lack of safety and union protection, and eternally low wages. "How many lives have been compensated for what appears to be cheap 'Made in China'?" the author asks. "The limits of challenge for China should be at the medal-awarding pedestal of the Olympic Games, the R&D of high-tech products, and not in using lives to challenge the limit of low cost for 'Made in China.'" Like other commentaries of this kind, there is an explicit antagonism directed toward the state-capital relationship, whether foreign or domestic. But the essay nonetheless ends with a call for action: "When can that character 'Made' be turned into 'Created?' What beautiful words, 'created in China!' I, we, every single Chinese . . . we have a long way to go, and our burden of responsibility is heavy (*renzhong er daoyuan*)."[109] The invocation of the real cost of "Made in China" here serves to heighten the urgency for "all Chinese" to participate in the movement away from the present. The march toward "Created in China," then, fully enacts the ideological force of the global-national imaginary, for it is through concrete actions taken up by "every single Chinese" that nation branding is to materialize its proffered national vision.

CONCLUSION

The "Made" to "Created" rhetoric triggered more sneers from Lang Xianping. In the same TV program on Guangdong Satellite, he points out that the success of Germany and Japan in overcoming their "fake" image had to do with their demand for precision in serving their "wartime machineries" – a tradition lacking in China, which is trying to "construct high buildings from the plains." For him, China's model can only follow that of Taiwan, a sort of "mistress" (*bang dakuan*) economy, because the "exploitive division" is too hard to overcome.[110] Lang's distrust of the rhetoric here speaks quite pointedly to the unequal global relations of power that underlie the global-national imaginary "From Made in China to Created in China." As an ideological formation that has come to reconfigure the WTO-era Chinese state, this imaginary reflects the subtle yet complex working of IPR in proffering a particular vision for the nation. What grants discursive power to the notion of "Created in China" is a temporality of progress specifically associated with the brand. Not only does the IPR regime serve as a legitimizing structure for the brands' intangible value; it also offers a developmental path that requires a strong state to guide the nation toward a future glorified by nation brands.

In this sense, the cultural work of IPR in shaping the "From Made in China to Created in China" discourse prompts us to rethink the productive rather than invasive workings of globalization qua cultural imperialism. While the transnationally produced "Made in China" brand crisis is not directly attributable to IPR, the conjoined temporalities of the nation and the brand had come to naturalize this label in the form of a globally circulated nation brand. After all, the crisis of "Made in China" is a crisis of authenticity in that the global imaginary of the brand has destabilized the state's "natural" claim to the nation. It is by resorting to a global-national imaginary – one that simultaneously corresponds to the global consumer-citizen and conforms to the financializing temporality of the brand – that the state is able to reconstitute itself as an agentive force in steering the nation toward an IPR-friendly future. In other words, IPR's cultural work has not only produced a schism between the nation and the state, it has also prescribed how the state may go about restoring its tie to the nation – by aligning its own citizen-subjects to fit with an IPR-friendly national vision. What is privileged in the nation-branding discourse, therefore, is the subject position of the domestic entrepreneurs who are deemed most qualified to shore up the legitimacy of the state. In this process, the working-class subjects behind the "Made in China" label are marginalized even though the objectification of their labor constitutes the foundation for the rise of the "Made in China" nation brand itself.

The working of the IPR regime, however, is not limited to shaping the state imaginary for the nation. Its cultural manifestation also includes the transnational practice of counterfeit culture – a culture of circulation that is bound to contest the homogeneous temporality of development on which the nation-branding project is predicated. Indeed, the "fake" incidents at the Beijing Olympics, along with numerous other "China fake" stories that consistently erupt into the global media spotlight, are powerful reminders that between "Made in China" and "Created in China" looms the specter of "Faked in China." Just as the brand can be subject to heterogeneous meaning-making practices that disrupt the value regime based on intangibility, the nation can also be re-imagined by various subjects and publics in ways that challenge the state-sanctioned trajectory of IPR progress. While these publics conjure up alternative visions for transforming the social world that is WTO-era China, their interactions with the project of nation branding also enact the contradictory cultural effects of IPR, and indeed the unequal relations of power that persist in contemporary globalization.

TWO

From Bandit Cell Phones to Branding the Nation: Three Moments of *Shanzhai*

TWO THOUSAND EIGHT WAS AN EVENTFUL YEAR FOR THE People's Republic of China. The made-for-TV global spectacle of the Beijing Olympics, preceded by governmental efforts in combating natural disasters like the January–February snowstorm and the Sichuan earthquake, afforded state media ample reasons to memorialize the year in more or less grandiose terms. Curiously, however, a different proclamation surfaced in the mediascape – 2008 was to be remembered as the "Year of Shanzhai."[1] The official English paper *China Daily* ran the following story on December 9, offering a glimpse into its meanings:

> It's a cold Sunday morning. Mr. Phony turned off his hiPhone alarm, put on Kabba suits and Adidos shoes, grabbed a coffee from the KFG downstairs and came back in a hurry for the latest episode of the popular sit-com Ugly Wudi. No spelling mistakes above. Products imitating famous brands have not been uncommon around China for a couple of years – and now they have a unified name, a *brand* if you like, "Shanzhai" (my emphasis).[2]

While it is no news that China has an abundance of counterfeit objects like "hiPhone" and "Adidos," the reporter seems most intrigued by the fact that they are now grouped under one name. This name – what is likened to a "brand" – consists of two characters: *shan,* literally meaning "mountain," and *zhai,* translatable as "village," "stockade," "fortress," or "stronghold." A Chinese speaker perhaps needs no expert knowledge of Chinese classics like *Water Margins* (*Shui Hu*) to understand the word's connotation: "Shanzhai" refers to the home of the bandits. More often than not, these outlaws are the Chinese equivalent of Robin Hood. Having offended the rich and the powerful, they flee from court rulings and retreat into the mountains to set up their base for counterattack. Hence the name "mountain stronghold."[3]

How has "the bandits' mountainous home" come to represent the identity of counterfeit goods? Some have traced the word's modern origin to the colonial city of Hong Kong, where Cantonese is the dominant dialect. There, small-scale "Shanzai" (Cantonese spelling) workshops, referred to as "mountain-village factories," are said to have emerged in the 1960s at the foot of Lion Rock Mountain.[4] Specializing in "light industry products like watches, toys, and garments," these factories emblematized a transition to a mixed economy within Hong Kong's developmental history.[5] It is only in recent decades that the term has been popularized in Mandarin, the official tongue of mainland China.

To be sure, numerous alternatives for "fake" have long existed in the Chinese lexicon, such as "wei" and "jia." More recently, Hu Ge's 2006 online video, "The Bloody Case that Started with a Steamed Bun," has pioneered a "digitized parody" movement and given rise to the neologism "egao."[6] Literally meaning "reckless doings," the term is a transliteration of the Japanese word "Kuso" ("shit"), which came into mainland China via Taiwan.[7] Compared to "egao," whose use is often restricted to online video spoofing, "Shanzhai" is known to have a more "adhesive power," capable of absorbing other imitating behaviors into its signification.[8] For example, copycat cultural productions, especially television shows based on Euro-American formats, are also incorporated into the category of Shanzhai culture. A case in point is 2006's hugely popular *Super Female Voice* (or *Super Girl*), which is retrospectively called the "Shanzhai *American Idol*."[9]

It is not difficult to detect a commonality among these myriad Shanzhai forms: whether it is the pirated hiPhone, the parodied art house film, or the popularly voted *Super Girl*, what unifies them under "Shanzhai" is their ostensible appeal to "the people." Indeed, numerous media accounts have come to label these cultural productions "grassroots," "subculture," and "resistance," both in China and abroad.[10] One question that remains unanswered among a growing body of scholarly work[11] is why Shanzhai has arisen at this particular moment to denote objects and practices that had been around for a long time. For example, markets famous for selling fake brand-name clothing and accessories, such as

Beijing's Silk Street (chapter 4) and Shanghai's Xiangyang Street, have been popular since the 1980s. There has also been no shortage of news reports about official crackdowns on counterfeit goods, especially before and during the Beijing Olympics. Yet the domestic media frenzy generated by Shanzhai seemingly outshone that of the Games in 2008. Its sheer scale would suffice to invite a more critical inquiry into the formation of the discourse itself.

To pursue this inquiry, I draw attention to the multi- or transmedia character of this new "brand name" for the fake. Notably, Shanzhai is simultaneously a discourse *about* new media – from cell phones to the internet – and a discourse *mediated by* these new media, as well as their older counterparts such as television and print. While Shanzhai's signifying journey is not reducible to the new media realm, an articulation of its relationship to these media certainly helps to contextualize its spectacular rise in contemporary China. For this reason, I have chosen to focus on three significant moments in Shanzhai's formation: the emergence of Shanzhaiji (short for "Shanzhai shouji," that is, "Shanzhai handset," also known as "bandit cell phones," as CNN puts it)[12] in the informal sector of southern China, the online archive of Shanzhai artifacts, and the news coverage of Shanzhai by CCTV (China Central Television). These moments are by no means distinct from one another, nor do they capture the entirety of the continuously unfolding Shanzhai phenomenon. They do, however, bring to light the interactive character of China's new media landscape, especially after the country's official accession to the WTO in 2001. Taking seriously Shanzhai's manifestations in these media sites and artifacts, I aim to identity the various subjects, agents, and publics that have engaged themselves in its making. In doing so, I return Shanzhai to its material sites of production, so as to delve further into the historical forces that shape its meanings.

My argument is that the Shanzhai discourse, co-configured within and across a multiplicity of media platforms, produces a set of ideological contestations that emblematize the cultural dilemma of the postsocialist state. While the emergence of Shanzhaiji and the online explosion of Shanzhai culture conjure up a collective imaginary, this imaginary has come to disrupt the state's long-standing claim to "the nation" as a signifier for "the people." The representation of Shanzhai by state media

2.1. An iPhone-Android hybrid displayed as an example of Shanzhai cell phones at the Bi-City Biennale of Urbanism/Architecture, Shenzhen, 2014.

therefore manifests the working of the ideological state apparatus in incorporating the Shanzhai discourse into the state's post-2001 nation-branding project. Together, these moments of Shanzhai shed light on the postsocialist state's operation amid the intensified contradictions of globalization after its WTO entry.

THE RISE OF SHANZHAIJI

Almost all media stories about Shanzhai in the 2000s have traced the term's contemporary origin to the rise of Shanzhaiji in southern China, particularly the Special Economic Zone (SEZ) of Shenzhen. Despite the ubiquity of the name, Shanzhaiji is notoriously hard to define. While global brand knockoffs like Nokla and hiPhone obviously belong in the category, many no-name others are also granted the label. Sometimes they are distinguishable by looks, since they often sport striking design

features. Others are simply cheaper phones made by small-scale manufacturers, albeit often equipped with more functions than their more
expensive counterparts.[13]

For the purpose of this analysis, I follow Cara Wallis and Jack Qiu
in understanding Shanzhaiji as products of the informal mobile phones
sector in southern China.[14] In many ways, this sector pioneered the rise
of Shanzhai culture in WTO-era China. The story of its rise reveals a
complex process of global, national, and local struggles. However, most
accounts thus far tend to discuss the phenomenon strictly as emblematic of a "Shanzhai economy," in separation from a "Shanzhai culture."
This distinction between the economic and the cultural obscures rather
than illuminates the important interconnections between the two. Scott
Lash and Celia Lury have suggested that in today's "global culture industry," culture is "thingified" – the superstructure has collapsed into
the economic base.[15] Our everyday encounters with commodities, particularly branded commodities, become an experience at once cultural
and economic. While Shanzhai is not a brand name per se, the way in
which it operates has an analogical as well as referential relationship with
that of a corporate brand. The economic production of this "brand" is
necessarily a cultural process, just as the cultural meanings it generates
are intertwined with the political-economic conditions from which it
has emerged. Therefore, I argue that Shanzhaiji is part and parcel of
Shanzhai culture and should be subject to cultural as well as economic
analyses.

From an economic standpoint, perhaps the most striking character
of Shanzhaiji is its low price, attributable to its defiance of legal doc-
trines, both the globalized IPR laws and state regulations and tax codes.[16]
But Shanzhaiji production is more intricately tied to its birthplace of
Shenzhen, a city that occupies a unique position in the globalization
of southern China. Bordering Hong Kong at the southern tip of the
Guangdong peninsula, Shenzhen was one of the first SEZs set up in the
Pearl River Delta in conjunction with Deng Xiaoping's 1978 launching
of the Reform and Opening Up policy. The city has since absorbed many
multinational corporations' subcontracting chains that had originally
relocated to Hong Kong in the 1960s.[17] Not only did the large factories
set up in its vicinity benefit from state policies favoring foreign direct

investment (FDI), they also brought large numbers of (predom
female) peasant migrants from inland Chinese provinces to Sh
in search of jobs in the export processing sector.[18]

The presence of global brand manufacturers in Shenzhen has helped
shape the Shanzhaiji sector in important ways. For example, veteran
technicians previously hired by global brand subcontractors often enter
the Shanzhai sector as contributors of operational knowledge. Sometimes the factory facilities and the subcontracted workers themselves
are also employed at night to produce Shanzhaiji.[19] If these aspects
point to the intimate connection between the Shanzhaiji sector and the
multinational corporations (MNCs) that produce global brands, other
features of the former also work to contest the latter's global operation.
For instance, one of the key cost-cutting features of Shanzhaiji is the
use of a multifunctional motherboard-software combo sold by a Taiwanese company, MediaTek (MTK). Tsai Ming-Kai, the inventor of the
technology who founded the company in 1997, is nicknamed "the father
of Shanzhaiji."[20] Not only did the technology significantly lower the
industry's entry barrier, it also sharply reduced the research and development (R&D) timeline. Before long, MTK started selling the chips in bulk
to small-scale manufacturers in Shenzhen. With investments from local
entrepreneurs of the Pearl River Delta, these makers soon established
a "fully integrated, large-scale Shanzhai cell phone industrial chain,"[21]
one that is said to have cracked the "foreign techno-monopolistic advantage."[22] Consisting of a flexibly organized network of software engineers, designers, and suppliers, Shanzhaiji's "modularized" model of
production is able to churn out a large quantity of phones at as little as
one-third of the cost for "legit" brands.[23]

Given these circumstances, it may not be an exaggeration to call the
clustered industry of Shanzhaiji a corporation without legal incorporation. Like many MNCs, the production of Shanzhaiji relies on a core
technology, an integrated supply chain, an R&D network, and a design
team. The sector also inherits if not co-exploits the technical and manual
workers employed by many MNCs' subcontractors. Shanzhaiji's production, rather than being demarcated by boundaries that distinguish an
inside and an outside, indeed depends on a constellation of several global
"vectors."[24] Most visible among these vectors are the flows of capital (in

the form of FDI or in the stock of MTK, a publicly traded company in Taiwan) and the movement of labor migrants and regional merchants or financiers.

What makes Shanzhaiji a more intriguing phenomenon, however, is the local and provincial media attention it triggered. These reports on Shanzhaiji have played no small role in the cultural production of the "brand." Just as MNCs deploy mass media for the transmission of meanings and lifestyles associated with their brands, the local coverage of Shanzhaiji has helped to establish Shanzhai's status as a bandit logo. Among these narratives of Shanzhaiji, often mentioned is Shanzhai's roots in ancient China, where "peasants would rise up in arms against despotic rules by occupying a mountain to become kings themselves."[25] The invocation of this "pre-modern" sensibility is accompanied by the idea that the Shanzhai strategy is based on "villages surrounding the city," pointing to the widely held belief that the peasantry held the key to success during the Maoist revolution.[26] The operation of the sector is seen as akin to guerrilla warfare – it responds quickly to market shifts and flexibly ducks official crackdowns, which have been frequent and pervasive in Shenzhen from 2006 onward. Its composition of thousands of small enterprises is also distinguished from the "foreign" Fordist-style mass production.[27] The law-defiant ethos of Shanzhaiji's production is further seen as cutting into the profits sought by global brands, which depend on the IPR regime to lay claim to their intangible values.[28]

To be sure, these narratives have romanticized Shanzhaiji production to an extent; its real working conditions are often no better than those facilities subcontracted by global brands,[29] especially for the underpaid migrants who produce the surplus value that profits a handful of local or regional entrepreneurs. However, the source of the enthusiasm for the "brand" is worth pondering, considering that much of it stems from Shanzhaiji's market success vis-à-vis its legit counterparts, particularly the state-sponsored "national brands" (*guochan pinpai*). Back in 1987, when the analog cell phone sector first emerged, a domestic cell phone industry did not exist in China. Motorola had enjoyed a market monopoly in the nation until the first Chinese digital cellular communication network was established in 1994. After that, Nokia and Ericsson joined in the competition, splitting the Chinese handset market

in three. Four years later, in 1998, the State Council issued a set of policies to promote the development of a domestic manufacturing sector
for mobile phones.[30] One of the follow-up measures stipulated that 60
percent of the phones produced in foreign-owned factories must be exported.[31] The goal, of course, was to leave room for national brands in the
domestic market. When these state policies took effect, the market share
of national brands showed a visible increase, exceeding that of the global
brands for the first time in 2003. However, the victory was short-lived, as
the share dropped from 60 percent to 37 percent within a year, a decline
attributed to the questionable quality of national brands and their pace
of innovation, which lagged behind the global brand manufacturers.

It was in this context that Shanzhaiji unexpectedly rose to compete
with both national and global brands. While it beat national brands in
its speed of R&D, thanks to the MTK combo and the flexible industrial
network, its low cost and daring design also appealed to what Jack Qiu
calls "the information have-less" – "migrants, laid-off workers, retirees
and students from low-income families" who have integrated mobile
phones into their "modes of communication and ways of life," transforming a former "elite privilege" into "basic instruments necessary to
human existence itself."[32] Migrant workers constitute no small part of
these groups, numbering 274 million in 2014 according to China's official statistics. Adding to the mix are "second generation" migrants (the
descendants of the first-wave migrants in the 1980s), who are increasingly
visible in the media as a social group that straddles a lost connection to
the countryside and a sense of rejection by city folks. Prior to the advent
of mobile technologies, migrants had to rely on limited public phones or
dormitory landlines to stay in touch with their friends and families. The
convenience of a handset was surely welcomed, even if the phone might
cost more than their monthly salary (around the equivalent of $100).[33]
According to a 2007 investigative report, 90 percent of China's migrant
workers were in possession of a handset.[34] Many of these phones were
noted to be of the cheaper Shanzhai "brand."[35]

Shanzhaiji is not just attractive to the "information have-less" for
its low cost. For example, such distinct features as extra-strong signals
and extra-long batteries are particularly important, because they allow
continuous use in factories and rural areas where signals are weak and

battery charging difficult. The additional functions of radio, television, MP3, and games also provide entertainment for those who have limited social resources at their disposal.[36] While some migrants claim they do not know much about brands and only follow friends in buying what is cheap, others say they do so because they cannot afford real brands but still want to look trendy.[37] These factors, combined with an affordable phone plan typical of the developing world,[38] indeed substantiate Shanzhaiji's status as "a prototypical 'working-class ICT (Information Communication Technology).'"[39] Not surprisingly, by 2008, the market share of Shanzhaiji was nearly 30 percent, surpassing several leading national brands that are more directly supported by the state.[40]

To be sure, not all migrant workers are in favor of Shanzhaiji. Some second-generation migrants, for instance, are reported to be shying away from Shanzhaiji products because the ownership of genuine global brands would better enhance their image in the eyes of the urbanites.[41] But the appeal of Shanzhaiji does not stop with the migrants, either. Even though the cell phone is much less of a status symbol now than it was in the 1990s, it has become a fashion marker for youths who are constantly susceptible to "the new." The desire for looks has come to trump the expectation of quality, as replacing the phone once per year allows the owner to keep up with the latest trends.[42] This fashion consciousness is a key reason for the cost-friendly Shanzhaiji's popularity among many urban youths in second- and third-tier cities as well as the vast countryside, where the income level is typically lower than in megacities such as Beijing and Shanghai. Besides its reach into China's inland, the demand for Shanzhaiji also extends beyond the national borders. In fact, the "bandit" phones are widely popular in the developing world, from Southeast Asia and India to the Middle East, Russia, and Africa. In Dubai, an entire street is reportedly set up as part of the Shanzhaiji sales network.[43] It is only understandable that malls specializing in Shanzhaiji in Shenzhen's Huaqianbei district are provided with multi-lingual signs to welcome its "global marketing team."[44]

The embrace of Shanzhaiji by the transnational "information haveless" points to a sort of "globalization from below," a "dark flow" that "appropriates globalization, repetitively reduplicating and deconstructing it."[45] This success in the global market, ironically, is precisely what the state had hoped to achieve. Jiang Zemin, Deng Xiaoping's successor, first brought up the notion of "going out" (*zouchuqu*) in 1992 as a key strategy for China's long-term economic growth. Central to the plan is the idea of "utilizing foreign resources through the opening of the global market" in order to "compensate the limitation in the domestic market." Formally presented in 1997, the policy clearly indicates the state's intent to shore up the global expansion of "the enterprises with strengths" (*you shili de qiye*).[46] Supporting a handful of domestic mobile phone manufacturers – as part of the globally burgeoning ICT sector – is in line with this strategic vision. China Bird (*Bo Dao*) was one of the leading handset producers that fell into this category. In 2004, as the No. 1-selling national brand, Bird was boasting about its success in following the call of "going global."[47] Though self-promoted as "the fighter jet of handsets" (*shoujizhong de zhandouji*), it was unable to sustain its market position for long. Despite the claim that its exports had been rising, the company began experiencing significant revenue losses in 2005. The reason for its failure, aside from the answering tactics of global brands like Nokia, was largely the competition coming from Shanzhaiji.[48] In this sense, Shanzhaiji has claimed the domestic and global market in a manner attempted, but not successfully implemented, by the state.

Perhaps more unsettling to the state is the idea that the Shanzhaiji community has come to manifest an "alternative national identity."[49] "Buy Shanzhai to show your love of our country," for example, was a tagline that appeared in a late-night television ad for one of the leading knockoff brands, iOrgane (an intentional misspelling of "orange.")[50] Some consumers were also reported to have chosen Shanzhaiji for patriotic reasons. Even former users of legit domestic brands were sometimes converted to "brand Shanzhai" supporters, as the latter often turned out to be better in quality, albeit at a lower price. When a former Shanzhaiji producer, K-Touch (*Tianyu Langtong*), joined the rank of legit companies in 2007 – thanks to the State Council's termination of the handset licensing regulation – it went on to achieve great market success and began unabashedly advertising on official channels like CCTV. Rather than being chastised as a bandit, however, it was described by *China Enterprise News* as offering a few lessons to other (state-supported) domestic enterprises in their combat with foreign brands.[51]

In this light, it is tempting to cast the rise of Shanzhaiji as a grass-roots upheaval targeted at the state. However, it is also undeniable that Shanzhaiji's success has indirectly benefited from state policies that brought the flow of FDI into the Pearl River Delta, which provided the informal sector with technical support, operational capacity, and migrant-workers-turned-consumers. What calls for more attention, then, is that the celebration of Shanzhaiji as an embodiment of the masses did not emanate directly from the interpellation of the state. Indeed, the state's attempt to counter global competition by way of promoting a few national brands has failed to achieve its intended outcome. What has emerged is a contestation between a consumer subject position for national brands, interpellated by the state, and a working-class subject position that Shanzhaiji has made visible. This contestation points to a fissure between the state's long-standing claim to represent the interests of "the people" – by aligning them with the interests of "the nation" – and "the people" of the "information have-less," who have made Shanzhaiji a market success.

A "BRAND" FOR "THE PEOPLE"

The story of Shanzhaiji, then, manifests the agency of a population typically thought of as a "vulnerable" social group (*ruoshi qunti*).[52] Surely it would be an overstatement to claim that any kind of community formation can easily take place through the "isolated connectivity" of the mobile phone.[53] Even as the handset connects users with their already existing social networks while enriching and expanding their circles of interaction, what it provides is often an "immobile mobility," which by no means transforms the unequal social constraints faced by many of the "information have-less."[54] Nonetheless, as the cultural signification of Shanzhai expands beyond the realm of handsets, the signifier has also come to embody the wishes, desires, and creativity of "the people" in unexpected ways. Indeed, its subsequent explosion in media culture, particularly on the internet, has lead many to proclaim that Shanzhai represents a "grass-roots carnival in the age of Web 2.0,"[55] an explosion of popular culture reformatted as "user-created content,"[56] and a "paradigm shift" that reverses conventional media flows.[57] From this, a sense of optimism often ensues; "the people" – in this case understood as netizens (or "net people," *wang min*) – are seen as in control of "the production of meaning"[58] as they create, transmit, and share "Shanzhai-ed" content on blogs, forums, and commercial and news websites.[59] "I 'Shanzhai,' therefore I am!" is but one slogan that captures this sense of enthusiasm.[60]

Present in these accounts is the tendency to map the utopian fantasies associated with "new media" onto Shanzhai without taking account of the very particular material and cultural conditions that gave rise to its form and content. I would suggest that Shanzhaiji did not *accidentally* become the first key Shanzhai object to attract media attention. The fascination it generated was at least in part due to the "newness" of the cell phone itself, as an emblem of the so-called digital revolution. While the same kind of "newness" can be attributed to the internet, it does not follow that Shanzhai had to become the default label for the myriad online activities of imitation that it later came to signify. In other words, an explanation for such wide adoption of this label calls for a more critical engagement with the particularity of Shanzhai as a discursive formation.

What may be observed here is a distinct mixture of temporalities that speaks directly to China's postsocialist situation. The signifier of Shanzhaiji simultaneously conjures up a folk imaginary of the anti-court bandit and a post-Fordist imaginary of the digital revolution. The latter is specifically manifested in the widespread perception that "new media" technologies are endowed with a historical mission to help China overcome the drawbacks of its delayed industrialization. The global outlook of an "informationalized capitalism,"[61] after all, has promoted numerous government initiatives in ICT development. This techno-utopian vision, coupled with the similarly revolutionizing "bandit" narrative, has enabled a seamless transmedia migration of Shanzhai from the handset market to the internet. As such, Shanzhaiji is transformed from a media product into a cultural object – a transformation that is facilitated in part by the hybrid nature of the signifier "Shanzhaiji" itself, one that combines a pre-modern construct with a postmodern technology.

Notably, it was also within Shanzhaiji's mixed temporalities that a different conception of creativity became discernible. Since at least

2005, Shanzhaiji had already been a widely discussed topic on Chinese internet forums and major news sites, as well as more official outlets. While some of the websites covering Shanzhaiji are dedicated to its technologies, production, and distribution, many others are more interested in presenting its looks. Major internet services such as NetEase, Tencent QQ, and Sohu have established a tradition of displaying the annual "Top Ten" of Shanzhaiji. The ranking is often determined by how "shocking" (*leiren*) the phones appear to the eye. Accompanying the photos are often brief descriptions of their unique features, along with a commentary on the "bold creativity" that is manifested in such exaggerated looks and functions.[62]

The notion of "creativity" here must be read more carefully. At the very least, it encompasses two layers of meanings: one is the more commonly accepted definition, "the ability to produce original work"; the other is simply the ability to copy. However, neither of these corresponds to the individual-based conception of creativity often found in the globalizing discourse of the "creative industries."[63] While many of the Shanzhaiji designs are imaginative in their own right, they are never attributed to any single inventor or Shanzhai company. Nor has anyone complained about this lack of recognition. It appears that there is a tacit understanding among the Shanzhaiji constituents that the ideas came from a *community*, not an individual. For those Shanzhai phones that are unabashedly knockoffs, a community of meaning makers is likewise assumed. In this case, the "shock value" stems from the ability of the viewers to recognize the level of similarity between the brand-name version and the Shanzhai-ed one. The status of Shanzhaiji as a visual object therefore privileges the social and the interpersonal rather than the rational and the individual.[64]

The online archives of Shanzhaiji provide a useful lens to explain the rise of Shanzhai as a dominant signifier for a multiplicity of imitative acts. At work is what Henry Jenkins calls "a turn back toward a more folk-culture understanding of creativity" defying the "privatization of culture" that stemmed from the origin of intellectual property in the Industrial Revolution.[65] The constituents of Shanzhaiji, in other words, have used the new medium of the internet to transform the cell phone into an artifact of visual culture. The way in which they achieved this is more reminiscent of pre-modern forms of folk knowledge production than the individuated types more often associated with Western modernity. This mode of cultural production also speaks to Lee and LiPuma's observation that postmodern circulation serves more than transmitting already constituted cultural forms; it produces culture through its own signification.[66] In this light, the internet not only serves as a medium for Shanzhaiji's "representation"; it indeed participates in producing Shanzhai itself as a cultural form, by offering a space for "interpretive communities" to generate meanings about Shanzhaiji.[67]

As Shanzhaiji is transformed into a cultural object through online circulation, Shanzhai also takes on a performative mode of signifying "the people." An imaginary of the "net people," often conjured up by the internet medium in contemporary China, finds a perfect match in the already circulating discourse about Shanzhaiji as a folk-originated IT sector and a working-class ICT. For example, a widely circulated list of Top Ten Shanzhai events of 2008 included myriad imitative acts taken up by people from all walks of life in different parts of the country, from a peasant-initiated Olympics "torch relay" in a village in Henan province to a college student's posing as a "goddess" via a phone camera.[68] From the pictures themselves, there is no evidence that the participants of these events had intended to publicize their actions explicitly as part of the culture of Shanzhai. It is rather the online cataloging that has recruited them under the Shanzhai banner. What legitimates the grouping is the identification of these acts as motivated by the desire to *produce one's own version,* whether it is impersonating a pop star like Jay Chow, putting up knockoff storefronts like "Pizza Huh," or appropriating symbols like the Bird's Nest (Beijing's Olympics Stadium).[69] In these instances, Shanzhai is not a preconstituted object that awaits representation by other media; it is a media object that arises from a collective meaning-making process, one that involves such cognitive endeavors as recognition, evaluation, classification, visualization, and description.

It is in this sense that we may further recognize Shanzhai's "brand-like" operation. As Celia Lury argues, a brand is "an abstraction that is made concrete in specific products and services."[70] Its rise in the second half of the twentieth century was informed by the growth of market-

ing as a "performative discipline," which came to reconfigure production by way of incorporating consumer information. In the 1970s, along
with the use of "communication media and information technologies"
to differentiate products, branding also shifted further away from an
emphasis on "stand-alone products" to inscribing "product mix" and
"services" with meanings. The rising role of intellectual property law,
especially trademark law, corresponded to this shift. Since a commodity
as a thing-in-itself cannot have rights, the law has to establish its rights
"by establishing relations between people." The value associated with
the trademark, then, is only realizable when the product is brought to
the market. The brand does not become a value adding, legally protected
entity until the branded object is exchanged in trade.[71]

Like the brand, Shanzhai is also "an abstract, intangible and dynamic
thing."[72] It is not a thing-in-itself, but rather an object that is formed in
transaction – that is, by the act of bringing an object to the online archive
of Shanzhai. This performative character enables Shanzhai to create a
"universe" not unlike the one conjured up by the online video parodies
associated with the *Star Wars* franchise.[73] The *Star Wars* fans Jenkins
speaks of appropriate and rework the characters and plots of the original
films, and sometimes make use of ancillary merchandise to infuse the
franchise with new meanings. Similarly, the networked publics of Shanzhai, in appropriating the sign for the naming of myriad imitations, also
participate in expanding the range of objects and actions that Shanzhai
can signify.

What is more remarkable, however, is that Shanzhai is able to operate as if it were a brand without the institutional backing of a corporation. In the case of Shanzhaiji, although its production also responds to
the needs and desires of working-class consumers, it does so not through
corporate-initiated market research but through a more organic process
whose foundation lies in the character and scale of the information have-
less. The fact that this mode of production defies trademark law only accentuates the alternative imaginary that the Shanzhai phenomenon has
brought forward. This is an imaginary of collectivity that corresponds
to the heterogeneous temporalities within China's postsocialist environment. Not only does Shanzhai hark back to the peasant uprisings
of a feudal past, it also quite powerfully brings back memories of the

Maoist utopian imaginary, according to which the seemingly "backward" masses (consisting primarily of the peasantry) are imbued with a sense of historical agency to catch up with – or even surpass – the West in achieving the goals of industrialization.[74]

While it would be far-fetched to argue that Shanzhaiji has brought forth the same kind of "mass subjectivity" that distinguished the Maoist revolution, the discursive formation of Shanzhai in China's WTO era does make visible a collectivity of a sort. Not only do Shanzhaiji's production and consumption make manifest a working-class subjectivity unique to the information have-less; Shanzhai's meaning-generative process also presupposes the presence of networked publics who engage themselves in meaning-making practices. This shared sense of agency – one that arises "within the masses" – is precisely what linked Shanzhai to a cultural form of "the people." Amid the celebratory discourse regarding Shanzhaiji's grassroots heroism, there is a noticeable lack of any association of the "brand" with a single individual (such as Robin Hood) or company (such as Ford). The occasional attribution to Tsai notwithstanding, the making of Shanzhaiji is portrayed as a collective endeavor, led by a "rebel army without a leader."[75] This tribute to a collectivity differs significantly from the individual-based conception of property that served as the foundation of IPR law in the West.[76] While the latter establishes the ownership of a brand in order for it to accrue *value* through trade, the movement of Shanzhai from cell phones to the internet has the opposite effect, disassociating the sign from its origin to accrue *meaning*. If trademark law relies on the distinction between the authorized and the unauthorized in order to validate the value of the real over the fake, the interpretive publics that have congregated around Shanzhai are more interested in the sign's shock value – a "value" that derives from a proliferation of meanings, generated through a collective process of recognition, interpretation, and creative reworking.

Thus, WTO-era China has not only witnessed the rise of Shanzhaiji as a challenge to state-supported national brands; it has also observed the eruption of "the people" in Shanzhai culture, a visibility of the working-class masses that contribute directly to the making of the brand. This eruption would ultimately create a schism within the state's longstanding claim to represent "the people" in the name of the nation. A case in point is a Shanzhai Spring Festival Gala that caught the media's attention in November 2008. The organizer proclaimed a "people's own" version of the Chinese Lunar New Year extravaganza, which made this Gala one of the most talked-about Shanzhai phenomena of the year. Featuring the country's best-known performers, the four-hour-long Spring Festival Gala, aired annually on CCTV, is one of the most watched and discussed (if not increasingly mocked) national televisual spectacles in post-Mao China. Over the years, the transformation of the Gala has mirrored CCTV's shift from a primarily state-subsidized and controlled model to one that relies more on corporate sponsorship and independent producers (see chapter 1).[77] If the Gala in its 1980s versions served as a secular ritual for a nation still recovering from the dramatic turmoil of the Cultural Revolution, it has now turned into a massive advertising machine that solicits skyrocketing sponsorship fees. For example, in 2006, inspired by the success of the *Super Girl* contest on Hunan Satellite TV, the CCTV Gala created a voting component, "My Favorite Program of the Spring Festival Gala," before auctioning it off to a pharmaceutical company for over RMB 45 million ($7 million).[78] This move among others suggests that even though the Gala has routinely addressed "the people of the entire nation" (*quanguo renmin*) and overseas Chinese (*haiwai qiaobao*) during its live broadcasts, "the people" for CCTV is now more akin to an audience-as-commodity sold to advertisers than to the national subjects it used to interpellate. This shifting identity of "the people" is what the Shanzhai Gala – a self-proclaimed "People's Gala Held by the People" – has made manifest.[79]

In this light, it is important to note that CCTV's own attention to the Shanzhai phenomenon in 2008 was another significant moment of Shanzhai's cross-media journey. The station first covered Shanzhaiji on its program *News in 30 Minutes* (*Xinwen Sanshifen*) in June 2008.[80] But what triggered the most follow-up reports was the inclusion of a two-minute segment in the station's 7 PM prime-time staple, *Network News Broadcast* (*Xinwen Lianbo*) on December 2, 2008. Not only did the number of print and official online sources on Shanzhai skyrocket after this coverage, numerous media accounts have pointed to this broadcast as the first time an official opinion was voiced toward a "popular phenomenon" (*minjian xianxiang*).[81] Baidu Baike (the home-grown version of Wikipedia) notes this as the moment that marked Shanzhai's entry into an "all-people time" (*quanmin shidai*, with *quanmin* translatable as "all the people").[82] Even the recording that later appears on the popular video-sharing site *Tudou Net* (one of YouTube's Chinese "knockoffs") is entitled "Shanzhai Handsets is in *Network News Broadcast!*" which demonstrates more than a hint of excitement.[83]

Certainly this enthusiasm is not uniformly shared; at least one blogger on the *Tudou* site has dismissed the segment as an indication of the station's lack of responsiveness. But the representation of Shanzhai on a program long associated with a sense of "authority and sacredness"[84] still calls attention to the ideological operation of state media in general and CCTV's shaping of the Shanzhai discourse in particular. If Bolter and Grusin's notion of "remediation" – "the representation of one medium in another"[85] – has alerted us to the interactions between new and old media types, what deserves more careful scrutiny is how CCTV reconfigures the meanings of Shanzhai by incorporating a discourse closely entwined with new media (mobile phones and the internet) into the realm of the televisual.

RE-BRANDING SHANZHAI FOR THE NATION

In CCTV's 2008 *Network News* coverage of Shanzhai, the reporter begins with the acknowledgment that "the emergence of Shanzhai handsets in 2003" and the output of Shanzhai products have transformed the term "from (describing) a kind of economic behavior to a form of sociocultural phenomenon."[86] Another reporter then appears in front of a cell phone wholesale market in Beijing, offering to take the viewer in for a look. As the camera pans over the market's exterior and interior, the voiceover tells us that ten thousand customers visit here daily, and most of them are in search of Shanzhaiji. Inside, a conversation takes place between a female journalist, a male journalist, and a male vendor. The vendor's image is shown through a lenslike frame, which appears to have been captured by a hidden camera. A transcript on screen accompanies this sequence and subtitles the following conversation:

Female journalist: Which one sells better?
Vendor: Of course this one (Shanzhaiji). [*Parenthesis in original.*]
Female journalist: Why?
Vendor: [It's] cheap! [It] can impress people! [If] you show it to some
    layman who doesn't know, this IS "real"! [*Brackets added.*]
Male journalist: But does this kind (Shanzhai cell phone)
    have inspectional testing? [*Parenthesis in original.*]
Vendor: No.

The anchor then relates that the market for Shanzhaiji is expanding, and one cannot presume that these phones do not contain any technical features. Indeed, the viewer is quickly informed about Shanzhaiji's many additional functions, such as extra-long standby time, dual SIM cards, and multi-megapixel cameras. This is followed by an interview with an IPR legal expert, who confirms that copying others' patented "external features" is patent-infringing behavior.

The program then moves from the cell phone market to the internet, where "all kinds of phenomena characterized by imitation keep churning out, forming a distinct Shanzhai culture." Several Shanzhai examples online are displayed on screen, among them BaiGooHoo, a combination of Google, Yahoo, and Baidu (the "Chinese Google"). The anchor goes on to cite an online survey done by *China Youth Daily* and *QQ Net,* which indicated that 30 percent of the respondents deemed Shanzhai a "fake-brand" culture while 50 percent endorsed it with optimism. The report concludes that "various aspects of the Shanzhai market," such as inspection and consumer rights, indeed demand "further regulation and management."[87]

At first glance this representation of Shanzhai on CCTV is a well-balanced piece of journalism, one that seemingly passes no judgment upon Shanzhaiji or "Shanzhai culture." Its mode of representation, however, invites a closer look. Despite CCTV's commercialization, it is well known that the *Network News* show remains a highly controlled program; not only is the coverage of "negative things" in China somewhat infrequent, their appearance is also more carefully scripted and shown.[88] Even though the "bandit" and "anti-court" stance is present in much of the online discourse surrounding Shanzhai, the CCTV coverage has portrayed the phenomenon in a more nuanced light than the typical "state oppression of online dissident" story that is frequently found in

Western media headlines. Although the Shanzhai advocates are not to be equated with the many online activists that Guobin Yang discusses in his comprehensive study,[89] a more critical examination of CCTV's treatment of Shanzhai also defies the binary opposition, which typically casts the Chinese state as a villain that specializes in cracking down on activists-turned-victims.

For this reason, I subject the CCTV news piece to a symptomatic reading, in Louis Althusser's sense of the term.[90] My aim is not only to uncover the ideologies at work in shaping Shanzhai's meanings, but also to complicate the often taken-for-granted transparency of state media in representing the voice of the state. Treating the CCTV report as a visual text, I argue that the coverage of Shanzhai works to reconstruct the state's authority by resurrecting it as a protector of "the people" and a leader for the nation. It does so in three steps. First, in the conversation inside the market, the hidden camera, carried by the reporter in disguise, invites the viewer to identify with its point of view in attempting to distinguish the "real" from the "fake." The word "Shanzhai" is not enunciated in this scene. Rather, it is inserted in parentheses to ensure the proper acknowledgment of the difference between the two. This inscription marks a third-party enunciation of Shanzhai, one that disrupts the identification of the viewer with the camera's viewpoint. When invited to read the subtitles – which operate as a form of televisual pedagogy – the viewer is established as a subject of knowledge, who can now distinguish one (Shanzhaiji) from the other (the legit product). Viewers are thus led to believe that they could be easily deceived – much like the camera is – just by "looking" at the items without "listening" to the state. Their position as knowing subjects depends on the protection of a third-party entity, one that shields them from the deception of Shanzhai by giving the latter a name – the "fake."

Second, when the program moves on to discuss "Shanzhai culture," it makes a specific reference to the online survey results. In doing so, the netizen publics of Shanzhai are replaced by a statistical abstraction, corresponding to a primary mode in which "the people" is represented in the modern nation-state as "population." In this way, "the people" becomes an abstracted, disembodied object on screen. By illustrating the numerical divide between those who are "for" and "against" Shanzhai culture, the screen forces viewers to disengage from their own identity as part of that "people," a self-objectification that also distances them from Shanzhai's original signified – "the people" as the working-class makers and users of Shanzhaiji and as the networked publics that proliferated the Shanzhai discourse.

Finally, the invocation of "consumers' right to know" is particularly significant as a concluding theme. A consumer-subject, as constructed from the beginning of the news segment, is one who needs the state – the third party – to disclose fraud, regulate the market, and exert quality control. Viewers, then, are invited to assume their subject position as "consumer-citizens" – a position that, as Jing Wang argues, has been promoted by the state since the 1990s as a new embodiment of "the people."[91] In this way, the program reduces the productive discourse of Shanzhai to an abstraction while installing an institutional relation between the state and the consumer in its place. It is this protective relation that allows the state to re-emerge as an entity whose interests are aligned with those of "the people," because the-people-as-consumers are now at the mercy of Shanzhaiji, whose illicit status is further cemented by the voice of an IPR expert. The culture of Shanzhai, shaped by a multitude of working-class as well as netizen subjects, is then replaced by a social contract between the state and the consumer-citizen; the latter's security is dependent upon the former's exercise of law, whether it be through inspection, regulation, or rights protection.

This reading by no means suggests that CCTV's ideological work is all-powerful in suturing the viewer into its discursive framework. After all, the viewership of *Network News* has seen a dramatic decline, partly because it is known to present a "machine-made image."[92] Parodies of *Network News* are frequently circulated online and via microblogs, not least as part of the "egao" movement. Although the segment on Shanzhai was re-posted online on at least two video-sharing websites, this TV-to-internet migration only received around ten thousand hits. Nonetheless, what this reading offers is a glimpse into the historical conditions that are shaping the Chinese state following its WTO entry. These conditions are even more clearly manifested in CCTV's follow-up effort in reconfiguring the discourse of Shanzhai: the first print publication on the subject in March 2009. Entitled *Shanzhai is Coming* (*Shanzhai Laile*), the book was edited by the programming committee of CCTV's highly regarded talk show series, *Chinese Finance and Economics Reports*. The preface to the book affirms that "Shanzhai" is a culture "rooted in the people" and an expression of "the aspirations of people on the bottom rim of the society."[93] But the emphasis is clearly on the notion that "the people's wisdom" can be extremely benevolent to the nation, if developed and utilized properly. The success of the Shanzhai model is acknowledged, but it is deemed "harmful" to domestic industries as well as to "the entire China brand" in the long run.[94] The "manufacturing nation" of China, whose cheap labor is exploited to "produce so-called high-value products," needs to aspire to a future of "Created in China." This is a project that requires "a proper understanding of Shanzhai," one that contributes to the upgrade of "Made in China."[95]

Implicit here is an unquestioned acceptance of the link between creativity and value, and by extension, the global IPR regime that legitimizes it. Under this regime, as Laikwan Pang points out, creativity is detached from meaning production and exchange, instead being "reified as intellectual property which the rights holders own and can benefit from."[96] This understanding of creativity is what underlies the nationwide adoption of the policy "From Made in China to Created in China" (chapter 1), now embraced by various levels of government to move the nation from producing the world's branded products toward creating the nation's own IPR-eligible brands. The language of the CCTV report reflects these broader policy concerns, which have informed such government-backed projects as urban creative clusters, cultural tourism, city branding, and new media innovations from video games to animation.[97] The sanctioning of the value-making capacity of creativity, which guides the policy directives, has precluded the CCTV report from acknowledging the meaning-making capacity of the Shanzhai publics. Replacing the self-proliferating discourse of Shanzhai is an ossified "culture of the people," wherein culture is understood less as meaning-generative practices than as profit-oriented cultural capital. This reworking of Shanzhai's meaning also depends on an ideological separation of "Shanzhai economy" from "Shanzhai culture," which works to transform the subjectivity of "the people" – one that Shanzhai has come to signify – into an objective resource to draw from for the purpose of nation building. In this way, "Brand Shanzhai" is rendered at the service of "brand China," since the Shanzhai economy presents important lessons for branding legit national products that would buttress the nation's competitive advantage in the world market. The potential of "the people," once invoked as a cultural force capable of creating meanings, is now a productive force more suitable for advancing China's position in the global "value adding" chain of branded commodities.

It is important to recognize that what enables CCTV's channeling of the "Shanzhai" energy back to a developmentalist project is an appropriation of a global structure – specifically that of IPR but also a neoliberal conception of consumer citizenship – to subsume a local discourse into a national narrative, even though the local phenomenon is itself influenced by global-national contestations. The story of Shanzhaiji emblematizes this paradoxical effect of globalization most vividly. To borrow Fredric Jameson's language,[98] Shanzhaiji's "resistance" to the state by way of competing against state-sponsored national brands is linked directly to the operation of global capital (in the form of FDI, among others); yet it is against the encroachment of the same global capital (in the form of global brands) that the state seeks to enforce its own legitimacy, by shoring up a national industry of legit brands to strengthen the national economy. It is precisely this contradictory working of globalization that presents an ideological predicament for the state. Under the global hegemony of the IPR regime, the WTO-era state must play by the rules of TRIPS (Trade-Related Aspects of Intellectual Property Rights) in order to maintain its global standing. The increased frequency of crackdowns on counterfeits in conjunction with the global media event of the Beijing Olympics reflects precisely this pressure for the state to perform its IPR duties (see chapter 4). On the other hand, the Shanzhai discourse has offered an alternative approach to counter the hegemony of the global brands, one that is characterized by a defiant attitude toward IPR rather than an obedient one. Faced with this eruption of "the people," the state must also reposition itself in relation to Shanzhai so as to re-emerge a legitimate leader for "the people" – one that will not only ensure their safety in consuming cell phones but will also re-direct their energy toward "proper" national ends.

What results, as the CCTV report demonstrates, is a fixation of "Shanzhai economy" as a sector to be regulated by the state, in the name of protecting the consumer-citizen, as well as a simultaneous subsumption of 'Shanzhai culture" into a narrative of national progress. This ideological reworking comes at the expense of a more serious engagement with the alternative cultural vision that the Shanzhai publics have put forth. This is the vision of a collectivity that distinguishes itself from the individuated notion of property promoted by Western modernity, a collaborative mode of cultural production versus a neoliberal framing of consumer-citizenship, a transnational class of information haveless over and against a few global brand owners, and an understanding of culture as meaningful practices not bound by the one-dimensional pursuit of profit. Interestingly, the CCTV book on Shanzhai does not acknowledge any single author, nor does it include an exhaustive "works cited" section. Rather, its postscript invites all those who had written the many online and print media reports referenced in the book to contact CCTV for compensation for their work.[99] This detail, while revealing the haste in which the book was brought to press, also manifests CCTV's desire to present the report as a "product of everyone's collective effort."[100] While this can be interpreted as yet another attempt on the part of CCTV to represent "the voice of the people," it has also unwittingly paid tribute to the anonymous collective body that produced the Shanzhai discourse. Here we may discern an opening for a different way of engaging Shanzhai, one that recognizes its collective vision for cultural production rather than dispersing that collectivity into individuated consumer subjects or objectifying it as a resource for national development.

CONCLUSION

The Shanzhai discourse has by no means reached an end point in the ever-shifting mediascape of WTO-era China. More recently, Shanzhaiji is noted to have played a role in the Arab Spring uprisings, the ripple effect of which reportedly led to more crackdowns in China of activities related to the so-called Jasmine Revolution.[101] Certainly the complex

2.2. An "Apple brand" counterfeit money inspection machine on display as an (ironic) emblem of Shanzhai culture at the Bi-City Biennale of Urbanism/Architecture, Shenzhen, 2014.

structural reasons for revolutionary upheavals cannot be reduced to the possession of bandit cell phones, nor should the routine coverage of state repression be taken uncritically as grounds on which to generalize the Chinese state's coercive apparatus. As Jing Wang points out, the post-Mao state is better seen as operating through a "systemic, regulatory form of governance."[102] I have examined three moments of Shanzhai to illustrate that this operation of the state is itself subject to global-national ideological struggles following China's 2001 WTO entry. What Shanzhai makes visible is a contested field in which myriad forms of media and types of publics participate in the production and negotiation of meanings. From mobile phones to the internet and state television, each medium has contributed to the Shanzhai discourse in ways that are specific to its characteristics as a communicative form. The Shanzhai publics, emerging from the Shanzhaiji sector and the online community of Shanzhai practices, have conjured up an imaginary of collectivity that challenges the national subject positions promulgated by the state – in this case, those of brand-creating entrepreneurs and individuated consumers. At the same time, the state's project of interpellation, manifested through such policy initiatives as "Created in China," is itself governed by the global structure of IPR.

What these struggles have come to reveal, then, is the contradictory working of IPR through the imaginary of the brand. Not only does it impose an "illicit" status upon Shanzhai, it also lays out the path to be undertaken by the Chinese state – that is, the state must transform a nation that specializes in making (or "faking") into one that can take pride in its ability to produce IPR-eligible nation brands. This hegemonic operation of IPR is discernible in the state media portrayal of Shanzhai, which works to re-align the state with "the people" by turning Shanzhai's meaning-generative performativity into a value-generative "creativity." Shanzhai's culturally productive force is thereby subsumed into the national-developmentalist project, "From Made in China to Created in China." It is this project's internalization of IPR's value-producing cultural logic that has helped shape CCTV's construction of the state as an agent for national development, by transforming Shanzhai from a signifier of "the people" into a brand for the nation. Within this ideological maneuvering, it is the individuated subject position of the consumer that has come to eclipse that of the migrant workers who contributed to the early success of Shanzhaiji. If the state thus reconfigured is bound to fail to acknowledge the alternative construction of "the people" that Shanzhai's cultural formation has brought forth, what has induced this failure is nothing other than the hegemonic operation of IPR.

What makes IPR culturally imperialistic, then, is not so much the invasion of a unified "Chinese" culture by the penetrating force of a global structure. Rather, cultural imperialism is manifested in IPR's work in enabling competing subject positions within the nation-state while privileging certain national subjects as worthier of the state's recognition than others. In this sense, the state not only "acts as well as reacts,"[103] but also interpellates and is interpellated. The Shanzhai moments I have documented here may be seen as a particularly salient enactment of IPR's effects in intensifying the discordance between the nation and the state. But the kinds of cultural struggles that emanate from them, which lay competing claims to the national, are by no means unique in making manifest the ideological contestations between counterfeit culture and the nation-branding project of WTO-era China.

THREE

Crazy Stone, National Cinema, and Counterfeit (Film) Culture

CRAZY STONE IS A LOW-BUDGET COMEDY FUNDED BY THE HONG Kong pop star Andy Lau.[1] Despite its low-profile cast and marketing, it achieved unexpected box office success and generated a wealth of discussion on the future of Chinese cinema. In particular, it was seen as introducing a new era for "genre films with Chinese characteristics"[2] as opposed to imported Hollywood blockbusters. The emergence of this "Chineseness" marks a break from dominant notions of Chinese cinema as a globally marketed nation brand – a joint venture of global Hollywood and the postsocialist state. In this chapter, I examine the film as an enactment of China's counterfeit film culture in order to delve into the making of an alternative national imaginary. I argue that the temporal distance between the acknowledgment of the "fake" and the recognition of the "real" activates a performative subjectivity. This disjunctive mode of being in the nation disrupts the homogeneous temporality on which nation branding's interpellation ultimately depends. To get at this contestation between a counterfeit film culture and nation branding through cinematic means, I will first analyze the rise of "Chinese cinema" as a global brand – a process more indicative of Hollywood's reigning global hegemony than representative of China's appearance as a national subject on the global screen.

"CHINESE CINEMA": FROM GLOBAL BRAND TO FILM CULTURE

Despite the long-standing practice of filmmaking in the geopolitically defined space of modern China and its historically, territorially, and diasporically linked locales such as Hong Kong, Taiwan, and the Southeast

Asian countries, the field of studies loosely identified as "Chinese cinema" emerged no earlier than the late 1980s in the English-based academy of the West.[3] The 1985 "breakthrough screening of *Yellow Earth*" (a collaboration by fifth-generation auteurs Chen Kaige and Zhang Yimou) in Hong Kong is often noted as the beginning of this "culturally defined national brand" in global circulation.[4] Over the past few decades, films that claim one or more notions of "Chineseness" (often in terms of their production) have increasingly become "exemplary sites in the study of cinema and the national."[5] In line with the predominant intellectual tendency to deconstruct the nation, this scholarship has yielded many sophisticated accounts aimed at pluralizing (or transnationalizing) the "national."[6] At the same time, the ongoing effort to deterritorialize "China" and "Chineseness" also reflects the desire to deploy their signifying power in legitimizing a field of inquiry.[7]

However, simply demonstrating that there is more than one China on- or offscreen does not reveal how the label "Chinese cinema" privileges particular understandings of Chineseness while excluding others. Among other things, it is at least worth noting that the intellectual discourse on "Chinese cinema" gained its currency soon after the integration of the People's Republic of China (PRC) into global capitalism after 1978. In some sense, the entry of "Chinese cinema" as a "distinctive brand name" into "the international marketplace" – constituted by the Oscars and the international festival circuit[8] – coincided with the integration of the nation into the world economic system. The appearance of films by award-winning directors like Chen Kaige and Zhang Yimou in the "'foreign' section of major North-American video rental chains" represented the "selective incorporation of a Chinese filmmaking elite into an American-dominated global film industry that was becoming increasingly multicultural."[9] In this sense, the brand production of Chinese cinema in the 1990s–2000s may well be seen as the "sign of a *cross-cultural* commodity fetishism."[10] The deconstruction of "Chineseness" in "Chinese cinema," in other words, is more symptomatic of the latter's fetishistic global brand power than explanatory of the historical and cultural conditions from which it emerged.

In some sense, the production and circulation of "Chinese cinema" as a global brand mirror that of goods labeled "Made in China." Much like the majority of commodities produced in China's export-processing zones, many crafted representations of the Chinese nation intended for international festivals were (and still are) rarely distributed and screened publicly within the PRC. If the making of the "Made in China" brand has to do with an intricate state-capital negotiation (chapter 2), the making of "Chinese cinema" is often negatively related to the state, whose regulatory role in the cultural sector is emblematized by the long-standing practice of censorship. Many of the "art house" films made by graduates of state-affiliated film academies typically evade state-level sanctions and aim directly at foreign festival exhibition. Only after they have been internationally recognized do some of them re-circulate back into the domestic market, first through pirated video compact discs (VCDs) and later via DVDs. In other words, there is a significant break between the globally circulated "Chinese cinema" brand and the collective imagining of the Chinese nation through film viewing, particularly among those who constitute the state citizenry "proper" – that is, those individuals more directly subject to state interpellation by virtue of residing within the state's sovereign borders.[11]

Given these circumstances, it is of some value to move the "parameters of a national cinema" from the realm of the production toward that of consumption.[12] Rather than continuing to deconstruct "Chinese cinema" as a globally visible nation brand, it is more useful to understand the "national" as a dynamic cultural process involving internal forces like historical narratives, state policies, and economic infrastructure as well as international ones primarily manifested through Hollywood's transnational reach.[13] These forces converge in the making of "the film culture as whole," which concerns "the activity of national audiences and the conditions under which they make sense of and use the films they watch."[14] This approach invokes such sociological questions as what films ("domestic" or "foreign") are available for what audiences to see, and how they are viewed and received within the "communicative space" demarcated by a national sovereignty.[15]

In WTO-era China, this "film culture" approach allows us to probe the ways in which counterfeit culture – a transnational culture of circulation – plays a role in the re-configuration of the nation cinematically. Film culture, for Tom Ryall, encompasses "the immediate contexts in which films are made and circulated such as studios, cinemas and film journals, and those contexts which have to be constructed from the material network of the culture, the philosophies and ideologies of film."[16] Since at least the 1990s, counterfeiting practices such as video piracy have constituted a major segment of the "material network" that supplies a great many audiences of postsocialist China with a wide range of viewing experiences.[17] In the first decade following China's WTO entry in 2001, the legacy of pirate VCD/DVD viewing also came to inform cinematic production and aesthetics.[18] Since 2005, this network has been partially supplanted as well as compounded by the state-promoted expansion of broadband internet, whose bit-torrent-rendered circulation and blogosphere-enabled interface even more dramatically expands the sphere of film reception and discourse.

Certainly access to and participatory use of these technologies are largely limited to urban Chinese who possess both economic and cultural capital. But their class/spatial privilege is congruent with their status as the default target consumers for Hollywood imports as well as the re-nationalized state film industry. It is thus important to parse out the kinds of hegemonic struggles at work in laying claims to the national, and how these nation-making activities intercept class politics that may or may not be confined within the national space.

Hollywood has long had a hegemonic presence in the Chinese nation-state, both historically and in the present. As early as the Nationalist-ruled Republican Era (1911–1937), Hollywood's global expansion into the colonial city of Shanghai was a key force in shaping an incipient local film industry.[19] This expansion came to a halt after 1949, when anti-imperialist sentiment was shored up by policies that promoted Soviet films, though film attendance for the latter was reportedly lower in places like Shanghai.[20] In the 1950s, the shift in the center of cultural production from Shanghai to Yan'an indeed extended the influence of Hollywood style and content on the nationalized filmic production and its reception, and this influence persisted during and after the Cultural Revolution.[21]

In 1994 the Chinese state opened up the national market to ten Hollywood blockbusters annually, an event that generated contentious media debates about these movies' "impact on the Chinese film industry and on Chinese society more generally."[22] A few years later, however, with the box office success of such Hollywood "megafilms" (*dapian*) as *True Lies, Forrest Gump,* and *Titanic,* "imported films had become essential to the survival of the Chinese film industry."[23] Not only did Hollywood imports generate a sizable profit for China Film Export and Import Corporation, accounting for "60 percent of its $12 million revenue" in 1994, their success also "carried over" to "domestic releases."[24] As Yeh and Davis point out, the policy that promoted Hollywood imports was "not just a political decision to open China to the world but an economic strategy to save the film industry from its worst slump since the 1950s."[25] The profits from foreign film distribution are often expected to "cover domestic film distribution losses."[26] In an era that saw the rise of multiple alternative forms of entertainment such as "karaoke bars, discos, video parlors, [and] pirated videos," it is understandable that this spillover effect was particularly welcomed.[27]

China's WTO entry has shaped the Chinese cinematic landscape in profound if not unprecedented ways. Under the Hollywood-backed bilateral U.S.-China agreement, China was required to "quadruple film imports to 40 films per year" upon its 2001 accession; the number increased to fifty in 2005.[28] Audiovisual import tariffs were reduced, the domestic market was opened to foreign distribution, and investment policies were revised to allow foreign ownership in film companies up to 49 percent.[29] China Film Group, the re-organized monopoly, was in part a state response, by way of re-nationalization, to the perceived rise in global competition.[30]

Amid the increasing interdependence between Hollywood's interest in prying open the Chinese market and China's state mandate to revive the national film industry, a strand of "Chinese popular cinema" emerged at the end of the 1990s, exemplified by director Feng Xiaogang's *hesuipian* (or "New Year Films"), referring to light-hearted comedies set for release during the Spring Festival, the Chinese New Year. While far from being a favorite among Chinese critics, Feng's three "New Year" films released from 1997 through 1999 regularly achieved box-office figures that surpassed those of many Hollywood megafilms.[31] Though the ample use of Beijing slang and in-jokes in Feng's films means that their popularity is often concentrated in Northern China, his work is nonetheless seen as a beacon of hope for the Chinese film industry to "beat Hollywood at its own game."[32]

The success of Feng's films is no doubt a complicated phenomenon, particularly considering that they fit squarely between three categories of films on the domestic market: (1) the *zhuxuanlu* or "main melody" films that are directly sponsored by the state to "instill patriotism" but that are almost never popular among audiences; (2) the art-house brand that is favored by film festivals abroad but, as mentioned above, is rarely seen on public screens in China; and (3) Hollywood imports, embraced by many Chinese urbanites.[33] Despite their popularity films like those by Feng have been insufficiently studied, especially when contrasted with the scholarly attention to art-house or experimental films, even though they could potentially "open up alternative readings of what constitutes Chinese cinema."[34] As Rui Zhang argues, Feng's films' "crowd-pleasing aspects may work not just to manipulate but to keep certain progressive and critical issues before the public."[35] Fans of Feng's films often exhibit a level of sophistication in "sorting through a variety of cinematic and cultural codes and conventions"; they are typically attuned to the "parodic and intertextual references to Hollywood hits" and the occasional "metacinematic" commentaries in Feng's films.[36] Indeed, Feng's "popular cinema can be considered a site where both the hegemonic power of ideological control and non-mainstream culture are struggling for a voice."[37] Nonetheless, Feng's cinema, while feeding a "transnational imaginary" to the fantasy of local audiences,[38] has not been successful in overseas markets. This is likely because "Westerners are apparently far less inclined to consume images of a China that looks not so different from any other contemporary urban milieu."[39]

It was not until 2002, with martial arts megafilms like *Hero* and *House of Flying Daggers,* that a new global appeal was achieved for the "Chinese cinema" brand.[40] For instance *Hero,* by the former art-house auteur Zhang Yimou, "set the box office record for a Chinese domestic film by grossing RMB245 million ($29.59 million)."[41] Its simultaneous opening on over two thousand screens "marked the biggest [opening] of any foreign-language import and set a record for an Asian film in North America."[42] Certainly, backed by transnational investment and distribution networks, directors like Zhang have achieved "partial autonomy" from the state's cinematic infrastructure.[43] However, as Yuezhi Zhao points out, "the 'Chineseness' of these films underscores the success of the capitalist culture industry on a global scale," especially as the representation of "Chinese history and culture" in *Hero* is "one viewed from the perspective of the rulers and the co-opted."[44] This is indeed a reading shared by many critics inside China.[45] A more nuanced reading, such as that of Wendy Larson, points out that "culture" (and specifically "xia," the folk martial art culture) as it is portrayed in *Hero* – appearing as a story within the story through the Qin King's imagination – mirrors the global power relations that overdetermine the "inauthenticity" of culture constructed for the global gaze.[46] This reading strikes an uncanny chord with the domestic reception of *Hero* and later *The Promise* (by Chen Kaige, the director of the acclaimed 1980s classic *Yellow Earth*).

To be sure, these two so-called fifth-generation filmmakers have brought about the era of "blockbusters with Chinese characteristics,"[47] global-audience-friendly spectacles featuring the grandiosity of dynastic China. And yet, regardless of their box office success, "the Chinese audience was at once captivated by the films' spectacle and disappointed by their lack of substance, sophistication and socio-cultural relevance."[48] *The Promise,* in particular, became the target of the first widely influential "egao" parody online, "The Bloody Case that Started with a Steamed Bun" (chapter 2). It would therefore be problematic to deem these films "popular" solely based on their sales figures; they have hardly succeeded in achieving the status of the "national-popular," in the Gramscian sense of the term. Under these conditions, the breakout of *Crazy Stone* as a popular cultural event in 2006 calls for further reflections on the hegemonic formation of the national in WTO-era China's film culture. This culture, characteristically, is entrenched in the transnational practices of counterfeit and piracy. Counterfeit (film) culture thus presents a privileged site for examining how an "ensemble" of cinematic practices and institutions interact with one another in ways that are sometimes "mutually supportive" and at other times competitive, if not "self-consciously oppositional."[49] Before I probe into the effect of this culture on the national imaginary, however, I will first provide a brief account of the methodology that I bring to the examination of the film *Crazy Stone.*

What informs this methodology, which is inspired by the framework of remediation, is nothing other than the interactions between counterfeit culture and nation branding as they are manifested in the specific realm of cinema.

As I have described in the introduction and chapter 2, counterfeit culture is a culture of circulation that is at once abstract and performative. When manifested in China's film culture after its WTO entry, counterfeit culture finds embodiment in the following contestations. On the first level, there is the state's interest in reviving a national industry to counter Hollywood, as part of the "Created in China" campaign. This re-nationalization entails cracking down on the counterfeit industry as a way to ensure profitable returns for state-sanctioned national films and to support the state's effort in bringing China closer to the rank of the international community of nations (chapter 2). Second, the piracy industry is understood to subvert global Hollywood's distributional regime; it is alleged to cut into Hollywood's profit and therefore is a central issue of contention between the Chinese state and the U.S. representatives in WTO disputes. Third, video piracy, though not directly in opposition to the state, makes available a range of cultural products that are otherwise censored, regulated, or contained by the state. These state actions take the form of sponsorship for "leitmotif" films, outright bans on sensitive materials (such as works by several art-house auteurs), or trade restrictions over the imports of foreign items, particularly those from Hollywood.

In this sense, counterfeit culture comes into contact with the state and its interests in nation branding on multiple planes, directly or indirectly. To an extent, pirated films have not only come to share an illegal status with censored materials but also provide a distributional network for these materials.[50] For example, state censors have routinely accused the art-house brand of Chinese films of portraying a backward China. Banned from the public screen, these films often find their way back into the film culture via pirated discs. The internationally celebrated sixth-generation auteur Jia Zhangke, for one, has taken note of this potentially "liberating effect of film piracy" on the future of Chinese cinema.[51] At the same time, the prevalence of pirated film viewing has informed the state's desire to build a brand of national cinema that is simultaneously culturally specific and spectacular enough on screen, for only such films can ensure box-office success globally and therefore be in a position to compete with Hollywood's hegemony.[52]

Laikwan Pang, a leading cultural critic on piracy in China, is particularly dismayed by the impact of counterfeit culture on the fate of national cinema. Acknowledging Chris Berry's call for reconceptualizing Chinese cinema as "a multiplicity of projects . . . bound together by the politics of national agency and collective subjectivity as constructed entities,"[53] Pang questions whether piracy could render possible "any form of collective cinematic agency" in the nation's future.[54] Her argument stems from a nuanced analysis of piracy as characterized by "dissemination and disorder," not by the Foucauldian "docile body" that Linda Williams describes as typifying contemporary cinema's working in the United States.[55] While Pang acknowledges the potential of piracy in disrupting "the orderliness of capitalism," she ultimately argues that its own "violence and unmanageability" does not promote "a self-empowerment of the people" and is detrimental to "the cultivation of a healthy and vigorous film industry in China."[56]

While film scholars like Yingjin Zhang have critiqued Pang for her disregard for "consumer agency,"[57] I would suggest that what deserves more attention is the specific impact that "non-disciplining" counterfeit practices have on the film culture of the PRC. Pang may have moved too quickly to dismiss this culture as reproducing capitalism's ideology and exploitative logic before articulating how it operates. A particular insight in Pang's analysis is that as an emblem of the "contradictions of globalization" piracy instantiates the difficulties of "a (post)Socialist state" in coping with "the dilemma between ideological control and economic activities," the latter's success being "a major pillar legitimizing the state's authoritative sovereignty."[58] And yet when it comes to what may contribute to a healthy national film industry, Pang has relied on two assumptions. First, she presupposes that a vigorous film culture is dependent upon the state, even when the state itself is chiefly interested in strengthening its own power (by sanctioning transnational capital's influx, for example) rather than that of "the people" to whom it is in principle held accountable. Second, she implies that the pirated films most desired by audiences are necessarily mindless Hong Kong and Hollywood entertainment, imbued with "prejudices" like "racism, chauvinism, and homophobia," if not "capitalist greed."[59]

What analyses of this kind leave out are the complex system of pleasure in Hollywood films, on the one hand, and the indeterminate linkage between state sponsorship and "critical" cinema, on the other. Certainly Hollywood may be critiqued for its standardized output of tropes and clichés. But the utopian promises that many of its narratives present are far too significant to be cast aside when it comes to the question of its global operation.[60] Likewise, while in many national contexts the state has played a crucial role in promoting a more introspective (if not art house) kind of filmmaking than Hollywood, it does not follow that a critically engaged national film culture can only be the product of state intervention. Today, abundant border-crossing cultural products and transnational cinematic co-productions often generate competing narratives about the nation. In China's case, the co-existence of these narratives is largely attributable to pirate DVD circulation in the past and (illicit) downloading and streaming in the present. Before questioning whether this counterfeit film culture is empowering or disempowering for the nation's people, it is necessary to understand how it enables ways of imagining nationhood that may differ from those propagated by the state or Hollywood. In other words, to get at a more critical evaluation of its impact, we need to first describe this piracy-saturated film culture.

A question then arises as to why we should get at this description through the prism of a particular film or text. An alternative route, one may suggest, is to examine the film culture itself empirically. A more conventional sociological study of counterfeit film culture would likely proceed to investigate the actual producers, distributors, consumers, institutions, channels, and interactions that make up the material network. This kind of approach is meaningful to the extent that it helps to unveil the social structures that enable the exchange of filmic commodities and discourses – the kinds of exchange that give this culture a tangible form. Nevertheless, this approach methodologically lacks the ability to explain what gives rise to these acts of exchange historically and culturally.

Part of the difficulty lies in modern sociology's disciplinary assumption that social systems consist of rational actors who undertake conscious actions to achieve particular ends. What follows from this assumption is an attempt to map out the actors' interests and motivations rather than an exploration of the psychological, unconscious dimensions that pre-inscribe these actions. These dimensions, as theorists from Freud and Simmel to Althusser and Jameson have argued, constitute the cultural order that is not readily discernible by the actors themselves. In other words, a sociological description of counterfeit film culture is unlikely to provide insights into the actual workings of this culture, because these workings have to do with historical and structural forces that are often unknown or unintelligible to the social agents within it.

Alternatively, literary criticism offers a way to interrogate the historical, structural, and psychic workings of culture through the method of "symptomatic reading." Analogous to the psychoanalytic treatment of patients, this method understands literary texts as symptoms of the culture from which they emerged, whose "cause is of another order of phenomenon from its effects."[61] A symptomatic reading does not take a particular text's intended or perceived meanings for granted but rather seeks to uncover what makes these meanings possible. The analysis of texts as symptoms of cultural contexts aims less to arrive at a "correct" or "best" reading – the typical goal of traditional "close" reading than to achieve knowledge about the social world that shapes and is shaped by the texts and their production, distribution, and reception. In the words of Fredric Jameson, this is an approach that allows the analyst to overcome, if only temporarily, the separation between texts (both literary and social) and their contexts – a separation that is itself a fiction of capitalist modernity. It prompts us to discern "media" texts (such as films) in terms of the way they triangulate (rather than merely represent or reflect) the narrative, the media system (autoreferentially), and the social totality in which subjects find themselves.[62]

Jameson's methodological insight finds an upgrade, as it were, in Bolter and Grusin's model of "remediation" in the converging multimedia circuit of film production and reception.[63] As various types of media are increasingly "commenting on, reproducing, and replacing each other,"[64] remediation, as "the mediation of mediation," serves as an apt way to re-organize the routine demarcation of the cultural spheres as production, distribution, and consumption. To be sure, the boundaries between these spheres are never impermeable in the first place. But new media or digital practices have no doubt made these porous boundaries more visible. From online promotional campaigns and star-related events to hypermediated contexts of consumption (such as the internet and DVDs) and reception (blogs, forums, online and print media reports), a number of new environments have emerged to allow a re-thinking of the kinds of "conversations" that "help construct the meanings by which and in which people . . . as the multifarious agents in those cultures – actually live."[65] In this sense, remediation serves as a useful model to re-orient an approach to contemporary film culture that is sensitive to its multimedia environment. It attunes us to the representational media system, the signifying chain of media messages, and the geopolitical referent (the "real") simultaneously.[66]

I employ remediation as a critical approach to interrogate *Crazy Stone* as a prime artifact of counterfeit film culture – a culture that has come to shape WTO-era China's national imaginary in particular ways. Not only is the film's narrative driven by the local omnipresence of counterfeit goods; its director, style, production, circulation, and popular reception all point to the role of transnational piracy in reorganizing the nation's film culture at large. A close examination of this artifact and the ways in which it remediates counterfeit culture would thus offer a glimpse into that culture and tell us a few things about how it operates in specifying "possible ways of acting in and understanding the social world" that is China in the WTO era.[67]

COUNTERFEIT (FILM) CULTURE THROUGH "REMEDIATION"

Production/Distribution: A Successful "Battle" against Piracy

While often described as a film with "no stars, no famous director, no big investment,"[68] *Crazy Stone* is far from starless. Its chief financier is Andy Lau, a famous Hong Kong pop singer and actor.[69] With the intent to promote "first-time Chinese directors," Lau founded Focus: First Cut, a project jointly financed by his own company Focus Films and STAR

TV, a subsidiary of Rupert Murdoch's News Corporation.[70] Operating under a total budget of $3.2 million each year, Lau handpicks six film scripts to be put on screen using "high-definition video technology."[71] When *Crazy Stone* premiered during the Ninth Shanghai International Film Festival (June 17–25, 2006),[72] many reporters arrived to take photographs of Andy Lau as an audience member but ended up "putting down the camera" to join in a frenzy of laughter.[73] The film's opening also coincided with the final games of the eighteenth FIFA World Cup (June 6–July 9), an attention grabber in China that caused many imported blockbusters to delay their theatrical release to avoid a sizable falloff in the summer market. But since the low-budget *Crazy Stone* did not have much flexibility, it went ahead as scheduled. Originally targeted at "student audiences" alone, the film became a surprise hit at the box office.[74] Part of its boost may have come from a poster featuring Andy Lau, who urges the audience to "come quick to see the *Crazy Stone* after watching the ball (game)."[75] Even without stars in its cast, the film no doubt capitalized on Andy Lau's brand power.[76]

Upon its nationwide release on June 27, 2006, *Crazy Stone* brought in RMB2 million in the first weekend. It went on to gross an impressive total of RMB20 million ($3 million), which amounted to a 300 percent profit ratio. According to a manager from Warner China Film HG Corporation who was in charge of the film's distribution, this was not only a miracle for domestic films but a rarity among global blockbusters as well.[77] Some have attributed the film's box office success to its ingenious marketing, which remediates televisual and online media in creative ways to thwart the challenge of piracy. As the film's distributor, Warner China Film HG Corporation spent "1.4 million RMB on obtaining the domestic copyrights (excluding cable)" and "1.6 million on . . . copying and promotions."[78] The film's official DVD was released within two weeks of its premiere (an event co-funded by Focus and Star Chinese Movies Network). Even the price was set close to that of a pirate copy – RMB10 ($1.50). Due to its low-profile release and starless cast, the film had briefly escaped the piracy industry's attention upon its opening. As its fame grew, however, it became increasingly known to have induced a large number of formerly "piracy-only" audiences to enter the movie theater or even purchase the official DVD.

This was reportedly achieved by the distributor's re-ordering of the standard marketing sequence, which typically goes from the "mass media" to "film channels and theaters" and to "moviegoers," by inserting "professional critics" and "internet groups" into the mix. This sequence allows the professional critics to exert an impact on mainstream media and movie buffs, who then utilize the internet groups to achieve word of mouth.[79] A series of free screenings was held on June 27 and June 28 in major cities like Chongqing, Chengdu (both located in Sichuan province, where most of the film was shot), Changsha (in Hunan Province), Shanghai, and Beijing. As part of the plan to promote the film through television and internet websites, for the first time "common" folks in China were also given free tickets to the film in designated theaters and invited to review it online afterwards.

In part thanks to these marketing measures intended to bring pirate DVD consumers back into the theater, *Crazy Stone*'s box office figure climbed to RMB6 million within ten days of its release. Following its success in major cities like Shanghai, Beijing, Shenzhen, Guangzhou, and Hangzhou, many theaters in lower-tier cities originally scheduled to open the film in the second round asked to put it on sooner than planned. Journalists' and bloggers' participation indeed helped to "speed up rolling of the 'stone'" within the first two weeks, bringing the ticket sales up to ten million.[80] Even when imported blockbusters like *Superman Returns* opened on July 11, many theaters still had to increase the showings of *Crazy Stone* to satisfy audience demand. When another major summer feature, *Mission Impossible 3*, came out on July 20, a theater in Beijing sold only 64 percent of its seats, whereas *Crazy Stone* maintained an 80 percent capacity.

By August, the box office already approached RMB20 million, making *Crazy Stone* the highest-grossing domestic film in the first half of 2006, beating such Hollywood blockbusters as *Poseidon* and *Ice Age 2*. The "*Stone* Phenomenon" became a popular topic for leisure-time discussion. Many reportedly saw the film more than once. To be sure, the film might have benefited from being screened within the time frame of the nationwide "Exhibition of Excellent Domestic Films," held from June 20 to July 10, during which the release of foreign (Hollywood, that is) films was prohibited and only state-sponsored "main melody" (or leitmotif) films were scheduled in theaters.[81] Back in 2004, the same mechanism had helped boost the box office for Zhang Yimou's *The House of Flying Daggers.* But this so-called protection month could not have produced *Crazy Stone*'s success single-handedly, since the audience for "main melody" films typically comes from government-arranged viewings.[82] In fact, Hollywood blockbusters that open before "blackout" periods often maintain high attendance rates. In 2007, for example, *Pirates of the Caribbean* and *Transformers* largely reduced the protection month to an empty term without much substance.

The unexpectedly high profit for the low-budget *Crazy Stone* generated a heated debate in the media about the state of Chinese cinema. What particularly came under attack was the paradoxical combination of big investment, bad reviews, and high box office gross typical of numerous blockbusters (or "megafilms") that came out since 2003 – the year that saw the success of the multi-million-dollar *Hero.* Compared to these epics with significantly more resources at their disposal, *Crazy Stone*'s promotional campaign was meager at best. Not only was its "pre-opening promotion . . . too low-key," it also failed to exploit "the elements of commercial comedies" by making and publicizing trailers to "warm up the market."[83] Some fans even claimed that they did not see any heavy promotion at all. But its box office figures, rather than beginning to dwindle after the opening weekend as with most blockbusters, instead climbed steadily over time. No wonder some critics have come to cite *Crazy Stone* as an instance in which "word of mouth," stemming from the good "quality" of the product, is "the most effective means of spreading a brand."[84]

Certainly *Crazy Stone* was in no position to compete with big productions in terms of absolute ticket sales; it did not make it onto the 2006 Top Ten list. However, the film did appear on the Top Ten Domestic list, numbering ninth as of December 29 at RMB23 million ($3.5 million). While the number itself is nothing compared to the winner, Zhang Yimou's *Curse of the Golden Flower,* whose screening in December alone grossed RMB240 million ($31 million), its popularity was understood to be against all the odds – that is, defying the combo of big production, heavy promotion, and stars.[85] Speaking to this popularity, if not its "brand" effect, are the "over one million words worth of review essays" that poured out from internet forums and film circles.[86] Douban, one of the frequently visited websites for amateur critics to share ratings and reviews of film, music, and books, gave it a rating of eight out of ten, higher than the average of all of Feng Xiaogang's films.[87] Popular websites such as Baidu, Sina and NetEase have launched forums or discussion threads dedicated to *Crazy Stone*. Many bloggers also continue to post articles or comments on their own blogs as they watch it repeatedly on DVD, online, or on television to this day. Fans of the film came to identify themselves as "*Shi Shi*" or "*Shi Fen*," referring to "*Stone* Powder" and "*Stone* Lion" respectively, each playing off of one character of the Chinese word *Fen Si*, or "Fans" (with the pronunciation of "Shi" approximating "Si"). A resident of Beijing even reportedly bought over a hundred copies of *Crazy Stone* DVDs to give away to pedestrians.[88] According to many moviegoers, it was not the media propaganda that brought them into the theater but rather what their friends had told them about the film.[89] Numerous lines spoken by the film's central characters became in-jokes among fans in daily life and online, as may be seen from their responses to one another's blogs and forum posts.

To get a sense of the film's torrid reception, one only needs to look at a thread that started on July 13 on Baidu Posting Board under the heading "Crazy Stone." Entitled "A proposal for supporting *Crazy Stone*," the initial post reads: "Don't watch the bt[BitTorrent]-downloaded video. Don't watch the pirated DVD. Go to the movie theater. If possible, go watch it again. Then buy an official DVD, because this is a milestone for Chinese cinema." This post is immediately followed by the comment: "It is so hard for Chinese films to have such a standard. Let's not obliterate this talented director with piracy." Another contributor states: "I'm going again on Sunday . . . then I'll buy a DVD! Chinese cinema is one hundred years old. This is truly a director unseen in a hundred years!" Many claim to have seen it through all means possible – in the theater, online, and on DVD. Many more call upon others to "Support domestic films!! Support official copies!!" Several respondents (self-identified as in their twenties) who had purchased only pirated DVDs prior to *Crazy Stone* claim that this would be their "first official DVD." Another one exclaims: "Hope this is not the last crazy stone for China!" Yet another: "Support new directors. We need a new cinema! Hope China gets ahead of Korea again!"[90]

The "*Stone* phenomenon," in this sense, presents a case in which the "publicness" of cinematic experience is facilitated by the often piracy-enabled activities that take place in private homes, such as DVD watching and illicit online streaming. As new media sites such as forums and blogs remediate print culture but do so in an anonymous manner, they allow a public sharing of private thoughts, whose "disorder" and "uncontrollability" mirror Pang's characterization of the counterfeit industry. This is reminiscent of what Yu Haiqing has called "media citizenship" – that is, a heterogeneous, fractured public sphere enabled by new media technologies, one that is "mobile and flexible" so as to "make actors and actresses situated in particular spaces" not only "visible subjects" for the state but "invisible subjects" situated in networks.[91] For Yu, despite its elitist makeup, the Chinese netizen community, which comprises just a small fraction of all internet users and is even tinier compared to the rural and uneducated population, does present possibilities for transforming "actual" reality through "virtual" actions and "for re-imagining the nation."[92]

Considering the momentum for "supporting the domestic film industry" generated around *Crazy Stone,* a critical question arises: What is it about the film that enables this production of the national imaginary? After all, while many other films are also watched and talked about a great deal in these hypermediated environments, few have been able to generate such an outpouring of patriotic feelings in cinematic terms. Complicating the matter even more, this imagination of the nation is not restricted to China's geopolitical borders. Numerous members of the Chinese diaspora have embraced the film just as enthusiastically if not more. A typical comment from an overseas Chinese reads like this: "If I return to China next year, I want to see the cinematic *Stone* too. Good films can only be watched in the movie theater."[93] What gives rise to this identification with the "national" clearly has more to do with cultural reasons than with the mechanisms of marketing and promotion. To get at the cultural forces that helped shape the "*Stone* event," the reception of the film becomes a crucial site of investigation; for it is within the outpouring of amateur reviews that competing claims to the national are made, contested, and solidified. What made *Crazy Stone* such a powerful landmark for national cinema was its ability to carve out a unique brand of "Chineseness." The kind of "Chinese cinema" that *Crazy Stone* fans have deemed the film to pioneer not only distinguishes itself from the globalized national image-making called for in international art-house circles, but also differs significantly from the state-promoted film productions aimed at offsetting the global hegemony of Hollywood.

The Local/Real versus the Transnational/Copy

One of the key themes that arose from the reception of *Crazy Stone* has to do with its dual character: at once a "realist" representation of the local and a "copied" style, alleged to have been borrowed transnationally via piracy. On the one hand, the film is routinely characterized along the lines of "realism of the absurd," – that is, "using an unserious form to reflect on serious social problems,"[94] or as a work "rooted in reality" that presents "the intense collision in real life."[95] Often noted is the film's deployment of "unrealistic means to depict very realist issues"[96] to penetrate "into a real world,"[97] and to portray the "authentic existence" (*shengcun benxiang*) of the lower classes.[98] A Shenzhen writer, among others, claims that the film allows him to see the "sickness of the society, the absurdity of reality, and the craziness of humanity" in the same way as the classical novel *Dream of the Red Chamber* (aka *The Story of the Stone*) did for the renowned modernist writer Lu Xun.[99]

On the other hand, the film is frequently alleged to have copied the style of Guy Ritchie in such cult classics as *Lock, Stock and Two Smoking Barrels* (1998) and *Snatch* (2000),[100] especially the famous "Boris the Blade's escape" sequence toward the end of *Snatch*.[101] The charge first appeared in an online post titled "CRAZY STONE or Crazy Copying?"[102] in which the author expresses disappointment at the film's "naked copying" – "the story, the camera use, even the setup of each person's weird accent! Isn't it ironic that the film that was copied is called *Snatch*?"[103] Another blogger states that *Crazy Stone* is a "bad" copy of Ritchie's two films, and believes that although Ritchie is "internationally famous," he is "little known among Chinese audiences," giving the director Ning Hao the opportunity to copy so daringly without cutting into the film's popularity. According to this blogger, the instances of copying are "so numerous that those who have seen these two films will understand immediately."[104] A contributor to a Sina forum, pointing to the blog post above, urged everyone to buy pirated copies of the film.[105] The most severe diatribe occurs in a post called "Copied! Bro, *Crazy Stone* is the most Deceptive Work." The author is outraged that Ning Hao does not even deny he is copying, and is dismayed that "a half-Chinese version of *Snatch*" has fooled his fellow Chinese people.[106]

In response to the "copying" charges, Ning claimed that he wrote the script for *Crazy Stone* back in 2000, at which time he had not seen *Snatch*.[107] The original idea was to make something more like a Hong Kong (or "foreign") thriller[108] – a fact likely related to Ning's teenage experience of watching Hong Kong films in video parlors, before the soon-to-follow onset of the "DVD era."[109] Buying DVDs was known to be one of his great hobbies, though he also claimed to have been too busy making money (by producing music videos) to watch most of them.[110] When Andy Lau, the film's star financier, was first presented with the script, he was concerned that it was too much like a Hong Kong film; he reminded Ning to "localize the story."[111] After that, Ning and his team spent three to four months "experiencing real life" (*tiyan shenghuo*) so that they could make the script "more Chinese" and "closer to the lives of common Chinese people."[112]

During the script rewrite, some of Ning's friends pointed out that the film looked more like one of Ritchie's, a director who is one of Ning's personal favorites, than a Hong Kong film. He and his crew tried numerous other possibilities, but decided that Ritchie's model offered the best dramatic effect.[113] He came to understand it as a learning process, and increasingly saw the film as a "genre film." For him, it was natural that "the best options for making one particular type of film under certain circumstances would share some similarities." Therefore, Ning and his crew decided not to bother trying not to be like Ritchie.[114] Instead, they worked toward "making a good film" and "creating more full-blown characters" than those in Ritchie's work.[115] In another setting, Ning referred to the movies of Guy Ritchie, Quentin Tarantino, and Emir Kusturica as a specific "school" about "play" and "black humor." As "world cinema reaches this particular stage, and the reality of China also arrives at this stage," he stated, "it is inevitable that this type of movie should emerge."[116]

It is worth noting that Ning's defense of his "copying" relies on a historical-temporal claim – that China is at a "stage" where such "black humor" genre films are bound to arise. His assertion is that rather than being motivated to copy stylistically, the *Crazy Stone* story is an attempt to remediate the "real." It is the local reality that calls for the Ritchie-esque rendition. A son of steel workers from Taiyuan, an industrial city of the inland Shanxi Province (where Jia Zhangke is also from),[117] Ning once stated that "growing up in a factory," he knew well the "hopeless" condition of the laid-off workers who came to his home every day to play mah-jong (a common leisure activity among the retired and the elderly). Naturally, he thought of these "real people" as a first step to "localize the characters" as well as the story.[118] An avid reader of "social news," Ning often incorporates news stories into his screenwriting, many of which are "in themselves black-humored enough" to him.[119] *Crazy Stone*, for one, contains numerous examples drawn from newspaper reportage,[120] the most prominent of which include a robbery scene masked as "house moving" at the beginning of the film and a "Coke prize" con staged on a cable car ride.[121]

Interestingly, *Crazy Stone*'s successful "localization" is often noted as closely linked to the global figure of Hollywood. For example, an author from Sichuan believes that, unlike "many of our films [such as the mega-productions of martial arts films that] often tell real stories in a 'fake' manner," *Crazy Stone* has learned from "many Hollywood films [that] can tell fake stories" with a masterful "verisimilitude of plots and details."[122] Others argue that Ning has cleverly filled a "bone structure" derived from foreign films with "authentic, domestically produced blood and meat."[123] Still others suggest that *Crazy Stone* exemplifies a sort of "counterfeit professionalism" contrasted with Hollywood's "profession-alism proper" – a counterfeit film style that mirrors the "overabundance of . . . fake brands in contemporary China."[124]

The linking of the film's "counterfeit" Hollywood style to the per-vasive counterfeiting practices in China is noteworthy, considering that the reviewers of *Crazy Stone* often invoke foreign films that have never been released inside China, including *Snatch* and *Barrels*. While access to these films is certainly available for overseas Chinese who also con-tribute to these online forums, large numbers of "*Stone* fans" do confess their extensive exposure to China's piracy-saturated film culture. In the over eleven thousand reviews on Douban, for instance, many viewers refer to things like "training in spoken English" and "preparing for exams" in their comments, which are experiences more likely found among a domestic rather than diasporic audience. These audience members also appear to have little affiliation with the relatively small academic film circle, which would have granted them routine access to foreign film materials.[125] Most of the viewers, judging from their responses to the accusations of Ning's imitative style, have no qualms about this "borrowing." Some point out that it is those who want to show off their knowledge of foreign films who are propagating the accusations. Others offer exaggerated versions of "copying" to point out the absurdity of the copying claim. One such post states: "If Russia had the October revolution, was China's Communist revolution copying? If the West had capitalism, is socialism with Chinese characteristics' then copying?"[126] Numerous films are noted to have engaged in similar acts of copying, from Ritchie's to Quentin Tarantino's *Pulp Fiction* to Zhang Yimou's *Curse of the Golden Flowers*.[127] Many support Ning's contribution to Chinese cinema, noting it to be "concise and smart" and capable of creating a genre distinct from China's typical "traditional dramas."[128] Although some believe that its copying is "representative" of films "made in China," others argue that it is at least a fun-to-watch movie, which is unusual for Chinese films.[129] Some of the fans came to know Ritchie's films only after reading about them in the online debate, and they asked whether it was *Crazy Stone*'s own fame that triggered the copying charges.[130]

A more detailed comparison that focuses on "the localization of filmic techniques" can be found in an essay published in *Movie Review*. The author claims that Ritchie's *Snatch* broke Britain's all-time box office record (this is not backed by any evidence). Even though London is the background for *Snatch* and *Barrels*, it is not the London that is known for its "prosperity and civilization," but "rather another side" – "the daily lives and psychological conditions of people living on the bottom of the society in this modern metropolis."[131] Inspired by Ritchie, *Crazy Stone* also features "a few central characters who are little people struggling at the bottom of Chongqing . . . a city that really has local Chinese characteristics," with many convincing details that "this can only happen in China."[132]

The author references an oft-analyzed scene at the beginning of the movie, where Xie Xiaomeng, a pretentious art photographer, tries to hit on a pretty girl on an aboveground, river-crossing cable car. Rejected, he accidentally drops a Coke can out of the window, initiating a closely knit sequence of events.[133] The author notes that this "parallel montage" (by which he means overlapping editing) is deployed by both directors, and compares the "Englishness" of the music in Ritchie's films and the "Chineseness" of the music used in *Crazy Stone,* such as the "Sinicized" version of Tchaikovsky's "Four Little Swans" (rendered on Pi Pa, a folk instrument).[134] Agreeing with many other critics and fans, he notes that the sequence in which Maike, the "international master thief," descends from the ceiling to steal the stone is reminiscent of Tom Cruise's act from *Mission Impossible.* In conclusion, he attributes *Crazy Stone*'s success to its ability to localize the "filmic techniques of Guy Ritchie" while "truly remaining close to Chinese people's everyday-life situations and inner-psychological experiences" – an invaluable contribution to "the development of Chinese cinema."[135]

This comment invites a closer look at the film's "realist" portrayal of Chongqing and by extension the Chinese nation. Many viewers have come to read the city, whose "lively development" is caught "between the old and the new," as "a microcosm of the entire nation."[136] Even one of the few commentators who dislikes the film and laments its "vulgarity" thinks the director's excessive portrayal of several fight scenes is a direct representation of the abundant social disputes that are in actuality often resolved through violence.[137] Most fans share the view that "*Stone* is a film only the Chinese can understand," because so many of the funny incidents come from "life moments" that are familiar to a "Chinese" audience.[138] One example they offer is that in Hong Kong, where cultural experience differs greatly from much of mainland, the film only grossed HKD130,000 ($16,700) during the first week, and did not surpass HKD200,000 until two weeks later – a big contrast to its mainland success.

The idea that a film so "Chinese" indeed relies so much on "foreign" influences and does so through counterfeit means enacts the Jamesonian paradox that while "Hollywood films" typically constitute "the form" of "external hegemony," they often also serve as "the source of resistance to internal hegemony."[139] What can be discerned from the viewers' celebration of the film's "Chineseness" is a sense of dissatisfaction with cinematic representations of the nation that are deemed "unreal," be it the directly state-sponsored "main melody" films, the Hollywood-inspired martial arts epics of Zhang Yimou and Chen Kaige, or the "counter-Hollywood" Feng Xiaogang brand of urban films. A question worth probing is, What makes *Crazy Stone* more "real" as a representation of the nation than these other cultural productions? And how may this desire for the "real" conjure up a different mode of being in the nation?

Performative Subject in "Real Space" and "Real Time"

I would suggest that the interplay between "realism" and "copying" brings forth a complex set of spatial-temporal tensions that demand careful unpacking. For one thing, much of the claim about the film's "realism" stems from a sense of place – that is, "real space." At the same time, the representation of this "real space" depends on what may be termed a televisual aesthetic predicated on "real time." While the accusation that this "real time" aesthetic was copied from *Snatch* depends on the viewers' having seen the original, the recognition of "real space" also relies on the viewer's having been there. In both cases, there is a temporal distance between a present moment of cinematic spectatorship and a previous moment of knowledge acquisition. The conjunction between the two in the *Crazy Stone* event, I argue, activates a critical mode of engaging the social. This mode of engagement, specific to China's counterfeit film culture in the WTO era, gives rise to a performative subjectivity that in turn reconfigures the national imaginary in profound ways.

Central to the production of this subjectivity in counterfeit film culture is what Homi Bhabha has called a "doubling" of time.[140] For viewers to assert their judgment of a copying act, they must already be implicated in two temporal frames: one in which they saw the original and one in which she is exposed to the copied. In the case of *Crazy Stone*, its "original," *Snatch,* is itself often made available through counterfeit practices, whereas the "copied" visual aesthetic is paradoxically what enables the film to capture the "real."

The style of *Crazy Stone* has been characterized as "slightly exaggerated," featuring "restless editing often accompanied by swish wipes."[141] Several critics have attributed this style to Ning's background as a veteran MTV director.[142] Throughout *Crazy Stone,* Ning makes abundant use, often at lightning speed, of sharp crosscutting, jump cuts, and split screen for parallel actions, which gives the film a jerky touch that is somewhat atypical of either the domestic "main melody" films or the art-house brand of Chinese cinema (with its now almost standardized long-take aesthetic). The use of overlapping edits demands the audience's close "attention to the extremely complex plot" with "multiple switcheroos."[143] Most importantly, "showing an event . . . and then replaying it from the points of view of different characters involved," requires the spectator's "keeping track of characters in various places at the same time."[144] As Hu Ke, a professor from the Communication University of China notes, multi-angle replay of this kind is comparable to the televised live broadcast of a soccer game.[145]

This televisual "liveness" positions the viewer as a spectator who is present in time but absent in space. As the event (for example, the fall of the Coke can from the cable car) unfolds repeatedly from the different viewpoints of the participants, viewers are repeatedly pulled back in time, as it were, to observe the happenings "live," over and over. They are, in other words, present in the time of the event more than once. This heterogeneous experience of the "same time" would not have been possible if they were present in space, in which case they would only have had access to one specific viewpoint in the singular "real time," much like a live audience would at a sports event.

The simultaneity across space enabled by this temporal presence and spatial absence, on the other hand, also activates a sense of "heightened and spatialized perception."[146] The inland city of Chongqing that is the stage for the film is a mountainous harbor town on the Yangtze River located in Sichuan province.[147] As Ning himself and numerous viewers point out, it is the city's own stratified spatial character that lends authenticity to an otherwise unfathomable story. In this sense, the spectator is sutured in the narrative flow through a spatial presence – "being-there," thanks to a directed navigation of the urban landscape.

This spatial experience becomes particularly significant when the real spaces that serve as the backdrop for the *Crazy Stone* story, as many have noted, are those typically obscured or unseen in much state-sanctioned cultural production; they are certainly not featured in the dynastic costume dramas or in the popular "urban" films by Feng Xiaogang.[148] The majority of the scenes in *Crazy Stone* take place in urban environments that are decrepit at best. Not only is the jade stone itself found in the factory's restroom, but several important scenes are shot in filthy toilets.[149] The prominently displayed figure of the "toilet," as Zhang Jie, a Shanghai critic points out, serves as a "magnifying glass" that affords the audience unusual access to the "real."[150]

Certainly "realist" scenes that depict developing-world conditions of this kind are present in many experimental and avant-garde digital videos or in the work of the so-called urban generation.[151] However, these depictions often feature an art-house style, exemplified by the work of the renowned sixth-generation auteur Jia Zhangke. (Jia himself was more or less inspired by the Taiwanese maestro Hou Hsiao-Hsien.) What distinguishes Ning's film from these representations is simply that *Crazy Stone* indeed reached a much larger domestic audience, both in terms of its direct cinematic public and those exposed to its media coverage. These publics are unlikely to be patrons of the underground venues where the more experimental films are screened.[152] Indeed, the display of "dirty motels, toilets, and bath houses," motivated by Ning's unabashed sense of the "real" – both "real space" and "real time" – even reportedly led some Chongqing residents to complain that the film might do harm to "the impression of the city" among their countrymen.[153]

To this complaint Ning responded that audience should find those spaces "not dirty at all, but in fact even lovely." Calling *Crazy Stone* "a film of black humor," Ning stated that he "wouldn't have chosen pretty places," though he also "found Chongqing's architecture to be quite grand," not unlike that of Hong Kong.[154] This reference to Hong Kong in some ways echoes one of Deng Xiaoping's famous quotes, in which he envisioned the creation of "several Hong Kongs" inland, as part of the

Reform and Opening Up.[155] The former colonial city has long been part of a futuristic urban imaginary for many mainland Chinese.[156] But Ning's statement situates Chongqing alongside Hong Kong rather than depicting it as a place that has to catch up with it. This understanding of spatial co-presence can also be linked to Ning's admiration for the city's ability to capture "time" geographically:

> Chongqing is a mountainous city with a much-stratified topography. The arhat temple (where the stone exhibit was held) is likely from the Ming-Qing dynasties. Behind it are buildings from the fifties or sixties. Behind them are those from the eighties or nineties. And behind those are the ones from the past two years. Just from this one glance, you see three hundred years.[157]

For Ning, Chongqing's distinctive stratification enables a direct visual representation of the city's history – a history closely entwined with that of the nation. An ancient capital for the southern kingdom of Ba, Chongqing did not achieve more than a marginal status in modern Chinese history until 1937, when it became the nationalist government's alternate capital at the onset of the Second Sino-Japanese War (1937–1945). The Guomindang government successfully deployed the city's wartime development to spatially and discursively create a "microcosm of the nation," and in doing so legitimized its position as the nation's modernizer.[158] After the so-called War of Resistance (a more locally familiar name for the Second Sino-Japanese War), the city became the site of intense Nationalist-Communist struggles, which resulted in the death of numerous key members of the Communist Party. Hence, a line of "Red revolutionary" narratives continued after 1949. In the post-Deng reform, economic power engines like Shenzhen and Shanghai again eclipsed the city. It was only upon the state's decision to "go west" that Chongqing resumed a strategic position in the nation's developmental vision. In 1997, three years after the launching of the Three Gorges Dam project and three years before the state officialized the policy to "expand and develop the west," Chongqing became the fourth municipality under the direct jurisdiction of the central government – a designation that was in sync with the nation's impending entry into the WTO.

Originally, Ning planned on going to three other cities – Wuhan, Guangzhou, and Chengdu – but he fell for Chongqing upon the first visit: "[It is] not too old, not too new, not too ordered, bursting with hot steam, as if anything can happen."[159] While "the ultra-modernized cities of Beijing and Shanghai"[160] are too "standardized," cities like Taiyuan (the capital of Ning's home province Shanxi) are "not new enough."[161] The "hot and scorched" Chongqing, however, is "a city in transition," and only there can "such a twisted story happen."[162] In other words, Ning seems fully aware of Chongqing's position in the nation's developmental path as it is transformed from a "backward" inland harbor town to one that resembles the more "advanced" coastal metropolises. However, Ning also discerns the possibility of compressing multiple temporalities in the city's layered structure – a spatialization of time that offers a perfect backdrop for the *Crazy Stone* story.

Crazy Stone's spatialized temporality of Chongqing, combined with its meticulously constructed simultaneity across space, intensifies the viewing subject's presence in the city/nation in such a way as to acknowledge the time of historical passage. There is a significant difference between this representation of history and the historical dramas that pervade contemporary China's screen cultures. The latter, one might argue, conform to what Homi Bhabha calls a "pedagogical" narration of the nation, which positions "the people" as an a priori object in the nation's "continuist, accumulative" tradition.[163] However, it would be more apt to say that *Crazy Stone* enacts Bhabha's notion of a "performative" mode of engaging with "the national sign."[164] Rather than turning the viewer into a spectator of the nation's past glory, *Crazy Stone* conjures up the nation in its "enunciatory 'present,'" thereby situating the subject in a temporality of "in-betweenness" – more specifically, between the original/real and the copy/fake.[165]

To illustrate the making of this performative subject, it may be worthwhile to look at an intertextual reference in *Crazy Stone* that is read by many as a paradigmatic example of the film's "spirit of parody" – the rehearsal and performance by the SOE (state-owned enterprise) employees at the gem exhibition. The scene is overwhelmingly interpreted as mocking a well-known dance number called "Thousand-hand Kwan-yin" (Kwan-yin is a Buddhist goddess of mercy).[166] In *Crazy Stone*, upon the discovery of the jade, the factory official decided to "use the jade to set the stage, and let the economy do the show (*feicui datai, jingji changxi*)." This is a modified version of a key official slogan since the

1990s, "let culture set up a stage on which the economy can perform the opera (*wenhua datai, jingji changxi*)." The revival of local traditions in this form is often part of the local and national governments' intent to generate tourism income while attracting investments by overseas Chinese.[167] This "economization of culture" – that is, the transformation in the conception of culture from ideology to profit-generatiing capital[168] – is portrayed in the film through the following sequence shot in the temple: A female employee gathers a dozen women workers of various ages (and a feminine-looking man with glasses) for a rehearsal. All the performers are dressed in dynastic costumes similar to those in the "Thousand-hand Kwan-yin" number. Baotou, the protagonist, has just grudgingly accepted the duty to guard the stone in the temple, which he believes to be a "dump." He gets into an argument with a female employee who is training the performers for the Kwan-yin show. The factory head, Xie Qianli, eventually pulls them apart, stating "we are all here for work."[169] Later in the film, the troupe perform the "Thousand-hand" dance to the theme song for the popular TV show *The Legend of the Wooden-Fish Stone* (*Muyushi de Chuanshuo*).[170] On-screen, accompanied by the well-known lyrics praising the beauty of the stone, are the far from beautiful troupe members (including the man with eyeglasses) posing awkwardly as goddesses. For some, the intertextual irony here points to the poignancy of the predicament faced by these laid-off workers.[171] For others, it embodies the Bakhtinian "carnivalesque" – an inversion of order that works to deconstruct the official motive to turn culture into capital.[172]

While I agree that these instances accentuate the film's self-distancing from a state-propagated relationship between economy and culture, more is at stake in making visible the performativity of "the people" in their engagement with "national traditions." Seen from the perspective of official narratives, the jade stone, the temple, and the Kwan-yin performance are signifiers of the nation's past. It is the "historical" value embedded in these "traditions" that is now upheld as cultural capital from which "the nation" may extract affective (that is, nationalistic) as well as economic profits. These values are typically indoctrinated into "the people" through their identification with the national body, in its self-imagined temporality of past, present, and future. As the Chinese critic Gan Yang argues, this equation between "tradition" and "what is past (*guoqu*)" presupposes an understanding of the past that "is already preformed."[173] For the past to exert its presence, it must engage in a constant self-reproduction, since the real past itself can never be retrieved. This reproduction of the past – what Gan calls "inauthentic temporality" – ultimately produces an "inauthentic being" in the present.[174] In *Crazy Stone*, however, one may observe an inversion of this "inauthentic presence." The sequence depicting the workers training to become performers and the Kuan-yin performance that highlights the body of the grotesque together make visible the very "reproducedness" of the "past," now repackaged as "tradition." The factory official's enunciation – "we are all here for work" – accentuates the commonality between the labor of SOE factory workers and the labor of performing the national "tradition." The worker-bodies in training to become performative bodies destabilize the inauthentic being to which a profit-motivated reproduction of the "past" indeed corresponds. As such, the aura of "tradition" is disrupted, and its reproduction qua commodification made abundantly clear.

The making visible of the commodification of the past also ambiguously portrays the figure of the state. One instance in the film that exemplifies this ambiguity is when the character Sanbao arrives in Beijing, at Tiananmen Square, on a mission to claim what he believes to be a Coke lottery. The background music for the scene is a children's song from the 1970s, "I love Beijing Tiananmen," an immediately recognizable "main melody" tune that is characteristic of the high Maoist era. Sanbao, alone and confused, is shown tugging his collar to offset the blowing wind, against the backdrop of the square. This scene generated a Baidu discussion thread, among others, in a forum dedicated to *Crazy Stone*. One viewer points out that the buses shown in the background are of an older design, a kind that has disappeared from the streets even in provincial towns and that could not have appeared in 2003 Beijing. A follow-up post concurs that Ning, working within budget, likely used CGI (computer-generated imagery) to insert Sanbao into an older documentary or film clip shot on the square. Most other follow-up commentators agree, reasoning that this less-than-ten-second scene could not have brought Ning and his crew to Beijing and that Tiananmen Square could not have been so empty as to have only one person in front of the camera.[175] In another thread, one post cites the lyrics for the song, "The great leader Mao Ze-dong, leading us marching forward," to which a later post responds: "the great leader has led us to this state (*dibu*), haha, how ironic!"[176]

What makes this scene so "ironic" for this forum contributor, as well as many others? For one thing, the Maoist-era lyric, "march forward," is juxtaposed with Sanbao's lonesome presence in front of Tiananmen Square. He was lured to the square by the Coke fraud – an empty prom-ise that cannot be realized, much like the failed Maoist dream of national self-determination, of "getting ahead" of the West by way of hyper-in-dustrialization. The present state of being in the nation is thus refigured in the Coke can, as the nation's developmentalist project today is increas-ingly conditioned by the terms of transnational capital, among them the individuating, privatizing processes that depart from the Maoist vision of collectivity in great measure. The fact that this scene appears shortly after the sequence in which Baotou went searching for Sanbao in the lat-ter's squalid home only serves to reinforce the gap between the utopian vision of a former era (as represented by the children's song) and the present experience of those living in real space.[177]

At the same time, Sanbao's spatial presence in Tiananmen Square is judged to be "forged" precisely because of a temporally determined recognition – that of the outdated look of the bus. The question is not whether the charge is valid, since it is debatable whether these old-style buses had indeed faded from public view by 2003, or whether this scene is CGI-rendered or shot on location. Rather, this kind of place-specific recognition depends upon knowledge that is acquired from a historical-temporal presence – of having been there, as embodied, living subjects in the nation. It is by identifying particular markers of history (such as the old-style buses) that viewers substantiate their subject status as those who have retained a continuous presence in the national space.

The claim to temporal presence here conjures up the possibility for a performative way of engaging history. This possibility is crystal-lized in a sequence that takes place not long before Sanbao's Tianan-men Square scene.[178] It happens after Heipi, disguised as a visitor to the stone exhibition, distracts the security and crowds in the temple for his fellow Xiaojun in order to swap out what they believe to be the real stone. The attempt is unsuccessful, as Maike intervenes and stops

Xiaojun at the very last minute. When Baotou returns to the temple, he scolds the eyeglass-wearing security guard and sends him away. As he steps away from the pedestal on which the stone is displayed, he freezes for a split second – and so does the crowd behind him – to the sound of a bell. When he starts walking again, a close-up tracking shot of his face is interspersed with a series of outlandish images.[179] At the end of the third and the last of these series, Baotou turns around to face the pedestal and eventually walks back to it. The Pi Pa tune that accompanies him speeds up as he comes closer to the stone. As Baotou looks down at the stone, a close-up shot reveals a cigarette mark on the stand made by his co-worker Sanbao earlier in the film. Baotou has previously put the stone in a specific position to cover it up. Now that the mark is visible, it serves as proof that the stone has been moved, and by extension that the real stone has been swapped for a fake one. As these thoughts are going through Baotou's mind (so the viewer presumes), on screen is a frontal close-up of his face as it changes expression. Behind him, the crowd appears as an array of bodies moving around in slow motion, leaving ghostlike traces. As Baotou's anxiety intensifies, the crowd comes to a standstill and eventually morphs into red pigments and light shadows, into which Baotou's body falls back, as if into a tunnel, against a high-pitched Peking opera tune mixed with heavy metal guitar.[180]

This moment surely appears as something of an anomaly in a largely narrative-based genre film. One blogger has used the Chinese idioms "spider threads and horse traces" (*zhusi maji*) and "sky horse racing through the sky" (*tianma xingkong*) to interpret the imagery.[181] However, this seemingly out-of-place sequence is crucial for advancing *Crazy Stone*'s narrative. Without it, Baotou would not have suspected the authenticity of the stone on display. His realization of the fact is enabled by something akin to a miracle, in a dramatic interruption of time. There is more than a bit of Benjaminian resonance here, particularly the idea of the "zero hour" (*Stillstellung*) or "standstill," signaling "a revolutionary chance in the struggle for the suppressed past."[182] Understood in terms of a "shock," Baotou's absence from the historical event (the swap of the stone) is compensated by a constructed presence in time, which is captured by the freeze-frames in the background. Aided by this rupture of time in suspension, he enters into "history" itself by constructing it as "that which is fulfilled by the here-and-now [*Jetztzeit*]," and not succumbing to its progression through "homogeneous and empty time."[183]

However, there is an ambivalence in this temporal construction, because Baotou's "historical consciousness" turns out to be false – he is convinced at this moment that the swap took place during the incident stirred up by Heipi, and he later mistakenly takes Sanbao's note to be the evidence that Sanbao is in possession of the stone. His "false consciousness" culminates when he returns what he believes to be the real stone and gives the copy to his wife, telling her: "It is fake!" It is the viewer who is in the position to discern that the real stone is precisely the one that now belongs to her. The closing scene finds Baotou's wife gently leaning her head on his shoulder, looking content even after being told that the stone is fake. For many *Stone* fans, this is a moment of "true feeling (*zhenqing*)."[184] A Douban contributor, among others, claims that Baotou's wife, as the "only non-crazy person in the film" who does not have the same maddening desire, thoroughly deserves the real gem.[185] This point is concurred with by most of the follow-up comments, even though some suspect "there can't be people of this kind in real society."[186]

What makes this narrative closure appealing to the fans, I would argue, has to do with the idea that the real stone is extracted from the network of a commodity economy and re-cast into a gift exchange. As anthropologists Lee and LiPuma have noted, "gifts neither presuppose a totality nor are necessarily instrumental in creating one," except under capitalism, where "the social" is reified as "society."[187] The market value of the real stone derives from its status as an artifact of history. But this value is ultimately unrecognized by the people who exchange it as a gift, which by definition does not create a surplus.[188] In their approval of Baotou's wife – the person with "true feeling" – as the final possessor of the "real," *Crazy Stone*'s fans display an appreciation for the kind of sociality that the gift of the real-and-yet-taken-to-be-fake stone is expected to signify. This recognition of the signified further breaks down the arbitrary distinction between the real and the fake. Even as the fans occupy the all-knowing subject position that allows them to lay claim to the truth, they have expressed a defiant attitude toward that claim and instead embraced the stone as a performative object whose referent is "true feeling" itself.

Indeed, the gifting of the real stone points to "particular and particularistic modes of sociality – ways of constructing social units and imagining their integration" that are "intrinsically linked to a mode of temporality that is heterogeneous, contextual, and immune to any uniform standard of measurement."[189] It is worth noting that this is the second time that the real stone is transformed from a commodity to a gift. The first exchange took place when Xie Xiaomeng, having swapped the real stone for a fake one that he purchased from a stand outside the temple, gave it to his love interest, Jingjing. This scene is justifiably seen as a direct reference to the counterfeit markets pervasive in China.[190] More important, however, is that the practice of counterfeiting serves as a driving force in the narrative and indeed creates the condition of possibility for the transformation of the stone into a gift. The same industry also thwarts Maike in his attempt to steal the stone.[191] In one oft-referenced scene, Maike, who descends from the ceiling, discovers that the rope is too short for him to reach the stone, because the "unscrupulous vendor" who sold him the rope had obviously cut it short. Later, in a split-screen sequence, Maike is shown trapped in an air duct while his alter ego, the local thief Heipi, donning the outfit that originally belonged to Maike, struggles to get through an underground sewer. The two eventually meet on the ground, facing each other, speechless. This spatial co-presence of the "global" and the "local" arguably mirrors the conditions that give rise to the Shanzhai industry in Southern China (discussed in chapter 2). If Heipi can be understood as an embodiment of Shanzhai, his literal underground situation is created by a double entrapment: a statue of Pharaoh placed by Baotou and Sanbao on the one end, and Maike's BMW on the other.[192] Heipi's release was dependent upon the removal of the BMW by the police – representatives of the state, which has raised trade barriers to remove foreign products from the market to make room for domestic cell phone brands.[193] But the flaw in his "hit and run" tactic is vividly illustrated in the closing sequence in which we find him, having snatched some bread from a bakery, running on a circular highway while the bakery owner chases after him on a motorcycle.

National Cinema and the Nation Brand

Not surprisingly, it is local thieves like Heipi who became heroes for many of *Crazy Stone's* supporters.[194] One of Heipi's most talked-about lines is in reference to the Hong Kong clothing brand Baleno (*bannilu*). In an early scene, when Daoge scolds Heipi for adopting "a sexy look" by wearing a flashy outfit and instructs him to be more "low-profile" as a newbie in the trade, Heipi replies: "It's a brand, all right? Baleno!"[195] In another instance, when Heipi is drinking with his friend in front of a BALENO neon store sign, he spots the drunk Jingjing and Xie Xiaomeng walking home together (a sight he apparently informs Daoge about in time for the latter to catch the two in bed not long after.) Just these two snippets were enough to exert "negative impact" on Baleno, for upon hearing Heipi's line, "the sub-middle class" reportedly decided to distance itself from the brand.[196]

In an article from the magazine *China Brand* (*Zhongguo Pinpai*), one contributor comments that Andy Lau, as Baleno's spokesperson, had the good intention of inserting a product placement, but ended up annoying the management of Baleno because the brand was now considered a "tasteless" trademark favored by a stupid thief, who likely bought it from a "street vendor." Even with a "loud foreign name," the author argues, the brand still stands for "good quality at a low price," and many who wear it are actually dreaming of global brands like Levi's. The film's bad publicity for the brand "was no more than a trigger," and the unskillful handling of "the public relations crisis" was a reflection of more serious problems in the young brand's "long-term strategy." By contrast, foreign fast-food giants like McDonald's and KFC still have no trouble making a huge profit despite a series of scandals concerning their illicit use of material and labor, in part thanks to "the domestic consumers' blind preference for anything foreign." In conclusion, the author cautions that the long-term cultivation of China's local brands will be a long and difficult process, and "the most valuable asset for Chinese enterprises in the age of economic globalization is not factories or equipment but rather a strong brand."[197]

The linking of the *Crazy Stone*-generated Baleno incident to that of the nation brand signified by "Created in China" is perhaps more than a coincidence. The all-powerful nation branding discourse has encroached in this instance upon the public conjured up by *Crazy Stone*.[198] This is evident in the responses among the film industry experts to the film. For them, *Crazy Stone* presents tremendous hope for "domestic cinema" even as its "distinctive" style is understood to have derived from the incorporation of many of the "cutting-edge foreign cinematic elements";[199] presumably "for the first time," it has "allowed a Chinese audience nurtured by Euro-American cinema to experience the national pride" of seeing a "domestic entertainment film" on a par with those of the advanced world.[200]

To probe into the "mystery" of the film's popularity, the Chinese Film Association held a conference that featured representatives from Focus: First Cut and Warner China Film HG, as well as numerous film critics and media scholars.[201] A professor from Tsinghua University proclaimed that "if there are twenty such domestic films each year, the habit of film watching among domestic audiences will be changed fundamentally; imported blockbusters will no longer be their first choice."[202] Likewise, a film literature professor believed that *Crazy Stone* "stood for a successful breakthrough by local films in the siege of Hollywood big productions," which came as a result of more people's changing attitude toward commercial blockbusters, from rejection to acceptance.[203] Others encouraged young filmmakers to "expand local resources" in order to "attract local audiences," as "entertaining films" like local comedies promised "a huge consumer market" and had the ability to "establish an industry."[204]

Certainly not all film scholars were in favor of *Crazy Stone*. One line of criticism came from Huang Shixian, a professor from Beijing Film Academy, who blamed Ning at a conference for commercializing his work too early and not following more of an artistic route, as he had done in his previous art-house films.[205] Those who believed that the film does not have enough social significance echoed his view.[206] But more often than not, Huang's point is refuted by audiences who believe that "films do not have to always have to carry the function of 'cultivating the spirit'"; so long as "they are grounded in the masses, they can win the audiences' applause," even without "big directors and international stars."[207] For others, *Crazy Stone* has grasped the "pulse of common people's lives," and can be contrasted with films by "those directors who have turned middle-class . . . and can no longer see such reality, hence making only films that fool themselves rather than entertaining the masses."[208] One critic even invokes Mao's famous doctrine that "arts and letters should serve the people and the masses, and not always be about the emperor and his entourage, or literati and their lovers," and suggests that the principle needs to be adjusted to changing historical conditions.[209] This comment echoes Ning's own assessment in attributing the success of the film to its ability to "speak to the audience," 90 percent of whom were presumably part of the "grass roots."[210] For him, "there is no separation between art and commerce in cinema, only between films that are entertaining and those that are not."[211]

Ning's stance on cinema as entertainment assumes a curious position between the long-standing state belief that "cultural workers" should educate the masses through producing "socially significant" arts, on the one hand, and the more recently globalized entertainment market that ostensibly caters to transnational masses, on the other. *Crazy Stone*'s own encounters with the state point precisely to the tension between the state's desire to educate and elevate the "masses" and a commercial mandate to offer what the "masses" enjoy the most so as to maximize the rate of return. For instance, the film was originally called "Thief of Thief" ("*Zei Zhong Zei*"), playing off "*Die Zhong Die*" or "Spy in Saucer," the Chinese translation of the Hollywood film *Mission Impossible*."[212] While the name was intended for more market effect based on a reference to the Hollywood blockbuster, it was not approved because of the inclusion of the word "thief," which potentially presents a "bad influence."[213] This led a blogger to categorize *Crazy Stone* as "a very commercialized genre film with Chinese characteristics, one that follows the rules of the socialist market economy."[214] A censorship report (though one whose veracity cannot be confirmed) appeared on the online forum Mtime in 2009 as a repost from a scriptwriter's blog. It lists such state recommendations for revision as "illustrate the theme of the overcoming of the evil by the righteous," "eliminate all crimes and curses," "revise the parts containing violence and sex," "redesign the scenes that contain panhandlers," "portray the employees of the soe in a more positive manner," and "reduce the number of smoking scenes."[215] One blogger lamented that "after seeing these, what kind of hope can you have for Chinese cinema?"[216]

However, a post on Tianya Club, a popular online community, attempts to complicate the contemporary effect of state regulations of this kind. Calling *Crazy Stone* "a big poisonous weed that propagates liberalism," it is "written in the classical style of the Great Proletarian Cultural Revolution," and as the forum contributor who reposted the piece in English suggests, it would surely "strike fear in anyone who was involved in the making of this film" if it were a product of 1968.[217] The original piece chastises many of the film's depictions of state policies and ends by urging the State Bureau of Radio and TV to ban it immediately. But most comments from the four-hundred-odd follow-up posts have come to read it as a spoof. This has led the forum contributor to comment that "in a state of post-modernist politics in China . . . it is just no longer possible to write this sort of thing and expect that the public will take it seriously."[218]

The invocation of "postmodernist politics" here may be seen as pointing to the performative subject in the making, vis-à-vis the pedagogical work of state interpellation. As Arif Dirlik and Xudong Zhang point out, "Chinese postmodernism" shares "an antirevolutionary repudiation of a socialist modernity" with the postmodernism that emerged from the late capitalism of the West. But "what may make Chinese postmodernity unique is that, within a postsocialist situation, postmodernity itself may serve as a site of struggle between the legacy of the past and the forces of the present."[219] The making of the performative subject in the production, circulation, and reception of *Crazy Stone,* both official and illicit, precisely mirrors what Bliss Cua Lim calls "immiscible temporality" – a "commingling" of insoluble times that refuses to succumb to, and indeed challenges, the homogeneous time proffered by capitalistic modernity.[220] The emergence of this performative subject within the spatial-temporal configurations of *Crazy Stone* is therefore indicative of the possibilities for a postmodern cultural artifact to preserve as well as rejuvenate the nation's historical experience in search of an alternative modernity.

CONCLUSION

In the spring of 2012, Chongqing, the city that provided the setting for *Crazy Stone*, became the center of international attention when Beijing ousted the city's party chief Bo Xilai. Bo, of course, was known for launching the "Chongqing model of development," an experiment, rooted in the city's strong working-class base and his own background as a "red princeling," that attempted to shift from a "Guangdong-style" neoliberal model to one that is more equitable and sustainable. It included such measures of "socialist renewal" as granting urban residency and benefits to over three million rural migrants, and was joined by "Singing Red" and "Striking Black" (*changhong dahei*), two related campaigns aiming to revive socialist morale and clamp down on corruption and organized crime, respectively. The "Singing Red" campaign, in particular, built on many already widely practiced grassroots forms of popular culture that "have been inspired by and made reference to China's revolutionary past," such as "the voluntary group singing of revolutionary songs in public spaces."[221]

The kind of "yearning for social justice, equality, and a sense of community" that these practices embody has no doubt conjured the possibility of a different national-popular culture, if not "a new subjectivity," much like the one put forth by the cinematic public for *Crazy Stone*.[222] Yet Bo's efforts encountered fierce opposition from within the party-state and a hostile neoliberal global media environment, which collaborated in orchestrating his downfall. Hence, the sociohistorical forces that gave rise to the "Chongqing model" were reduced to a sensational murder trial that unfolded on Weibo (China's major Twitterlike microblogging site) in the form of a well-scripted family drama.[223] One could not help but discern a parallel between the (increasingly commercialized but still controlled) state media's production of the Bo Xilai case as a spectacle and the Chinese film industry's response to *Crazy Stone*'s popularity, which was overwhelmingly to see it as a new opening for nuturing a commercially viable national cinema for China. Since the success of *Crazy Stone*, there has indeed been a boom in dialect comedy films in China's domestic film market, a trend that Liu Jin has identified as "regionalization or localization."[224] Ning himself has also moved on to make big-budget films like *Silver Medalist* (2009), *Guns N'Roses* (2012), and *No Man's Land* (2013), all of which featured key cast members of *Crazy Stone* and won big at the box office. This trajectory seems to confirm several critics' observation that films like *Crazy Stone* offered nothing more than a "sanctioned social release" for an audience consisting primarily of middle-class, internet-savvy youths.[225] To be sure, as Beijing-based critic Li Yang points out, the "gamified" narrative of chasing the gem works to erase the class and spatial "stratifications" otherwise present in the text and aids in the ideological construction of a middle-class fantasy.[226] But casting *Crazy Stone* in this light alone would perhaps be no different than succumbing to the official narrative of the Bo Xilai "scandal," which leaves out the intense ideological struggles that underlay the event itself.

I have attempted an investigation into the complex formation of the *Crazy Stone* phenomenon, particularly as it intertwines the (cinematic) nation-branding project and the material configuration of a counterfeit (film) culture in WTO-era China. What this event has made visible, indeed, is the fissure between the pedagogical time of the nation brand and the performative time of counterfeit culture. While the self-legitimating discourse of nation branding positions the national cinematic public as one that awaits state indoctrination, the national-popular phenomenon of *Crazy Stone* has come to challenge this state-sanctioned national imaginary by promulgating an alternative mode of being in the nation; nation branding dedicates itself to the transformation of "the people" into one that would uphold the financializing principle of the IPR regime, whereas the aftermath of *Crazy Stone* has worked to destabilize the homogenizing temporal logic of "development" and "progress" implicit in the slogan "From Made in China to Created in China."

The global-national imaginary of nation branding is observably at work in subsuming the energy generated around *Crazy Stone* into building a domestic cinematic industry based on market-oriented entertainment value – itself serving to shore up the state's global-national legitimacy. In doing so, those aiming to promote nation branding cinematically have missed out on an opportunity to pursue a national vision of a different kind, one that is perhaps more in line with the project of socialist renewal promoted by the Chongqing model. This failure

of recognition, however, is more attributable to the hegemonic operation of IPR as a cultural system than to the lack of alternative cultural
claims to the national, which are made apparent by the transnational
Chinese viewership for *Crazy Stone*. Indeed, the aim of cultivating a
cinematic nation brand that can compete with Hollywood is integral
to China's "current soft power drive," which "foregrounds an (apparently) depoliticised notion of 'culture'" in the effort to "downplay or
even explicitly suppress ideological differences in the global symbolic
arena."[227] This self-essentializing national vision, with a fixated focus
on commodifying the nation's "image," may be seen as resulting from
IPR's value-producing conception of culture, which understands the
national primarily as a resource for generating profit. This economized
understanding of national culture, now more closely connected with
the state's attempt to legitimize itself, has not gone unchallenged among
the publics of counterfeit culture, who insist that the national can be re-
negotiated as a site for meaning (and not just profit) making. In fact, the
cultural contestations between nation branding and counterfeit practices, which stem from the contradictory workings of IPR as a culturally
imperialistic regime, are discernible in multiple cultural spaces that
extend beyond the cinematic realm.

FOUR

Landmark, Trademark, and Intellectual Property at Beijing's Silk Street Market

IN PREVIOUS CHAPTERS, I HAVE EXAMINED THE MANIFESTATION of counterfeit culture in a variety of media forms. These media traverse different social spaces and encompass a range of commodities and symbolic forms, from cell phones and the internet to television and film. Their workings speak to Lash and Lury's claim that the global culture industry operates through a "mediation of things."[1] In this mode of production, culture is "thingified," which implies that commodities have become meaningful objects in and of themselves. In this chapter, I suggest that counterfeit culture also takes "place" as a specific product of the global culture industry – that is, it is produced and consumed in specific locales that are also entrenched in processes of meaning production. The conception of counterfeit culture as a "culture of circulation," then, also entails the re-consideration of the sites of production and consumption as nodes within the cultural circuit. While counterfeit culture's site of production is receiving increased scholarly and journalistic attention (a realm into which chapter 2 has offered a glimpse),[2] the numerous informal markets for the transaction of fake goods remain understudied. This negligence is what this chapter hopes to remedy.

The Silk Street market is an urban destination in Beijing known for its sales of counterfeit global brands. Located in the diplomatic quarter of the capital city, the market first emerged in the 1980s, in the beginning years of the Dengist reform. After China's accession to the WTO in 2001 and as part of Beijing's efforts in preparing the nation's capital for the 2008 Olympics, the city decided to transform the original street market into an eight-story shopping plaza. This process of transformation was fraught with tensions and struggles, especially between individual vendors, the municipal government, and global brand owners. While these struggles bring the internal contradictions of the nation-branding project as an ideological formation to light, they also point to alternative visions for the nation that contest the cultural logic of intellectual property. To probe into these cultural contestations, the spatial history of the market, which is entwined with the re-integration of China into the global system, is a good place to begin.

THE BIRTH OF SILK STREET

Silk Street (or Xiushui Jie, in Mandarin Chinese) has had no shortage of media attention since China became a member of the WTO. To locate the market's exact origins, however, has proved to be a challenging task.[3] This lack of official history speaks in some ways to the spontaneity that characterizes the market's birth. One legend has it that in 1982 a peasant convinced a security guard at the nearby American embassy to let him sell some potatoes on the east side of the Xiushui alleyway so that he could pay up his child's tuition. Soon, eight other vendors joined in, first selling fruits and vegetables on the ground, then on flatbed tricycles, and finally, in 1986, setting up actual stands.[4] Nobody expected this tiny alley – at the time no more than five hundred meters long and eight meters wide – to become an "internationally famous commercial street."[5]

In the years that followed, a growing number of vendors came to the alley with more diversified merchandise, from key chains to antiques. By the spring of 1983 the alley was already packed with vendors. As a consequence, the Chaoyang District government of Beijing saw it necessary to exert some form of regulatory control. On August 15, 1985, the city granted the traders commercial licenses. Officials even put up a white banner at the entrance that displayed the slogan "Civilized Commerce, Hygiene Maintained, Guaranteed Quality and Quantity, Reasonable Pricing." By 1999, as more items such as crafts, clothing, and accessories became available for sale, the Beijing Administration of Industry and Commerce (AIC) entered an official record of the space as a "collective trading market."

In many ways, former Chinese Prime Minister Li Peng's claim that the market "is a window of China's Reform and Opening Up"[6] is not far from the truth. The nationwide developmental policies put forth by Deng Xiaoping in 1979 included a central component: the downsizing of state-owned-enterprises that constituted the mainstay of the socialist economy. The disintegration of the "iron rice bowl" system gave way to a booming "individual economy" (*geti jingji*), officially listed in 1979 as a complementary sector to the state-socialist economy.[7] The number of "independent entrepreneurs" (*getihu*) increased from 140,000 to over two million between 1978 and 1981. As the national government made further efforts to promote the private sector, the number of "independent entrepreneurs" jumped to over ten million by 1987. This was the group that made up the majority of traders who had come to occupy Silk Street.

The early success of Silk Street vendors had in large part to do with the market's location in the "first diplomatic quarter" (*diyi shiguanqu*) of the capital city. After all, the state's intent to "open up" brought an influx of foreign diplomats, tourists, and visitors, many of whom found lodgings in this district reserved for expats and embassy personnel.[8] This foreign presence constituted a major customer base for the market, known at one point as "the fire lane for the American Embassy."[9] Likely because of the popular demand for silk products among foreign consumers, "Silk Street" soon came to replace "Xiushui Jie" as the alley's official nickname.[10] Not only was the market a tourist favorite for local specialties, it also became the only place in Beijing where foreign currency could be exchanged under the table and even directly used for purchasing goods.

The international makeup of Silk Street's customers, however, is but one aspect of the market's global character. Indeed, the rising fame (or notoriety) of Silk Street had everything to do with the post-1979 emergence of the export processing zones in southern China – the primary production site for the "Made in China" brand. According to several veteran traders, in the mid-1990s, traders from the south began to bring "fake brand-name clothes, watches, and glasses" to the market.[11] The sources for their goods were mainly of two kinds: one was "pure faking by imitation," that is, wholesale copying of "real brands"; the other was "excess order" (*shuai dan*), which consists of copies made by local factories using the extra materials provided by foreign companies.[12] These "excess copies" were known as "fake real" goods – ones that contain the "same blood" (that is, the same materials) as authentic goods, albeit without authentic trademarks. Because the materials that went into these products were "real," they were often of good quality but sold at significantly lower prices than those with a licensed trademark. Many of these goods were also trendier than those available in mainstream department stores at the time. Since traders were quite good at keeping up with consumers' changing whims, they were soon able to establish the market's reputation as a place for "fakes of quality" (*jiamao buweilie*). This reputation in turn attracted more customers, both from Chinese provinces outside of Beijing and from abroad. As its fame grew both domestically and overseas, the market garnered such titles as "Little Hong Kong in Beijing" and "Little Paris in the Capital."[13] The thousands of daily visitors who frequented Silk Street generated millions of dollars in revenue. The sales were even sustained through the 1998 Asian financial crisis, when many other street markets in the city went into a recession.

For many, the market's continued success lies in its specialty in selling "Chineseness" to foreigners. What exactly this "Chineseness" means, however, is a bit hard to pin down. On the surface, the name "Silk Street" itself seems to suggest that it refers to the local "traditional," "ethnic," or "folk" character of the goods on display.[14] Some of the vendors, however, came to see the market's "Chineseness" in a different light. One vendor, for instance, told *China Youth Daily* that he once thought the foreigners (or *laowai,* in colloquial Beijing dialect) who came to Silk Street were "stupid" because they would rather come to this "open-air" market for products that they could buy for the same price in department stores. Only later did he understand that it was the "relaxing" atmosphere of the market that made the experience special, and therefore "cultural."[15] He Wei, a Beijing-based economics professor, has characterized Silk Street as an "indigenous" market, a place that enables interaction of a more "intimate" kind.[16] Whether it is haggling or multilingual small talk, this shopping experience is quite different from the orderly procedures of "purchasing, ticketing, standing in line, and making a payment" in a standard department store, where customers are often subject to a form of "control."[17] This understanding may be linked to historian Rosalind Williams's account of the rise of department stores in fin-de-siècle Paris, where the introduction of fixed pricing transformed the social interaction of "haggling" between people into a "response of consumer to things."[18] At this moment of Western modernity commodities came to replace "art and religion" as objects that promised to fulfill the desire for a "finer, richer, more satisfying life" beyond the basic need for "physical survival."[19] In contrast, what drew large numbers of Westerners to Silk Street were not just commodities, but rather the cultural specificity of the goods and of the place. Its allure had less to do with "Chinese" folk objects or counterfeit brand-name products than with the disorderly street bazaar atmosphere, which was quite distinct from that of the overly regimented department stores.

The rise of Silk Street's cultural identity, then, reflects a production of local culture within globalization, in that the meaning ascribed to the space – as a sign of "locality" – is not directly construed by those who reside within it but by those who come from outside. Many Beijing residents, including Professor He, who celebrates the market's "distinct flavor," have never been to the market, let alone been a regular customer there. More often than not, a Beijing local will tell you that the market's "most attractive business" is the cheap fake brands and not the traditional arts and crafts. This "inside knowledge," while shared among the locals, is nonetheless produced *for* them, since the primary customer base for fake brands is foreign visitors to the city/nation.

In this sense, it may be useful to think of Silk Street as a "heterotopia," one that operates through "a system of opening and closing."[20] On the one hand, it is "not freely accessible like a public place," considering that the vendors "must have certain permissions and make certain gestures,"[21] such as paying rent or consenting to governmental regulations. On the other hand, despite its ostensible "openness," it attracts visitors who are endowed with a specific body of knowledge – that of the global brands, for example. In the market's early days in the 1980s, this knowledge was certainly more extensive among foreign visitors than Beijing locals, who were yet to experience the bombardment of global brand images that ensued in the 1990s. For many of Silk Street's visitors from the developed world, especially North America, Australia and Europe,

IPR-infringing acts in their own countries are more visibly inscribed with criminal meanings than in developing countries like China, where the global IPR regime is still attempting to inculcate the same sense of guilt. For a tourist, Silk Street is a space where the "illicit" trading of counterfeits is "both absolutely sheltered and absolutely hidden, kept isolated without however being allowed out in the open."[22] This excitement about the fake as something exotic is also compounded by the typical tourist demand for souvenirs, which often calls for a distinct sense of the "local," marked by visible signs of "cultural" if not "traditional" distinction.

It would appear that it is the understanding of Silk Street as a haven for the consumption of *otherness* – both "counterfeits" and "traditions" – that enables the production of "Chineseness" by the market's foreign patrons. This understanding, in turn, became widespread among many Beijing residents, who had come to see the place through the eyes of an outsider. Silk Street, then, can be seen as another instance in which cultures of circulation – counterfeit among them – came to shape the national imaginary through a constellation of global networks. The making of Silk Street as a local tourist landmark indeed depended upon a complex glocal network of knowledge and commodity production. Later, it would give rise to a series of property struggles never foreseen by the market's early tenants.

THE STRUGGLE OVER THE "SILK STREET" PROPERTY

Perhaps the only Beijing residents who did not see the market as chiefly a tourist destination were the vendors who worked and traded at Silk Street on a daily basis. Their occupancy of the urban space, however, had been precarious at best.[23] As early as 1987, when business at Silk Street was booming, rumor had it that the city government intended to demolish the market because it was lacking in hygiene standards and fire prevention measures. Faced with allegations of this kind, the vendors organized themselves into an "Association for Independent Laborers" to enforce a no-smoking rule throughout the entire market. This self-organizing work had some visible effects, as the district and municipal officials decided that the market was "not as chaotic" as they had thought, and that it merely needed a face-lift rather than demolition. The renovation of Silk Street first appeared on the city's agenda in 1997, a year before the Public Security Bureau (the city police) announced a plan to rebuild the market due to its hidden fire hazards. *China Youth Daily* reported on May 29, 1999 that the aim of the renovation was "to eliminate the scenic deficiencies" in the market's infrastructure so as to fulfill the capital's overall beautification goals.[24] The market was to be rebuilt "in its original location" without forfeiting much of its "original flavor," and the commercial space would be expanded, with added service facilities for finance, food, and communication, among other activities.

This official plan, however, obscured some of the underlying tensions involving Silk Street's reputation as a counterfeit bazaar. At the time, China was striving to join the WTO, and in the minds of the Beijing officials the blatant sale of fake brands at Silk Street was no doubt an unpleasant smudge on the nation's IPR image. The publicity surrounding the market's renovation in some sense reflected the city's intent to take more control of the management of this "counterfeit" reputation. Moving the market indoors appeared to be a reasonable solution. As an official in charge told *China Daily* in June 1999, the plan was to relocate the market in a five-story mall-styled building. In order for the new site to blend in with the surrounding urban environment, its design would feature no "traditional Chinese" characteristics, as such additions would likely incur additional cost.[25] But the authority was also worried that the commercial vitality of the market might be affected by the move, as was the case for Ya Bao Road Market, another street bazaar in Beijing. Now the impending WTO entry provided the final push, as the city decided that the market's continuing prosperity required stricter "regulations" over its distribution channels, which would eventually work to disrupt Silk Street's IPR-offending routines.

As the city's cleansing plan unfolded, the uncertainty of Silk Street's future also prompted the traders to act. They invited a handful of Beijing intellectuals to a conference on July 19, 1999, to speak out on the market's "existential value." The outcome was a set of slogans intended to help Silk Street find a way to position itself "culturally." One of these slogans linked the market with other Beijing-specific tourist activities – "Climb Great Wall, Eat Peking Duck, Stroll Silk Street (*deng changcheng, chi ka-*

oya, guang xiushui)."[26] Another one described Silk Street as "a twentieth-century Qingming River Painting carved out by the scissors of Reform and Opening Up."[27] The reference to the Qingming River Painting was clearly meant to suggest that the culture of Silk Street was on a par with the vibrant twelfth-century street life in the famous painting from the Northern Song dynasty rendered by the renowned artist Zhang Zeduan (1085–1145).

"Cultural" work like this seemed to have halted the city's beautification scheme temporarily; a delay was announced by the market's official administrator, Jianwai Community Economics and Management Center in 2001. But the continued sales of counterfeits at Silk Street led to a series of stringent crackdowns. Just before the May Day holiday (International Labor Day) in 2001, the city issued an order to ban the selling of fakes of five major global brands – Nike, Adidas, Polo, Boss, and Tommy Hilfiger – at Silk Street. The vendors had twelve days to put an end to their "illegal acts." Without much dissent, they proceeded to put the counterfeit items on sale at half-price or even lower. When reporters from *China Business Herald* came to the market on May 8 and 9, they saw no trace of these particular fake brands, as well as fewer counterfeits of other items.[28]

Just when crackdowns like this triggered more speculation over the market's demolition, a city notice came on July 29, 2003, announcing that a real-estate development company named Xinya Shenghong had been granted the right to reconstruct this section of the capital.[29] Although it was unclear whether Silk Street was part of the "reconstruction," the vendors again decided to fight for their right to stay. They organized two more conferences, one on the "folkloric way of life in Beijing" on September 27, 2003 and the other on the "intangible assets of the Silk Street Market brand" on April 10, 2004.[30] Numerous Beijing academics joined forces with them, including several prominent legal scholars who put together another conference with the theme "New Silk Street, New Olympics," and called for more cautious handling of the Silk Street case.[31] As the conference participants pointed out, the market was a brand for the city, if not the nation, one that was created by independent traders over the past twenty years.[32] Again invoking the idea that Silk Street was "carved out by the scissors of Beijing's reform," they argued that the bazaar embodied "the mode of production and lifestyle of the masses."[33] The consensus was that if the market were to be torn down, an important urban landmark would be lost.

These efforts to retain Silk Street's original form appeared to have little effect in changing the market's destiny. In 2003, the Municipal Commission of Development and Planning, along with other land administration departments, approved the construction of the new Silk Street Plaza. While it was only two years before the new building opened (on March 19, 2005), the bazaar-to-plaza transition was not as smooth a process as the municipality had imagined. For what this transformation entailed was a significant change in Silk Street's meaning – from a name for a place to a brand for a landed property. The tensions and contradictions that arose within this transformation of meanings were crystallized in a lawsuit over the "Silk Street" trademark, one that brought forth a set of entangled issues of public space, national interest, and private ownership.

A trigger of the lawsuit was a high-profile auction on June 21, 2003, where five of the five-square-meter stalls in the future Silk Street plaza were sold at RMB3 million ($456,000) each. The developer Shenghong received 40 percent of the auction income (the equivalent of $912,000), which led its chair, Zhang Yongping, to boast that Silk Street was more expensive than Manhattan.[34] The investors' interest in renting stalls in the plaza was overwhelming, according to Xiushui Haosen Clothing Co., the company in charge of the plaza's operation. Taking advantage of the plaza's apparent popularity, Haosen signed contracts with numerous tourist agencies that targeted foreign customers, so that they would include the plaza in their Beijing tour itineraries. The news of the auction dumbfounded the occupants of the old Silk Street. One of the traders did a calculation and estimated that it would take thirty years for him to earn back the auction price.[35] While the developer had offered the original Silk Street vendors some discount in prices and sponsorship in bank loans, no more than twenty of them decided to move into the new plaza. Meanwhile, new vendors from Shanghai, Zhejiang, and Guangdong were reportedly in touch with the developer, some demanding as many as "hundreds" of stalls.[36]

While many old vendors believed that the "sky-high prices" constituted "severe infringement upon the intangible assets" of Silk Street,[37]

Sun Jiangang, the head of Beijing Yelusheng Commerce and Trade Ltd.,
decided to file a lawsuit against the developer as well as the manager
of the new plaza. Having read about the auction, Sun appealed to the
district's Trademark Office (part of the Beijing AIC), claiming that the
organizers had infringed upon his company's trademark. When he did
not receive enough attention, he supplied the office with further proof,
including a trademark registration. In interviews, Sun claimed that if the
new plaza were to be engraved with the three words "Xiu Shui Jie" (literally "elegant water alley," the name of Silk Street in Chinese characters),
it would definitely constitute a violation of his "trademark rights."[38] It
turned out that Sun was hoping to use the "Silk Street" trademark for a
different mall he had planned to build in the city, one that would "attract
venders from all around the country" and imbue the trademark with
even more "Chinese national characteristics." A representative from
Shenghong later revealed that the developer had been aware of Sun's
trademark registration but decided not to bother with it: "Everyone
knows Xiushui Street refers to this place, on Jianwai Avenue; it can't
possibly be elsewhere." He claimed that Sun had asked to partner with
Shenghong in the reconstruction project, but Sun himself denied any
contact of the sort.[39]

Shenghong's representative also pointed out that the developer had
registered the "Xiushui" trademark before Sun.[40] According to official
records, Shenghong's application for the Xiushui trademark was approved on December 31, 1998, and Sun did not obtain his until 2001.
While Shenghong's trademark was valid between April 28, 2000 and
April 27, 2010, Sun's was valid from November 28, 2002 to November
27, 2012. However, the two registrations had different classifications.
Shenghong's trademark was classified under the thirty-fifth (advertising, industry, industrial management, and office affairs) and thirty-sixth
(insurance, finance, currency affairs, and real estate affairs) categories.
But within the thirty-fifth category, it was filed under "supporting business for industry and commerce" and "office affairs," but not "sales (on
behalf of others)," to which Sun's trademark belonged.[41]

Based on this detail, Sun filed a lawsuit against Shenghong, demanding an RMB3.5 milion ($560,000) fine and a public apology in the news-
paper *Beijing Daily*. His charges included the unauthorized display of the

characters "Xiu Shui Street" on the plaza and the illegitimate use of these characters in the promotional materials for the new building. He also claimed that since the plaza's opening, Beijing AIC had found numerous fake brand-name goods at the market, which "severely tarnished" its brand owner's long-standing reputation.[42] Shenghong, in its defense, asserted that the use of "Silk Street" was adopted from the name of the original market, which stemmed from its geographical location, No. 8 Xiushui East Street. In fact, it was the Beijing Planning Commission that recommended the name "Xiushui Street" to Shenghong, which had originally planned on using the name "East Bridge Road Comprehensive Commerce Building."[43] The legal counsel for Haosen, the building's future manager, also argued that the plaintiff did not have any previous relationship with the market, and therefore its trademark registration was driven by malicious motives.[44] For the defendants Shenghong and Haosen, since Silk Street was much better known as an urban locale than as a registered trademark, it was only appropriate to continue using the name as a marker of the place in tourist promotion.

On December 8, 2005, the court dismissed the plaintiff's charges based on the understanding that Silk Street "is a famous tourist destination and not a trademark."[45] The foundation of the market, the court held, preceded the trademark registration; its reputation as a tourist and shopping destination had evolved over an extended period of time. The developer and manager's use of the name for the new plaza was therefore legitimate, because it was meant to describe the nature of the service that had long taken place at the market. Unconvinced by this verdict, Sun appealed for a second trial, which took place on April 10, 2006. He argued that Silk Street was not a mall or a supermarket; instead of selling its own products, it was indeed using the "Xiushui" trademark to promote goods sold by the traders. The first verdict, according to Sun, contradicted itself by stating that the use of the name was simultaneously a description of the market's geographical location and an appropriate label to enhance the plaza's publicity. To this, the court's second ruling, announced on June 9, 2006, responded that the service provided by the new plaza was a continuation of the original market, and that it was similar to malls and supermarkets. Therefore, the ruling in the first verdict was upheld.[46]

The lawsuit and its rulings, while leading some legal scholars to call
for further specification in IPR laws, more importantly pointed to the
question of Silk Street's ownership: To whom does Silk Street belong?
The answer to this question varies depending on whether one understands "Silk Street" to be a street name, a place, a trademark, or a brand.
As Yuan Jiafang, a law professor, stated in a 2000 article in *China Trademark,* the issue ultimately came down to the "intangible asset" of the
Silk Street market.[47] For the four hundred vendors at Silk Street, it was
their collective effort that had cultivated the brand equity over the years;
therefore, in the words of one vendor, this asset did "not belong to any
individual."[48] However, once Silk Street was perceived as a "cultural
landmark," its preservation as "a valuable symbol of Beijing's social life"
immediately became a matter of "public interest," which was in principle
subject to the protection of the government.[49] But the government had
no involvement in the market's day-to-day operation, and should therefore have no business in owning the "brand." Would it not be better, Yuan
asked, to prohibit the trademark "from being registered by any organization or individuals," so that business opportunists could not step in to
take possession of it?[50]

While questions of this kind were posed by many who struggle to
understand the ownership issues that surround the market, the fate of
Silk Street has nonetheless revealed a privatization process. The rhetoric
of protecting the public interest, it turns out, has only served to mask a
complex web of government-business alliances, which transferred the
ownership of the Silk Street trademark to the hands of a few state-backed
companies. In 2004, when plans for the future Silk Street Plaza were
firming up, several investigative journalists were able to uncover an intricate interest matrix behind the bazaar-to-plaza transition. A central
figure in this matrix appeared to be Guo Liwen, the general manager
of the Jianwai subdistrict office that oversaw the original street market.
She later became a shareholder in Tianwei Lida, an investment branch
of Haosen, the company that was to become the operational manager
for the new plaza. Guo, then, clearly played the double role of a public
servant and a private business representative. This public-private "partnership" was also reflected in the government's arbitrary selection of the
developer Shenghong to construct the new plaza, a choice not subject to
any open bidding whatsoever.[51]

To be sure, certain "democratic" processes were in place to ensure that the traders could get their voices heard. But a public hearing about the market's safety concerns, scheduled to take place on July 15, 2004, mysteriously turned into two less formal "discussions." Even so, the vendors elected their own representatives to take part in these discussions, preparing hundreds of pages of background material and inviting more legal and economic experts to join the fight. A former People's Congress member from the district also spoke out on their behalf, stating that Silk Street's supposed violation of city regulations against fire hazards could not have occurred because the rules were not yet in place when the market was first set up.[52] The vendors also argued that back in 1988, the district government had required each of the 140 private entrepreneurs to contribute RMB3000 ($450) to the construction of a fire-prevention booth. Since then, they had been paying a sizable fee to their administrator in addition to Beijing's city taxes. They demanded to know how these funds were used if not on fire prevention. They also called into question the qualifications of the developer and its use of the "Silk Street" name for the new plaza. More than one trader held the view that "the intangible asset that belongs to us traders has been carved up!"[53]

Yet Silk Street's demolition became imminent after August 19, 2004, when the government and vendors reportedly "reached an agreement." Many traders had no choice but to plan for their next move. When interviewed, some vendors were confident that old customers would find them in the new location, while others were dismayed about their prospects. On the eve of the demolition, some traders attempted to stay at the market to "fight to the death" before they were taken into police custody.[54] When a bulldozer came to tear down the Xiushui Market sign on the morning of January 6, 2005, hundreds of traders, citizens, pedestrians, and media crews braved a snowstorm to gather at the market. While many donned heavy-duty down jackets to protect against the freezing temperatures, several old traders wore T-shirts that bore the characters "Protest Demolition" (*dizhi chaiqian*) to put their bodies on display in front of the media zone designated by the police.[55] Before the market sign came down, a police officer lowered the national flag that was waving on the spot and carefully folded it before leaving the platform to make space for the bulldozer. At around noon, after the departure of the police, the crowd dispersed and most onlookers returned to their daily routines. It was not until then that the protesting traders started to pack up. There was some talk about marching down to Tiananmen Square, but no one actually took the lead.[56]

The vendors' embodied presence at Xiushui Alley's demolition site was no doubt more than a nostalgic gesture toward a disappearing site of local folk culture. Their bodies in public served as a powerful reminder of the struggles that underlay the bazaar-to-plaza transformation. For these traders, Silk Street was a space in which they had cultivated a particular kind of local culture. Joining them in this cultural production were the global tourists who had come here for a taste of "Chineseness," be it fake or folk. However, this process also created the conditions for perceiving the market less as a physical space and more as an "intangible asset," to the extent that even the vendors themselves adopted this language in the effort to keep Silk Street intact. This change in perception seems crucial in shaping the ongoing property struggles at the Silk Street site. On the one hand, the legal dispute over the use of the Silk Street trademark at the new plaza depends on the conception of "Silk Street" as a trademark – that is, as intellectual property. On the other hand, once understood to be an urban landmark and a source of the city's tourist revenue, Silk Street was brought into the realm of public interest, which is in principle subject to state regulation and protection. In both of these re-conceptions, the locality of the market becomes an abstracted form that is detachable from its original locale. The notion of deterritorialization, as discussed in the introduction to this book, again best describes this transformation, as the culture of Silk Street is lifted out of its geographical confines to become a culture of circulation.

In the state-sponsored bazaar-to-plaza transformation, however, the intangibility of the "Silk Street" brand appeared to have encroached upon the physical space itself. Deterritorialization, then, takes on an even more literal meaning – that of displacing some of the most important cultural producers of Silk Street from their place of production. This second sense of deterritorialization is directly tied to the state interest in cultivating a proper national image in preparation for the Olympics. What allows the state to claim ownership of the market and subsequently transfer this "intangible asset" to private entities is precisely the abstracted notion of the brand. Here, the discourse of branding – proffered by the global-

ized IPR regime – plays a significant role in legitimizing the state action
of demolishing the Silk Street site. Once re-cast through the lens of a
branded property – a landmark-signifying trademark – the market's culture is transformed into a kind of value-generative resource, linkable to
the interests of the "general public" – itself an abstraction akin to "the
people" as it was deployed in state media's representation of Shanzhai
culture (chapter 2).

This generalized notion of "the public" is precisely what was contested on the day of Silk Street's demolition. The protesting vendors
there appeared as a collective, embodied subject who refused to be abstracted in the same way that Silk Street was taken to signify a brand for
the city and for the nation. Their conflicts with the police manifested a
fissure between the difficulty of claiming ownership over the market and
their nominal status as citizens of the state. One must remember that the
key reason for the traders' failure to secure ownership of the Silk Street
brand was their "loose organization."[57] This kind of collectivity did not
fit with the individual-based conception of property found in Western-
originated IPR laws. In the craze to rejuvenate the capital city in order
to stage a global-national spectacle par excellence, the state appears
once again incapable of conjuring up an alternative national imaginary,
one that would allow Silk Street to flourish in its distinctive form. As
the open-air market became reterritorialized – that is, subsumed into a
privately owned and operated shopping plaza – its fate was to become
more closely entwined with the project of nation branding in the years
to come.

RE-BRANDING SILK STREET FOR THE BEIJING OLYMPICS

Before the grand opening of the new plaza in 2005, Zhang Mao, then the
deputy mayor of Beijing, proposed "Silk Street" as the official English
name to replace the market's pinyin transliteration, "Xiushui."[58] The
emphasis on "silk" as a self-Orientalizing code of "tradition" was very
much in line with the display of "Chineseness" at the Olympics opening
ceremony a few years later.[59] Also closely linked with the Games was
the expectation that Silk Street would be frequented by predominantly
English-speaking Olympic tourists. Today, upon exiting the Yong An Li

4.1. The new Silk Street plaza.

subway station visitors are greeted with the sign "Silk Street Pearl Market," along with the Chinese characters *"Xiushui Jie"* (Xiushui Street). Visible in the plaza's underground parking lot is the slogan "Welcome to the Silk Street Pearl Market – Merchant's Bird Nest!" As if to solidify this reference to the official stadium of the Games, the real Bird's Nest also appears in the background on the same neon-lit billboard, with the new Silk Street plaza in the foreground. A subtitle at the lower left-hand corner displays the phrase "One Dream, One Shopping Paradise," obvi-

4.2. Neon sign on display in the parking lot of the new Silk Street plaza.

ously invoking the central motif for the 2008 Games, "One World, One Dream."

It was not easy to change the face of the market from a bazaar for illegal fakes to a shopping paradise for the Olympics. Back in 2003, not long after the Beijing Organizing Committee for the Games released its logo design, 134 unauthorized clothing items bearing the emblem were found at Silk Street. Numerous legal struggles with global brands over the years have reinforced the Silk Street administration's determination to transform the market into a more legitimate tourist destination. A central figure behind this process was the general manager for Haosen, Wang Zili, who also served as Silk Street's chief public relations spokesman.[60] Wang devised a two-pronged strategy for Silk Street's turnaround: on the one hand, the market was to become "an element of Chinese culture" by "using Chinese flavor" and "Chinese elements" to

attract "outside guests"; on the other, by introducing discount stores for
international brands and turning the market's unofficial outlets into legit
ones, its "fashion atmosphere" would be enhanced to attract "domestic
guests" to the officially licensed brand-name stores. In other words, the
future of Silk Street would rely on a combination of "Chinese culture"
and "foreign fashion" – "full of Chinese flavor outwardly, and full of foreign flavor inwardly."[61]

In 2006, Wang began to launch the first prong of the turnaround
plan by inviting the so-called time-honored brands of Beijing (*Beijing
laozihao*) to set up branches at the market. Meanwhile, he increased
the percentage of stalls specializing in "folk commodities" such as silk,
china, and tea so as to change the orientation of the market from "fake"
to "folk." A rental discount of 20 percent or more was offered to these
"old" brands, and only one of each goods category would be chosen to
be included in the market. Wang also announced plans to expand the
Silk Street operation overseas. The idea was to adopt a "tourism commerce" model, which would allow Silk Street to bring its affiliated "time-
honored" brands to foreign locales. Considering that many old brands
were facing operational and developmental difficulties despite their "rich
historical and cultural" heritage, international showcasing opportunities
of this kind had proven quite attractive.[62]

Along with the cultivation of the market as a destination for "folk"
brands, there was an effort to crack down on counterfeits and promote
licensed sales of real brands. In March 2007, over one hundred stalls
selling unlicensed branded items were reportedly eliminated. According
to Wang, traders who obtained license agreements from international
brands could benefit from a year of free rent, and those developing their
own brands would get a 10–30 percent reduction in their rent. Not only
did the administration put forth a development strategy for intellectual
property protection, it also set up an RMB30 million ($4.5million) IPR
protection fund to help traders adapt to selling "national," "licensed,"
and "time-honored" brands.[63] As a result of these efforts, by June 2007
a total of ninety traders were persuaded to convert their stalls from fake
to folk.

The management presented its vision for Silk Street in a new slogan:
"Cultural Xiushui, Fashionable Xiushui, Branded Xiushui, and Innova-

tive Xiushui (*wenhua Xiushui, shishang Xiushui, pinpai Xiushui, chuangxin Xiushui*)." The percentage of traders who had turned legit quickly rose to as high as 77 percent among the shoe vendors and 95 percent among those selling luggage and bags. To recognize this "working progress in China's IPR protection," Paul Ranjard, the chair of the IPR working group of the European Union's Chamber of Commerce, came to the market on January 18, 2007 to present awards to forty traders before applauding Silk Street as a "model" for others to emulate.[64]

Clearly Silk Street's goal was to turn itself into an "incubator for China's nation brands" in order to allow the latter to "march into the world."[65] Thanks to rent discounts and other incentives, traders began to produce and sell their own brands quite successfully. Branded pearls like "Hong Rui Fu" and "Yu Qian" had already become hit items among the attendees of the 2006 Beijing Summit of the Forum on China-Africa Cooperation for their "global brand" quality and low price. Clothing vendor Hua Shijun, who had been a partner in 80 percent of the fashion stalls at Silk Street, invested RMB10 million ($1.6 million) in the cultivation of the "Ding Zhong" brand, which was soon lavishly displayed on giant LCD screens in his luxury store, alongside other world-famous fashion icons.[66] It came as no surprise that the market was designated in January 2007 by the city government as a "Special Commercial Street in Welcoming the Olympics."[67] That year, the annual sales figure was estimated to be above RMB1 billion (about $16 million). The "silk zone" of the market was expanded in July to accommodate a thousand-square-meter tailoring and made-to-order area for the purpose of serving "high class" Olympic guests. On January 23, 2008, a "Silk Street" brand, whose products included tea, jewelry, ties, and shirts, became an official brand, the license for which was granted to selected traders in the market.

What marked the beginning of Silk Street's Olympics festivity was a "mobilization meeting" held at Chang'An Theater on January 23, 2008, 200 days before the Games. In front of numerous municipal, commerce, and intellectual property law enforcement officials, manager Wang presented a slogan to over one thousand vendors and sales staff, highlighting the importance of Silk Street as a key venue for the Beijing Games and emphasizing that "serving the nation's guests is a glory above all."[68] As if to secure this "glorious" representation of the nation, numerous language and etiquette training sessions became the daily routine for the five thousand sales staff at the plaza. Random tests were conducted to ensure that each person was qualified to provide basic bilingual tourist information. Also enforced were rules known as "Three Necessities and Eight Prohibitions" and "Olympics Security and Protection Rules"; the former stipulated requirements on clothing, language use, and smiles, while the latter offered specific instructions on how to keep the thieves out of Silk Street (by "looking out for your neighbors," for example.) These rules and regulations were even printed on index cards so that salespeople could carry them around as an immediate reminder. The stringency of these rules led some traders to call their workplace the "[Communist] Party School" (*dangxiao*) or the "Huang Pu Military Academy."[69]

While these measures worked to transform Silk Street into a disciplinary space of surveillance, they also mirrored the re-territorialization of the market from a spontaneous constellation of glocal networks to a space-specific production of the national imaginary. Even though none of these measures was sufficient to erase the traces of counterfeits at Silk Street, they helped to construct a new IPR-friendly image of the plaza that could be positively linked to the Olympics as a global-national spectacle. As manager Wang put it, unlike the opening ceremony of the Olympics, which allowed the world to "observe Chinese culture from a distance," Silk Street offered an opportunity for visitors to "touch, experience, and consume Chinese culture up close." Together, Silk Street and Zhang Yimou (the award-winning filmmaker who directed the Olympics opening ceremony) were co-producing nothing less than a "panoramic display" of Chinese culture.[70]

There is certainly a parallel between Zhang's cinematic rendition of the nation as an object for the global gaze and the selling of "Chinese culture" at Silk Street as an object for global tourist consumption. This is another instance in which the internalized gaze of the "foreigner" comes to re-shape the national self, or rather how the nation is to be represented to its domestic and international publics.[71] Re-conceived as a representative sign of the nation on display, Silk Street's own clothing brand also blended itself seamlessly into the global-national event. According to the market's official records, eighty of the one hundred foreign media who had come for interviews during this period had reported on the "Silk Street" brand. During the opening ceremony, delegations from Nauru and Venezuela donned made-to-order "Silk Street" brand outfits, while Ethiopians wore the brand at the closing ceremony. Ji Mingren, the stall manager for a store called "No. 1 Silk Street," saw these as early indicators of the brand's "international success."[72] The sales staff even joked that their workplace had become "a subfield" of the Olympics.[73] Their metaphor echoed that of Fox News, among other U.S. media, which reported that haggling at Silk Street had become a new sport for the Games. This was not entirely an exaggeration, considering that from August 1 to August 25, over a million customers shopped at Silk Street, with an all-time daily record of fifty-three thousand on the nineteenth. A total of twenty-five national officials and first ladies visited the market between August 3 and August 26, some stopping multiple times to pick up their made-to-order outfits and pearls. Among them, former U.S. president George H. W. Bush's visit on the eleventh no doubt attracted the most media attention.[74] His trip to Silk Street was seen as an acknowledgement of the market's IPR protection work, a shift in "America's long-time critical attitude toward China's IPR issues."[75] Star athletes, including many NBA celebrities, came to the market and used their medals to bargain for discounts.[76] Athletes and officials also gave many salespeople souvenir pins from various nations, which they proudly wore on their red uniform vests, competing with one another to see who got the most.

Between August 1 and August 25, Silk Street received a total of over 880,000 foreign customers, and the sales figures during the two months' span before and after the Games reportedly surpassed RMB200 million ($32.1 million). This gave manager Wang a good reason to compare the market's constant breaking of its thirty-year record in customer numbers and sales to the athletes' record breaking on the sports fields. He called Silk Street the winner of "the fifty-second gold medal," in addition to the fifty-one earned by Chinese athletes (and in turn, the National Sports Committee).[77] Numerous media outlets reported on the market's transformation from a fake-brand clearinghouse to a mall full of "China's time-honored brands" and goods with "Chinese traditional flavor."[78] *China Intellectual Property News*, among others, described it as a "leap from an IPR troublemaker to its protector."[79] A silk vendor noted that the most attractive products for foreigners remained those of "Chinese national flavor," which led him to reference the saying "Only that which belongs to the nation belongs to the world."[80] The items that were most likely taken to embody the "national flavor," besides silk, were "Chinese characters, chopsticks, kites, tea leaves," that is, things appearing to be "most common to our [Chinese] eyes" but "new and strange" to "foreign friends."[81] A vendor of panda-themed souvenirs, for example, was particularly pleased that the store's sales doubled during the Olympics.[82]

CCTV, which had assigned a reporter to "Silk Street watch," featured the market's daily activities quite prominently in its evening news.[83] When a sales girl had a picture taken with former president Bush, the photograph also made its way into *Chang'An Avenue*, a documentary aired in January 2010 to pay tribute to the thirtieth anniversary of the Reform and Opening Up.[84] At the end of the documentary, the picture is displayed to conclude the story of a successful Silk Street vendor who made enough money from the market to have purchased six properties for her family: "Many such wealth-creation stories are circulated here. These vivid stories combine to make up the changing history of this long avenue, this city, and this nation."[85] Personalized Silk Street narratives like this, in other words, have become an integral part of the post-Olympics media celebrations of the nation's economic development.

While the Chinese press predominantly emphasized the "successful" outcome of Silk Street's new branding strategy, the "foreign" press came to see it in a different light. For instance, the International Anti-Counterfeiting Coalition compiled a list of twenty English-language news reports on the sales and shopping of knockoffs and other items at Silk Street, from August 11 to August 28. Among them, the *Washington Post* pointed out that as one of "the capital's most beloved tourist destinations," Silk Street became famous "not for its silk" but "for the knockoffs."[86] *Sky News* reported that despite the officially prescribed "stiff fines and jail terms," fake Fuwa (a set of five Olympic mascot figures) key chains could be found at a Silk Street stand ostensibly selling "Tiffany silver"; offenses like this, for the reporter, were no less than a slap in the face of the Chinese government, which "has paid little more than lip service to intellectual property laws" and now has had its own Olympic trademark counterfeited.[87] Only one article, from the *Wall Street Journal,* mentioned the re-branding measures taken up by the market's administrators.

When interviewed about news like this, the chair of the plaza's developer, Zhang Yongping, came to Silk Street's defense. While he granted that counterfeiting issues at the market were serious, he also drew a parallel between the demand for illegal drugs in the United States and the demand for fakes in China. Emphatically, he pointed out that the source of the problem was the customer demand for fake brands, particularly among visitors from overseas. Zhang's dichotomous construct of "foreign versus Chinese" notwithstanding, a search of Beijing Olympics–related content on websites like YouTube would indeed yield quite a few personal videos that vividly portray foreign tourists' experience of haggling for counterfeit goods at the new plaza.[88] Clearly the rebranding of Silk Street by way of constructing a heavily regulated space for consumption did not succeed in eradicating counterfeit bargains at the market. The continuation of these practices also points to the limits of nation branding as an image makeover project. For one thing, the plaza management's desire to promote Chinese-themed merchandise that caters to foreign consumers seems at odds with its accusation that the same group of consumers demand counterfeit brands. The government's attempt to wipe the nation's IPR-offending record clean by constructing a "cultural Chineseness" has hardly worked to displace the perception of Silk Street as a paradise for fakes among foreign tourists and journalists alike.

What brought these tensions to the fore was a high-profile lawsuit brought jointly against the plaza's management by Burberry, Chanel, Gucci, Louis Vuitton, and Prada. The case generated so much media frenzy prior to the Games that it was touted as an unprecedented success story for combating trademark infringement in China. A closer look at the legal controversies surrounding the case would indeed offer a deeper insight into Silk Street as a site of meaning production amid the local practice of fake sales, the state branding of the nation, and the global operation of IPR.

GLOBAL BRANDS VERSUS SILK STREET FAKES

In April 2005, the five luxury-brand owners sent agents to Silk Street and obtained hundreds of bags and garments bearing well-known logos through "notarized" purchases – that is, the items were bought in the presence of a third-party notary representative. They issued a warning letter the following month to Silk Street's management, Haosen, specifying the stall numbers and demanding that these "rights-violating" acts be terminated. In June, however, the agents were able to find the same type of goods at these stalls again. After some deliberation and further collection of evidence, the brand owners decided to file a lawsuit in November 2005, asking for an RMB2.5 million ($310,000) fine from Haosen and the five stallholders combined. Three months later, the Beijing Municipal No. 2 Intermediate People's Court ruled that the defendants were guilty and would be subject to an RMB100,000 ($12,500) penalty. Although the fine was significantly lower than requested, the brand owners did not appeal again. According to their legal representative, the American lawyer Joseph Simone, this was because they cared less about money than that the court had held the landlord co-responsible and liable. Another pleasant surprise for Simone was the short time it took for the case to be decided; this kind of efficiency was unheard of and could very well "mark the beginning of real change" for IPR enforcement in China.[89]

Hailed by the *Financial Times* as a "landmark" case,[90] the "global brands versus Silk Street" lawsuit became one of the most highly publicized IPR events in pre-Olympics Beijing.[91] The *World Intellectual Property Organization Magazine* even listed it as one of China's "Top Ten" IP lawsuits in 2006. While the laws applied in the case were not new, they had never been "earnestly applied before."[92] Legal scholars also endorsed the court's judgment as one that was based on a more "reasonable" logic than in previous similar litigation.[93]

Among the abundant press coverage of this "first ever trademark dispute between prestigious foreign brands, Silk Street, and the traders," one report from *China Intellectual Property News* provides an animated description. The author uses the title "Silk Street 'Li Gui' meets 'foreign Li Kui' (*Xiushuijie 'Ligui' zaoyu 'yang Likui'*)" to invoke the ancient myth of a famous ghost catcher, Li Kui. Legend has it that Li Kui once caught a ghost, called Ligui (*gui* literally meaning "ghost," with a similar pronunciation as Kui), who was posing as Li Kui, the ghost catcher.[94] The subtext of the report, then, is that the real ghost catchers in the lawsuit were the foreign brand owners, whereas the Silk Street vendors had been the ghosts to be caught.

An unequivocal association of "authenticity" with "justice," as indicated in this and many other media accounts, brings into focus the ambivalent figure of the state, whose legal ruling had ostensibly worked to protect the interests of the "foreign Li Kui" while penalizing the domestic "imposters" at Silk Street. This state endorsement of global brands speaks prominently to the symbolic significance of the lawsuit, for it was the nation's IPR image that appeared to be at stake. The case happened at a particularly sensitive time; not only was 2006 an important year for China to fulfill its WTO promises, the World Intellectual Property Day of April 26 was also just around the corner when the first verdict came out. A number of other high-profile IPR events were taking place as well, among them the signing of a $1.2 billion "licensed software" deal between Microsoft and Lenovo (the much-touted national brand of computers) – another celebrated sign of China's IPR progress.[95]

The global representation of the nation in terms of its ability to handle IPR infringement cases gracefully, then, was of particular concern to the state. As one Ministry of Commerce official put it, IPR protection is a "significant international relations issue that impacts the national interest."[96] As China "enters a phase of increased international trade disputes," IPR has become "a major means by which all economic entities participate in international competition"; it is key to "the cultivation of the nation's core competitive capacity," which paves the way for the nation's independent "scientific innovation" and "economic development."[97] In the words of another official, "as we move from a big manufacturing nation to a *powerful* manufacturing nation," IPR protection is not just a "reaction to international pressure"; the fact that not only fake foreign brands but also fake domestic brands were sold there hindered the cause of "cultivating the nation's own brands" (my emphasis).[98]

Accounts like these, again, have seamlessly subsumed the Silk Street case into the pervasive nation-branding discourse, "From Made in China to Created in China" (chapter 1). On the one hand, this subsumption further manifests the growing influence of the WTO on the Chinese state when it comes to IPR issues. While the influence is certainly discernible in China's expanding body of IPR laws, it is also more visible at the level of national image shaping, especially when that shaping's global audience consists of world-renowned luxury brand owners. On the other hand, these accounts also depict Silk Street as representative of the "underdeveloped market economy and legal environment" of China, whose fate is at the disposal of the more "advanced" IPR regime that is now tightening its grip on "regional fake-producing industries."[99] The impending "IPR storm" not only requires that national enterprises "wake up" and stop relying on foreign brands, but also demands that consumers exercise their "national self-respect" in supporting their own nation brands.[100] In other words, the "golden age" of Silk Street, once a "microcosm" of China's folk trade, was officially over. The kind of "dangerous 'infringement-style prosperity'" it engendered would now have to be terminated because of IPR laws.[101] However, this particular way of reshaping the meaning of the lawsuit has elided two contradictions that emerged within the legal struggle between the plaintiffs and the defendants. These contradictions only surface when we probe deeper into the narratives that arose from the litigation itself.

The first contradiction stems from the ambiguous relationship between the new plaza and its stall renters – specifically, whether the plaza management was in support of stall renters' sales of fake brands. A central point of contention had to do with the notion of intentionality. According to China's trademark laws, "*intentional* behaviors providing conditions that facilitate others' infringement of registered trademarks, such as storage, transportation, shipping, and hiding, are considered trademark-infringing activities" (my emphasis).[102] The plaza management's defense focused precisely on the claim that they "did not *intentionally* provide" such conditions.[103] Their evidence included the termination of the five vendors' contracts as well as written pledges from one hundred other vendors that they would be subject to a $50,000 fine if they engaged in selling counterfeits.[104] They also presented pictures of the prominently displayed notices that the plaza administration had issued to prohibit sales of trademark-infringing goods.[105] However, the plaintiffs argued that Haosen, as "the developer and operator of the mall" that was obligated to "stop its tenants" from "selling counterfeit goods on its premises," did not terminate the five tenants' leases "until the lawsuit was filed."[106] The lack of action, then, constituted the ground for their claim of intentionality.

Haosen's legal representatives attempted to counter the claim by arguing that the company did not have the administrative capacity to "search or confiscate the goods sold by the traders."[107] The violations, they asserted, resulted from "the various measures taken by independent traders to evade proper administration" by Haosen, not because of the latter's intentional facilitation.[108] Wang Zili, Haosen's general manager, who himself acted as the company's legal counsel during the second round of litigation, argued that only if the traders were proved to be selling the fakes "publically and visibly" could Haosen be accused of facilitating the sales.[109] In order to demonstrate the "covert" nature of the fake sales,[110] Wang emphasized such measures as the implementation of surveillance cameras throughout the building, which marked the "progress" made at Silk Street in terms of IPR protection and distinguished the new plaza from its older, open-market version.[111] Wang's personal assistant also told the *Financial Times* that Haosen only had the responsibility to "report on" counterfeit sales, not to "terminate" them, because "the right to search and confiscate items" belongs only to state authorities.[112]

These claims failed to convince the judge, who decided that Haosen, as the leasing entity, did not immediately stop the infringement activities upon being notified by the brand owners. As the plaintiff's lawyer Joseph Simone explained, this ruling was based on the notion of "landlord liability," a new strategy for tackling trademark infringement globally. While it was "relatively new in China," the strategy "had been successful in the United States and other more developed countries" in combating counterfeit sales at "flea markets" and more recently "in established offices and apartment blocks on Canal Street and elsewhere in New York City." Generally, China's criminal code "precludes the use of criminal sanctions against violations that are deemed too small in scale"; therefore small vendors, such as those in the former Silk Street bazaar, could not be convicted for selling fakes. But in the case of the new plaza, Haosen

was the property manager that "knowingly" provided "business premises to counterfeiters."[113] This made it possible for the court to establish
landlord liability.

The establishment of landlord liability brings back the question of
Silk Street's ownership. The fact that Silk Street can now be conceived as
a landed property at all reveals that the bazaar-to-plaza transformation
was indeed a process of privatization, despite the city's ostensible claims
to protect a "public" interest. This privatization comes through most
clearly in Haosen's intent to demonstrate its status as a business entity,
not a government unit. As one journalist pointed out, if Haosen is a
private enterprise that has a "leasing relationship" with the government,
the two should share liability for infringement; however, if Haosen is a
political-administrative unit of the government that oversees the vendors, it should be charged with "administrative negligence" rather than
infringement liability.[114] The fact that the court held Haosen responsible
for infringement and not negligence, and that the city government itself was not held responsible, implied that the corporation indeed was
perceived as a private landlord of sorts, not a governmental entity (despite its quasi-military training of the sales staff). This, then, contradicts
the municipality's claim to protect the presumed "public interest" associated with the "Silk Street" trademark. In addition, since the ruling
is intended to thwart counterfeit sales at the market, it also potentially
cuts into its real source of tourist attraction, which is what originally
contributed to the making of Silk Street as a landmark for the city, one
that is in principle to be protected by the municipality.

The irony, of course, is that what enabled the establishment of landlord liability in the lawsuit was precisely this legalized ownership of Silk
Street as private property. Back in Silk Street's old days, such ownership was non-existent. Instead, the vendors were loosely organized as
a collectivity, subject to the administrative oversight of the municipal
subdistrict government. In this original state, the market was an urban
space directly regulated by the state; it was "public" in the sense of not
being in principle owned by any individual or corporation. It was only
after the plaza reconstruction that it came under the purview of private
corporations (Shenghong, the developer, and Haosen, the manager). The
idea of Silk Street as a landmark for Beijing served as nothing more than

a rationalization for the building of the new plaza. In this transition, a "public interest" was transformed into a private property. This privatized ownership of a space that should in principle be public was in some sense the source of the dispute over the relationship between Haosen and the vendors in the "global brands versus Silk Street" lawsuit.

Another contradiction arose from the Silk Street management's narrative in its own defense. On January 28, 2006, likely in an effort to secure the use of the "Silk Street" trademark for its newly introduced clothing line, Haosen changed its name to Silk Street Apparel Market Ltd. (SSAM). In the meantime, its attempt to get the court to revisit the lawsuit turned out to be futile, as the second verdict on April 18 affirmed the decision made in the first ruling. The case then became "the first time a Chinese court has penalized not just the vendors of fake goods but also their landlord," with whom the brand owners now wished to work more closely "to set up more effective anti-piracy safeguards."[115] Given his effort to demonstrate the IPR progress at Silk Street, the manager Wang Zili would certainly have embraced this idea of collaborating with global brands. However, in his interviews with the Chinese press, he was quick to point out that as many as 80 percent of the consumers who knowingly came to the market for fakes (*zhijia maijia*) were "foreigners."[116] Since the market's administration had no control over these buyers who "viciously" (Wang's words) requested fakes, the government would need to adopt a different set of rules for them as well. IPR protection, for Wang, ought to be a joint effort between "the market, the traders, and the government," and SSAM itself could not be the sole bearer of responsibility.[117]

Claims like this have not been uncommon; foreign tourists are often blamed as the major source of demand for fakes. It is also often pointed out that these tourists come from the same advanced nations that are propagating IPR law enforcement in China. In such remarks, what emerges is a dichotomous construction between the "Chinese" as producers and sellers and "foreigners" as consumers of counterfeits. This understanding of the "Chinese people" is much different from the implicit concept of the "Chinese nation" in the nation-branding discourse. That discourse, as I showed in chapter 1, calls for the nation to become the creator of brands. This transformation depends upon the state's standardization of its legal institutions according to the decrees of the global IPR regime on the one hand, and the commodification of a distinct Chineseness based on self-Orientalized "traditions" on the other. In contrast, for many Silk Street defendants, from the chair Zhang Yongping and the manager Wang Zili to the vendors attempting to save the old Silk Street, insufficient knowledge of global brands became a marker of national *difference,* an alternative "Chineseness" of a sort. This recognition, rather than seeking to compensate for China's lack of IPR knowledge, as in the state's version of nation branding, affirms it as a source of national-cultural distinction.

The contradiction in Silk Street's bazaar-to-plaza transition, in other words, lies in the distance between the codes of "Chineseness" in the Silk Street rebranding measures and the IPR-defiant "Chineseness" that emerged in the defense's statements in the Silk Street lawsuit. This contradiction ultimately manifests itself as a two-tier conflict, between the "Chinese people" and the Chinese state on the one hand, and between the "Chinese" working within the state's sovereign borders and the "foreigners" on the other. When interviewed in 2001, some old vendors were vocal about their antipathy towards the government's banning of counterfeit sales: "It is the foreigners who come here for fake brands that have sustained Silk Street. If we aren't allowed to sell brands, what can we sell in the future?"[118] Naturally, Wang's call for increased governmental actions to regulate foreigners' buying habits was unlikely to win the favor of the vendors. Even if all were in agreement to exert more direct legal measures in controlling foreigners' consumption of fakes, the task itself would be easier said than done. The difficulty, of course, lies in the foreign nationality of these consumers of counterfeits, who are not immediately subject to rules set up by the Chinese state. In other words, the imaginary of a global consumer citizen for the "Made in China" brand (chapter 1) is harder to realize in practice than the state might wish, because there is an asymmetry between the state and the figure of the globally mobile tourist. The conflict between "the people" and the state, then, is simultaneously compounded by transnational tourism and IPR-based demarcations of national differences. This conflict was to play out more intensely in the aftermath of the "global brands versus Silk Street" lawsuit.

THE VENDORS' REVOLT

After winning the landmark Silk Street case, the five brand owners joined twenty-three other major apparel brands to form a coalition to collaborate with the Beijing Intellectual Property Office in implementing more "cost-effective [IPR] enforcement work."[119] On June 7, 2006, they signed a "fake-busting agreement" with SSAM, in the presence of European Trade Commission representatives and the vice minister of China's Ministry of Commerce. The first contract of its kind between brand owners and a sales outlet, the agreement was expected to serve as a model for IPR protection in other Chinese cities in the future.[120] The agreement contained a proposal to include a "two strike" rule in leases, which would grant landlords "the explicit right to suspend the operations of an outlet after a first offence and to terminate the lease after a second offence."[121]

The signing of the agreement was seen as a key accomplishment of China in the area of IPR protection – a message delivered by the minister of commerce personally.[122] However, lawsuits continued to plague the plaza's administration after the much-publicized event. Only three days after the signing, for instance, the French company Chemise Lacoste, which was not part of the coalition, sued SSAM and five vendors for infringement, demanding a fine of RMB100,000 ($12,476).[123] The year after, in October 2007, The North Face won another case against SSAM, based on claims similar to those filed by the five luxury brands in 2005.[124] Despite the ongoing legal struggles, though, vendors continued to sell counterfeits at the market, leading SSAM to seek other means of enforcement to avoid the time and money involved in future litigation. Upon consulting with IntellecPro, a local IP law firm that often represents global brands, SSAM came up with the idea of signing a court-recognized "resolution agreement" to penalize the traders by temporarily closing down their stalls.[125] Signed in the beginning of December 2008, the agreement stated that whenever trademark owners presented notarized evidence of infringement, the market would have to shut down the specified stall's operation for seven days.[126]

On December 15, 2008, SSAM received five notices indicating that thirty vendors at the market were selling fakes. When ordered to shut down their shops, the vendors refused, pointing out that a mere picture displaying some goods could not possibly suffice as evidence of infringement. One vendor said she could not even say the names of the brands whose fakes she was accused of selling, and that considering she paid a fee of RMB100,000 ($15,000) as a guarantee for not selling fakes at the stall, the risk was too high for her to partake in such violations.[127] Despite the vendors' resistance, SSAM went ahead and closed down the stalls. In response, the vendors filed a lawsuit against SSAM, claiming that the market's administration did not have the right to terminate the operation of their shops. The language they used to describe the role of the market strikes a curious resonance with the defense of SSAM in the 2005 lawsuit filed by the global brands. At the time, SSAM pronounced itself to be a mere leasing entity that only had the responsibility to report on counterfeit sales, not to terminate them. By signing the "fake-busting" contract, SSAM appeared to have overstepped its "landlord" status and taken on the role of a governmental unit to order stall closures. The vendors, then, had appropriated the legal discourse that stemmed from a state decision to challenge the self-assigned regulatory role of SSAM. By bringing SSAM to court in defense of their right to continue their practices, they re-established their own status as citizens of the state.

Some of the vendors' defense took a more physical and confrontational form. Starting February 4, a dozen of self-identified Silk Street traders began to stage protests every day at the IntellecPro office, even threatening the personal safety of its employees.[128] On the first day, they were not able to get past the receptionist, thanks to police intervention. The day after, however, they succeeded in getting through; they even "banged on the walls and swore at the staff." According to "one vendor's clandestine cellphone recording," the protesters lectured a senior partner of the firm "on the need for intellectuals like him to respect workers." The same kind of class-specific antagonism could also be discerned in the protest signs; some of these accused the "fake-busting" firm to be a "people-busting company," while others suggested that the "fake protection of rights" was no more than "putting on a show." One vendor carrying a fake Dolce & Gabbana bag told the reporter that "We don't read English. We don't know what the letters mean. We just think it is pretty."

As if to back up this juxtaposition of Chinese ignorance against foreign knowledge toward global brands yet again, the manager Wang Zili, when interviewed, pointed out that two-thirds of the 15 million shoppers at the market were foreigners.[129]

The same kind of "anti-foreign" attitude is also displayed in an open letter issued by SSAM to the five brand owners. The letter zeroes in on one single individual, Joseph Simone, who had been acting as the brand owners' legal representative. It accused Simone of being an "international Wang Hai,"[130] mocking him as a version of the domestically famous "professional consumer of fraud."[131] It also pointed out that Simone's demand for an RMB30,000 ($4,000) security deposit from each trader was against "Chinese law" and had been "rejected by the Chinese government and the vendors" back in 2005.[132] Emphasizing that the "Silk Street problem" was "made by the West" because of foreign consumers' demand for fakes, SSAM now decided to seek "Chinese solutions," which also demand "international collaboration."[133]

The letter is not unique in its nationalistic tone; an online legal forum post, for example, also cautions "foreign lawyers practicing in China" to halt their "Wang Hai" behavior and submit to Chinese authorities.[134] It does, however, mark a shift in SSAM's attitude toward "foreigners" – from one that borders on obsequiousness (displaying Chineseness "up-close") to something close to chauvinism (invoking "Chinese laws and solutions"). In this narrative Simone appears as an individual embodiment of "the West" over which the Chinese state apparatuses could exercise their power. At work is an ambivalent self-defense mechanism not so different from what was demonstrated in the "Made with the World" ad discussed in chapter 1. Again, one cannot help but bring Lu Xun's famous story "Ah Q" to bear on this rhetoric. A reading of the letter through the spirit of "Ah Q" would sound something like this: China may not be able to defeat the bigger and more powerful global IPR regime, but it can surely get a few foreign lawyers in order; therefore, China is still stronger than the foreign nations.

On February 6, 2009, seven traders got their case heard at Beijing Chaoyang District People's Court. The court ruled on April 24 in favor of the vendors, who demanded a public apology, RMB28,000 ($4,200) in compensation, and reputational damages of RMB5,000 ($760). Subsequently, ssam agreed to a settlement and promised a payment of 10,000 rmb ($1500) to each trader by April 30. However, trader victories of this kind did not put an end to trademark-related conflicts at the plaza. On February 15, 2009, when ssam again exercised its stall-closing power upon discovering the sale of fakes, more violent protests broke out on the ground floor. An old woman stall renter commented: "This market is vicious. We are losing money in it every day now, and they still want to close us down. Will they let us live?" When the police were brought in to restore order, what appears to be so abstract a global concept as the trademark had manifested itself in local conflicts of the most visceral kind. Contentious as it might be, the intensified struggle between the state and "the people" (in this case embodied by the vendors) at Silk Street would soon take another dramatic turn unanticipated by its domestic or international observers.

WANG ZILI'S ARREST AND THE FILM *SILK ALLEY*

On August 4, 2009, Beijing's major media outlets received a letter from the ssam manager Wang Zili, the man who had been Silk Street's pr chief since the opening of the new plaza.[135] The letter charged Zhang Yongping, Silk Street plaza's chair, not only with evading taxes for three years but also making rmb300,000 ($45,000) in profit per year by charging the tenants outrageous rent. Zhang immediately responded to these charges by holding an "explanatory" meeting that night. He presented tax receipts from the year before, as well as a tax-exemption certificate from Chaoyang Shuangjing Tax Service issued in 2005, which waived the plaza's "operational tax, city construction tax, and educational fees addition" for the three years between August 2005 and July 2008. Wang's letter also stated that after his hasty resignation in July, Zhang had been hunting him down, likely because of Wang's possession of inside knowledge of Zhang's illicit deeds. Zhang's representative quickly denied such actions, arguing that it was Wang's inability to turn the market around that had led to his resignation.[136]

Nonetheless, rumors (presumably spread by Silk Street vendors) began to circulate on the internet that Zhang Yongping had "escaped with a huge amount of money," forcing him to hold a plazawide meeting on August 6 to clear the air. After that, numerous postings and threads on the Silk Street website and the popular Baidu forum began to appear, disclosing Wang Zili's secret receipt of "black money" in support of sales of fakes. Yet in a recording from July 16, Wang said to Zhang: "I have never taken any money from traders, nor have I done anything to harm you."[137]

On December 21, 2009, the Beijing police tracked down and arrested Wang in Inner Mongolia. In a trial that took place on January 20, 2010, a trader from Silk Street accused Wang of being at once a promoter and a beneficiary of counterfeit sales at the plaza.[138] Wang was eventually sentenced to four years in prison in 2012, though he reportedly still wished to fight back. The press, however, held the viewpoint that the government had been backing the plaza chair Zhang all along. On the surface, Wang's sentence appeared to be another case of "killing the chicken to warn the monkey," a typical measure by the state to contain wide-ranging "unhealthy" activities from bribery to counterfeiting. But it may also well be the case that Wang served as a scapegoat for the nation's long march toward the "rule of law." After all, when IPR offenses are so intimately linked to the nation's global image, the state is in need of a constant, visible, and performative repetition of crackdowns on counterfeits to shore up its own domestic legitimacy.[139]

However, it would be reductive to interpret this as another instance of the Communist state's oppressive apparatus. Other evidence, such as the 2009 government-sponsored film *Silk Alley,* would point again to the ideological momentum of the nation-branding project – which some might argue is a much more effective means of reaching "the people." Set on location in the actual plaza itself, the film tells the story of a self-made Silk Street vendor who befriends an American lawyer, not knowing that his new friend is charged with a mission to collect evidence of IPR infringement activities at Silk Street. After a series of dramatic events, from perceived betrayal and lawsuits to heartbreaks and reunions, the vendor ends up transforming his fake-selling business into one that specializes in "Chinese"-style clothing designed by his daughter (who gave up the opportunity to study at New York University to stay and help her father). Numerous government representatives attended the film's first day of shooting on October 21. The State Administration of Radio, Film

and Television, which financed the film, aired it in March 2010 on its affiliated film channel, CCTV6. It continues to be available today on such
video sharing sites as 56.com.[140]

One of the most dramatic moments in the film takes place when
the lawyer Thomas is called into court to testify to the brand owner's
profit loss. Instead of affirming the estimated amount stated in the
charges, he proclaims that counterfeits have actually helped spread the
brand's reputation in China, "the world's biggest market." This moment
is significant in part because the lawyer's sudden change of heart had
something to do with the fact that the vendor and his family had previously saved him from a life-threatening heart attack. More important,
however, is that this description of "China" transforms the nation from
a producing body – figured most prominently in "Made in China" – to a
consuming body, as the potential market for global brands. The nation
then becomes, yet again, an object of "foreign" desire, no different from
the "Chinese-styled" items that are celebrated as assuring Silk Street's
future success. The repositioning of the practice of counterfeiting in this
representation of the national self has again subsumed an otherwise self-
affirming counterculture into an imaginary of "the people" whose primary identity takes the form of "the consumer."

CONCLUSION

The conception of the nation as a desirable market for global brands
in the film *Silk Alley* is quite different from the kind that Silk Street's
counterfeit cultural publics have brought forth. In turning their lack
of IPR knowledge into a source of national distinction, the original tenants of Silk Street conjured up a national imaginary that runs counter to
the state's IPR-conforming efforts to build a brandable national culture.
As in the case of *Crazy Stone* fandom, the vendors' defense of their rights
to Silk Street challenges the state's nation-branding scheme, which positions "the people" chiefly as a pre-configured object of national pedagogy. By laying claim to Silk Street as a place in which they reside and
conduct everyday business, they reconstitute themselves as embodied
citizen-subjects within the nation. In doing so, they enable a place-based
understanding of the national community, significantly different from

the branded imaginary proffered by IPR that has helped shape state policies aimed at transforming the nation into an "intangible asset."

The state-sponsored reconstruction of Silk Street as an Olympics-related tourist destination is emblematic of the contradictions that underlie the nation-branding project. While relying on rhetoric to preserve the brand of an urban landmark that is in principle public, the state indeed assisted in the privatization of this public interest. Ironically, it was this spatial privatization that allowed the global brands to extend the institutional reach of IPR protection, thus undermining the state's default role in representing and protecting the interests of its citizen-subjects. This may be seen as another manifestation of the culturally imperialistic forces of IPR in engendering a split subject status of the postsocialist state, discussed more extensively in chapter 1. If the discursive formation of the slogan "From Made in China to Created in China" reflects IPR's work in simultaneously destabilizing the state's claim to the nation while prescribing the route toward restoring this nation-state "hyphen," the Silk Street case exemplifies the failure of the state to accommodate a different vision for national culture than the one that it has internalized as the "norm"–that is, a brandable kind of "Chineseness" typified by "time-honored" traditions, which appeals to the eyes of foreign tourists and therefore generates economic value for the city and the nation.

This branded imaginary can be situated again in China's recent "soft power drive," whose distinct emphasis on strengthening the national "image" (in handling IPR issues or otherwise) precludes a conception of "culture as a site of struggle between antagonistic social forces over the fundamental directions of society."[141] By privileging a notion of "Chineseness" in line with the production of the orientalist "Other" within the global culture industry, Beijing's re-branding of Silk Street projects a national vision that is far removed from the many citizen-subjects who inhabit the city itself. This process of deterritorialization, which was followed by state-sanctioned reterritorialization, speaks to the "instrumentalization of spatial practices" demanded by the "global city discourse," which renders Beijing "a product that can be produced and managed rather than a vast area of urban space where people dwell."[142] However, the vendors' claims to the national, which invoke their presence in the city and nation as grounds for their citizen-subjectivity, defy such a reified conception of national difference. By appropriating the language of IPR in describing the space in terms of a collectivized "intangible asset," they point to the persisting possibilities for resistance in postsocialist China in undermining the homogenizing logic of global modernity. Indeed, competing visions for the national as a site for difference making under the cultural conditions of globalization are emerging from the visceral struggles between the vendors and the state.

In this sense, the struggles at Silk Street again emblematize the cultural dilemma for the Chinese state. While IPR's cultural logic proffers a value-productive vision of national culture for the state, it is simultaneously re-worked by the transnational publics of counterfeit culture who give rise to an alternative formation of "Chineseness." This alternative formulation is predicated less on the sanctity of IPR-protected values than on a meaning-generative conception of culture – in this case, the collective making of an urban landmark. While it may be far-fetched to claim that this production of space immediately presents "radical alternatives to the present,"[143] it does point to the continuous need to investigate how and why enduring practices of this kind are deemed less desirable by the state in its attempts to re-claim its national legitimacy than those more in line with the branded imaginary of IPR. In other words, we must pay further attention to the hegemonic forces that are at work in shaping the cultural formation of the postsocialist state, whose search for an alternative modernity remains subject to the unequal relations of power within contemporary globalization. This cultural formation of the state has arguably taken a new direction as China enters the second decade of the twenty-first century.

Conclusion: Cultural Imperialism and the "Chinese Dream"

THIS BOOK HAS BEEN CONCERNED WITH THE CULTURAL EFFECTS of globalization on WTO-era China. Specifically, I have examined the interactions between nation branding and counterfeit culture – two cultural formations that are produced within the ideological mechanism of the globalizing IPR regime. Rather than "invading" a self-contained national culture, this regime operates to intensify the disjuncture between the nation and the state. On the one hand, China's post-2001 "From Made in China to Created in China" campaign results largely from the IPR regime's interpellation of a state subject through the global imaginary of the brand. On the other hand, counterfeit culture, a transnational culture of circulation whose status derives from a referential relation to the brand, also induces multifarious national imaginaries that challenge the state vision for the nation.

As my analysis has shown, the cultural contestations between nation branding and counterfeit practices manifest themselves in a series of *countering* acts. For one, the state counters global brands by building the nation's own brands. The goal of nation branding – as seen in the promotion of domestic brand-name cell phones, the production of "Chinese megafilms," and the cultivation of "Chinese-flavored" merchandise – is to nurture IPR-friendly commodities of distinct "Chineseness" that can compete with those already established within the global IPR structure. At the same time, the publics that create and consume counterfeit culture also partake in the countering of the global regime of the brand. Their spirit of defiance toward IPR's underlying cultural logic can be discerned in the making of Shanzhai culture, the reception of *Crazy*

Stone, and the affirmation of the Silk Street Market as a site of cultural production. The resulting discordance between the state and the nation from the contestations between these two countering acts is what I have been calling a "cultural dilemma." It is this discordance that speaks most pointedly to the contradictory cultural effects of IPR in the WTO-era Chinese context and that therefore sheds new light on the persistence of cultural imperialism in contemporary globalization.

In the introduction to this book, I have referred to Tomlinson's critical assessment of cultural imperialism as operative through the modern social imaginary. For Tomlinson, "the process of the spread of capitalist modernity involves not an invasion of 'weak' cultures by a 'stronger' one, but almost the opposite – the spread of a sort of cultural decay from the West to the rest of the world."[1] The "weakness" of capitalist modernity manifests itself as "a failure of cultural will," a "vacuous social imaginary" incapable of resolving its internal contradictions.[2] I have tried in this book to articulate a process through which this "weak" culture is "spread" through the IPR regime. Such a process is emblematic of the workings of the global culture industry in that it is chiefly mediated through the institution of the brand, which restructures the social imaginary in the further service of capital accumulation.[3]

Partly following Tomlinson's attempt to debunk the notion that cultural imperialism involves the West's invasion of self-contained – often "Third World" – "national cultures," I have placed my analytical focus on the level of the nation-state. In distinguishing the state from the cultural production of the nation, I have aimed at complicating the conception of the state as a singular sovereign that centrally exercises its political power. While I agree with Aihwa Ong that "sovereignty is manifested in multiple, often contradictory strategies that encounter diverse claims and contestations, and produce diverse and contingent outcomes,"[4] I have also illustrated the ways in which the postsocialist state is implicated in the branded imaginary that stems from the global system of IPR.

If the brand constitutes the cultural form through which the IPR structure exerts its power globally, practices of counterfeiting, as part of the ongoing process of "globalization from below," also conjure up a site of contestation. I have attempted – in the discussion of Shanzhai, for instance – to attend to the material settings within which participants of counterfeit culture engage in meaning-making practices that are often themselves defiant of state-sanctioned projects. What these subjects and publics demonstrate is not so much the semiotic potential of the counterfeit to displace the aura of the original as the production of distinct national imaginaries. These imaginaries not only offer competing cultural narratives about the nation, but also present alternative cultural visions that contest what is proffered by the IPR-supported global culture industry.

Therefore, rather than reducing the workings of cultural imperialism to the erosion of national differences, I have paid more attention to how these alternative visions are made to appear less desirable and legitimate than those that fit with the established cultural norms of global modernity. To some extent, this is a process of homogenization that threatens to erase the potential for national difference making. But the pressure for China to "become the same" is only one side of the coin. I have argued that a significant resource from which WTO-era China's counterfeit-cultural publics conjure alternative national imaginaries is the heterogeneous temporalities that inform their meaning-making practices. The national visions they present, which are distinct from the one offered by nation branding, are imbued with the possibility to challenge the homogeneous temporality and underlying cultural assumptions of the IPR regime. The problem is not that this difference-making potential does not exist within global homogenization, but rather how and why it is subsumed within the discourse of nation branding, which is itself a manifestation of IPR's branded imaginary. The "imperialist" dimension of globalization, then, does not manifest itself through the cultural subjugation of one weaker nation-state to a more powerful one. Instead, the unequal relations of power within the global IPR system operate through a series of culturally productive mechanisms that exert contradictory cultural impacts on the Chinese nation-state.

One useful way to articulate the effects of these productive forces is to describe IPR's impact as simultaneously a countercultural production and a counterproduction of culture. By "countercultural production," I refer to the kind of disjunctive conceptions of time that arise in discourses about counterfeiting practices (such as Shanzhai, *Crazy Stone,* and Silk Market). They are disjunctive in the sense that they emerge as spatiotemporal registers that are distinct from the "homogeneous, empty" time that structures the IPR imaginary of the brand. The Shanzhai discourse predicates itself simultaneously on an imaginary of the "pre-modern" bandit and an adoption of the "postmodern," post-Fordist, modular mode of production. The fandom of *Crazy Stone* conjures up the desire for a temporal presence that performs and enlivens rather than ossifies and commodifies the "past." The defenders of Silk Street as a space of cultural production, while not directly invoking time-specific frameworks, nonetheless deploy an "anti-modern" stance – a collectivist conception of property and a defiance of IPR knowledge – to contest both the regulatory regime of the global brand and the self-Orientalizing logic of the "time-honored" nation brand. In all of these instances, there is a refusal to conform to global modernity's one-dimensional production of culture. What these practices affirm instead is an understanding of what culture does – that it generates meanings. This conception departs from the instrumentalized notion of culture that is sanctioned and naturalized by the IPR regime. It is this affirmation of cultural difference that points to alternative ways of imagining the national as a site of hegemonic contestation against the global system of IPR.

A legitimate follow-up question, then, is, Who is delimiting what is seeable, sayable, and imaginable on the part of the WTO-era Chinese state? As we enter the second decade of the new millennium, the global forces that inform WTO-era China's state vision are often more specifically embodied in the figure of another nation-state: America. In the 2008 financial meltdown, numerous Chinese publications on cultural development invoked the 1930s Great Depression as the moment Hollywood emerged as a powerful sector of the economy of the United States.[5] As the rhetoric goes, the opportunity now exists for China, which is to follow Korea's footsteps (in the aftermath of the Asian financial crisis in the 1990s) to rise up through heavy investment in the "culture industries." The invocation of Hollywood here is far from coincidental, for despite its much transnationalized operation, Hollywood is still perceived as a cultural symbol of America, whose shadow has come to loom larger than ever in the global-national imaginary of WTO-era China.

In some sense, there is hardly anything surprising about this strong imaginary presence of "America" in the WTO-era Chinese context, considering that the cultural industries that originated in the United States constituted a primary target of attack in earlier critiques of cultural imperialism. Even though such frameworks as "cultural globalization" and "cultural pluralism"[6] have come to challenge the premise of the "cultural imperialism" thesis on the basis of contraflows (referring to the flow of cultural products *to*, rather than *from*, the West), glocalization, hybridization, and active audiences, among others, the enduring cultural influence of the United States in the post–Cold War world order remains keenly felt but difficult to analyze. Part of the difficulty has to do with what Amy Kaplan describes as the "absence of the United States in the postcolonial study of culture and imperialism," which "reproduces American exceptionalism from without" and fails to consider its expansionist projects as an integral part of European colonialism.[7] This failure to pay attention to the specificity of American imperialism is also discernible in the tendency of the "global-localism" framework to overemphasize the role of (European) imperialism in destabilizing the nation-state as a geopolitical entity, while neglecting to acknowledge the structural inequality (especially U.S. domination) in the global economic system.[8]

There is, in other words, a continuing need to further examine the hegemonic operation of the cultures of American imperialism in global contexts, particularly on the level of nation-states.[9] This is an effort to which I hope *Faked in China* has contributed to some extent by focusing on the case of WTO-era China, a nation-state that is more often imagined to be a contender for global hegemony with the United States. As I have illustrated in chapter 1, "America" and the "American consumer" figure prominently in the post-2001 formation of China's nation-branding project, "From Made in China to Created in China." But this complex global-national ideological formation defies the dominant framework of postcolonial studies, whose primary concern has been the colonial legacies of the British and French empires. To be sure, even though Mao's anti-imperialist rhetoric was often quite clearly targeted at America, the United States has never colonized China – that is, if colonization is strictly understood in terms of the occupation of territories and the displacement of sovereignty. However, this does not mean that China is exempt from the conditions of "coloniality" – a cultural "logic"[10] that persists beyond "historical colonialisms" and continues to exert influence through "imperialism without colonies."[11] Paying particular attention to the enduring influence of coloniality, *Faked in China* can be seen as participating in a global project of decolonization, which grounds itself in the material struggles of the Third World, from which China has emerged as a key figure since the 1955 Bandung conference in Indonesia.

At the same time, postcolonial perspectives on nation-state formation, particularly those that delineate the enduring cultural impact of historical colonialisms in contexts such as India, have undeniably informed the analytical focus of this book, which privileges the global-national over the global-local as a site of struggle.[12] As I have examined in chapters 2, 3, and 4, competing claims to the national, which are themselves produced at the intersection between the global and the local, bring into view a complex negotiation of power in which the state and the citizenry are both subject to and challenge the parameters of the global culture industry sanctioned by IPR. In this sense, my approach reflects an attempt to account for China's own "colonial modernity"[13] by turning to the continuing anti-imperialist struggles in the WTO-era Chinese context. This approach departs from the more frequent mode of inserting China into the "'postcolonial' template," which sees its dynastic past as an unproblematized equivalent of imperial Britain or France.[14] Instead, it argues that China must be seen as much a "victim" as an agent, a contradiction that is itself to be discerned at the level of the nation-state.

Indeed, I will argue in this conclusion that it is through an emphasis on cultural struggles at the site of the national that cultural imperialism may best retain its relevancy as an analytical framework for understanding contemporary globalization. As Tomlinson reminds us, it is through a "colonisation of the social imaginary" that globalization can be characterized as cultural imperialism, a process that takes place less on the level of "individual consciousness" than on the plane of "institutionalized practices."[15] I have shown throughout this book that the nation-state is one of the institutional formations that are subjugated to such "colonizing" processes, whose workings through the IPR regime are as uneven as they are contradictory. While the objects and processes I have analyzed are primarily drawn from the first decade of the second millennium, it is my hope that the analytical perspectives I have developed can help to generate more critical reflections on the persisting influence of cultural imperialism, particularly as manifested through the figure of "America" and the imaginary of the "American Dream."[16]

CULTURAL IMPERIALISM THROUGH THE IMAGINARY

In 2012, China's new president Xi Jinping introduced the "Chinese Dream" (*zhongguomeng*) as a new buzzword for his administration. The first official "announcement" came rather unexpectedly. After Xi's visit to an exhibition entitled "Road to Revival (*fuxing zhilu*)" at the National Museum in Beijing on November 29, he gave an unscripted speech, the entirety of which was later broadcast on CCTV's *Network News Broadcast*. Xi opened his speech by sharing his thoughts on the exhibition itself, which featured China's modern history from the imperial invasions at the end of the nineteenth century (in the form of the Opium War, among others) to the founding of the Chinese Communist Party and its leadership in building the People's Republic of China. "The exhibition has reviewed the past, displayed the present, and declared the future of the Chinese nation," Xi stated, before touching on each of these time frames more specifically, including the nation's "suffering" in the modern era (often referred to as "the century of humiliation") and the ongoing need to adhere to the "correct path" of "socialism with Chinese characteristics." It is at the moment when "we look to the future" that Xi invoked the "dream":

> Nowadays, everyone (*dajia*) is discussing the Chinese Dream. What is the Chinese Dream? In my view, to achieve the great revival of the Chinese nation (*zhonghua minzu*) is the grandest Chinese dream (*Zhongguo meng*) of the Chinese nation (*zhonghua minzu*) in the modern era. For the long-cherished wishes of many generations are combined and embodied in this dream, which manifests the integrated well-being of the Chinese people, and is the common wish of every single son and daughter of China. History tells us that the fate of every one of us is closely connected to the state (*guojia*) and the nation (*minzu*). Only when the state is well and the nation is well can everyone be well.[17]

For a term that was to become "the Chinese Character of the Year for 2012,"[18] the first appearance of the "Chinese dream" figure is perhaps most unusual in its apparent lack of originality. Not only has Xi seemingly drawn on an ongoing conversation that "everyone" is engaged in

C.1. Street posters for the "Chinese Dream" in Shenzhen. The characters visible in the first one from the right state that "only when you have a (nation-)state can you have a family" (*you guo cai you jia*).

rather than offering something entirely new, the phrase is also too close a copy of its American counterpart, as numerous Chinese and Western observers were quick to point out. *The Economist* even went so far as to suggest that Thomas Friedman of the *New York Times* might have been an immediate source of inspiration for Xi.[19] The best-selling author's piece, "China Needs Its Own Dream," appeared just weeks before Xi's 2012 inauguration; it warned that "if Xi's dream for China's emerging middle class – 300 million people expected to grow to 800 million by 2025 – is just like the American Dream (a big car, a big house and Big Macs for all) then we need another planet."[20] To be sure, the phrase had appeared previously in books published in the United States and China, including Helen Wang's *The Chinese Dream: The Rise of the World's Largest Middle Class and What It Means to You* (2010, in English) and Liu Minfu's *China Dream: Great Power Thinking and Strategic Posture in the Post-American Era* (2010, in Chinese).[21] But it is Friedman's article that was most frequently cited in the state media's top-circulating news publications, including *Reference Works, Frontline,* and *Globe.* Admittedly, despite its ostensibly condescending tone, the main point of Friedman's article is in fact to stress the importance of sustainable development for China. But why did so many commentators see this American journalist's call for a "different Chinese dream" as so important that they immediately interpreted the new president's first public "dream" speech as an official response?[22]

The answer to this question is perhaps best provided through the analytical model of the global-national imaginary I developed in chapter 1. If the global imaginary that helped shape the state's vision for the nation – "From Made in China to Created in China" – is a branded imaginary promulgated by the IPR regime, what has prefigured the "Chinese dream" is arguably another globally hegemonic discourse, that of the "American Dream." After all, for *The Economist* and for many others, the only nation-specific "dream" that can lay claim to global recognition is the American one. For this reason, even though the "Chinese Dream" discourse is not directly connected to the IPR regime, the cultural conditions of globalization that shape the state's national vision in these cases indeed have much in common. In both instances, the Chinese state is interpellated, as it were, by a globally operative cultural regime even as it seeks to reclaim and reinforce its own legitimacy through formulating distinct visions for the nation. In the nation-branding campaign, the vision of "Created in China" works in conjunction with the global consumer confidence crisis of "Made in China" to secure the state's subject position as a guarantor of the nation's development towards an IPR-friendly future. Likewise, the linking of President Xi's "Chinese Dream" to the comment by Thomas Friedman is indicative of a global-national ideological formation at work, subjugating the state to the pursuit of a "middle-class" version of an "American Dream" while allowing it to reinforce its subject position as the leader of the nation and its "people."

The working of this global-national imaginary can be discerned in Xi's first "dream" speech and his subsequent repetitions of the phrase. In the passage cited above, the invocation of "history," or more specifically the nation's "century of humiliation" exhibited at the National Museum, offers a backdrop for stressing the idea that the "fate" of "every Chinese" is "closely connected to the state and the nation." While China's "great revival" is, in the first iteration, the "grandest Chinese dream of the Chinese *nation*," it is also an expression of the "integrated well-being" of the Chinese *people*. Here, Xi has made both a clear distinction between the nation and the state and an attempt to reinforce an alignment between the people and the nation, as if the link needs to be restored. This attempt became more pronounced at the National People's Congress, when Xi downplayed the nation as "dreamer" and emphasized that "the Chinese dream is the people's dream," a statement that prompted the English-language media to adopt "Chinese Dream" as the preferred translation as opposed to the earlier version, "China Dream."[23] Nonetheless, the oscillation between the nation and the people has persisted in Xi's later public addresses on the topic.

These incongruent articulations of the identity of the "dreamer" are perhaps better seen as symptoms of what I call a "split-subject" status of the state, whereby the interpellation of the citizenry is itself subject to the ideological hailing of a global imaginary – in this case, the American Dream.[24] I have argued that this split bespeaks the contradictory impact of globalization. What is culturally imperialistic about this operation is not so much that a global imaginary, be it an IPR-sanctioned brand regime or the American Dream, is imposed upon the state in its engineering of a unified national identity. It is that the unequal relation of power manifests itself as a productive force, at once disrupting the hyphen between the state and the nation while proffering a specific kind of national vision, one that the state has deemed to be the most effective in re-establishing its tie to the nation. In the case of the Chinese Dream, this vision appears to be one that conforms precisely to an "American middle class" version of the "good life," which Friedman has seemingly "denied" China – a denial that numerous Chinese commentators have seen fit to contest by endorsing Xi's national dream in turn.

With this in mind, the Chinese state's adoption of the "dream" signifier becomes emblematic of the link between U.S. imperialism and cultural imperialism in contemporary globalization. As Tomlinson points out, globalization is a "far less coherent or culturally directed process" than imperialism "proper," which is a "purposeful project" aimed at the "spread of a social system from one centre of power across the globe"; rather, globalization "happens as the result of economic and cultural practices which do not, of themselves, aim at global integration, but which nonetheless produce it."[25] The globalization of the American Dream can be said to operate as such an unintended process. To be sure, the political-economic process through which the "American Way of Life" has come to appear as the "Global Familiar" has a well-documented history.[26] The U.S. government, after all, has long supported Hollywood for its potential to advertise American consumer goods globally, as recorded by early accounts of "media imperialism" and more recent critiques of "global Hollywood."[27] The discursive formation of "globalization" has also to do with the "spaceless universalization" of American values since the nineteenth century.[28] However, this does not mean that there is necessarily an orchestrated process at work in promulgating something as specific as the American Dream to other parts of the world, including China. What I have suggested instead is that the "American Dream" functions as an "imaginary social signification," in Castoriadis's sense of the term, not unlike the branded imaginary of IPR. While its global visibility is closely tied to the U.S. state's various intended projects of global integration (seeking global markets for American products, for example), its cultural work is more aptly described as operating through an internalized cultural logic. The fact that global media representatives like Friedman and *The Economist* so easily laid claim to the universal appeal of the American Dream – an appeal that seemingly resonated with the Chinese commentators – speaks precisely to the internalization of such an imaginary. This cultural logic is indeed comparable to the distinction between the brand and the fake, which is so naturalized through the workings of the IPR regime that even an unauthorized "Apple Store" selling real products in Kunming was deemed to be a "fake" (as recounted in the introduction).

In this light, it is less important to inquire whether Friedman's call for China to "dream differently" actually informed Xi's conception of the Chinese Dream than whether this Chinese appropriation of a globally dominant signifier presents a *difference-making* possibility. This is a question that Xudong Zhang has taken up by arguing that the only way to avoid reducing the Chinese Dream to a copycat version of the American Dream is to situate its emergence in a world-historical context in which the people of the Third World, who have been "structurally

kept outside the dream of the 'middle class,'" are "beginning to engage
in the construction of their own life worlds."[29] In other words, what
deserves more attention is how the discursive formation may help shift
the terms of who can dream and what can be dreamed, despite its apparent adoption of a hegemonic rhetoric presumably owned by America.
A similar attempt to locate the sites of struggles for difference making
has motivated my analysis of the counterfeit cultural publics and their
production of alternative national visions. But the persisting influence
of cultural imperialism, whether working through the imaginary of the
brand or the American Dream, appears to have rendered these alternative visions less desirable for a state that has decided to follow a developmental path more in line with the trajectory of global modernity.

These global-national tensions, embodied in both the discursive formation of the "Chinese Dream" and the cultural formations of "faked
in China" artifacts, are played out most vividly in a 2013 Chinese film,
Zhongguo Hehuoren. While its Chinese title literally translates as "Chinese Partners," its English name, *American Dreams in China* (ADIC),
is particularly revealing about the global-national ideological struggles that have helped shape the "Chinese Dream" rhetoric. Moreover,
the film's narrative, which is organized around an IPR dispute that is
itself based on a real-life lawsuit, points to the myriad ways in which
global imaginaries such as IPR and the American Dream have worked,
sometimes in converging ways, to produce competing national visions
for China. A careful examination of the film as a cultural text, then, will
help us further discern China's cultural dilemma in the WTO era even
as we move beyond the time frame that is the first decade of the twenty-
first century.

IPR AND *AMERICAN DREAMS IN CHINA*

ADIC is a fast-paced urban film that was widely celebrated in the media as
a domestic hit for having beaten *Iron Man 3* during its opening weekend.
It tells the story of three 1980s Chinese college graduates who join in a
partnership – over three decades and through various struggles – to form
New Dreams, an English test preparation school modeled on New Oriental Education & Technology Group (a Chinese equivalent of Kaplan,

Inc.). The film went on to earn RMB500 million (close to $100 million) at the box office, even though its reception was not uniformly positive. As in the case of *Crazy Stone*, the film's popularity generated suspicion that it had copied a Hollywood production – in this case *The Social Network* (2010; directed by David Fincher) – in terms of style and plotline.[30] Both films, after all, are based on real stories of several young college graduates' entrepreneurial success and the deterioration of their friendship during the process. Both narratives also prominently feature one or more IPR lawsuits faced by the protagonist: in *The Social Network*, Mark Zuckerberg is accused of stealing the idea of Facebook from his Harvard schoolmates, in addition to being sued by one of his former partners for the unfair dilution of the latter's shares; in *ADIC*, New Dreams is charged with copyright infringement due to the use of unauthorized test-preparation material in its own tutorials. Both films portray their main characters as eloquently defending themselves against their opponents during settlement talks – a plot element that grants them an on-screen victory of sorts, despite the actual outcome of the (real-life or cinematized) lawsuit itself, which in both cases involved the defendant's payment of a sizable sum for settling out of court.

Peter Chan, the director of *ADIC*, while admittedly an admirer of *The Social Network*, has dismissed copying charges of this kind by stating that one of his previous films, *The Warlords* (2009), had already adopted a similar style. More important, the original script for *ADIC* came from Xu Xiaoping, who wrote the story based on his real-life experience as one of the Beijing-based company's co-founders. Established in 1993, New Oriental is a private company that joined NASDAQ in 2006. Boasting an online network of 9.2 million registered users and 2.7 million enrolled students in 2014, it is known for preparing large numbers of Chinese students for their TOEFL (Test of English as a Foreign Language) and GRE (Graduate Record Examination).[31] Many of those students would go on to obtain a visa to study in America. Michael Yu Minhong, the CEO of New Oriental, was named one of the nation's honored entrepreneurs in an awards ceremony with the theme "From Made in China to Created in China" (see chapter 1). This recognition likely had to do with the company's reputation of having transformed itself from a "pirate" into an "innovator." In fact, it is well known that Educational Testing Services (ETS), the American nonprofit in charge of TOEFL and GRE, took New Oriental to court in 2001 for copyright infringement. Yu reportedly went to ETS in person with the hope of convincing ETS's general counsel that foreigners like him could not win in China.[32] However, the Beijing Municipal Court proved Yu wrong by requiring New Oriental to pay $1.25 million in damages.[33] It was not until 2007 that ETS officially authorized New Oriental to incorporate its TOEFL Practice Online into its curriculum.

This lawsuit made its way into the story of New Dreams – an unmistakable cinematic version of New Oriental. The producer of *ADIC*, Han Sanping, is the CEO of China Film Group and the chief figure behind almost every Chinese megafilm in the past decade. Han first requested the script from Xu in March 2012, before hiring two other writers to add "more drama and conflict" to the screenplay.[34] One of these writers was Zhou Zhiyong, a co-writer of *Crazy Stone* who had won a national award for that script (chapter 3). While Zhou's presence in the production team may serve to explain why IPR is such a key element in *ADIC*, just as it was for *Crazy Stone*, the thematic choice also reflects the way in which IPR frequently operates as a distinct reference point for conjuring China's WTO-era national imaginary. Indeed, even though the bulk of *ADIC* covers the college life, romances, friendship, and business partnership of the three main characters over the thirty-year span 1979–2003, the scenes that feature IPR struggles between New Dreams and the American plaintiff are of crucial importance in structuring the narrative of the film as a whole. As such, IPR functions as a key node that connects the film's titles in Chinese and English; it is by "winning" (albeit figuratively) an IPR battle with America that the "Chinese partners" can ultimately lay claim to success in realizing their "American Dreams in China."

This linkage between IPR and a Chinese version of the American Dream is evident in the seven-minute-long introductory sequence that precedes the appearance of the film's Chinese title. In this scene, an officer from the American embassy carefully examines the protagonist Cheng Dongqing's passport during an interview – a standard procedure during one's application for a visa to study in the United States. The sequence is intercut with two other visa interviews conducted by the same officer, of Cheng's two best friends from college (who later become his partners): Meng Xiaojun and Wang Yang. While Meng obtains a visa and Wang withdraws his application, Cheng's interview ends with the officer stamping the word "rejection" into his passport. As Cheng slowly leaves the visa window, disappointed, he informs us in voice-over: "He [the visa officer] would not have imagined that after twenty years, help-ing people to go to America would become what I do best." Immediately, a rock version of the *Internationale* ensues, accompanying the entrance of the three partners into a big stadium, where Cheng (now the CEO of New Dreams) is to deliver a speech about dreams. Through Cheng and Meng's voice-overs, we learn about what New Dreams does – "teach-ing English to the Chinese" – and how well it does it, with students scor-ing so high on American standardized tests that "the Americans" have come to suspect that they are cheating. We also learn that three-quar-ters of the Chinese students studying in America are graduates of New Dreams – a statistic presumably matched by that of New Oriental[35] – and its "flags have been hoisted all over America" (including one that Wang has just placed on screen for "Wisconsin").

The clear emphasis of the sequence is on Meng, who now coaches students on how to succeed in obtaining a U.S. visa, as he himself did in the opening scene. A series of flashbacks, narrated by Cheng, reveals that Meng comes from a family for whom America is a "legacy"; Meng's grandfather returned from studying in America in 1925, as did his father in 1955, and each later gave his son an English dictionary as a gift. Then we see Cheng himself, microphone in hand, speaking live to the stu-dents of New Dreams: "What are dreams? Dreams are what make you happy, even when you are just trying."[36] When Wang's voice-over leads us back to "twenty years ago," we return to the American visa office. As the three exit the interview room and walk into a waiting area where a U.S. map is displayed, we hear Cheng's narration again: "Meng Xiaojun said he love[s] America. What he meant was, '*loved*'" (*aiguo* is the past tense of *ai*, or "love" in the present tense in Chinese). "But I," he contin-ues, "the 'Godfather of Studying Abroad' as they say, have never been to America." As Wang pulls Cheng away from the waiting room, Cheng's voice-over tells us: "Today, America is suing us."

The scene quickly cuts to a brightly lit conference room on the top floor of a skyscraper (located in Manhattan, as revealed later in the film).

The words "EES Sues New Dreams for Theft of Educational Materials: 2003 New York Meeting," appears as a title superimposed on-screen,[37] when a female American lawyer poses the question: "Mr. Cheng, do you acknowledge that your company used unauthorized test materials from my client, Educational Exams Services of Cornell, New York, so that Chinese students would have an unfair advantage during exams?"[38] When Meng and Cheng rush their responses in English simultaneously, rendering their words barely intelligible, a white-haired Caucasian man sitting at the end of the table (later revealed to be Mr. Bernard, presumably the head of EES) begins to speak: "Mr. Cheng, I know you had a mediocre academic record. The school you founded enabled half a million Chinese students to study in the United States. To them you may be a hero. To me, you are a thief."

As the camera pans to the three Chinese partners at the table, Meng's voice-over brings us back to 1979, when Cheng Dongqing "was still a loser" ("loser" is spoken in English) from the countryside who "failed the National College Entrance Exam twice." We flash back to Cheng Dongqing in his hometown, kneeling in front of the village elders as his mother urges him to become the "peasant he's meant to be." When Cheng's mother finally decides to let Cheng try a third time, Meng speaks again in voice-over: "Americans will never understand, heroes in China can kneel down, or can even crawl underneath someone's crotch." As a close-up of Cheng's bitter smile fills the screen, a rock song by Cui Jian (often considered the "father of Chinese rock") accompanies the narrative transition to 1980s Beijing, when Cheng joins other college freshmen to arrive at Yan Jing University (unmistakably mirroring the prestigious Peking University, attended by several founders of New Oriental) and only then is the film's title, "Chinese Partners," displayed in the foreground.

This long introductory sequence is significant in that it serves to organize the narrative time of the entire film by orienting the viewer to the "present day" of 2003, when the IPR lawsuit is taking place. By this time, China had already joined the WTO and was preparing itself to host the much-anticipated 2008 Olympics (depicted later in the film by a brief shot of a newspaper article about Beijing's successful bid). While one may argue that both the WTO and the Olympics represent the world's recognition of China's rising stature within a global community of nations, they also embody the established global system of power to which China must now be subject and of which the cultural regime of IPR is part. Such a framing of the "now" (or the "modern") as the time of IPR renders the other plots of the film a series of non-linear flashbacks, told through the three protagonists' personal voices and displayed on screen as a set of temporal and spatial heterogeneities. What may be observed, then, is a juxtaposition of the globalizing – if not "empty and homogeneous" – time of the modern, in which IPR is a central anchor, and the heterogeneous time that is specific to each locale, whether it is Cheng's hometown village (1979), the Yan Jing University campus (1988), or other places and periods featured in the film.

For Chinese critic Song Fagang, this narrative structure has the effect of heightening the conflict between New Dreams and the American company. Even though the IPR scenes constitute a mere "one-seventh" of the film's total length, the conflict leaves the audience with a strong impression, even a sense of "triumph over America."[39] This impression is especially fortified at the end of the film, when Cheng delivers a passionate speech in English at the final EES meeting scene, one that renders the American plaintiff speechless. Filmgoers around the country reportedly responded to the ending with standing ovations, a phenomenon that Song attributes to the film's strategic construction of the "national pride." Clearly, IPR has played a uniquely symbolic role in shaping a structure of feeling that has laid claim to the national. Indeed, I would argue that the framing of ADIC, which accentuates the IPR dispute between China and America in the "present," emblematizes the homogeneous temporality that is proffered by IPR's branded imaginary (chapter 1). Much like the nation-branding discourse "From Made in China to Created in China," which does not go uncontested by the multifarious publics and temporalities of counterfeit culture, ADIC enacts a complex set of negotiations between the national and the global, which simultaneously sanction IPR as a value-producing cultural regime and evoke a performative Chineseness to challenge the unequal relations of power that IPR represents.

These negotiations can be discerned in the two remaining sequences of the EES meeting. In the first one, the American lawyer informs Cheng that EES "has issued a warning to all U.S. universities of the possibility that New Dreams students have cheated on the TOEFL and the GRES." "You can't issue such a notice," interrupts Meng, who claims that this is a "violation of the fundamental principle of American law." Mr. Bernard intervenes by acknowledging Meng's "good thinking," which to him is evidence of Meng's having received "a good education in the United States." He goes on to share "some interesting facts about Chinese culture" – namely, that China's "imperial exam system" bred a "tradition of cheating with many documented techniques on how to cheat." As if offended by Bernard's condescending tone, Wang stands up and says he's going to "take a leak."

The scene then cuts to another flashback set in 1988, when Cheng, already graduated, had become an English lecturer at his university and his application for a U.S. visa had been rejected twice more. His girlfriend Su Mei returns to their small teacher's dorm room with the complaint that "the newest tutorial for TOEFL is ridiculously expensive." While this mention of the high price of the "original" is only a subplot of the sequence (in which Cheng receives a *Penthouse* magazine from Meng and tries to hide it from Su), it nonetheless offers a rationale for New Dreams' "copyright infringement" later. After all, if it had not been for the purpose of making the tutorials more affordable for the Chinese student population, New Dreams would not have "stolen" copyright-protected material from ETS, just as Shanzhaiji, the "bandit" cell phones, would not have taken off among China's working class were it not for their combination of high tech and low price (chapter 2).

Through various flashbacks, we learn about Meng's failed attempt to achieve the "American Dream" in the United States, which brings him back to China and to New Dreams – a name proposed by Meng for Cheng's school. In 1999, when the partners realize that some of their use of unauthorized EES material for their own TOEFL and GRE tutorials might present "a hidden hazard for the future," Meng comes back to New York to settle the issue with EES. However, not only does a customs officer at the airport single him out for a special inspection, but Mr. Bernard never grants him a meeting, despite having him wait an entire day at his office. In a telling scene, we see Meng walking across Times Square when a big electronic sign catches his attention: "Sina Corp. to join NASDAQ for public trading." (Sina, of course, is one of China's biggest internet service providers; it also owns the popular social media platform, Sina Weibo, a homegrown Facebook-Twitter hybrid.) Upon his return, Meng presents Cheng with the idea of making the company public, but Cheng decides to hold off. The disagreement between the two escalates into the breakup of the partnership later in the film. Only when Cheng is confronted with the EES lawsuit (in 2003) are the three reunited, in a car soaring toward the Manhattan skyline with Wang exclaiming, "New York City, here we come!"

Thus begins the film's grand finale: the IPR "battle" between the representatives of EES and New Dreams. Outraged by the EES's demand for $15 million in damages, Meng takes his two friends during the lunch recess to the restaurant where he once worked as a busboy. Relaying his experience of being given no more than coins as tips, Meng laments: "Only when you swing the hammer at the New York Stock Exchange will they see you, recognize you, respect you." Upon hearing Meng's apology for the idea of bringing New Dreams public for selfish reasons, Cheng responds: "After lunch, we will go take down America." As the EES meeting resumes, Cheng offers Bernard a "formal apology": "We acknowledge that we committed copyright infringement, and are prepared to settle." He then hands the lawyer a book of IPR law and asks her to test him on "any clause you want." As he recites several clauses perfectly, Cheng tells them that he had memorized the entire text on the plane coming here, using a skill that he's developed since the age of 18, when he memorized the whole Xinhua English dictionary. "For your information, I was only considered mediocre among my peers," Cheng continues. "Chinese students are extremely adept at taking exams. You can't imagine what they are willing to go through to succeed. You don't understand Chinese culture." At this point, Meng informs Mr. Bernard that "regardless of the final ruling, this meeting marks the start of our formal partnership." Encouraging EES to enforce its copyrights in the Chinese market, Meng tells the group that the purpose of their trip is "to educate you about one thing: China has changed. Unfortunately, you are still stuck in the past."[40]

The climatic moment arrives when Cheng reveals his decision that New Dreams will be issuing its initial public offering (IPO) in New York that same day, because the lawsuit has attracted attention from potential investors from Wall Street, who will see the company as one that takes responsibility for its mistakes. While Cheng predicts that only when New Dreams becomes the world's largest educational service corporation will Americans like Bernard "show us the respect we deserve," he nonetheless concludes his speech on a more personal note. Going public, it turns out, is his way of reclaiming dignity for his "friend" – "the best man of my generation" who was almost "destroyed" by America. Calling himself a risk-averse *tu bie,* or "soft-shell turtle," "terrified" even as he speaks, Cheng tells a speechless Mr. Bernard that "the playing field has never been even," but "some things are so important that they force us to overcome our fears."

Numerous Chinese critics have found these IPR scenes overly heavy handed and indeed attributable to the director Peter Chan's "Hong Kong" style of filmmaking, often seen in martial arts films in which the principal kung fu master typically beats a "foreign devil" in a climatic sequence.[41] Others, however, have found it a fair representation of "China's rise," even "one of the best films that represent the 'Chinese Dream.'"[42] Still others are troubled that the realization of the "Chinese Dream" appears to be based solely on recognition by America, more specifically NASDAQ, which reduces "the spirit of the Reform Era" to a single dimension of "entrepreneurship."[43] This "distortion" is something that several critics again attribute to Chan's Hong Kong identity, which "overly dramatizes the East's admiration for the West" rather than seeing New Oriental's experience, and indeed mainland China's transformation in the past three decades, as struggles between "tradition and modernity."[44]

While these criticisms no doubt help to illuminate the depoliticized mode of storytelling in ADIC (which may be more attributable to Hollywood's influence), the complex ways in which the IPR dispute figures in the construction of "Chineseness" within the characters' ostensible pursuit of the "American Dream" seems to be underexamined. I have analyzed this negotiation of the national within a globalizing cultural system throughout this book; now it is more prominently expressed in the "Chinese Dream" discourse, which manifests quite distinctively the contradictory workings of globalization as cultural imperialism. ADIC, as a cinematic component in the "Chinese Dream" discourse, is best seen as an allegory of WTO-era China's cultural dilemma. This dilemma, crystallized in the contestations between the state project of nation branding and the transnational practice of counterfeit culture, finds a symptomatic expression in the film's narrative. Like the clashes between nation branding and counterfeit culture, which largely stem from competing visions for the nation in terms of its relations to time, ADIC can be seen as a cultural attempt to negotiate the competing temporalities that are emerging in the "Chinese Dream" discourse – which is, after all, a debate about China's future.

THE "CHINESE DREAM": A CULTURAL DILEMMA

Given the film's explicit invocation of the "dream" signifier, it is tempting to see ADIC as lending subtle support to the "mainstream state ideology" that is the "Chinese Dream," as some critics have argued.[45] Yet this kind of analysis falls short in mapping the historically specific conditions that give rise to a cultural artifact like ADIC. After all, the "Chinese Dream" discourse, as documented in William Callahan's *China Dreams,* is a heterogeneous formation that involves a variety of actors whose voices can hardly be captured by the notion of "mainstream state ideology." A more pertinent question, which a group of young cultural scholars in China convened in June 2013 to reflect upon, is how and why contemporary "popular cultural productions" like ADIC have come to participate in the construction of "an American imaginary."[46] Indeed, the presence of this imaginary, as several critics have noted, can be seen in two other hit films of the same year that also feature "America" quite prominently. One is *Finding Mr. Right,* whose Chinese title literally translates as *Beijing Meets Seattle (Beijing yushang Xiyatu),* paying explicit tribute to the 1993 Hollywood romantic classic, *Sleepless in Seattle.*[47] The other is *So Young (Zhi Qingchun),* in which the female lead has two consecutive boyfriends who have chosen America over their relationship, presumably in pursuit of their own American Dreams.[48]

Compared to these productions, for which "America" remains a backdrop for "Chinese" stories, ADIC's treatment of the "American imaginary" is arguably more direct and more ambivalent at once. While director Peter Chan's "postcolonial" Hong Kong identity may very well have informed his staging of an "East-West duel" over IPR, Chan's experience in America may also serve as a more immediate source of inspiration. After all, Chan was trained at UCLA, and after such huge Hong Kong successes as *Comrades: Almost a Love Story* (*Tian Mimi*), he had an unsuccessful run in Hollywood before returning to mainland China in search of new opportunities. He was first asked to be a producer for ADIC, but decided that he would direct it himself, in part because he had wanted to make a Chinese version of *Citizen Kane* since his school days. For Chan, "Kane's era" – a period that exemplifies the "capitalist myth" of "rags to riches" – "was America's Reform and Opening Up." While looking for China's "Kane," however, Chan realized that even though China's three decades of economic boom had made plenty of Kane-like "lucky scoundrels," it was impossible to bring these stories, which are often entangled in seedy transactions between money and power (perhaps not unlike the kind discussed in chapter 4 regarding the privatization of Silk Street) onto the Chinese screen. The script for ADIC offered a perfect opportunity to "localize" *Citizen Kane,* which for him is a story that depicts the turbulence of the times through the struggles, gains, and losses of an individual entrepreneur. Besides, the topic of learning English collectively also makes good material for comedy.[49]

If Chan's reading of *Citizen Kane* in relation to American history appears idiosyncratic, his own experience of "defeat" in America explicitly helped shape the character Meng Xiaojun. In one particularly telling sequence early in the film, Meng challenges a college professor during a lecture on "contemporary America" in the 1980s. Upon hearing the professor's thoughts on anti-black and anti-Asian racism in the United States,[50] Meng rises from his seat and asks: "Have you been to America? You have only read about America in the books, no?" As his friend Wang also stands up to quote a famous line by Mao, "Practice is the sole criterion for testing truth," in support, Meng continues: "The so-called American Dream ["American Dream" is spoken in English] means that everyone has an equal opportunity to embrace a dream. In the whole world, only America can achieve this." When the professor tells Meng that he is "too young, too naïve," Meng promises: "I will definitely go to America [spoken in Chinese]. I'll find out for myself [spoken in English]." As it turns out, not only has "America" reduced him from a lab assistant to a busboy, it is through the business partnership with his Chinese friend that he is able to regain his dignity. It is precisely this ambivalent attitude toward America, shared by Chan in real life and Meng in the film, that the film's English title has come to reflect; it is about "American Dreams" *in China.* As Chan explains why he favors this title: "People feel that the 'American Dream' must belong to America, but America's economy is already saturated . . . the American Dream was what happened in America in the last century . . . but now this 'American Dream' is taking place in China every day."[51]

Chan's comments here resonate with a common interpretation of the film's motif that one can realize the American Dream on Chinese soil.[52] This is a motif that departs from previous representations in Chinese popular media, which typically portrayed Chinese protagonists leaving China for America in search of their dreams.[53] What is curious about Chan's description, however, is the unquestioning characterization of China's present in terms of America's past. This is perhaps why several critics in China have found the film to lack inspiration for constructing a more Chinese-specific dream. After all, the success of the three "Chinese partners" is still conveyed through their realization of an American Dream – whether it is the entrepreneurial spirit of starting New Dreams or the final triumph over an IPR lawsuit by way of capitalization at the New York Stock Exchange. In other words, "America" is still imagined as "a powerful 'Other'" for a story purportedly about the "rise of China."[54] Due to this binary construction of "America versus China," as cultural critic Wang Yan points out, the film has perhaps missed out on an opportunity to re-imagine a "different" China within a postcolonial global order.[55]

In this sense, rather than attributing the film's incongruous construction of a "Chinese Dream" to the director's "Hong Kong" identity, it is necessary to question whether (post)coloniality is a not a condition limited to Hong Kong but in fact impacts the Chinese nation-state more generally. Indeed, the film's narrative failure to escape the imaginary "Other" that is America ties this cultural text to the broader discursive formation of the "Chinese Dream" more closely than its English title suggests. Even though the participants in the "Chinese Dream"

C.2. Street posters in Shenzhen for the "Chinese Dream" rendered in folk style, seen outside of a construction zone at Huaqiangbei, the retail hub for Shanzhai phones.

discourse are "involved in a raucous debate of the direction of China's future," many of these "dreamers" still hold that the "main goal" is to "surpass the United States economically, militarily, and politically."[56] Thus, *ADIC* can be more usefully read as representing the impossibility of the nation's breaking away from a pre-occupation with "America" as a telos of progress, a temporality that speaks powerfully to the continuing presence of coloniality.

This is not to say that aspirations for the national to become a site of difference making do not exist in the "Dreams" discourse. As Callahan argues, a key value promoted in the "Dreams" debate is precisely China's own "characteristics" or "national conditions," something that "outsiders cannot understand" and that therefore would require "the Chinese perspective" to engage in "global ideological battles."[57] The negotiation of national difference in a global context can indeed be discerned in numerous flashback sequences in *ADIC*. These moments, which often feature meticulously re-constructed spaces, bring forth heterogeneous temporalities that contest the film's IPR "present," in the same way that counterfeit cultural practices have conjured differently imagined temporalities for the nation that challenge the state project of nation branding. Two of these sequences, which take place in two 1990s New Dreams "classrooms," stand out most prominently. One location is a Kentucky Fried Chicken (KFC) in 1993 Beijing, where one can "buy a piece of chicken and sit all day." The other is a derelict factory building that formerly belonged to a state-owned enterprise, which Cheng illegally occupied in 1994 as the first "campus" for New Dreams. Wang, whose voice-over introduces both scenes, describes Cheng's appropriation of these spaces as "taking advantage of an 'American Grandpa'" (that is, Colonel Sanders) before "taking advantage of the state." This "double" appropriation, reminiscent of Shanzhai cell phone makers' reworking of global brands to compete with state-supported nation brands in chapter 2, bespeaks the film's attempt at negotiating a national difference that departs from the state's efforts in constructing the "Chinese Dream."

A telling scene takes place on a hot summer day in the deserted factory, where Cheng delivers a moving speech to a group of watermeloneating students. Abandoning the written draft that Meng has prepared for him, Cheng begins by speaking of himself as someone who "never dreams" but knows so much about failure that he can talk about it without a prepared text. He references statistics that highlight the national-specific conditions faced by students in China, such as the competitive National College Entrance Exams, which eliminate millions every year (including Cheng himself, twice). As he concludes the speech with the motto Seek Hope in Despair (which belongs to New Oriental in real life), heartfelt applause breaks out in the factory turned classroom. This emotional sequence comes to an abrupt end when two policemen arrive at the site, demanding to see the person in charge. The officers take Cheng and his partners in for questioning, because they have set up the school without proper authorization. During the confrontation, Meng, who had returned from America not long ago, invokes the notion of "rights violation" and threatens to sue the police but only elicits the response: "If you are so capable, why would you come back?" Cheng, on the other hand, effusively apologizes to the officer, even offering to pay whatever fine might be required. As the three leave the police station, Cheng says to Meng: "This is China. Your 'American' way won't work." Curiously, upon hearing this, Meng decides to stay and join the Chinese partnership.

In this staged confrontation with a state entity, "China" appears as a signifier for the nation that breaks from "China" the state, not unlike the "Chineseness" produced in the various forms of counterfeit culture analyzed in this book – that is, artifacts and discourses that lay claim to the national in ways that do not align with the state project of nation branding. In fact, Meng's ready adoption of the American way, clear from the beginning of the film, is even more pronounced after he joins the partnership, continuously proposing development plans for New Dreams. Cheng, in a voice-over, admits that he is accustomed to saying yes to Meng's proposals because he trusts that Meng's experience in America allows him to "see things" that he and Wang cannot. However, when it comes to Meng's desire for New Dreams to be No. 1 in the educational business so that it can issue stock, Cheng finally manages to say no, presumably because "the time is still not right." The "say no" rhetoric is reminiscent of a popular nationalist discourse from the 1990s that took its name from a best-selling book, *China Can Say No: A Choice of Politics and Attitude in the Post-Cold War Era,* by Song Qiang, Zhang Zangzang, and Qiao Bian (1996). If the "ultranationalistic and xenophobic sentiment" exhibited by the real-life "say no" crowd, as Dai Jinhua points out, contradicted "the state's pursuit of an open-door policy aimed at drawing in overseas capital" as it prepared to join the WTO, a similar divide can be discerned in Cheng's defiance of Meng, whom he has long regarded as his idol (as revealed explicitly in the opening visa interview scene).

Throughout the film, Meng has asked Cheng repeatedly: "Do you have a dream?" But Cheng never offers a clear answer, even opting to give public speeches about "failure" instead, both in the factory turned classroom and in the stadium during the opening sequence. Meanwhile, after Meng's own failure in America, he develops stage fright upon returning to China. Deprived of the ability to deliver public talks, he chooses to conduct nothing but private mock visa interviews. It is Cheng who now takes on the role of a charismatic speaker, tirelessly telling self-deprecating jokes, often about his failed love life. The transfer of public

speaking ability from Meng to Cheng can in some sense be seen as mirroring the movement of the "American Dream" discourse to the Chinese
context; it is now China (the state) that is in a position to speak openly
about dreams to a collective audience (the nation), unlike the American
Dream, whose discursive power is confined to the private individual. At
the same time, Cheng's ostensible replacement of the "dream" signifier
with an emphasis on "failure" also decidedly breaks from the state's rhetoric. After all, despite frequent attempts on the part of the new administration to re-cast itself as a promoter of dreams among the "Chinese
people," many social media users still see Xi as propagating "a dream for
strengthening the nation" (*qiangguo meng*), one that has nothing to do
with "ordinary" Chinese.[58]

In this sense, by distancing itself from the state's appropriation of
the American Dream rhetoric, Cheng's invocation of "China" to defy
Meng's "American way" conjures an alternative Chineseness that is not
unlike the kind presented by the participants in Shanzhai culture and
the old vendors at Silk Street. Just as these publics have come to challenge the IPR-friendly vision of nation branding, which shares a developmental trajectory with Meng's plan for New Dreams, Cheng's "Chineseness" proffers a different conception of culture that undermines the
IPR regime's value-producing logic, which the state has blindly accepted
as given. A most telling representation of this new cultural vision takes
place in KFC, the "birthplace" of New Dreams where Cheng first started
gathering students. It is here that Cheng uses Chinese transliterations to
help students memorize English words, by turning "ambulance" into "*an
bu neng si*" ("I cannot die") and "pregnant" into "*pu lai ge nan de*" ("got
a male one"), among others.[59] The linguistic adaptation of English, not
uncommon among English learners in China, parallels the spatial appropriation of KFC – a transnational fast-food company often invoked
as a symbol of globalization. While the transliterated words become
a "Chinese way" to "conquer" English by way of "creolization," the re-
purposing of KFC has turned an otherwise highly disciplinary social
space into a place of meaning making. In moments like this, set in a
meticulously constructed past, we have a glimpse into a different way to
imagine what "culture" might mean for the nation – not the kind of "ossified" past that the new Silk Street Market employed to re-brand itself,

but more like the dynamic engagement with history that is presented in *Crazy Stone*. Just as the '80s–'90s Chinese popular (rock and folk) music played throughout *A DIC,* which evokes a distinct collective memory of the era for many, these moments present an understanding of culture as generative of meanings. It is through highlighting the social practice of meaning making that they offer the possibility of conjuring "different ways of belonging and different ways of becoming," and indeed different "modes of belonging to time and space."[60]

With this in mind, the final IPR "battle" scene in the film, which is set in the "present," becomes a more pointed confrontation between the various claims to "Chineseness" that are predicated on "different temporalities and different modalities of belonging to time."[61] Cheng's recitation of IPR law, which comes after his "official apology" for New Dreams's IPR offense, enables him to criticize Mr. Bernard for his ignorance of "Chinese culture" – specifically, the inability of "foreigners" to imagine the hardship that the Chinese students are willing to endure.[62] By emphasizing the technique shared by reciting English dictionaries and memorizing IPR laws, Cheng renders IPR's hegemonic status comparable to that of English, the lingua franca of contemporary globalization (despite the increasing and often state-orchestrated spread of the Chinese language globally). Cheng's display of this "Chineseness," then, serves to rebut the charges of cheating that EES has brought against the Chinese students in a different manner than Meng, who challenges the procedural lack of due process on the basis of "American law." In the end, it is Cheng's memorization – illustrative of his "Chinese" way – that ultimately impresses if not defeats the "Americans."

However, this countering of "American law" by way of a performative "Chineseness" not only does not undermine the premise of IPR but in fact manifests an internalization of its value-producing cultural logic. As Cheng's speech indicates, it is the EES lawsuit that has helped New Dreams to obtain attention from potential investors from Wall Street. Even the $15 million compensation that EES is seeking from New Dreams is positively linked to the company's future market value, because the higher payment would purportedly lead Wall Street to evaluate the company more favorably. Such mention of the future can be contrasted with Meng's speech to Mr. Bernard that "China has changed" and yet "you are still stuck in the past." For Meng, America has not come to terms with a changing China because its attitude is stuck in a proto-orientalist mindset, as indicated in Bernard's invocation of the "imperial exams" and the "tradition" of cheating. But for Cheng this outdated attitude is precisely something that New Dreams, and indeed China itself, can exploit as a future growth opportunity.

While Meng suggests that EES tap into the Chinese educational market, already one of the biggest in the world, Cheng proposes that New Dreams, by entering the U.S. capital market, will be en route to become "the world's largest educational service corporation." If Meng's suggestion is reminiscent of the objectification of China as a nation of consumers for global brands in the film *Silk Alley* (chapter 4), Cheng's plan for New Dreams is demonstrably more ambitious and yet more "intimate" – that is, it is ultimately motivated by personal reasons, to reclaim the respect that America owed to his friend. When Cheng tells Mr. Bernard that "the playing field has never been even," he is simultaneously exposing America's façade of "equal opportunity" – whose true nature Meng has learned the hard way – and the global IPR structure in which China finds itself. This uneven power relationship, indeed, is what China must "overcome" in order to assume a proper subject position in the world of nations. However, the film's narrative closure does not seem to present a plausible opening for China to do so. At the end of Cheng's speech, he describes himself as a "*tu bie*," which literally translates as "a turtle of the earth," with the term "earth" (*tu*) connoting the local, the countryside, the unsophisticated. While this self-identification appears to be Cheng's way of affirming his peasant origins, he ultimately resorts to one of Meng's mottoes in the film: "Some things are so important that they force us to overcome our fears." Those "important things," of course, are none other than "dignity and respect." These values are later reiterated through the words of Su Mei (Cheng's love interest) who is quoted as saying: "No matter what you do, you can't let go of your dignity." This is a curious arrangement, considering that Cheng's pursuit of Su (who is played by Du Juan, the first Asian supermodel to appear on the cover of the French *Vogue*) constitutes a central plot line of the film. Not only does the courtship manifest Cheng's "dream" philosophy, revealed in the opening speech – "if you try, you are happy"; his energy for setting up New Dreams also largely derives from his breakup with Su (over the phone, when she was studying in the United States and around the same time that China failed to obtain the rights to host the 2000 Olympics). Su, with a distinct blend of Chinese aura and international appeal has thus come to embody "the rules that cannot be changed or controlled," something that one "can embrace but cannot possess."[63]

Cheng's self-identification as a *tu bie* can thus be seen as laying claim to a locally derived national identity to challenge the global forces of homogenization, not unlike the way the original vendors at Silk Street Market turned their lack of IPR knowledge into a marker of national-cultural distinction. But Cheng's decision to regain America's respect for Meng by subjecting New Dreams to the whims of Wall Street is perhaps more indicative of the "uneven playing field" that continues to limit the extent to which one can re-imagine the nation's relation to time. As several Chinese critics point out, Cheng's speech offers little more than the "psychosexual pleasure" of "conquering America" and indeed the world.[64] After all, the future value of New Dreams still depends on subscribing to the global regime of financialization, a condition that "China" (the state) must heed if it wishes to obtain global recognition; it means having to adopt the homogeneous temporality proffered by IPR, which serves as an admission into the global financial market, at the expense of dismissing the heterogeneous temporalities that inform alternative cultural visions for "China" (the nation).

This impossibility of imagining the nation's future beyond the temporal logic of IPR again crystallizes what I have been calling WTO-era China's cultural dilemma. At work is a contestation between a developmental blueprint that the state must adopt by internalizing the global culture industry's instrumentalized conception of culture, and the kinds of meaning-making practices that persist in shaping cultural visions for the nation in spite of that blueprint. The hegemonic workings of the branded imaginary of IPR, then, manifest themselves in their influence on the state, which limits its ability to recognize the cultural possibilities that present alternative means to challenge IPR's globalizing regime. This failure of cultural imagination is perhaps most clearly seen in the kind of "industry expert" responses to films like *Crazy Stone* and ADIC that see them as examples for boosting the national "cultural" output

in audiovisual production, hence paving the way for realizing a "cinematic Chinese Dream" that would strengthen the nation's soft power
globally.[65] It is also discernible in the CCTV reports on Shanzhai, which
sought to rework the creativity of "the people" as a value-generating asset
for the nation, as well as in the rebranding of Silk Market, which turned
a local market rich with meanings into "intangible assets" if not cultural
codes for global tourist consumption. At work in these apparent attempts
at "creating" culture is a counterproductive conception of culture as a
source of value. In line with the state-promoted march toward "Created
in China," these processes project an image of an IPR-friendly future
as already pre-figured and therefore something to be obtained through
progress and development. The drive to transform culture – variously
defined as tradition, heritage, or symbolic repertoires in general – into
"cultural goods" in order to generate profit thus results in a condescending attitude toward those countercultural practices that are incongruent
with the globally hegemonic trajectory set up by IPR. The state's aim
of producing a "branded nation" of the future therefore works to deplete
resources that may help shape different, more meaning-generative visions for the nation.

DOING CULTURAL STUDIES OF THE
STATE IN GLOBALIZATION

The speedy diffusion and mutation of the Chinese Dream discourse
in contemporary China and its intricate connection to the American
imaginary will surely demand more critical attention in the years to
come. What I hope to have brought attention to in my analysis of ADIC,
a distinct cultural product of the moment, is the working of a globally hegemonic imaginary – that of the American Dream – in setting the terms
for the Chinese state in its imagination of the nation's future. In many
ways, the film's ideological participation in the state-promoted "Chinese Dream" discourse shares much with that of the post-2001 nation-
branding campaign, "From Made in China to Created in China." Both,
one may argue, privilege the subject position of "creative" entrepreneurs
represented by figures like Michael Yu, the CEO of New Oriental who
served as a major inspiration for ADIC. In fact, the ending of the film

features a series of "then and now" portraits of an ensemble of successful Chinese entrepreneurs – among them Yu and his New Oriental partners, as well as Jack Ma (Ma Yun), a former English teacher who was soon to become the richest man in China when Alibaba, the e-commerce company he founded fifteen years before that is known for selling counterfeit goods, issued a record-breaking IPO at the New York Stock Exchange on September 19, 2014. "Their story is perhaps also your story," says an intertitle that precedes this portrait sequence. While audience responses to this message have ranged from "inspired"[66] to "disgusted,"[67] the glorified on-screen parade of these "Chinese partners" certainly underscored the film's English title, "American Dreams in China."

To treat this cinematic production as a direct vehicle for the state-propagated Chinese Dream, however, would be to miss out on an opportunity to discern the global-national ideological tensions that underlie the discursive formation itself. Indeed, ADIC is best analyzed as a symptomatic text that bespeaks the culturally imperialistic forces at work in delimiting the extent to which China may negotiate a national difference within the homogenizing logic of global modernity. The founders of New Dreams, after all, have failed to conjure a different "future" than what has been prescribed by the financializing regime of the global culture industry, despite their attempts to say no to the Americans by way of a performative, even meaning-generative, Chineseness. Likewise, the WTO-era Chinese state's intent to upgrade China from a manufacturing nation to a brand-creating powerhouse entails a dismissal of those counterfeit cultural practices that are deemed incompatible with IPR's value-productive conception of culture. The cultural dilemma faced by the postsocialist state in globalization, then, may be ultimately described as the impossibility for the state of reconciling the contradiction between an internalized pressure to adhere to the mandates of global modernity and the continuing claims to the national, which are made by the various publics who are engaged in meaning-making practices that defy the globalizing cultural regime as well as the state's attempt to conform to it.

Ending the book on this "impossibility" for the state, however, would be to fall into the same ideological trap that has pre-configured the domestic reception of the "Chinese Dream" discourse. A glance at Chinese-language social media easily yields a wealth of "anger and cynicism" directed at the Chinese state; many posts, for instance, simultaneously denounce Xi Jinping's "Dream"-speak as irrelevant to the individual Chinese while chastising the government for failing to have turned that dream into reality more quickly.[68] By invoking the state as a singular agent responsible for the nation's problems, this seemingly antistate stance becomes a form of "essentializing," which turns the state into "a permanent fixture."[69] The legitimacy of the state, in "criticisms" of this kind, is shored up not by the imposition of a state ideology upon the citizenry but rather by an imaginary of resistance that perpetuates the status quo instead of opening up the possibilities for change.

This fixed conception of the state is precisely what I wish to challenge by rethinking the WTO-era Chinese state itself as a cultural formation in globalization. Indeed, the dramatic transformation of contemporary China must be treated not as an internal problematic within a monolithic state, but rather as a historical process deeply embedded in global contradictions. Whereas the unequal power relations of globalization – what I have described as the persisting workings of cultural imperialism – continue to influence the configuration of the nation-state, I hope to have delineated a number of situations in which the WTO-era Chinese state and its citizenry are participants in the making of globalization rather than mere recipients of its "cultures." This is what makes cultural studies, the approach adopted in this book, a more productive way to engage the multidimensional processes that we have come to call globalization. For it is precisely by acknowledging the dynamism of culture that we may bring human agency back into the picture, which would enable us to re-imagine a new kind of nation-state, if not a new kind of hyphen in between the nation and the state.

In this sense, I see this book as taking a different spin on the so-called rise of China discourse, which is increasingly prevalent on both sides of the Pacific. The newfound global visibility of China as a non-Western nation-state not only destabilizes the territorial origins of cultural studies but also affords us the opportunity to develop a different model that takes more seriously the questions of state legitimacy and national cultural formation in global contexts. Indeed, a critical assessment of the global conditions that reshape the national imaginary is a crucial step toward envisioning alternative forms of international or transnational political praxis. Globalization, despite its problematic ideological resonance, must continue to be examined with rigor. Only then can we channel to more critical ends the various interconnectivities that it promotes. Only then can we reshape its representational forms and lived experiences into world-making projects of a different kind.

Crazy Stone Synopsis

CRAZY STONE FOLLOWS A MULTI-LINEAR NARRATIVE, WITH THE progression of events structured around the overlapping actions of several different characters. It tells the story of competing attempts by several local petit outlaws and a professional thief from Hong Kong to steal a precious jade stone found in the bathroom of a run-down state-owned enterprise on the verge of bankruptcy. The factory official Xie Qianli decides to display the stone publically, recruiting the workers as performers while putting some of the factory's inventory on sale. In doing so, he hopes to avoid the fate of having to sell its land to a real estate developer, Feng Dong (Chairperson Feng), within three weeks. To disrupt this plan, the scheming Feng, with the help of his liaison, Four Eyes, hires Maike, an "international master thief" from Hong Kong, to snatch the stone. However, upon his arrival at the airport, Maike's luggage is taken by three local thieves. Therefore, he has to replace all his gadgets (a Batman-style outfit, a wireless webcam and a climbing rope) through purchases from local vendors, who claim their goods are of "reliable quality." The three local thieves, now equipped with Maike's advanced equipment and informed of the stone exhibit, join in the treasure hunt by checking into a motel next to the temple where the exhibition is held. Their room happens to be adjacent to the one occupied by Bao Shihong (nicknamed Baotou), the protagonist factory security guard entrusted by official Xie to organize a squad of factory workers to protect the gem.

Meanwhile, Xie's son Xie Xiaomeng, a pretentious art photographer turned tabloid reporter, successfully switches out the real gem with a "high-quality" counterfeit copy (*gao fang zhen*), which he bought for 200 yuan from a vendor in front of the temple. He then gives it to Jingjing, a girl whom he has been courting since the beginning of the film. Jingjing turns out to be the girlfriend of Daoge ("big brother Dao"), the leader of the three-thief gang. He finds out about the affair, beats Xie up, and mistakenly judges the stone to be a fake. Heipi ("black skin"), the foolhardy one in the gang, comes up with the idea to swap the "real" stone out with this "fake" one. As the gang proceeds with the plan, Maike executes his, driving a BMW that Feng Dong has loaned him to the temple and parking it above a manhole. When lowering himself down from the ceiling of the temple (as many viewers point out, in the style of Tom Cruise's character in *Mission Impossible*), Maike is outraged by the fact that the rope he purchased from the local vendor is shorter than expected, making it impossible for him to reach the gem. As he curses "jianshang" ("unscrupulous merchant") to himself and finally grasps the gem with a stick, Xiaojun, the third member of the petit-thief gang, snatches it from him and places the "fake" into the exhibition box while setting off the alarms, forcing Maike to escape the scene. In a rush, Maike gets stuck in an air duct, while Heipi, wearing Maike's outfit, is trapped in a sewer and cannot get out until a few days later. As Daoge presents the "real" stone to Chairperson Feng in hope of getting the money, a jewelry appraiser judges the stone to be a fake. In shock, Daoge goes back to interrogating Xie Xiaomeng. Upon learning that he is the son of the factory head, Daoge decides to hold him hostage and ask his father for the real gem. But he quickly finds out that the father, who has been accustomed to his wasteful son's various trickeries in the past, does not believe him at all.

It is Baotou who discovers that the stone has been swapped. Meanwhile, Sanbao, a co-worker of Baotou's who is obsessed with winning a lottery, picks up a Coke can in the motel room previously occupied by the three-thief gang. Upon seeing the "Fifty-Thousand Reward" notice printed on the back of the tab, he leaves a note saying "We now have money!" for Baotou, and takes a twenty-hour train ride from the city of Chongqing, where the film is set, to Beijing to claim the prize. What he does not know is that the Coke can was one of the standardized trick items used by the gang to con commoners into bidding money for a prize (however unsuccessful the attempt might often be, as a sequence in an early part of the film indicates).

Upon seeing Sanbao's note, Baotou is convinced that Sanbao has replaced the real stone with a fake one. His search for Sanbao leads him to his ramshackle residence. When Sanbao returns to the motel, Baotou, not knowing where he has been, engages him in a violent exchange. As they finish off the fight, Baotou asks for the stone, but his interrogation is cut off as one of their co-workers spots Xie Xiaomeng's gem swap caught on a security camera. Baotou then goes to the police for the missing Xie, but soon receives a phone call from Xie himself. Taking the line from Xie, Daoge asks Baotou to bring the stone to exchange for Xie in the evening. As Sanbao and Baotou leave their rooms, Sanbao passes by Xiaojun in the motel's hallway, a Coke in hand. Upon realization that he was cheated by Xiaojun and the others, Sanbao storms into the three-thief gang's room to find Xiaojun (left there by Daoge and Heipi to keep an eye on Xie) and proceeds to beat him up, catching sight of the kidnapped Xie. As both Xiaojun and Xie are taken to the police, the ecstatic Baotou reclaims the "real" gem and puts it back onto the exhibition stand, and later gives what he believes to be the "fake" one to his significant other, a woman who works as a bus conductor.

In the meantime, Maike, who finally frees himself from the air duct, even meeting his alter ego Heipi as the latter climbs out of the sewer, calls his client to report on the "minor incident" he encountered. He promises to get the stone back, since his "business motto" is "honesty and integrity" (*chengxin*). But his contact, Four Eyes, has already been fired. Feng, in a hurry to close the deal, has offered the factory head a portion of the "hotel-style condominium" that is going to be built on the property. By the time Maike calls, Feng has taken charge of the stone as well as the factory's land. Unaware of this turn of events, Maike goes to Feng's office for the jade. He arrives right after Feng kills Four Eyes for fear of the latter's disclosure of his long list of secretive deeds. Maike and Feng engage in a standoff, in which Feng is killed and Maike injured. Maike then calls his client from his cell phone and discovers that he has killed none other than the client himself.

Just as Maike takes the elevator to retreat from the scene, he encounters Baotou, who has all along mistaken Maike to be someone hired by Four Eyes to spy on him. (This is because in the early part of the film, Baotou and Sanbao's factory car hit Feng's BMW, which Four Eyes was driving; Maike later used the same car to carry out his stone-snatching mission.) Baotou promised Four Eyes five thousand yuan to handle the accidents "privately" (*si le*). Now, Baotou comes searching for Four Eyes to deliver the money in exchange for his confiscated driver's license. (Previously, upon learning about the deal between the factory head Xie Qianli and the developer, he berated Xie Qianli for selling out at the public ceremony set to announce the stone's purchase by Feng. His possession of the money is likely a result of the factory's stone-generated profit, which allows Xie Qianli to repay the salaries owned to the employees, though this is not explicitly shown in the film.) He is carrying a bag of quicklime, which he originally planned to use as a "weapon" on Daoge during the transaction to swap Xie Xiaomeng for the stone. Daoge, however, has died trying to grab the bag from Baotou's shoulder while riding on a motorcycle.

Confronting Maike in the elevator, Baotou glances at the blood dripping down Maike's hand. When the elevator door opens, the two are frozen in a deadlock, apparently after some struggles. Awaiting them are the municipal police, who have been on stakeout to catch Maike. Maike's capture appears in the newspapers, turning Baotou into a heroic figure. Just as the host of a reward ceremony held for Baotou summons him to the stage for a speech, he finds himself happily urinating in a restroom, overcoming the prostatitis that has troubled him since the opening of the film. In the closing sequence, the starving Heipi, who had just found his way out of the tunnel, thanks to the police's removal of the same BMW that Maike parked on top of the manhole, robs a bakery with his typical hit-and-run technique. The film ends with a freeze-frame of a medium close-up of Heipi desperately running on a circular highway while chewing bread, with the baker chasing him on a motorcycle to the tune of the "Trepak" from Tchaikovsky's *Nutcracker Suite*.

The Opening (Copied) Sequence in *Crazy Stone*

THE SCENE IMMEDIATELY FOLLOWS A SHORT OPENING SEQUENCE in which Baotou visits a male doctor (played by the director himself) who checks on his prostatitis by penetrating him with a lubricated finger. Just as Baotou's screams and his pained face appear in a medium close-up, a piano soundtrack begins to strike several introspective notes, and the scene cuts to an aerial shot of the city from the perspective of a cable-car rider looking down. Accompanying the camera's smooth movement over the crowded, run-down residential buildings and busy traffic is Xie Xiaomeng's voiceover: "God [literally "Old Heaven"] is so not fair. I take the cable car [to cross the river] every day, but I have never seen you. Maybe [It is because] I have been paying too much attention to the scenery [of the city]. What can I say? – I am a photographer."[1] At the end of the last line, an extreme close-up of Xie's eyes, behind glasses, appears. He continues: "My name is Xie Xiaomeng. You can just call me Charles," while pulling the strap of his bag up on his shoulder. His pompous smile fades into an extreme close-up of a girl's rolling eyes as she turns away to look out the window. This is followed by a close-up shot of a Coke can being opened by Xie, as he continues: "Whenever I look at the city" – the scene quickly cuts to an almost level-angle shot of the buildings – "from this angle" – back to Xie's face – "I feel so strongly that the city is a mother. And we're living inside her womb." This line appears to disgust two middle-aged women on the car, and one of them murmurs: "Pervert."

Xie and Jingjing (whose name we find out later on in the film) then appear in a medium close-up, with Jingjing leaning against the back window of the car. (There are several other passengers in front of them, some in ethnic outfits.) As Xie moves from her right to her left, extending his right arm, Coke in hand, out the window, while leaning his body toward hers, he says: "I was just thinking about that [issue] when I looked up and saw you. Something about you touched me deeply. You know what it is?" A close-up of Jingjing's lips follows, as she again turns away, showing the headphones in her ears. "Maternal spirit. The glorious aroma of maternal spirit," Xie finishes his line. The camera cuts quickly to Jingjing's sneering lips as she turns toward him, pulling one of her headphones out, from which pours the sound of "Water That Makes You Forget Love" (*Wang Qing Shui,* a popular pop song by Andy Lau). Then a swift cut to her high heels shows her stepping on Xie's left foot, leading Xie to scream, his hand losing its grip on the Coke can. This is followed by a view of the cable car from the ground, with the can falling down toward the camera. As the can "hits" the camera lens, a heavy metal soundtrack is introduced, and the film's title (in both Chinese and English) appears in red against a background of cracked, rusty metal. As the metal falls toward the lens piece by piece, the screen fades into darkness.

The scene cuts to a high-angle shot of Four Eyes' hand opening a car door from the inside. His exit from the car is depicted by three distinct, consecutive close-ups, each from a different angle: his left foot steps out (eye-level), the car door shuts (close-up of the bottom rim of the door from the side of the car), and he checks himself out at the front mirror (low-angle). Then we find him pacing through a demolition site – the factory being torn down, where the factory head Xie Qianli has just found a piece of jade. A female employee jokingly accuses him of being partial, having built the men's bathroom with gems. Xie orders the workers to "bring it all down (*chai chai chai, dou chai le*)" and that someone send the gem to "Master Zhang" in the city for examination. (This entire sequence, from Four Eyes' coming out of the car to Xie's orders, is complete in twenty seconds, making it almost impossible for first-time viewers to follow everything.) Four Eyes acts pretentiously bossy to the workers before saying to Xie: "[Old] Xie, you are really something. [You] haven't paid anyone in eight months. Yet you are still doing such impressive work."[2] Xie responds impatiently: "What is it?" Four Eyes continues: "[Our] Chairman Feng understands your situation. He understands you can't pay back the loan. Seeing as you already mortgaged the land to us, [Our] Chairman Feng has drafted [another] contract. So sign it, and we'll call it even." As Xie looks at the paperwork, Four Eyes says: "I am telling you. Lay everyone off early. Now that would be a good deed."[3] Xie responds: "Don't we still have another three weeks? Such a fart-sized issue. What are you hollering about?" He shuffles the contract back to Four Eyes and calls out to the workers: "Chai [Bring it down]!" And down goes a wall right behind Four Eyes, accompanied by the workers' exclamations. Annoyed by the debris that is falling on him, Four Eyes yells: "Watch out!" – as he dusts himself off – "My Western suit!"[4]

As this sequence ends, a view from inside a microwave follows, with a male voice saying "Salute! Kow-tow . . . What? [You don't know anything?] I should just nuke you?" As the microwave door opens, Daoge holds up a puppy, saying "Heh, I am really going to do it!" as he puts the dog into the microwave and closes the door. The scene cuts to Daoge and two followers in blue uniforms bringing some furniture downstairs before nervously stopping on the ground floor of a residential building. A point-of-view shot from where they stand shows a policeman who is copying information at the front of their truck (which has a "House Mover" sign on its side). The camera cuts back to the three: "What are you looking at? Move!" orders Daoge. In a series of unsteady handheld camera shots, we see them come out to meet the policeman, who charges them for parking illegally. As Xiaojun shows his driver's license on demand, Daoge tries to ingratiate himself with the policeman by offering him a cigarette: "We are moving house. If we can't park here, where can we park?" Meanwhile, Heipi goes to the back of the truck, picks up a hammer and quietly moves toward the policeman from behind. Just as he raises the hammer to attack, a crashing noise accompanies a collision involving a BMW. As Heipi and the police look to their right, the camera follows their point of view and pans quickly to a slanting street nearby, where several men are shown running toward the site of the crash. Having seen that, the police shuts his notebook and says: "Rules are rules, even if you are moving house. Go!" as he gives back the license. When he leaves the scene on his motorcycle, Daoge curses and opens the truck's door.

The truck door then quickly cuts to a trunk door being opened by Four Eyes. He riffles through the trunk and finds a bottle of spray paint. He shakes the bottle and walks toward a wall, cursing: "Damn shit! Some people got to learn the hard way. [The original is "No crying till the sight of a coffin," a well-known idiom.] Dumb shit [Demolish you to death]!" He arrives at the wall, on which he sprays some characters in yellow: "Carefully arrange today's . . ." He decides to spray on the character "arrange" (*pai*) to change the right radical of the character so as to turn the whole figure into "demolish" (*chai*). As he continues to paint a circle around it (making it resemble one of the most prevalent signs in the areas inflicted by the Three Gorges Dam, as also seen in Jia Zhangke's award-winning *Still Life*), a shot from his right shows a van in the background slowly moving toward his car, with two men running behind it. As the van hits the car, Four Eyes turns and yells "Son of a bitch!" as he leaves the wall with the encircled "demolish" sign behind.

A female radio voice is heard as the image of the wall fades into an image of two hands holding a lottery ticket, announcing "The winning numbers for the fifth prize are. . . ." As the numbers go on, the hands move along with those on the ticket, and on the third number, the scene cuts to a front-view shot of Baotou driving a van, with Sanbao in the passenger's seat. Sanbao tears the ticket apart and Baotou sneers: "You'll be struck dead eight times by lightning before you win anything. [You are still buying?]" Sanbao retorted: "The doctor said you shouldn't even ride a bike, what are you doing driving a car?" "Aiya! Don't tell anyone. I'm practicing with the factory car," says Baotou. Sanbao taps on the radio, as the female announcer goes on: "A precious jade stone was found in a local handicraft factory. It's an extremely rare type of jade. . . ." Sanbao turns to Baotou: "Bao, they're talking about us!" "Are you nuts?" exclaims Baotou, "American dollars don't just fall from the sky!" Just as he finishes the line, an object breaks through the windshield from the sky, forcing Baotou to hit the brakes. A shot from the front finds Baotou, eyes shut, through the crack in the windshield. He slowly opens his eyes and looks at the crack in disbelief. Sanbao does the same. The radio starts to work again, intermittently playing "Water That Makes You Forget Love" (the same song played right before the Coke can fell out of the cable car). Baotou finds a crushed can beside him, and comes to realize what has happened. He and Sanbao storm out of the van, and Sanbao spots the cable car: "Bao! Up there!" The two start cursing at the tram moving by. As they do so with their backs to their van, it begins to move away down the slope. A few curses later, they turn back, and upon seeing the imminent crash immediately start chasing after the van. Their movement, crosscut with that of the van, is accompanied by a rock band on the soundtrack mixed with the sounds of Pi Pa (a Chinese instrument that resembles a banjo). As the van approaches the car, the running of the two men is shot in slow motion. When the collision takes place, a series of close-ups from several angles quickly jumps into a high-angle shot of the two vehicles.

Baotou's face appears on screen as he examines the damage, and Four Eyes is seen running toward the BMW. "Gutsy! Very high-tech!" he cries, "Auto-pilot!" He points to the car's brand: "Can't you see? You Bump Me, you Weep [the original is "Bie Mo Wo," which means "Don't touch me"]! Don't drive if you can't, you retard!" Four Eyes starts pushing Baotou, who pushes back: "Hey! Mind your manners. Don't scold me!" Four Eyes responds: "I'm scolding you. So what? So bloody what? You smashed my car, so I'm scolding you. And I'll beat you up!" He starts to push Baotou further, but is met with harsher blows from Sanbao, who pushes him to the ground. Baotou tries to stop Sanbao just as the policeman arrives at the scene. When the police asks if they "want to handle it officially or privately," Baotou quickly responds "privately." Four Eyes asks for RMB 8000 for the repair, but Baotou and Sanbao can only come up with three thousand in cash. Four Eyes then asks to keep Baotou's driver's license in case he runs away without paying the remainder of the money.[5] The sequence ends.

Silk Alley Synopsis

THE FILM OPENS WITH THE RED "SILK STREET" SIGN ON THE new plaza, followed by a zoom out to a shot of the busy Jianwai Avenue on which it is located. It is early morning, and the stalls in the building are still covered. Li, a Silk Street stall owner, is preparing breakfast, which includes freshly made soybean milk, for his nuclear family in a two-story luxury condo. He goes upstairs to wake up his daughter, whose bedroom is filled with fashion design sketches. Her long-anticipated TOEFL score is due to be released that day. The scene cuts to Thomas, an American lawyer, who is eating a Western-style breakfast (including fries) and taking pills to soothe some kind of discomfort. His British colleague, Mark, joins him and invites him to some "real Chinese" breakfast. (When offered soybean milk, he expresses some disgust at first.) Mark, who is being transferred back to the United States, gives him the location of Li's stall. He asks Thomas to collect more evidence for the counterfeited Rocker brand products sold there, even offering him a significant bonus. On the verge of early retirement after thirty years of working at the company DCA (an American firm whose full name is never specified), Thomas needs to prove himself capable, and the task seems to present exactly such an opportunity.

As Silk Street opens for the morning, the vendors and sales personnel begin to take down the covers of their stalls. A meeting to educate the vendors about intellectual property is about to take place. The market's manager, Zhang, receives a phone call about counterfeiting issues. He talks into his cell phone: "Those old traders, they have carried it on for so many years. [If] you all of a sudden want to raise intellectual property issues with them, they can't handle it."

Li drives his daughter to retrieve her TOEFL score. During the ride, she tries to persuade him to discontinue the selling of fake brands and set up his own brand or conduct licensed sales. He rebuts her by stating that the money he makes from the fakes will be used to support her education in the United States. He takes a call from Thomas, who later meets him at Silk Alley, having placed a big order for counterfeit Rocker goods. In an attempt to save the salesgirl who works for Li from an accident, Thomas falls on the steps in the market, resulting in a heart attack. Li takes Thomas to the hospital. They become friends over time, sharing stories of their daughters and family. Thomas even offers to send Li's daughter's college application to his ex-wife at New York University. When Thomas is released from the hospital, Li convinces his wife and daughter to host Thomas, twice-divorced and without a family, for the rest of his short stay in China. Thomas, though doing so betrays their friendship, continues his mission by asking Li to show him the factory where the goods are produced, claiming that his academic work at the State University of New York demands such data.

Li not only takes Thomas to his factory, hidden behind a locked gate whose opening requires a secret knock, but he has even staged a big welcome for "Professor Thomas." Thomas finally obtains enough evidence in the form of pictures of the factory. He sends them off secretly to DCA, which files a lawsuit against the market and Li himself, demanding RMB2 million ($304,000) in damages. Upon looking at the legal representative's address, which matches the one on Thomas's earlier order, the enraged Li rushes back home to question Thomas about his betrayal of his feelings and friendship. Thomas, awaiting Li, rationalizes that even though he is a friend, he has to do his job, and that the biggest cheating is Li's unauthorized use of the Rocker logo: "You stole their ideas, stole their trademark, stole their enterprise culture!" Li storms out in anger, leaving Thomas behind to suffer another heart attack. He eventually turns around, only to find Thomas in the hospital again, taken there by Li's daughter. She is now wavering about her decision to go abroad upon hearing Thomas's suggestion that with her creative talent, she can help build their family's own brand in China.

In the climactic court scene, Li confesses that counterfeiting is cheating, and in the end the person who is cheated is "one's own self."

The DCA representative accuses Li and Silk Market for costing the brand owner RMB10 million in profit. When Thomas comes to the stand, he surprises everyone by stating that this estimate is inaccurate. He argues that the loss is relative, and that Li's making and selling of counterfeits "helped the company cultivate the world's biggest market, China." Meanwhile, the daughter opens a letter from Thomas on her way to the airport, which encourages her to stay in China to realize her dream of becoming a designer.

After the verdict, which subjects Li to a RMB2 million ($304,000) fine, is announced, he and his wife pack up to leave the market, but are greeted by the manager and other vendors on the way out. The manager, patting Li's shoulder, offers him a discounted lease to build his own brand. Outside the market, just before Li boards his van, he finds his daughter waiting for her parents. With the Silk Street sign glittering in the background, the three embrace in tears.

At the end of the film, Li is shown talking to new clients at home about his newly rebranded business. His daughter, who now has her own line of "Chinese-styled" clothing, drags him to his new store. There, Thomas and his recently reunited daughter await their arrival. When Thomas's daughter asks how Li was able to get "back on his feet after only six months," Thomas responds: "That's the greatness of the Chinese people, their ability to rise from the ashes." Thomas is now bringing an $80,000 purchase order. His reason is that the clothes are "amazing" and "the design is so creative," and they will "one day turn the whole fashion world on its head." When Li arrives, the two friends, who had previously bonded as "Ge men'r" (Northern Chinese slang for "buddies") while taking shots of *bai jiu* (literally "white liquor," referring to strong distilled liquor) are finally reunited. Preceding the credits is a long shot of the plaza fading into the background as the electronic signage visibly projects "The Merchant's Bird Nest Welcomes You!"

Notes

Introduction

1. Barber, "The End of US Hegemony." The actual quote came from Gerard Lyons, the chief economist of Standard Chartered Bank.

2. Ronnie Polidoro, "Apple CEO Tim Cook Announces Plans to Manufacture Mac Computers in USA," *Rock Center with Brian Williams.*

3. Fredric Jameson, among others, has declared this collapse of the cultural into the economic and vice versa a representative condition of contemporary globalization. See Jameson, "Notes on Globalization," 60.

4. Bhattasali, Li, and Martin, *China and the WTO,* 4.

5. Appadurai, *Modernity at Large,* 39.

6. For a well-documented account of "Created in China," see Keane, *Created in China.*

7. For a recent anthropological study of the subject, see Lin, *Fake Stuff.*

8. Pang, *Creativity and Its Discontents,* 74.

9. Tomlinson, *Cultural Imperialism,* 69.

10. Lenin, "Imperialism."

11. Anderson, *Imagined Communities.* For a comprehensive anthology on studies inspired by Anderson and others, see Delanty and Kumar, *The SAGE Handbook of Nations and Nationalism.*

12. Anderson, *Imagined Communities.*

13. Ong, *Flexible Citizenship,* 40–41.

14. Appadurai, *Modernity at Large,* 33.

15. Ibid., 39.

16. Tomlinson, "Globalization and Cultural Identity," 273.

17. Ibid.

18. For a more detailed analysis of this event, see Yang, "The Politics of Exhibition."

19. Duara, "Legacy of Empires," 36–38.

20. Tomlinson, "Globalization and Cultural Identity," 276.

21. Appadurai, *Modernity at large,* 39.

22. For a detailed history of IPR, see May and Sell, *Intellectual Property Rights,* 43–74.

23. Maskus, *Intellectual Property Rights,* 1–3.

24. Biagioli, Jaszi, and Woodmansee, "Introduction," 9.

25. Tomlinson, *Globalization and Culture,* 1.

26. Ibid., 29.

27. For a more detailed analysis of this event in the context of globalizing IPR, see Yang, "China's 'Fake' Apple Store."

28. Castoriadis, *The Imaginary Institution,* 135–136.

29. Pang, *Creativity and Its Discontents,* 73.

30. May, "The denial of history." May references Marx in defining "reification" as the "abstracting of a particular set of relations into an ahistorical, naturalised (and hence non-political) set of occurrences," 40.

31. World Trade Organization, "10 things the WTO can do," 38.

32. Lee and LiPuma, "Cultures of Circulation," 193.

33. Maskus, Intellectual Property Rights, 6.

34. Vukovich, China and Orientalism, 11.

35. Ibid., 1.

36. Calhoun, Nations Matter, 156.

37. Gaonkar, "Toward New Imaginaries," 4.

38. Arnason, "Nationalism, Globalization and Modernity," 224.

39. Lee and LiPuma, "Cultures of Circulation."

40. A noteworthy example is Klein, No Logo.

41. Jenkins, Convergence Culture, 2.

42. Lash and Lury, Global Culture Industry.

43. Lee and LiPuma, "Cultures of Circulation," 192.

44. New Oxford American Dictionary, 3rd ed., s.v. "counterfeit."

45. Hopkins, Counterfeiting Exposed, 9.

46. World Intellectual Property Organization, "Understanding Copyright and Related Rights," 4.

47. The tendency to educate the general public about the illicit status of counterfeit copies is also discernible in the print and video materials included in a 2014–2015 exhibition entitled "Faking It: Originals, Copies, and Counterfeits" at the Fashion Institute of Technology in New York City.

48. Pang, "'China Who Makes and Fakes,'" 128.

49. New Oxford American Dictionary, 3rd ed., s.v. "counterfeit."

50. Lash and Lury, Global Culture Industry, 14.

51. Phillips, Knockoff, 8.

52. Office of the United States Trade Representative, Special 301 Report, 4.

53. Organization for Economic Cooperation and Development, "Magnitude of Counterfeiting and Piracy of Tangible Products: An Update," 1.

54. Hohnen, A Market Out of Place? 28.

55. Pang, "'China Who Makes and Fakes.'"

56. The Anti-Counterfeiting Group, "The Scale of Counterfeiting."

57. Reuters, Special Report: Faked in China.

58. Office of the United States Trade Representative, Special 301 Report, 35.

59. Midler, Poorly Made in China, 115–116.

60. Choate, Hot Property, 100.

61. Naim, Illicit, 117–118.

62. Phillips, Knockoff, 47.

63. For a more nuanced analysis about China's culture of copying that takes into account both historical and contemporary forces, see Bosker, Original Copies.

64. Philip, "What is a technological author?" 202–207.

65. Biagioli, Jaszi, and Woodmansee, "Introduction," 2. This introduction also provides an excellent overview of the growing critical scholarship on IP.

66. Dirlik, "Postsocialism?"

67. Ibid.

68. Anagnost, "Socialist Ethics," 179–182.

69. Harvey, Brief History of Neoliberalism; Lin, Transformation of Chinese Socialism.

70. Dirlik and Zhang, "Introduction: Postmodernism and China," 7.

71. Wang, China's New Order, 57.

72. Ibid., 83.

73. Zhang, "Nationalism," 342.

74. Rofel, *Desiring China*, 11, 164.

75. Wang, *China's new order*, 198n24.

76. Panitchpakdi and Clifford, *China and the WTO*, 2.

77. I thank Jason Loviglio for the inspiration to use this term.

78. Wang, "Culture As Leisure and Culture As Capital."

79. Jameson, "Notes on Globalization," 75.

80. Liang, "Beyond Representation," 171.

81. Chatterjee, *Nation and Its Fragments*; Desai, "Nationalisms and Their Understandings"; Desai, "Inadvertence of Benedict Anderson."

82. Chatterjee, "Nation in Heterogeneous Time."

83. Dirlik and Zhang, "Introduction: Postmodernism and China," 7.

84. Hayden, "A Generic Solution?" 489.

85. Hayden, "The Proper Copy"; Hayden, "No Patent, No Generic."

86. Latour, "Why Has Critique Run out of Steam?" 240.

1. "From Made in China to Created in China"

1. Bongiorni, "A Year without 'Made in China,'" 5.

2. Bongiorni, *A Year without "Made in China*," 24.

3. Following Guobin Yang, among others, I use "global media" in this book to refer to "the network of leading media corporations in the world that have a global reach and impact, such as BBC, CNN, *The New York Times*, and *The Guardian*." See Yang, "Power and Transgression," 174.

4. Watts, "Made in China."

5. Bongiorni, *A Year Without "Made in China*," 1–2.

6. Ibid., 2.

7. See Frank, *Buy American*.

8. The General Agreement on Tariffs and Trade (GATT), for instance, did not standardize this requirement for its participating nations until the Uruguay Round of Multinational Trade Negotiations (the Uruguay Round) in 1986.

9. Palmer and Nickel, "U.S. to Appeal WTO Ruling against Meat Labels."

10. Ibid.

11. Marx, "Capital, Volume One," 302–329.

12. Appadurai, *Modernity at Large*, 41–42.

13. Ross, *Fast Boat to China*, 26.

14. Asia Times Online, "China Surpasses US As Most Attractive FDI Nation."

15. Perkowski, "China Leads in Foreign Direct Investment."

16. United States Customs and Border Protection, *U.S. Rules of Origin*.

17. Koopman, Wang, and Wei, "The myth of 'Made in China.'"

18. Frank, *Buy American*.

19. Ibid., 233. In recent years, the popular revolt against corporate outsourcing has arguably generated more antagonism toward the MNCs themselves. In the debates leading up to the 2012 U.S. presidential election, however, "Made in China" remained a prominent scapegoat for both parties whenever America's hegemony was questioned. The notorious "Debbie Spend It Now" campaign ad for a Michigan senate candidate, which engendered numerous charges of racism in the Asian-Pacific community, is a case in point.

20. Linden, Kraemer, and Dedrick, "The case of Apple's iPod," 10.

21. Appadurai, *Modernity at Large*, 42.

22. Smith, *Millennial Dreams*, 39.

23. Cable News Network, "Made in China, Part 1."

24. Ibid.

25. Cable News Network, "Made in China, Part 2."

26. Anderson, *Imagined Communities*, 26.

27. Bhabha, "DissemiNation," 294–297.

28. Lash and Lury, *Global Culture Industry*, 182.

29. Ibid., 6.

30. Martin, *Financialization of Daily Life*, 197.

31. Lury, *Brands*, 2.

32. Klein, *No Logo*.

33. Doane, "Information, Crisis, Catastrophe," 252–261.

34. Aronczyk, "New and Improved Nations" 114.

35. Bongiorni, *A Year without "Made in China,"* 39–41. One moment of surprise came when the family could not "afford" to buy beach toys for the summer; they ended up clearing the "debris" of "other people's Chinese trash" on the San Diego beach, an experience they would not have had if they had gone "the traditional route," 132–133.

36. Ibid., 227.

37. Smith, *Primitive America*, 30–31.

38. Ibid., 31.

39. Bongiorni, *A Year without "Made in China,"* 221.

40. Ibid., 197.

41. Bongiorni has included a sample list of questions asked by this reporter. See ibid., 222.

42. Ibid., 223.

43. CCTV, "'Xiangxin zhonguo zhizao'" ["Chinese Products Are of High Quality"].

44. Ibid.

45. Ibid.

46. Dyer, "CCTV Opens 'Believe in "Made in China."'"

47. CCTV, *Shijie zhoukan*, "Meiguoren meiyou zhongguo zhizao" ["Life without 'Made in China'"].

48. Ibid.

49. Ibid.

50. Zhao, *Communication in China*, 151.

51. CCTV, *Shijie zhoukan*, "Meiguoren meiyou zhongguo zhizao" ["Life without 'Made in China'"].

52. Pan, "Yiyuzhe yanzhong de zhongguo zhizao" ["'Made in China' in Foreigners' Eyes"].

53. Gerth, *China Made*, 18.

54. Wang, *Brand New China*, 118.

55. Li, "Branding Chinese Products."

56. Wang, *Brand New China*, 33.

57. Ibid., 142.

58. See the elaborate introduction of the term in Gaonkar, "Toward New Imaginaries."

59. "Made in China ads."

60. Canaves, "Makeover Attempt For 'Made in China.'"

61. *Wall Street Journal*, "Melamine Discovered in More Milk Products."

62. *Beijing ribao*, "'Zhongguo zhizao' guanggao" ["'Made in China' Theme Underwent Changes"].

63. Yin and Li, "Zhongguo zai quanqiu toufang xingxiang guanggao" ["China Projects Image Ad"].

64. Li, "Ruhe tisheng wenhua ruanshili."

65. Hu, *Hu Jintao zai dang de shiqida shang de baogao*.

66. See a more elaborate application of this Lacanian notion in Yang, "The Politics of Exhibition."

67. ["'Made in China' Theme Underwent Changes"].

68. CCTV, "'Xiangxin zhonguo zhizao'" ["Chinese Products Are of High Quality"].

69. Yin and Li, "Zhongguo zai quanqiu toufang xingxiang guanggao" ["China Projects Image Ad"].

70. *Beijing ribao*, "'Zhongguo zhizao' guanggao" ["'Made in China' Theme Underwent Changes"].

71. CCTV, "'Xiangxin zhonguo zhizao'" ["Chinese Products Are of High Quality"].

72. Hong, Lu, and Zou, "CCTV in the Reform Years," 40.

73. Lull, *China Turned On,* 22.

74. Sun, "Dancing with Chains," 188.

75. Ibid., 189.

76. Ibid., 188.

77. Zhao, "The Media Matrix," 200.

78. Lu Xun's work is routinely taught in China's high-school Chinese classes. While not all those who have read *The Story of Ah Q* can articulate its historical significance and/or critical nuances, most high-school graduates are aware of the general storyline. For one of the more famous readings in the English language, see Jameson, "Third-World Literature."

79. Wangxiang dailiren [Agent of Delusion], "Yangshi tuichu 'Zhongguo zhizao' xilie zao pengji" ["'Made in China' Series Attacked"].

80. Zhao, *Communication in China,* 287–338.

81. Lang, "Zhongguo zhizao zai haiwai" ["'Made in China' Overseas"].

82. The three commentators on the program then pointed out that the choice of CNN as the media outlet for the ad made it even more ironic, since the channel had been known for its "China-bashing," for which it had been rebuked many times online the year before.

83. Keane, *Created in China,* 85.

84. Su, "Cultural resources," 307.

85. Keane, *Created in China,* 85.

86. Su cited a 2004 CCIA branding campaign in the form of a "wheaten food festival" in Taiyuan, a poverty-stricken coal-mining town in northern inland China's Shanxi province.

87. Keane, *Created in China,* 83, 170.

88. Ibid., 78. The plan was ratified in the fourth session of the Ninth People's Congress in 2001, the same year in which the country acceded to the World Trade Organization (WTO).

89. Ibid., 61, 78.

90. A key document in this regard is Mao's 1944 essay "Mao Zedong: Wei Renmin Fuwu" ["Mao Zedong: Serve the People"].

91. Keane, *Created in China,* 80–81. The promises of "Created in China" include "wealth creation, renewal of traditional resources, enhanced productivity combined with cleaner greener production, education curricula revitalisation, and the ever-present theme of industrial catch-up."

92. Ibid., 61.

93. Su, "Cultural resources," 312.

94. CCTV, "Kuayue Zhongguo zhizao" ["Across 'Made in China'"]. The opening sequence of the first episode emphasizes the role of Chinese labor in shaping the global economy by comparing the American average wage in the 1990s, $16 per hour, with the Chinese one, $0.50 per hour. This "attractive" human resource, priced at 3.1 percent of the US rate, not only comes in "great quantity," but also "quick-learning quality."

95. Qi, "Zhuazhu jiyu shixian Zhongguo chuangzao" ["Grasp the Opportunity to Achieve 'Created in China'"].

96. Si, "Cong Zhongguo zhizao dao Zhongguo chuangzao" ["From 'Made in China' to 'Created in China'"].

97. Wang, "Tisheng 'Zhongguo chuangzao' yingdui jinrong weiji" ["Elevating 'Created in China'"].

98. CCTV, "Kuayue Zhongguo zhizao" ["Across 'Made in China'"].

99. Meisner, *Mao's China and after.*

100. CCTV, "Kuayue Zhongguo zhizao" ["Across 'Made in China'"].

101. Qi, "Zhuazhu jiyu shixian Zhongguo chuangzao" ["Grasp the Opportunity to Achieve 'Created in China'"].

102. Bhabha, "DissemiNation."

103. Hu, "Cong 'Zhongguo zhizao' dao 'Zhongguo chuangzao' ["From 'Made in China' to 'Created in China'"].

104. Ibid.

105. Sun, "Shida zhanlue" ["Ten Major Strategies"]; Xun, "Jingji weiji xia Zhongguo" ["Crisis and Resolution of 'Made in China'"].

106. Lash and Lury, *Global Culture Industry*, 183.

107. Wang, *Yazhou Shiye* [Narrations of Chinese History], 313–314. Here, Wang questions Charles Taylor's distinction between the "secular time" presented in the political and economic imaginaries of John Locke and Adam Smith and the "higher time" of the age of religion. He poses the following question to Taylor: "Does the 'secular time' of capitalism include a 'higher time'? If we situate the fetishism of money in this problematic, the latter's power in dictating horizontal activities perhaps cannot be ignored."

108. The former consists of traditional industry leaders, like Liang Zhaoxian, of Galanz, a Guangdong-based microwave company, whereas the latter includes service industry types, such as Michael Yu Minhong, who became successful in founding New Oriental, an educational institution famous for TOEFL (Test of English as a Foreign Language) and GRE preparation for overseas college and graduate school applicants (more on this in chapter 5).

109. Zhang, "Cong 'Zhongguo zhizao' dao 'Zhongguo chuangzao' haiyou duoyuan" ["How Far Is It from 'Made in China' to 'Created in China'?"].

110. Lang, "Zhongguo zhizao zai haiwai" ["'Made in China' Overseas"].

2. From Bandit Cell Phones to Branding the Nation

1. Wang, "Shanzhai wenhua de yousi" ["Troubled Thoughts on Shanzhai Culture"], 39.

2. Xinhua, "'Shanzhai': Faking it for money or fun?"

3. Yu Hua, the renowned Chinese novelist who included "Shanzhai" (translated as "copycat") as one of the key lenses through which to dissect contemporary China, emphasized that as "a name once given to the lairs of outlaws and bandits," the term "has continued to have connotations of freedom from official control." See Yu, *China in Ten Words*, 181.

4. Lion Rock Mountain is a geographical landmark that has come to symbolize the identity of refugee migrants pouring into Hong Kong from all over China. See Luqiu Luwei, "Liaoliao Shanzhai" ["A chat on Shanzhai"].

5. Pang, *Creativity and Its Discontents*, 222.

6. An instant sensation, Hu's video mocks the award-winning director Chen Kaige's multi-million-dollar production, *The Promise* (2005). For a detailed analysis, see Gong and Yang, "Digitized Parody."

7. See Meng, "Regulating egao."

8. Wang and Xing, "Shanzhai wenhua zongheng tan" ["Open Discussion on Shanzhai Culture"], 62.

9. Tai Xing Xia Ke, "Shanzhai wenhua de minjian kuanghuan" ["Popular Carnival of Shanzhai Culture"].

10. See, for example, Barboza, "Knockoff Cellphones"; Farrar, "China's 'bandit phones'"; Canaves and Ye, "The Sincerest Form of Rebellion."

11. See, for example, Ho, "Shan-Zhai"; Lin, "Knockoff."

12. Farrar, "China's 'bandit phones.'"

13. Wallis and Qiu, "Transformation of the Local Mediascape."

14. Ibid.

15. Lash and Lury, *Global Culture Industry*, 4–7.

16. Barboza, "Knockoff Cellphones."

17. Cartier, *Globalizing South China*, 3–4.

18. See Pun, *Made in China*.

19. Barboza, "Knockoff Cellphones."

20. Lin, "Knockoff," 67.

21. Zhang and Ning, "Shanzhai shouji chanye diaocha" ["Shanzhai Cell Phone Industry Investigation"].

22. *Shouji daigong wang*, "Shanzhaiji shinian fazhan licheng" ["Developmental Path of Shanzhai Handsets"].

23. Gao, "Pouxi Shanzhai shouji shichang xianxiang" ["Dissecting the Market Phenomenon of Shanzhai Cell Phones"].

24. The concept of "vector" comes from the various writings of Paul Virilio, such as *Speed and Politics*. As McKenzie Wark explains, Virilio uses it to refer to "any trajectory along which bodies, information, or warheads can potentially pass." This is the formulation that I adopt here. See Wark, *Virtual Geography*, 11.

25. This is a quote by a Shanzhaiji sales rep. See Liu, "Jueqizhong de kunhuo: Shanzhai shouji jiang hequhecong?" ["Puzzle amid the Rise"], 44.

26. Ji, "Shanzhai zhongshengxiang: cong Shanzhai xianxiang kan zhongguoshi chuangxin" ["Panorama of Shanzhai"].

27. Ibid.

28. Qiu, "Wangluo shidai de 'Shanzhai wenhua'" ["Shanzhai Culture in the Network Age"], 127.

29. Wallis and Qiu, "Transformation of the Local Mediascape."

30. Chen, "Yidong dianhua zhizaoye: waishang zhijie touzi yichu xiaoying anli yanjiu" ["The Spillover Effect of Foreign Direct Investment"].

31. Xue, "Xinchanbu cheng bufa shouji xin paizhao, 3G shouji wu paizhao menkan" ["Ministry Will Issue No New Licenses"].

32. Qiu, *Working-Class Network Society*, 13.

33. Wallis, "'Immobile Mobility,'" 69.

34. He, "Nongmingong xinxihua shengcun baogao" ["Peasant Workers' Informational Survival Report"].

35. Zheng, "Shanzhai shouji weihe shou nongmingong xiongdi qinglai?" ["Why are Shanzhai handsets favored by peasant workers?"].

36. Qiu, "Wangluo shidai de 'Shanzhai wenhua'" ["Shanzhai Culture in the Network Age"] 125.

37. Zheng, "Shanzhai shouji weihe shou nongmingong xiongdi qinglai?" ["Why are Shanzhai handsets favored by peasant workers?"].

38. Castells, *Mobile Communication and Society*.

39. Wallis and Qiu, "Transformation of the Local Mediascape," 110.

40. Barboza, "Knockoff Cellphones."

41. Li, "Xinshengdai nongmin gong qingku e shenghuo" ["Peasant Workers' E-life"].

42. Hong, "Shanzhai shouji shi 'minzu yingxiong'?" ["Shanzhai Cell Phones are 'National Heroes?'"].

43. Sun, "Shenzhen zaixian da heishouji fengbao, jingxiaoshang jinchan tuoke konggui yingdui" ["Shenzhen Re-Stirred the Storm of Black Cell Phone Crackdown, Dealers Responded with Empty Counters"].

44. Ibid.

45. Chang, "Fake logos, fake theory, fake globalization," 233.

46. Chen, "Jiang Zemin 'zouchuqu' zhanlue de xingcheng ji qi zhongyao yiyi" ["Jiang Zemin's 'Going Global' strategy"].

47. Sun, "Guanzhu guochan shouji fazhan, tanqiu guochan shouji zouchuqu zhi lu" ["In Search of Ways of Going Global"].

48. "'Shouji zhong de zhandouji' anran pojiang, bodao jiannan shengcun" ["'The fighter jet of handsets' forced to land"].

49. Lin, "Knockoff," iv.

50. Barboza, "Knockoff Cellphones."
51. Zeng, "Tianyu: 'Shanzhaiji' moshi cheng diyu yangpinpai yitianjian? ["Tianyu: the 'Shanzhaiji' Model?"].
52. Qiu, *Working-Class Network Society,* 13.
53. Groening, "Connected Isolation."
54. Wallis, "'Immobile Mobility,'" 77.
55. Li, "Shanzhai wenhua: Web 2.0 shidai de caogen kuanghuan" ["Grass-Roots Carnival"].
56. Li, "Popular Culture beyond the Fortress."
57. Wu Yue San Ren, "Shanzhai wenhua shi yizhong fanshi zhuanhuan" ["Shanzhai Culture is a Paradigm Shift"].
58. Lin, "Knockoff," 206.
59. Currently existing online forums on Shanzhai include a Shanzhai Ba (*ba,* literally "bar") on *Baidu Tieba* (literally "Baidu posting bar"), an online bulletin board. The earliest post there dates from July 9, 2008, prior to most mainstream media coverage.
60. YunQingCheng, "Wo 'Shanzhai' gu wo zai" ["I Shanzhai, Therefore I Am"].
61. Schiller, "An Update on China," 113.
62. See, for example, Sohu IT, "Most Shocking Shanzhaiji."
63. See Wang, "The Global Reach of a New Discourse: How Far Can 'Creative Industries' Travel?"; Pang, *Creativity and Its Discontents.*
64. Pang, "'China Who Makes and Fakes,'" 124.
65. Jenkins, "Quentin Tarantino's Star Wars?" 288.
66. Lee and LiPuma, "Cultures of Circulation."
67. Fish, *Is There a Text in This Class?*
68. Xi Xiao Tang, "Wangyou ping 08 wei 'Shanzhai nian,' shida Shanzhai shijian chulu" ["Year 08 as 'The Year of Shanzhai'"].
69. For an ethnographic account of this "DIY (do-it-yourself) maker culture"

and its participants' identification with the "Shanzhai" mode of production in Shenzhen, see Lindtner, "Hackerspaces and the Internet of Things in China."
70. Lury, *Brands,* 8.
71. Ibid., 85–96.
72. Ibid., 96.
73. Jenkins, "Quentin Tarantino's Star Wars?"
74. Meisner, *Mao's China and after.*
75. Ah Gan, *Shanzhai Geming* [Revolution of Mode of Production], 30.
76. Pang, *Creativity and Its Discontents.*
77. Sun, "Dancing with Chains."
78. Lu, "Ritual, Television, and State Ideology," 119.
79. Lao Meng, "Shanzhai chunwan jiemu zhengji" ["Shanzhai Gala Program Call"].
80. Zhou, Zeng, and Jing, "Jingji banxiaoshi: jiemu shouji Shanzhaiji shichang" ["Half-Hour Economy"].
81. *Renmin wang,* "2008 Zhongguo 'Shanzhai' nian, meiti Shanzhai fengchao hen qiang hen badao" ["China's Year of 'Shanzhai'"].
82. *Baidu baike* [Baidupedia]. "Shanzhai."
83. *Xinwen lianbo,* "Shanzhai shouji jin xinwen lianbo le" ["Shanzhai Cell Phones Got into Network News Broadcast"].
84. Xia, "'Shanzhai' wenhua de chuanboxue jiedu" ["Decoding 'Shanzhai' culture"], 20.
85. Bolter and Grusin, *Remediation,* 47.
86. *Xinwen lianbo,* "Shanzhai shouji jin xinwen lianbo le" ["Shanzhai Cell Phones Got into Network News Broadcast"].
87. Ibid.
88. Hong, Lu, and Zou, "CCTV in the Reform Years," 49.
89. Yang, *The Power of the Internet in China.*
90. Althusser, *Reading Capital.*
91. Wang, "Culture As Leisure," 92.

92. Hong, Lu, and Zou, "CCTV in the Reform Years," 50.

93. CCTV Chinese Finance and Economics Reports, *Shanzhai Laile* [Shanzhai is Coming], iv–v.

94. Ibid., v.

95. Ibid.

96. Pang, *Creativity and Its Discontents*, 3–7.

97. For detailed examples, see Keane, *Created in China*; Pang, *Creativity and Its Discontents*.

98. Jameson, "Notes on Globalization," 75.

99. CCTV Chinese Finance and Economics Reports, *Shanzhai Laile* [Shanzhai is Coming], 205.

100. Ibid.

101. Lindsay, "China's Cell Phone Pirates."

102. Wang, "Culture As Leisure and Culture As Capital."

103. Zhao, *Communication in China*, 14.

3. *Crazy Stone*, National Cinema, and Counterfeit (Film) Culture

1. See synopsis in Appendix 1.

2. Song, "Fengkuang de Shitaou" ["*Crazy Stone*: A Very Commercialized Genre Film"].

3. Some of the earliest book-length publications include Clark, *Chinese Cinema*; Stemsel, *Chinese Film*; Berry, *Perspectives on Chinese Cinema*.

4. Berry, "Cinema: From Foreign Import to Global Brand," 297.

5. Berry and Farquhar, *China on Screen*, 14.

6. Lu, "Chinese Cinemas (1896–1996) and Transnational Film Studies"; Zhang, *Chinese National Cinema*; Metzger and Khoo, "Introduction."

7. Pang, "The Institutionalization of 'Chinese' Cinema."

8. Higson, "The Limiting Imagination Of National Cinema," 69.

9. Zhao, *Communication in China*, 163.

10. Chow, *Primitive Passions*, 59.

11. While I do not mean to equate the notion of "citizenry" with that of "residency," my emphasis here is less on the deterritorialized making of Chinessness via "flexible citizenship," à la Aihwa Ong, than on the effect of Hollywood hegemony in obscuring other means of cinematic nation making. I will return to the idea of citizenry with a more class-based focus later in this chapter.

12. Higson, "The Concept of National Cinema," 36.

13. Ibid., 38–42.

14. Ibid., 36.

15. Schlesinger, "The Sociological Scope of 'National Cinema,'" 17.

16. Ryall, *Alfred Hitchcock & the British Cinema*, 2.

17. Wang, *Framing Piracy*.

18. Zhang, "Playing with Intertextuality"; Pang, "Piracy/Privacy"; Xu, *Sinascape*; Li, "From D-Buffs to the D-Generation: Piracy, Cinema, and an Alternative Public Sphere in Urban China."

19. Zhang, *Screening China*, 38.

20. Clark, *Chinese Cinema*, 39–41. Even during the Maoist Era, when non-Soviet foreign cultural products were prohibited by and large for the public, Mao's wife was known to enjoy Hollywood films in private. See MacFarquhar, *Mao's Last Revolution*, 100.

21. Clark, *Chinese Cinema*, 137. For example, domestically famed director Xie Jin, whose work crossed over from the Maoist to the post-Mao era, often featuring melodramatic portrayals of heroism and everyday life, openly acknowledged the impact of American films (a great number of which he watched in 1930s Shanghai) on his filmmaking. See Stemsel, *Chinese Film*, 112.

22. Rosen, "The Wolf at the Door," 52.

23. Ibid., 54–56.

24. Ibid., 56. Rosen's term "domestic releases" likely refers to *guochanpian*, literally "state-produced films."

25. Yeh and Davis, "Re-Nationalizing China's Film Industry," 39.

26. Wang, *Framing Piracy*, 63.

27. Rosen, "The Wolf at the Door," 50.

28. Zhao, *Communication in China*, 163.

29. Ibid.

30. Yeh and Davis, "Re-Nationalizing China's Film Industry."

31. Zhang, *The Cinema of Feng Xiaogang*, 1.

32. Rosen, "The Wolf at the Door," 68.

33. McGrath, *Postsocialist Modernity*, 165–166.

34. De Kloet, "Crossing the Threshold," 66.

35. Zhang, *The Cinema of Feng Xiaogang*, 15.

36. McGrath, *Postsocialist Modernity*, 199.

37. Zhang, *The Cinema of Feng Xiaogang*, 15.

38. Zhang, *Screening China*, 320.

39. McGrath, *Postsocialist Modernity*, 196.

40. These films are characterized above all by huge production values and dynastic themes, and are often seen as attempts to emulate the success of Ang Lee's Oscar-winning hit, *Couching Tiger, Hidden Dragon.*

41. Wang, "Global Hollywood," 131.

42. Wang, "Understanding Local Reception," 300.

43. Zhao, *Communication in China*, 163.

44. Ibid., 165.

45. Osnos, "The Long Shot"; Zhang, "Yingxiong: xinshiji de yinyu" ["HERO: A Metaphor for the New Century"]; Cui, "Tianxia yingxiong shi guaren" ["The Hero of the World is the Emperor Myself"].

46. Larson, "Zhang Yimou's 'Hero,'" 184.

47. Berry, "'What's Big about the Big Film?,'" 224.

48. Wang, "Understanding Local Reception," 299–300.

49. Ryall, *Alfred Hitchcock & the British Cinema*, 2.

50. Pang, *Cultural Control and Globalization in Asia*, 104.

51. Zhang, *Cinema, Space, and Polylocality*, 166. In one of his later films, Jia has also self-reflexively depicted an exchange between the protagonist and a street vendor who sells pirated copies of his early work. Pang, *Cultural Control*, 104.

52. See, for example, Xu, *Sinascape*.

53. Berry, "'If China Can Say No, Can China Make Movies?'"132, cited in Pang, *Cultural Control*, 110.

54. Pang, *Cultural Control*, 110.

55. Williams, "Discipline and Fun," cited in ibid., 109.

56. Ibid.

57. Zhang, *Cinema, Space, and Polylocality*, 35–36.

58. Pang, *Cultural Control and Globalization in Asia*, 110.

59. Ibid., 109.

60. Jameson, "Notes on Globalization."

61. Jameson, *The Political Unconscious*, 26.

62. Jameson, *The Geopolitical Aesthetic*, 26.

63. Bolter and Grusin, *Remediation*, 5.

64. Ibid., 55.

65. Smith, *Clint Eastwood*, xii.

66. This direction is in line with the growing exploratory efforts in search of new methods and approaches in the field of Chinese cinema, where there is an increasing call for attention to both digitalized cultures and the venues for popular criticism they open up. See Leung and Yue, "Chinese Cinemas," 6; Leung, "Unthinking"; De Kloet, "Crossing the

Threshold"; Zhang, *Cinema, Space, and Polylocality*.

67. Smith, *Clint Eastwood*, xii.

68. Ma and Ding, "Fengkuang de Shitou: 'san wu' chanpin ruhe huoyi 300%?" ["How Did a 'Three Nothing' Product Gain 300% Returns?"].

69. Lau's stardom in Greater China (and indeed throughout East Asia) is comparable to that of Brad Pitt's in the United States.

70. Seno, "A Hong Kong Star Extends His Reach."

71. Ibid.

72. Guan and Zhu, "Fengkuang de Shitou 6 yue 30 ri qi dou ni mei shangliang" ["*Crazy Stone*, Starting June 30, Entertains Without Reservation"].

73. *Caijing shibao* [Business Times], "Wangluo faxing + 'egao' quanqian zhuti: shitou rang quanguo fengkuang" ["Internet Distribution + 'E Gao' Baiting Themes: *Stone* Makes the Whole Country Crazy"].

74. Wei and Zhu, "Fengkuang de Shitou piaofang tupo qianwan" ["*Crazy Stone* Box Office over Ten Million"].

75. hkfilmart.com, "Crazy Stone's Chinese Box Office."

76. In fact, Lau had expressed interest in making a cameo appearance in all of his First Cut films, but he was injured in the shooting of another action feature before *Crazy Stone* was completed, and therefore did not make the schedule. See "Fengkuang de Shitou zhuanlun" ["Special Comments on *Crazy Stone*"]. One of Lau's popular songs can be heard on several occasions as background music in *Crazy Stone*, which triggered immediate recognition among the audience, who were invariably amused by Lau's absent presence. See Wang, Liu, and Jiang, "Dianying Fengkuang de Shitou: yici chenggong de shangyepian tuwei" ["The Film

Crazy Stone: A Successful Breakthrough by Commercial Films"], 30.

77. Yuan, "Jingji banxiaoshi" ["Half-Hour Economy"] This high return made it stand out among the over four hundred productions made in China that year. See Coonan, "China Bound to Tradition."

78. Ma and Ding, "Fengkuang de Shitou: 'san wu' chanpin ruhe huoyi 300%?" ["How Did a 'Three Nothing' Product Gain 300% Returns?"]. Founded in 2004, Warner China Film HG Corporation was "the first Sino-foreign joint venture filmed-entertainment company in the history of the People's Republic of China. See TimeWarner.com, "Warner China Film HG Corporation." In addition to China Film Group, a state-owned enterprise, and TimeWarner, a transnational corporation, the third company in this partnership is the Hengdian Group, a Zhejiang-based township and village enterprise specializing in silk production that turned to the culture sector in 1995. See Hengdian Group, "About Us." Blending the film studio model with cultural tourism, Hengdian became the first entity of its kind in China on April 2, 2004, when the State Administration of Radio, Film, and Television announced the establishment of the Zhejiang Hengdian Film and Television Industry Experiment Zone. Quickly becoming a major production base in Asia for international film crews, the zone was also famous for creating opportunities for local village peasants to work as movie extras. See Zhao, *Communication in China*, 230–231.

79. Ma and Ding, "Fengkuang de Shitou: 'san wu' chanpin ruhe huoyi 300%?" ["How Did a 'Three Nothing' Product Gain 300% Returns?"].

80. *Caijing shibao* [Business Times].

81. *Jinghua shibao* [Beijing Times], "20 yu bu guochanpian jiang zhanying: Liang

Wenli houhui mei yan Tian Gou" ["Over Twenty Domestic Films to Exhibit"].

82. Zhu, *Chinese Cinema During the Era of Reform*, 88.

83. Liu, "Guanzhong repeng Fengkuang de Shitou: youxiu guochanpian zhanying daidong guanying rechao" ["Audience Applauds *Crazy Stone*"].

84. Bao, "Juanshouyu: Fengkuang de Shitou" ["Foreword: Crazy Stone"].

85. Xu, "Fengkuang de Shitou 'nishi' zouhong" ["Crazy Stone Becomes Popular Against All Odds"].

86. Wu, "Toushi wenlu – guanyu yingpian Fengkuang de Shitou" ["Dropping a Stone for Directions: About the Film Crazy Stone"]. Not only do online and print media accounts of its production and distribution abound, a search in the China National Knowledge Infrastructure databases also yielded over eighty reviews (most of which are positive) by film critics and media scholars published in academic journals and film magazines.

87. Feng's films are rated around seven on average, but the total number of raters for them is much larger than that of *Stone*.

88. Sun, "Fengkuang de Shitou: guochan dianying cong shehua huigui pingmin" ["*Crazy Stone:* Domestic Cinema Returns from Luxury to the Common Folks"].

89. Yuan, "Jingji banxiaoshi" ["Half-Hour Economy"] An employee of a foreign company in Shanghai reportedly said "I bump your lung" at a meeting, which is a line in Cantonese used by a key character in the film several times to express his anger at unfavorable situations. This behavior, apparently widespread in the white-collar community in Shanghai, resulted in not only a severe reprimand from the boss but also the issuing of a company-wide ban on "*Stone* language" at work. See Wang and Han, "Bailing yong Fengkuang

de Shitou duibai renao shangsi" ["White-Collar Employee's Use of *Crazy Stone* Dialogue Angered the Boss"].

90. *Baidu tieba* [Baidu Posting Board]. "Guanyu zhichi Fengkuang de Shitou changyi" ["A Proposal for Supporting *Crazy Stone*"].

91. Yu, "From Active Audience to Media Citizenship," 308.

92. Ibid., 310.

93. *Baidu tieba* [Baidu Posting Board]. "Guanyu zhichi Fengkuang de Shitou changyi" ["A Proposal for Supporting *Crazy Stone*"].

94. Kang, "Fengkuang de Shitou weihe ruci fengkuang?" ["Why Is Crazy Stone So Crazy?"], 80.

95. Ibid., 79.

96. Zhang, "Cong Fengkuang de Shitou shilun Zhongguo dianying de fazhan" ["Discussion on the Development of Chinese Cinema"].

97. Si, "Ping Fengkuang de Shitou: yi xifang de mingyi chaoyue" ["On *Crazy Stone:* Transcendence in the Name of Parody"].

98. Ge and Piao, "Fengkuang de Shitou xiaofei jiegou fenxi" ["An Analysis of the Consumption Structure of *Crazy Stone*"], 39.

99. Hou, "Caogen-shugen-jigen-wugen" ["Grassroots, Tree Roots, Thorny Roots, Rootless"], 133.

100. *Wangyi*, "Ninghao fouren Fengkuang de Shitou chaoxi Gai Ruiqi" ["Ning Hao Denies That *Crazy Stone* Copies Guy Ritchie"].

101. In this sequence, Tommy throws Turkish's milk carton out the truck window; it hits the windshield of the car driven by Bullet-Tooth Tony, with Boris the Blade in the trunk. As the car hits the wall, Boris escapes but remains blindfolded and bound. A parallel sequence shows Sol and his cohorts in a different car, as Sol,

challenged by Vinnie on his knowledge of guns, shoots a handgun through the car's ceiling. As the three passengers continue to argue, the car runs right into Boris – a scene observed later by Bullet-Tooth Tony and Cousin Avi in their sequence.

102. Yuchen. "[Zhuantie] Fengkuang de Shitou huo fengkuang de chaoxi?" ["Repost: *Crazy Stone* or *Crazy Copying*?"]. This post appeared even before July 17. Somehow the original post cannot be located, only a repost.

103. Ibid.

104. According to the same blogger, this and several other "copying" incidents reflect certain people's shameless pursuit of quick profits during the primary stage of China's industrialization of culture." See *Du erduo de gushi* [Stories of Wooden Ears], "Wo lai shoushuo Fengkuang de Shitou" ["My Comments on *Crazy Stone*"].

105. baohulutime, "Fengkuang de Shitou shi chetouchewei de buyaolian chaoxi" ["*Crazy Stone* is Completely, Shamelessly Copied"].

106. Yajun, "Chaode! Gemen'er, fengkuang de shitou shi zui yunong ren de zuopin" ["Copied! Bro, *Crazy Stone* is the Most Deceptive Work"].

107. *Wangyi*, "Ninghao fouren Fengkuang de Shitou chaoxi Gai Ruiqi" ["Ning Hao Denies That *Crazy Stone* Copies Guy Ritchie"], February 11, 2009.

108. Ning, "The Making of *Crazy Stone*.

109. *Xinwen chenbao* [Shanghai Morning Post]. "Fengkuang de Shitou" ["*Crazy Stone*"].

110. MuHe, "Fengkuang de Shitou de 'fengkuang' xianxiang" ["The 'Crazy' Phenomenon of *Crazy Stone*"].

111. Wu, "Fengkuang de Shitou daoyan shuo: Feng Xiaogang de youmo wo bugan bi" [Director of *Crazy Stone* Ning Hao says: I can't compete with Feng Xiaogang's Humor"]. Andy Lau first saw Ning's ear-

lier award-winning art-house work, *Mongolian Pingpong,* and discerned a penchant for comedy in him.

112. Ning, "The Making of *Crazy Stone*.

113. Ibid.

114. Ibid.

115. *Wangyi*, "Ninghao fouren Fengkuang de Shitou chaoxi Gai Ruiqi" ["Ning Hao Denies That *Crazy Stone* Copies Guy Ritchie"].

116. Gong, "Houxiandai yujing xia de kuanghuanhua xushu – jiedu dianying wenben Fengkuang de Shitou" ["Reading the Filmic Text *Crazy Stone*"], 34.

117. Chen, "Fengkuang de Shitou, mensao de Ning Hao" ["*Crazy Stone*, 'Secretly Sexy' Ning Hao"], 40.

118. Zhao, "Fengkuang de Shitou" ["On *Crazy Stone*"], 18–19.

119. *Xinwen chenbao*, "Fengkuang de Shitou" ["*Crazy Stone*"].

120. One of the journalists I spoke with pointed out that in contemporary China's print journalism, "scrutiny at a distance" (*yidi jiandu*) is a common practice, meaning that newspapers based in one locale may have greater freedom in reporting on sensitive social issues in another locale.

121. In the Coke scamming sequence, Heipi is disguised as a porter carrying a shoulder pole, a typical job taken up by peasants who have migrated to cities in Sichuan. In local dialect, these porters are nicknamed "the army of bangbang" (bang referring to the balancing pole). (Later in the film, a group of them outside the temple are bribed by Baotou, who suspects that they were the ones who reported a false alarm in order to snatch the stone.) On the cable car, as Heipi opens the coke can and discovers some words printed inside the tab, he turns to ask Xiaojun what it says. Acting like a stranger, Xiaojun tells Heipi that he has just won a prize of RMB50,000. Xiaojun then offers to buy

the tab from Heipi, at which time Daoge, another "stranger" on the tram, joins in and offers a higher price for the prize, even showing off a stash of cash. Daoge then turns to a woman sitting between him and Heipi, and suggests they chip in to buy the tab so that they can claim and split the prize. While this is taking place, the passengers who are sitting near the three begin moving toward the other end of the car one by one. Seeing that the woman between Daoge and Heipi hasn't moved, another woman comes back and whispers to her, eventually persuading her to join the others. Defeated, the trio sighs: "We have been scamming the whole morning and still haven't succeeded once!" Ironically, as the *Shenzhen Special Economic Zone News* reports, the same trick was played successfully on numerous bus passengers in 2008, indicating that in "real life," common people are not as vigilant as the ones depicted in the film. See Ma and Xue, "Cheshang chang shuanghuang shexia 'yilaguan' zhongjiang pianju" ["Con-Man Duo Set up 'Pull-Top Prize' Swindle on Bus"].

122. Wang, "Fengkuang de Shitou yu xiju jingshen" ["*Crazy Stone* and the Spirit of Comedy"], 14.

123. *Xinwen chenbao*, "Fengkuang de Shitou" ["*Crazy Stone*"].

124. MuHe, "Fengkuang de Shitou de 'fengkuang' xianxiang" ["The 'Crazy' Phenomenon of *Crazy Stone*"] It is worth noting that *Crazy Stone* was certainly not the first or only Chinese film to feature the existence of counterfeiting practices in the nation. Feng Xiaogang's *Big Shot's Funeral* (2001) and He Jianjun (a.k.a. He Yi)'s *Pirated Copy* (2004) are but two examples. *Big Shot's Funeral* features a sequence in which the protagonist You You refuses to sell an advertising spot to a Cantonese manufacturer of DVD players.

He claims that the machines are specialized for "super error correction," which suggests that they are meant for reading pirated copies. The manufacturer in turn accuses You You for "suppressing national industry" (*daji minzu gongye*). You You responds: "National industries like your kind might as well go bankrupt before too long!" He then announces that the ad spot will be used for a public service announcement. The next scene depicts the announcement itself: "Fight Video Piracy, Protect IPR." In a later sequence, a gang leader presses You You for an ad spot for his counterfeit bottled water, Le Ha Ha (a fake of the well-known domestic brand, Wa Ha Ha). When You You asks him why he needs such costly advertising for a fake product, he says: "You don't understand [capitalism]. With enough advertising, the fake becomes the real." While an ambivalent attitude toward IPR can be detected here, the film is better known for mocking Beijing's overcommercialization in general than for commenting on counterfeiting practices in particular. See Wang, "Big Shot's Funeral: China, Sony, and the WTO." For a reading of He's *Pirated Copy*, see Zhang, *Cinema, Space, and Polylocality*, 157–167.

125. The film circle in fact also depended on the pirated-DVD network for many visual materials, at least prior to the popularization of broadband internet.

126. shawnj, "Chaoxi nian" ["The Year of Copying"].

127. Zhang's lavish production was known to be based on the famous modern Chinese stage drama, *Thunderstorm*. See ChongQiWaWa, "Haokan ge pi" ["Entertaining My Arse"].

128. Internet Movie Database, "Reviews and Ratings for *Crazy Stone*."

129. shawnj, "Chaoxi nian" ["The Year of Copying"].

130. Ibid.

131. Wang, "Dianying shoufa de bentuhua" ["Localization of Filmic Techniques"].

132. Ibid.

133. See appendix 2 for details.

134. In addition to *Stone*'s opening sequence, the author also points out that Maike's journey from Hong Kong to Chongqing, which takes place within seconds, is portrayed in exactly the same way as Cousin Avi's trip from New York to London in *Snatch*.

135. Wang, "Dianying shoufa de bentuhua" ["Localization of Filmic Techniques"], 52.

136. Wu, "Xianshi zhuyi de yulehua biaoda" ["The Expression of Realism through Entertainment"], 114.

137. Li, "Fengkuang de Shitou su qie zao" ["*Crazy Stone* Is Vulgar and Flippant"], 29.

138. *Xinwen chenbao*, "Fengkuang de Shitou: yichang xianshi zhuyi de hongtangdaxiao" ["*Crazy Stone*: A Great Laugh of Neo-Realism"].

139. Jameson, "Notes on Globalization," 75.

140. Bhabha, "DissemiNation."

141. Elley, "Crazy Stone."

142. Wang, Liu, and Jiang, "Dianying Fengkuang de Shitou" ["The Film *Crazy Stone*"], 29. As a student in film school, Ning worked as a photographer and journalist for Channel [V], MTV's Asia branch, in 1999, and later on directed nearly one hundred music videos. See Sohu.com, "Ning Hao geren jianjie" ["Ning Hao Profile"].

143. Elley, "Crazy Stone."

144. Ibid.

145. *Dianying yishu* [Film Art], "Fengkuang de Shitou: heise de kuanghuan" ["*Crazy Stone*: the Carnival of Black Humor"], 74.

146. Jameson, *The Geopolitical Aesthetic*, 31–32.

147. The characters predominantly perform in the local Sichuanese dialect but different provincial accents are interspersed throughout.

148. Feng is known as one of the few directors working in the category of urban cinema – a genre considered underrepresented in contemporary domestic film. In Feng's more recent "New Year" films set in domestic or foreign cities, such as *Cell Phone* and *If You Are the One*, the urban landscape typically consists of luxurious condos, fancy hotel rooms, and trendy restaurants. See Feifeizhiyin, "Fengkuang de Shitou" ["*Crazy Stone*"], 13.

149. This is something not unfamiliar to those who live in or have visited China, especially its smaller cities and inland areas (including the city of Chongqing).

150. Zhang, "Fengkuang de shitou: dianying yuyan de kuanghuan" ["*Crazy Stone*: the Carnival of Cinematic Language"].

151. Zhang, *The Urban Generation*.

152. Zhang, *Cinema, Space, and Polylocality*, 211–213.

153. *Wangyi*, "Ninghao fouren Fengkuang de Shitou chaoxi Gai Ruiqi" ["Ning Hao Denies That *Crazy Stone* Copies Guy Ritchie"].

154. Ibid.

155. Deng, "Yao xishou guoji de jingyan" ["We Must Learn from International Experiences"].

156. In the film, besides the fact that Maike, the "international thief," is from Hong Kong, there is a scene in which the girlfriend of Daoge accuses him on the phone of not taking her on a shopping trip to Hong Kong as promised.

157. Ning, quoted in *Wangyi*, "Ninghao fouren Fengkuang de Shitou chaoxi Gai

Ruiqi" ["Ning Hao Denies That *Crazy Stone* Copies Guy Ritchie"].

158. McIssac, "The City as Nation."

159. *Renmin wang* [People Net], "Fengkuang de Shitou zhaoliang Zhongguo dichengben dianying shichang" ["*Crazy Stone* Lights up the Low-Budget Film Market of China"].

160. Ning, quoted in *Wangyi*, "Ninghao fouren Fengkuang de Shitou chaoxi Gai Ruiqi" ["Ning Hao Denies That *Crazy Stone* Copies Guy Ritchie"].

161. "Daoyan Ning Hao jiemi Fengkuang de Shitou" ["Director Ning Hao Decodes *Crazy Stone*"].

162. *Wangyi*, "Ninghao fouren Fengkuang de Shitou chaoxi Gai Ruiqi" ["Ning Hao Denies That *Crazy Stone* Copies Guy Ritchie"].

163. Bhabha, "DissemiNation," 298–299.

164. Ibid., 299.

165. Ibid.

166. Originally, the number was debuted by a dance troupe made up of twenty-one deaf-mutes. See *OpenV*, "2005 nian chunjie lianhuan wanhui" ["The 2005 CCTV Gala"]. After a sensational premiere at the Special Olympics in Athens in 2004 (as part of the eight-minute segment that introduced the 2008 Beijing Olympics), the troupe was later invited to CCTV's Spring Festival Gala (chapter 3) in 2005, and their performance was voted one of the most popular programs of the Gala that year. Many continue to watch it online and celebrate the "stunning," orderly beauty conveyed by the physically challenged yet highly disciplined, skillful performers. A later CCTV program, however, reported that the condition of eighteeen of the twenty-one troupe members, nine of whom were male, was caused by improper use of medicine during their youth. This news led some netizens to ponder the logic

of such "absurd events" taking place in "this 'great' nation." See QiCaiZhiLang, "Tianna, shui shi xiongshou???" ["God, Who is the Murderer?"].

167. Tan, *Southern Fujian*, 14; Ong, *Flexible citizenship*.

168. Wang, "Culture As Leisure and Culture As Capital," 83.

169. The actual exchange is as follows (I have added words omitted in the onscreen subtitles): *Baotou*: "This is a tourist spot! Too many [floating (*liudong*)] people is high risk! Detective work 101. Get it?" *Female employee*: "You're just a security guy watching over a stone. So what are you yapping about? Detective work? What we need is [exactly] tourist business. This way, you even save on advertising." *Baotou*: "Yes, you save on advertising. A rundown temple, its doors don't even close. How can we make this place secure?" *Female employee*: "If we were doing this in the Great Hall of the People, we wouldn't need you, would we?" *Xie Qianli*: "Stop this! Stop this arguing! We're all here for one thing. We're here to keep our jobs [literally, "This is all for work, OK?"]. Bao, we have so many guys hanging around doing nothing. Go on, put together a security team."

170. The song, sung by the nationally renowned singer Jiang Dawei, was once a huge hit on the CCTV Gala show, and is immediately recognizable to many viewers.

171. Wang, "Fengkuang de Shitou yu xiju jingshen" ["*Crazy Stone* and the Spirit of Comedy"], 14.

172. Huang, "Kuanghuanhua shixue xia de 'shitou' – jiedu Fengkuang de Shitou" ["Stone in Carnivalesque Poetics"]. On two other occasions, some factory employees who remain infatuated with their professional craftsmanship continue to draw elaborate renditions of histori-

cal figures and a map of the temple. Their actions are chastised by the factory head and Baotou, who claim that this is not the time for them to create works of art. These employees are subsequently recruited into the security team, and in the case of the man with eyeglasses, also into the performing troupe.

173. Gan, "Bashi niandai wenhua taolun de jige wenti" ["Cultural Discussions of the Eighties"], 19.

174. Ibid., 20.

175. *Fengkuang de shitou ba* [*Crazy Stone bar*], "Shitou li Beijing Tiananmen changjing faxian" ["The Tiananmen Square Scene in *Stone*"].

176. Ibid.

177. In the barely lit, tiny room, Baotou finds Saobao's mother preparing Chinese medicine for Sanbao's sick wife while asking him to expedite the reimbursement of their medical expenses.

178. The idea of examining this sequence through the lens of temporality came to me when I was attending Philip Rosen's presentation, "Violence, State Theory, and Cinema Theory."

179. These include a train, some residential buildings, a street lamp, a yellowish sky, a bridge, the jade stone on display, a running horse, an iron-wired web structure, and networks of electronic lines. All the images are compressed so that the whole sequence occupies less than one second, creating an overlapping effect that renders them indistinct and indeed only discernible when viewed using the "step frame" feature on a DVD player.

180. The next scene finds Baotou falling onto his bed in the motel room – a transition based on literal connections (the fall of Baotou's psychological state linked with his falling onto the motel bed) that is deployed in numerous other occasions in the film.

181. "Shitou dao muqian suo faxian de suoyou xijie [zhengli ban]" ["All Stone Details Discovered up to Now (Rearranged Version)"]. The former expression refers to hints left behind by happenings (such as spider threads and horse traces), and the latter is often used to describe a literary imagination that runs free. Understood in this way, Baotou's return to the stand in search of traces of the stone's exchange is aided by his own imagination "run free." Others have read Baotou's fall as indicative of his suicidal mental state; his desperation and fear are so intense he feels as if his body is being trampled by the train and the horse. See Zhong, "Fengkuang de Shitou, fengkuang de yinyue" ["*Crazy Stone,* Crazy Music"].

182. Benjamin, "On the Concept of History."

183. Ibid.

184. For example, this clip is posted on Youku with the title "True Feeling between Humans" (*renjian de zhenqing*). See http://v.youku.com/v_show/id _XMTU4MjEoNA−− html While the character "*qing*" can be justifiably translated as "love," I use "feeling" here so as to distinguish it from "*ai,*" the literal contemporary Chinese term for "love."

185. kissinger, "Bao Shihong de laopo zhen biaozhi" ["Bao Shihong's Wife is So Beautiful"].

186. Ibid.

187. Lee and LiPuma, "Cultures of Circulation," 200–201.

188. There is a link here to be made with Pierre Bourdieu (1977): "The preconceptual structures of the habitus provide the phenomenological base for what from an objective perspective is a 'misrecognition' that is constitutive of the social totality of exchange" (cited in Lee and Lipuma, 202).

189. Lee and LiPuma, "Cultures of Circulation," 202.

190. MuHe, "Fengkuang de Shitou de 'fengkuang' xianxiang" ["The 'Crazy' Phenomenon of *Crazy Stone*"].

191. In a later scene, Maike also claims the moral high ground as one who upholds "honesty and trust" as his business motto, even if sticking to this principle involves the killing of those standing in his way.

192. One commentator understands the Pharaoh and the BMW as referring to "power" and "wealth," respectively, and Heipi as an embodiment of the migrant working class. See Yimin, "Yingping xinshang: Fengkuang de shitou" ["Film Review Appreciation: *Crazy Stone*"].

193. In an online review that later appeared in the business magazine *Zhongguo Zhaobiao* (*China Tendering*), a blogger who works in the transportation/distribution business offers a reading of *Stone* as "a story about business competition." For him, Daoge embodies the figure of the new entrepreneur "without resources, without brand and real power" – indeed "petty thieves' when compared to state-owned enterprises and transnational corporations." The arts and crafts SOE owns the jade, much like real SOEs, which usually own "rare resources and market opportunities." But as the action of Baotou suggests, the SOE is only interested in maintaining the status quo, that is, "protecting the current assets." The son of the factory head asks his father for money whenever he is in need, much as "tertiary subsidiary companies" under SOEs easily obtain valuable opportunities from the mother company. The international thief Maike fails to adapt his world-class style and professionalism to the local environment, and by trusting local suppliers loses the opportunity to obtain the stone. Between the limitations of the SOEs and transnational

corporations, Daoge still fails to get the stone for two reasons. One is his emphasis on "caliber," which prevents him from realizing his subordinate Heipi's potential to snatch the stone in the most direct and simple way. The other is his emotional devotion, which prevents him from collaborating with the factory official's son, who obviously has ample resources at hand but little business ambition. See Qu, "Daoge weishenme shibai yu hulianwang chuangye" ["The Reason Daoge Failed and Internet Entrepreneurship"].

194. Huang Bo, the actor who played Heipi, later rose to stardom.

195. This scene also cuts immediately to a vendor selling an outfit to Maike with the claim: "A famous brand! Look how it stretches. You can't tear it!" Of course, the outfit was torn by the time Maike came out of his trap later in the film.

196. Sun, "Bannilu, Pulada, A Huo B Huo" ["Baleno, Prada, luxury fantasy"].

197. Piao, "Fengkuang de Shitou zashang le Bannilu" ["Baleno Crushed by Crazy Stone"]. Another author compares *Stone*'s effect on Baleno with that of *The Devil Wears Prada*'s on Prada, in relation to a 2007 Hong Kong film about counterfeits, *Luxury Fantasy* (*A Huo B Huo*, literally "A-level Fake, B-level Fake"), and concludes that Baleno, A/B fakes, and Prada represent "the past that is not so distant, the present that is very real, and the future that is in sight" for China's emerging middle class. See Sun, "Bannilu, Pulada, A Huo B Huo" ["Baleno, Prada, luxury fantasy"].

198. *Crazy Stone* is indeed mentioned in the CCTV publication *Shanzhai Laile* (chapter 2) as a paradigmatic example of "Shanzhai film."

199. CRI *Online*, "Fengkuang de Shitou zhuchuang renyuan xiao tan 'Shitou'" ["Core Creative Team Lightheartedly Discusses *Crazy Stone*"].

200. Yu, "Fengkuang de Saiche" [*"Crazy Racer"*].

201. *Dianying yishu* [Film Art], "Fengkuang de Shitou: heise de kuanghuan" [*"Crazy Stone*: the Carnival of Black Humor"].

202. Zhu and Wang, "Xiao zhizuo bo da shichang" ["Small Production Plays Big Market"].

203. Ibid.

204. Ibid.

205. Huang Shixian, quoted in *Dianying yishu* [Film Art], "Fengkuang de Shitou: heise de kuanghuan" [*"Crazy Stone*: the Carnival of Black Humor"], 75.

206. Song, "Fengkuang de Shitaou" [*"Crazy Stone*: A Very Commercialized Genre Film"].

207. See, for example, Kang, "Fengkuang de Shitou weihe ruci fengkuang?" ["Why Is *Crazy Stone* So Crazy?"], 81.

208. Sun, "Fengkuang de Shitou: guochan dianying cong shehua huigui pingmin" [*"Crazy Stone*: Domestic Cinema Returns from Luxury to the Common Folks"]. In the same article, the scriptwriter Lu Tianming is quoted as suggesting that domestic films can't all be "seafood, steak, and roast pork" but instead should improve on the making of "cabbage, rice, and pancake," which are more essential to "the daily spiritual pursuit of 1.3 billion people."

209. Bao, "Juanshouyu: Fengkuang de Shitou" ["Foreword: *Crazy Stone*"].

210. Dong, ed. "Quanguo piaofang po 1600 wan, Ning Hao: 'Shitou' zan feng wo mei zan" ["Ning Hao says: 'I am not making any money'"].

211. Liu, "Yi 'xiao' bo 'da' chushou bufan" ["Use the 'Small' to Challenge the 'Big'"], 28. Elsewhere, Ning also revealed that he did not think the film was all that perfect; he'd only give it a personal score of seventy-five (out of one hundred). See

Renmin wang [People Net], "Fengkuang de Shitou zhaoliang Zhongguo dichengben dianying shichang" [*"Crazy Stone* Lights up the Low-Budget Film Market of China"].

212. *Caijing shibao* [Business Times].

213. This seems to confirm a young Beijing critic's comment that "while films of government and police corruption were main staples of Hollywood, a film about Chinese police or high-level government corruption would guarantee a ban." See Zhu, *Chinese Cinema during the Era of Reform*, 83.

214. Song, "Fengkuang de Shitaou" [*"Crazy Stone*: A Very Commercialized Genre Film"].

215. Shao, "Dangnian Fengkuang de Shitou juben shencha yijian" ["Censors' Suggestions for the Script of *Crazy Stone*"].

216. Ibid.

217. Since the original post (in Chinese) on Tianya is no longer available online, I am quoting the comments and translation from *ESWN Culture Blog*, "Crazy Stone Is A Poisonous Weed."

218. "Crazy Stone Is A Poisonous Weed."

219. Dirlik and Zhang, "Postmodernism and China," 7.

220. Lim, *Translating Time*, 32.

221. Zhao, "The Struggle for Socialism in China: The Bo Xilai Saga and Beyond."

222. Ibid.

223. The dramatic conflict, as the "script" has it, centers on a love triangle between Bo, his wife Gu Xilai, and the city's police chief Wang Lijun.

224. Liu, *Signifying the Local*, 220–242.

225. Ibid.

226. Li, "Youxi: liudong de xiandaixing" ["Game: the liquidity of modernity"].

227. Zhao, "China's Quest for 'Soft Power,'" 21.

4. Landmark, Trademark, and Intellectual Property at Beijing's Silk Street Market

1. Lash and Lury, *Global Culture Industry*, 4.

2. See, for example, Lin, *Fake Stuff*.

3. According to one report, the street's name never appeared in records of dynastic China, nor can it be traced in the founding moments of the People's Republic. See *Zhongguo xiaofeizhe bao* [China Consumer News], "Beijing Xiushuijie, zuotian de chuanqi" ["Beijing's Xiushui Street: Legends of Yesterday"]. Another suggests that the original Chinese name Xiushui (literally "elegant water") came from the river on the west side of the nearby Temple of Sun. At the end of China's last dynasty, Qing (1644–1911), the land was known to be part of a vegetable garden owned by an aristocrat named Qi. In the 1950s, the northern portion of the land was devoted to the construction of a coal factory. As the Qi garden became the locale for constructing an "embassy district," it took the name from the river and became "Elegant Water" Alley. See Sun, "Xiushuijie" ["Xiushui Street"]. A security guard on duty at the former American Embassy nearby, however, told me that "Xiushui" really meant "Chou Shui" ["stinky water"], and that the name was euphemized in the 1950s. Yet another account relates to a rumor that the alley's origin had to do with Emperor Qianlong, who ordered its construction upon return from his famous southern tours. See Zhi and Li, "Xiushuijie de bian yu bubian" ["Change and Continuity of Xiushui Street"].

4. Lu and Xiang, "30 nian xiushui bianqian ji" ["The Thirty-Year Transformation of Xiushui"], 5.

5. Yu, "Xiushuijie: bumai jiahuo xing bu xing" ["Xiushui Street: Can It Not Sell Fake Products?"].

6. Quoted in Liang, "Xiushui: hongsheng jingcheng yi tiao jie" ["Xiushui: A Street that Lights up the Capital City"], 24.

7. Shen, "Duomian Xiushuijie – Getihu de mingyun bianqian" ["The Multi-Faceted Silk Street"].

8. Huang, "Banzhe zhitou zuo maoyi" ["Counting Fingers for Trade"]. For example, the American embassy was no more than thirty meters away. This location is emphasized in most media accounts about the market, likely because the United States is a major policing force for counterfeit practices in China.

9. Jiang, "Xiushuijie getihu" ["Independent Entrepreneurs at Xiushui Street"]. The scale of this foreign presence might not be on a par with that of the Pearl River Delta, whose key site is the city of Shenzhen (the location for Luohu Shopping Mall, a precursor of Xiushui). But Xiushui was noted to be unique for its "people-generated" spontaneity. See Li, "Xiushuijie: Gaige Kaifang de huohuashi" ["Xiushui Street: A Living Fossil for 'Reform and Opening Up'"].

10. The demand prompted traders to bring in large quantities of silk products from Zhejiang, a south-eastern province famous for silk production. Though the market did not adopt the official English name "Silk Street, Pearl Market" until 2005, from this point on I will use "Silk Street" instead of "Xiushui" when referring to the original market, while retaining "Xiushui" if the sources are dated prior to 2005.

11. Jiang, "Xiushuijie getihu" ["Independent Entrepreneurs at Xiushui Street"].

12. These companies typically supply more material than necessary to produce the order, so that those products with defects at the final quality checkpoint can be easily replaced.

13. Sun, "Beijing Xiushui shichang: ruhe chongxian zuori huihuang" ["Xiushui Market: How to Re-Create Yesterday's Glory?"].

14. Yu, "Xiushuijie: bumai jiahuo xing bu xing" ["Xiushui Street: Can It Not Sell Fake Products?"].

15. Liu and Zhou, "Xiushuijie miju" ["The Xiushui Street Conundrum"].

16. He Wei, "Fengyu xiushuijie" ["Xiushui Alley in Wind and Rain"]. Some have come to call the market an "'OK' Street," because English soon became the dominant language used in the market. Numerous regional dialects of China could also be heard there because of the multi-local origins of the vendors themselves. See He Nan, "Xiushuijie, 'OK' jie" ["Silk Street, 'OK' Street"], 49.

17. He, "Fengyu xiushuijie" ["Xiushui Alley in Wind and Rain"].

18. Williams, *Dream Worlds,* 66–67.

19. Ibid., 65.

20. Foucault, "Of Other Spaces, Heterotopias."

21. Ibid.

22. Ibid. In a way, this is akin to Foucault's example, the American motel where a husband takes his mistress.

23. A journalist told me that as the market grew, many owners of the stalls either sublet their spots or hired staff to oversee the daily transactions.

24. Liu and Zhou, "Xiushuijie miju" ["The Xiushui Street Conundrum"].

25. Tang, "Big Move Planned for 'Silk Alley.'"

26. *Zhongguo funu bao* [China Woman], "Xiushuijie: nengfou chongfu zuotian de gushi" ["Xiushui Street: Can Yesterday's Story Be Repeated?"].

27. *Jinghua shibao* [Beijing Times], "Beijing Xiushuijie zouguo fengyu 20 nian" ["Beijing's Xiushui Street Went Through Twenty Years of Wind and Rain"].

28. Li and Yang, "Beijing Xiushuijie fengsha wuda jia mingpai" ["Beijing's Silk Street Bans Five Major Fake Brands"].

29. Liu and Zhou, "Xiushuijie miju" ["The Xiushui Street Conundrum"].

30. Ibid.

31. *Silk Street Market,* "Silk Street Legends."

32. Geng and Jiang, "20 nian de luyou pinpai gai bu gai chai?" ["Should a Twenty-Year-Old Tourism Brand Be Demolished?"].

33. Ibid.

34. Liu and Zhou, "Xiushuijie miju" ["The Xiushui Street Conundrum"].

35. Ibid.

36. Sun, "Beijing Xiushui shichang: ruhe chongxian zuori huihuang" ["Xiushui Market: How to Re-Create Yesterday's Glory?"].

37. Deng, "Xiushuijie zhi tong" ["The Grief of Xiushui Street"].

38. Haosen did file for a name change, adopting "Xiushuijie" as its official company logo, on February 4, 2006, for reasons unknown. See *Beijing Ye Lu Sheng Commerce Ltd. vs. Beijing Xinya Shenghong Real Estate Development Ltd., Second Trial* (Beijing No.2 Intermediate People's Court, June 9, 2006). Available at: http://www.110.com/panli/panli_112957.html.

39. Li, "Toushi 'Xiushuijie' shangbiao jiufen" ["Probing the 'Silk Street' Trademark Dispute"].

40. Ibid.

41. Ibid.

42. Wen, "Butong 'Xiushuijie' lunzhan shui qingquan" ["Different Versions of 'Xiushui Street'"].

43. Zhou and Liu, "Xiushui miju zai diaocha" ["Re-Investigating the Xiushui Street Conundrum].

44. *Beijing Ye Lu Sheng Commerce Ltd. vs. Beijing Xinya Shenghong Real Estate Development Ltd., First Trial* (Beijing No.2

Intermediate People's Court, December 8, 2005). Available at: http://www.110.com /panli/panli_122698.html. Haosen had proceeded to file an application to rescind the registration to the national AIC's Trademark Evaluation Committee on June 26, 2005.

45. Ibid.

46. *Beijing Ye Lu Sheng Commerce, Second Trial.*

47. Yuan, "'Xiushui' yinggai shi shuide?" ["To Whom Should 'Xiushui' Belong?"], 9.

48. Quoted in Liu and Zhou, "Xiushuijie miju" ["The Xiushui Street Conundrum"]. Liu told me that the vendors' collective was also multifaceted. Some vendors rented the stalls from the beginning and relied on the market's business as their only source of income. Some leased the stalls to others and collected fees. Still others went there because of their personal connections, since after the market became famous, stall openings became difficult to come by. Liu Wanyong, in discussion with the author, June 3, 2010.

49. Yuan, "'Xiushui' yinggai shi shuide?" ["To Whom Should 'Xiushui' Belong?"], 9.

50. Ibid.

51. Shenghong reportedly did not obtain a mandatory Temporary Qualification Certificate for Real Estate Developing Enterprises, a prerequisite for construction projects, until after its application for the new building was approved, which indicated that it was "chosen" even before it established itself as a legitimate contender. See Zhou and Liu, "Xiushui miju zai diaocha" ["Re-Investigating the Xiushui Street Conundrum"].

52. Ibid.

53. Yuan, "'Xiushui' yinggai shi shuide?" ["To Whom Should 'Xiushui' Belong?"].

54. Jiang Xinjie, in discussion with the author, June 4, 2010.

55. Liu Wanyong, in discussion with the author, June 3, 2010.

56. Jiang Xinjie, in discussion with the author, June 4, 2010.

57. Deng, "Xiushuijie zhi tong" ["The Grief of Xiushui Street"].

58. *Xiushui xinwen* [Silk Street News], "Guanyu Wang Zili jubao shijian de jingji shengming" ["Urgent Notice Regarding Wang Zili's Disclosure Incident"]. I will refer to the market as "Silk Street" or "Silk Market" for events that have taken place since January 2005.

59. Yang, "The Politics of Exhibition."

60. In addition to being a former analyst for China's Ministry of Aviation Industry, Wang also holds an MBA degree; his background was noted as "over-qualified" for an administrator of an "independent entrepreneurs' market." See Lu and Xiang, "30 nian xiushui bianqian ji" ["The Thirty-Year Transformation of Xiushui"], 13.

61. Meng, "Xiushui: Beijing aoyun de di 52 kuai jinpai" ["Silk Street: The Fifty-Second Medal of the Beijing Olympics"], 77.

62. Gao and Zhao, "Xiushuijie dengdai 'laozihao'" ["Silk Street Awaits 'Time-Honored Brands'"].

63. Geng, "Beijing Xiushuijie rang laowai shu qi le muzhi" ["Beijing's Silk Street Got Thumbs Up from 'Lao Wai'"].

64. "Xiushuijie juxing baohu zhishi chanquan biaozhang dahui" ["Silk Street Holds Commendation Meeting for IPR Protection"].

65. Niu, "Wang Zili – Zhongguo diyi shewai shichang de 'yuhuo chongsheng'" ["Wang Zili – The Revival of China's No.1 Foreign-Directed Market"].

66. Geng, "Beijing Xiushuijie rang laowai shu qi le muzhi" ["Beijing's Silk Street Got Thumbs Up from 'Lao Wai'"].

67. Li, "Xiushuijie – Guojihua de gouwu zhi di" ["Silk Street – An Internationalized Shopping Destination"].

68. Xiushuijie [Silk Street], "Xiushuijie shichang chui xiang ying aoyun 'jijiehao'" ["Silk Street Market Blows the 'Assembly Bugle' to Welcome the Olympics"].

69. Niu, "Wang Zili – Zhongguo diyi shewai shichang de 'yuhuo chongsheng'" ["Wang Zili – The Revival of China's No.1 Foreign-Directed Market"]. "Huang Pu," a.k.a. "Whampoa," was a prestigious training institution for military officers in Republican China (1911–1937).

70. Gui, "Xiushuijie: aoyun chengjiu de 'shangye niaochao'" ["Silk Street: the Olympics-Made Merchant's Bird Nest"].

71. The production of "Chineseness" in both instances also speaks to John Tomlinson's argument that globalization, rather than destroying cultural identities, indeed creates and proliferates them. Tomlinson, "Globalization and Cultural Identity."

72. Deliveries were guaranteed within twenty-four hours, with over one hundred clothing workers and professional facilities working non-stop. The time was further reduced to eight hours during the Olympics. See Li, "Xiushuijie: Cong jia mingpai dao zhen pinpai" ["Silk Street: From Fake Famous Brands to Real Quality Brands"].

73. *Renmin ribao* [People's Daily], "Aoyun guibin guang Xiushui" ["Distinguished Guests of the Olympics Stroll Down Silk Market"].

74. *People's Daily Online*, "Silk Market Magnet for VIPs." Bush's visit was noted by manager Wang as the "best recognition" of Silk Street's progress in IPR protection, contrasting with the generally "critical attitude toward China's IPR issues" in U.S. media. See Li, "Xiushuijie: Cong jia mingpai dao zhen pinpai" ["Silk Street: From Fake Famous Brands to Real Quality Brands"]. Having bought seven silk nightgowns, some embroidered with dragon-and-phoenix patterns (at the discounted price of RMB2000), Bush sent a hand-written thank-you note to manager Wang upon his return to the United States. The letter was later displayed on the official Silk Street website: "I got home to the USA today. I want to thank you for all you did to help me then at the Silk Street Pearl Market. You made it very easy for me to shop. Please thank those delightful sales ladies. Good Luck!" See *Xiushui xinwen* [Silk Street News], "Xiushui aoyun zhuanti baodao" ["Silk Street Olympics Special Reports"].

75. Li, "Xiushuijie: Cong jia mingpai dao zhen pinpai" ["Silk Street: From Fake Famous Brands to Real Quality Brands"].

76. American swimming champion Julia Wilkinson said on a Fox Sports interview that vendors would accept a markdown of the price in exchange for an athlete's offer to let them "wear the medal." See Fletcher and Wilkinson, "Giving a Whoop About the Olympics."

77. Meng, "Xiushui: Beijing aoyun de di 52 kuai jinpai" ["Silk Street: The Fifty-Second Medal of the Beijing Olympics"], 76.

78. Hu, "Beijing Xiushuijie jie aoyun tisheng pinpai meili" ["Beijing's Silk Street Relies on Olympics to Raise its Branding Charm"].

79. Ibid.

80. Meng, "Xiushui: Beijing aoyun de di 52 kuai jinpai" ["Silk Street: The Fifty-Second Medal of the Beijing Olympics"]. The original line, first introduced by Lu Xun in 1934, was "The same goes with literature now. Those with local flavor may indeed easily become the world's, that is, to be recognized by other nations. Presenting them to the world is then ben-

eficial for China's activities." See Lu, "Zhi Chen Yanqiao" ["To Chen Yanqiao"], 391.

81. Huang, "Xiushuijie zui shou 'laowai' zhuipeng" ["Silk Street Most Hounded by 'Lao Wai'"].

82. Li, "Zhongguo techan Xiushui 'xiu'" ["Chinese Special Goods 'Showing' at Silk Market"].

83. Cha, "Shopping on Silk Street with Bush Sr."

84. In the section that uses Silk Street to illustrate the development of the city's "independent economy" since the 1980s, the closing shot features the picture prominently in the foreground.

85. *Chang'anjie (wu) dongjie gushi* [Chang'An Avenue – Episode Five: Stories of East Avenue].

86. Cha, "Shopping on Silk Street with Bush Sr."

87. Williams, "Counterfeit China: Fake Goods Rife."

88. See for example CharleysVideos, *OlympicsOrBust.*

89. Simone, "Silk Market Fakes – Light at the End of the Tunnel?"

90. Leary and Ma, "Luxury Brands Take On Landlords."

91. It was noted as one of the thirty "exemplar lawsuits" at the Convention for Institutionalizing Trademark Licensing and Public Rulings of IPR Violations, which took place on March 28, 2006.

92. Wan, "Xiushuijie baisu gei zhizao daguo de qishi" ["The Implication of Silk Street's Loss in Its Lawsuit for the Big Manufacturing Nation"].

93. One such case involved another shopping mall in Beijing, Chaowaimen Shopping Mall, which was sued by Louis Vuitton in January 2006. See *Louis Vuitton vs. Beijing Chaoyangmen* (Beijing No. 2 Intermediate People's Court 2006). In that case, while the final ruling was the same as in the Silk Street one, the court simply

concluded that once the mall management was informed of infringement activities on its premises, the proven existence of such activities afterwards constituted the mall's "subjective" aid, hence its indirect infringement. This is different from the Silk Street case in that there, the management's lack of action was considered as providing "objective" conditions for subsequent infringements. See Wang, "Lun changsuo tigongzhe goucheng shangbiao 'jianjie qinquan' de guize" ["On the Rules for 'Indirect Infringement' of Trademarks by Venue Providers"], 51. Louis Vuitton was also the plaintiff in another trademark lawsuit whose verdict came out in Shanghai almost simultaneously with the Silk Street final order, in which the Shanghai court held the defendant, Shanghai Carrefour Supermarket, liable for a fine of RMB300,000. See Zhao, "Xiushuijie yuanhe baisu?" ["Why Did Silk Street Lose?"].

94. Su, "Xiushuijie 'Ligui' zaoyu 'yang Likui'" ["'Li Gui' at Silk Street Meets 'foreign Li Kui'"].

95. Tan, "Xiushuijie dajia bushi weile mingpai" ["Striking Fakes at Silk Street Not for Luxury Brands"].

96. Feng, "Baohu zhishi chanquan juefei jinxian koutou" ["Protecting IPR Is by No Means Just about Talks"].

97. Ibid.

98. Wan, "Xiushuijie baisu gei zhizao daguo de qishi" ["The Implication of Silk Street's Lost Lawsuit for the Big Manufacturing Nation"].

99. Zhao, "Xiushui shichang zai diaocha" ["Re-investigating the Silk Market"].

100. Liu, "Xiushuijie shoujia an" ["Silk Street Fake-selling Case"]. Some positive examples were provided by Liu Guoquan, the head of the Guangdong Dongguan subbranch of the China Trademark and Patent Law Office, who pointed out that Dongguan, a city previously famous for

its "product imitation" industry, had entered an era of innovation and brand making five years before. The number of trademark registrations among Dongguan enterprises increased by over 30 percent, from 2,400 in 2004 to 3,800 in 2005.

101. Zhao, "Xiushui shichang zai diaocha" ["Re-investigating the Silk Market"].

102. Liu, "Xiushuijie susong'an" ["The Silk Street Case"].

103. Su, "Xiushuijie 'Ligui' zaoyu 'yang Likui'" ["'Li Gui' at Silk Street Meets 'foreign Li Kui'"].

104. Simone, "Silk Market Fakes – Light at the End of the Tunnel?"

105. The stallholders also presented their sales records, which indicated that they did not sell as many fake items as charged; considering that their stalls had already been confiscated, the fine was simply too high. Su, "Xiushuijie 'Ligui' zaoyu 'yang Likui'" ["'Li Gui' at Silk Street Meets 'foreign Li Kui'"].

106. Leary and Ma, "Luxury Brands Take On Landlords."

107. Su, "Xiushuijie 'Ligui' zaoyu 'yang Likui'" ["'Li Gui' at Silk Street Meets 'foreign Li Kui'"].

108. Liu, "Xiushuijie susong'an" ["The Silk Street Case"].

109. Liu, "Waiguo pinpai Zhongguo dajia diyi'an, Beijing Xiushuijie baisu" ["First Case of Foreign Brands Cracking Down Fakes in China, Beijing's Silk Street Lost"].

110. Silk Street Apparel Market Ltd. v. Chanel (Beijing Supreme People's Court, April 18, 2006). Available at: http://www .legaldaily.com.cn/misc/2008-11/17/con tent_983049.htm.

111. Liu, "Waiguo pinpai Zhongguo dajia diyi'an, Beijing Xiushuijie baisu" ["First Case of Foreign Brands Cracking Down Fakes in China, Beijing's Silk Street Lost"].

112. Liu, "Xiushuijie susong'an" ["The Silk Street Case"].

113. Simone, "Silk Market Fakes – Light at the End of the Tunnel?"

114. Liu, "Xiushuijie shoujia an" ["Silk Street Fake-Selling Case"].

115. Dickie, "Beijing Market Fights Piracy Verdict."

116. For instance, a French customer interviewed at the market said the chief reason for him to be there was the possibility of buying low-price clothing that was "not any different from real brands," and that many of his friends came to the market to buy for themselves or as gifts. See Zhao, "Xiushui shichang zai diaocha" ["Re-investigating the Silk Market"].

117. Ibid.

118. Tu, "Mingjie tansuo" ["Exploring Famous Streets"].

119. Simone, "Holding the Landlord Liable."

120. This signing event was also a new addition to China's initiative to combine criminal enforcement and civil measures in handling IPR cases, a decision announced the day before at the China-Europe IPR working meeting. See Shen, "Mande'ersen Xiushui duzhan 'dajia'" ["Mandelson Oversees 'Fake Strikes' at Silk Street"].

121. Simone, "Holding the Landlord Liable," 7.

122. *Zhongguo fushi bao* [China Fashion Weekly], "Beijing Xiushuijie deng lingshou shichang yu Ouzhou mingpai qianding dajia xieyi" ["Beijing's Silk Street and Other Retail Markets Signed 'Fake Strike' Agreement with European Luxury Brands"].

123. Friedmann, "Lacoste vs. Silk Street Plaza."

124. Zhang, "Xiushuijie beipan qinquan 'Bei Mian' fushi shangbiao" ["Silk Street Held to Infringe 'North Face' Apparel Trademark"].

125. Dou, "Xiushuijie shanghu pingqing lushi gao shichang" ["Xiushui Street Traders Hire Lawyers"].

126. If the trader pays a voluntary RMB 5,000 ($760) "rights protection" fee to the brand owners, the closure is limited to three days. See Gui and Liu, "Xiushuijie 'fengtan tingye zhengdun' fengbo" ["Silk Street 'Stall Closure for Reorganization' Disbutes: Notary for Fake-striking Rendered Suspect"]. See also Dou, "Xiushuijie shanghu pingqing lushi gao shichang" ["Xiushui Street Traders Hire Lawyers"].

127. Gui and Liu, "Xiushuijie 'fengtan tingye zhengdun' fengbo" ["Silk Street 'Stall Closure for Reorganization' Disputes: Notary for Fake-Striking Rendered Suspect"].

128. Li, "Yingte puluo cangcu huiying Xiushui 'fengtan shijian'" ["IntellecPro Responds Hastily to Silk Street's 'Closure' Incident"]. On February 3, 2009, a lawyer from the firm came to the market and engaged in an argument with numerous traders. One of the traders pulled out a Gucci-like shoe, whose brand was "Bei Jia Si" and whose picture was taken in the presence of a third-party notary representative, and threw it at the lawyer. See Dou, "Xiushuijie shanghu pingqing lushi gao shichang" ["Xiushui Street Traders Hire Lawyers"]. The traders revealed that they would be bringing a lawsuit against SSAM and IntellecPro, since it was written in the municipal "consumer goods and productive materials market regulations" that the market had no right to shut down the stalls. The notary agency's location in a different district was also brought up to invalidate the evidence for fake sales at the market.

129. Lafraniere, "Facing Counterfeiting Crackdown, Beijing Vendors Fight Back."

130. Beijing Silk Street Market Ltd., "Xiushui shichang zhi wuda pinpai quan-

liren de gongkaixin" ["Open Letter from Silk Street Market"].

131. Rofel, *Desiring China*, 144. Wang Hai is a young Chinese man who became nationally known for "fighting fakes" (*dajia*) in the 1990s. Taking advantage of a consumer protection law (newly passed in 1994) that requires fake-selling stores to pay double compensation to customers who return the fraudulent goods, Wang made a living from repeated buying and returning transactions of counterfeit products and eventually started his own consulting firm. For a more detailed analysis on how Wang legitimizes this consumer advocacy movement, see Rofel, *Desiring China*, 144–146.

132. Upon learning about IntellecPro's conduct, the letter states, the European Union representative is said to have announced at a 2007 IPR convention that twenty-three brand owners would terminate their relationship with the law firm.

133. Beijing Silk Street Market Ltd., "Xiushui shichang zhi wuda pinpai quanliren de gongkaixin" ["Open Letter from Silk Street Market"].

134. Jiang, "Xiushui shichang zhi wuda pinpai quanliren de gongkaixin; Pinglun: Waiguo lushi zai guonei congye ying shenzhong 'yang Wanghai' xingwei huanxing" ["Open Letter from Silk Street Market to the Rights Holders of Five Brands; Comments: Foreign lawyer practicing in China should be more cautious and slow down 'foreign Wang Hai' behaviors"].

135. As the manager of Silk Street, Wang's daily activities consisted mainly of receiving distinguished guests and engaging in interviews with foreign and domestic journalists. See Gui, "Xiushuijie: aoyun chengjiu de 'shangye niaochao'" ["Silk Street: the Olympics-Made Merchant's Bird Nest"].

136. Ren, "Lizhi zongjingli jubao Xiushui taoshui 2 yi: Xiushui shichang lianye fouren" ["General Manager Who Resigned Discloses Silk Street's Tax Evasion, Market Denies Charges Overnight"].

137. Another accusation in Wang's letter was that Zhang tried to take advantage of the state regulation for a tax exemption based on the percentage of downsized workers hired by recruiting 30 percent of all staff (nominally only thirty) from this pool, while putting the other hundred workers under the developer's name (Xinya Shenghong). To this, SSAM responded that only thirty-six staff worked for the company; the security and cleaning staff came from other "specialized" companies and did not belong to the management. Further, Zhang was said to not be in control of the corporation, as he was not the biggest shareholder. See Xiao, "Beijing Xiushuijie dongshizhang bei zhi taoshui 2 yi: shuiwuju cheng wei jie jubao" ["Chairman of Beijing's Silk Street Accused of CNY200 Million Tax Evasion, Taxation Affairs Claimed Report Never Received"].

138. *China Daily,* "Silk Street Fake Goods Retailer Claims He Was Management's Puppet."

139. The public display of justice is especially necessary when it comes to high-profile crimes, as attested by the 2012 Bo Xilai case.

140. See Appendix 3 for a synopsis of the film.

141. Zhao, "China's Quest for 'Soft Power': Imperatives, Impediments and Irreconcilable Tensions?" 21.

142. Pang, *Creativity and Its Discontents,* 149–150.

143. Dirlik, "Markets, Culture, Power," 25.

Conclusion

1. Tomlinson, *Cultural Imperialism,* 164.

2. Ibid., 174.

3. Lash and Lury, *Global Culture Industry,* 5.

4. Ong, *Neoliberalism as Exception,* 7.

5. See, for example, Chen, "Aosika qishi Zhongguo wenhua chanye" ["The Oscars Inspires China's Cultural Industry"].

6. Kraidy, *Hybridity.*

7. Kaplan, "'Left Alone with America,'" 17.

8. Pease, "New Perspectives on U.S. Culture and Imperialism," 26.

9. This is a point also emphasized in Kuan-Hsing Chen's work on "deimperialization." See Chen, *Asia as Method,* 24–25.

10. Mignolo, *The Darker Side of Western Modernity,* 20.

11. Ibid., 54.

12. See, for example, Chatterjee, *The Nation and Its Fragments.*

13. Barlow, "On 'Colonial Modernity.'"

14. While meaningful on its own, the latter perspective is ultimately based on "facile assimilation through non-recognition," because "colonialism's legalized racial discrimination and monopolistic economic extraction" was absent in imperial China. See Vukovich, "Postcolonialism, Globalization, and the 'Asia Question,'" 590.

15. Tomlinson, *Cultural Imperialism,* 162.

16. For a recent volume that mobilizes the imaginary as a critical category for American studies in a transnational context, see Bieger, Saldivar, and Voelz, *The Imaginary and Its Worlds.*

17. Xi, "Xi Jinping canguan Fuxing Zhilu zhanlan jianghua yuanwen" ["Xi Jinping's Speech at the Road to Revival Exhibition"].

18. *Economist* Briefing, "Xi Jinping's Vision."

19. Ibid.

20. Friedman, "China Needs Its Own Dream."

21. J. M., "The Role of Thomas Friedman."

22. *Economist,* "Xi Jinping's Vision."

23. Ibid. The phrase "China Dream," however, can still be found in English publications. See, for example, Callahan, *China Dreams.*

24. Here I am using "hailing" in Louis Althusser's sense to refer to the mechanism through which an ideology works upon and "'transforms' the individuals into subjects." See Althusser, "Ideology and Ideological State Apparatuses."

25. Tomlinson, *Cultural Imperialism,* 175.

26. Morley, "Globalisation and Cultural Imperialism."

27. Miller et al., *Global Hollywood,* 2.

28. Smith, *American Empire,* cited in Harvey, *The New Imperialism,* 47.

29. Zhang, "Zhang Xudong tan Zhongguomeng: zhongyu daole keyi tan mengxiang de shike" ["Zhang Xudong on the Chinese Dream"].

30. *Zhongguo wang* [China Net], "'Hehuoren' shangying 10 tian po 3 yi, yi chaoxi 'Shejiao Wangluo' ["'Partners' Grossed over 300 Million within Ten Days"].

31. New Oriental, "Overview."

32. Golden, "Test Prep in China," 63.

33. The amount was reduced on appeal to $750,000 in 2004. See Golden, "Test Prep in China," 63.

34. *People's Daily,* "Zhongguo Hehuoren" [*"American Dreams in China"*].

35. A 2008 biography of Yu Minhong, the founder, shares a widely known anecdote that two of three Chinese students studying in a famous university abroad would recognize Yu as their teacher. See Guo and Huang, *The Legend of Yu Minhong.*

36. I have taken the translation of this particular sentence from Xinhua Net. The speech also includes a self-deprecating

story of Cheng's pursuit of a woman in college who rejected him numerous times, a rejection that is plainly reminiscent of America's rejection of Cheng's visa application.

37. While the on-screen title displays *"Ting Zheng Hui,"* the Chinese translation for "Hearing," it is clear that the scene is not set in a courtroom in the presence of a judge, as it would be the case in an actual hearing. I have therefore opted for "meeting" as the translation here.

38. EES is of course a stand-in for the real-life ETS.

39. Song, "Guozu rentong beihou de wenhua zifu" ["The cultural conceit behind national identity"], 4.

40. In addition, Meng also suggests that today, Chinese students studying in America no longer wish to stay there but "want to go home" – a line that resonates with the film's calling upon overseas Chinese (just like Xu Xiaoping, the screenwriter himself) to return to their homeland for realizing their "American Dreams in China."

41. See, for example, Tian, "Zhongguo Hehuoren" [*"American Dreams in China"*].

42. *Guangming Ribao* [Guangming Daily], "Neihuo waileng" ["Hot Inside but Cold Outside"].

43. Wang, "Shidai jingshen de chouli yu bianxing" ["Abstraction and Distortion of the Zeitgeist"].

44. Tian, "Zhongguo Hehuoren" [*"American Dreams in China"*].

45. See, for example, Hu and Wei, "Cong yishixingtai chuanbo de jiaodu kan dianying Zhongguo Hehuoren dui 'Zhongguomeng' de jiangou" ["The 'Chinese Dream' in *American Dreams in China"*].

46. Zhang, "Dangdai dazhong wenhua zhong de Meiguo xiangxiang" ["The 'American' imaginary"], 43.

47. Despite having a different English title, *Finding Mr. Right,* it is almost entirely based in Seattle, where two people from Beijing fall in love.

48. Zhang, "Zai fansi 'Meiguomeng' zhong renshi Zhongguo" ["Understanding China by Reflecting on the 'American Dream'"], 8.

49. Wang, "Chen Kexin tan Zhongguo Hehuoren" ["Chen Kexin on *American Dreams in China*"].

50. The exact quote is: "America's racism can never be dissolved. If a white man sees three black men coming into the elevator together, he is going to flee the elevator just a moment before the doors close. For the whites, blacks are always lazy, ignorant, and a barbarian race. What about the Chinese in America? At least they are smart and diligent? But, they say, the Chinese took jobs away from the local residents."

51. Luo, "Zhongguo Hehuoren" ["*American Dreams in China*"].

52. Zhang, "Zai fansi 'Meiguomeng' zhong renshi Zhongguo" ["Understanding China by reflecting on the 'American Dream'"].

53. One example of this was a 1990s popular television show, *Beijing Sojourners in New York,* which is known for its opening tagline: "If you love someone, send him to America. If you hate someone, send him to America."

54. Zhang, "'Zhongguo jueqi' de minzu yuyan" ["A national allegory of 'China's rise'"].

55. Wang, "Houzhimin yujing xia de biaoshu jiaolu yu rentong weiji – jiedu dianying Zhongguo Hehuoren" ["The Expression of Anxiety and Identity Crisis in the Postcolonial Context"], 87–88.

56. Callahan, *China Dreams,* 58.

57. Ibid., 149–150.

58. Marquis and Yang, "Chinese Dream? American Dream?"

59. This is also a method adopted by real-life New Oriental teachers, including Xu Xiaoping, the original screenwriter, who has a cameo appearance in the film as one of the English instructors using this approach at New Dreams.

60. Grossberg, "History, Imagination and the Politics of Belonging," 157.

61. Ibid.

62. This emphasis on "Chineseness" is in line with earlier moments in the film that serve to accentuate the "Chinese" characteristics of Cheng's blend of entrepreneurship, manifested in, say, his rejection of Meng's advice to fire an old but underperforming employee, and his arbitrary use of veto power during a board meeting to stop the company from going public.

63. Zhuang, "Xindushi lizhipian de xiandai tujing" ["The modern vision of new urban motivation films"], 200.

64. Tian, "Zhongguo Hehuoren" ["*American Dreams in China*"], 42.

65. See, for example, *Guangming Ribao* [Guangming Daily], "Neihuo waileng" ["Hot Inside but Cold Outside"].

66. More than a few personal friends of mine living in China have used the term "*lizhi*" (meaning "inspirational" or "motivational") to describe their feelings toward the film. Several of them also mentioned, as did news reports, that many audiences greeted the film's ending with standing ovations.

67. Two authors, An Puruo and Xiang Shang, have used "*exin*" and "*zuo'ou,*" both of which mean "disgusted," to express their reaction to the film's ending sequence. Quoted in *Zhongguo wang* [China Net], "'Hehuoren' shangying 10 tian po 3 yi, yi chaoxi 'Shejiao Wangluo'" ["'Partners' Grossed over 300 Million within Ten Days"].

68. This sentiment is one that is arguably shared on the other side of the Pacific,

where recent polls indicate that "only about half of Americans now believe in the American Dream," and increasingly, "the phrase is just as likely to be used in irony as in earnest," despite President Obama's campaign promise "to reclaim the American Dream. See Marquis and Yang, "Chinese Dream? American Dream?" This cynicism is also shared by numerous Chinese friends I spoke with during a research trip to China in January 2014.

69. Herzfeld, *Cultural Intimacy*, 2.

Appendix 2

1. I quote from the DVD (overseas/Netflix) version's English subtitles, inserting content that has been left out or giving explanations, when necessary, in square brackets.

2. The last two sentences are my translation.

3. The full original line is "The earlier the death, the sooner the rise to pure heaven (*zao si zao chao sheng*)."

4. As some viewers note, this "Four Eyes" sequence seems to have borrowed some elements from *Missing Gun* (2002), a film by Lu Chuan that won critical acclaim in several domestic and international film festivals.

5. The entire movie can be viewed at http://www.56.com/u56/v_MzQoNzQzOTc.html.

Bibliography

Ah Gan. *Shanzhai Geming* [Revolution of Mode of Production]. Beijing: China CITIC Press, 2009.

Althusser, Louis. "Ideology and Ideological State Apparatuses (Notes towards an Investigation)." Translated by Ben Brewster. New York: Monthly Review Press, 1971.

———. *Reading Capital.* Translated by Ben Brewster. London: New Left Books, 1970.

Anagnost, Ann. "Socialist Ethics and the Legal System." In *Popular Protest and Political Culture in Modern China: Learning from 1989,* edited by Elizabeth J. Perry and Jeffrey N. Wasserstrom, 177–205. Boulder, CO: Westview Press, 1992.

Anderson, Benedict R. O'G. *Imagined Communities: Reflections on the Origin and Spread of Nationalism,* rev. and ext. ed. London: Verso, 1991.

Anti-Counterfeiting Group. "The Scale of Counterfeiting." *The Anti-Counterfeiting Group,* n.d. http://counterfeiting.unicri.it/docs/Anti-Counterfeiting%20Group.Scale%20of%20Counterfeiting.UK.pdf.

Appadurai, Arjun. *Modernity at Large: Cultural Dimensions of Globalization.* Vol. 1 of *Public Worlds,* edited by Dilip Ga-onkar and Benjamin Lee. Minneapolis: University of Minnesota Press, 1996.

Arnason, Johann P. "Nationalism, Globalization and Modernity." *Theory, Culture & Society* 7, no. 2 (1990): 207–236.

Aronczyk, Melissa. "New and Improved Nations: Branding National Identity." In *Taking Culture Seriously,* edited by Craig J. Calhoun and Richard Sennett, 105–128. London: Routledge, 2007.

Asia Times Online. "China surpasses US as most attractive FDI nation," September 25, 2002. http://www.atimes.com/atimes/China/D125Ad03.html.

Baidu baike [Baidupedia]. "Shanzhai." March 30, 2010. http://baike.baidu.com/view/268947.htm?fr=alao_1_1.

Baidu tieba [Baidu Posting Board]. "Guanyu zhichi Fengkuang de Shitou changyi" ["A Proposal for Supporting *Crazy Stone*"], July 13, 2006. http://tieba.baidu.com/f?kz=114130787.

———. "Shitou dao muqian suo faxian de suoyou xijie [zhengli ban]" ["All Stone Details Discovered up to Now (Rearranged Version)"], July 22, 2006. http://tieba.baidu.com/f?kz=116631151.

Bao Ran. "Juanshouyu: Fengkuang de Shitou" ["Foreword: *Crazy Stone*"]. *Zhongguo shuzi dianshi* [China Digital TV], August 2006.

baohulutime. "Fengkuang de Shitou shi chetouchewei de buyaolian chaoxi" ["*Crazy Stone* is Completely, Shamelessly Copied"]. Sina Entertainment Forum (blog), August 12, 2006. http://club.ent.sina.com.cn/redirect.php?tid=330689&goto=lastpost.

Barber, Lionel. "The End of US Hegemony: Legacy of 9/11." *Financial Times,* September 5, 2011.

Barboza, David. "In China, Knockoff Cellphones Are a Hit." *New York Times,* April 28, 2009. http://www.nytimes.com/2009/04/28/technology/28cell.html?_r=1&scp=1&sq=china%20hi%20phone&st=cse.

Barlow, Tani E. "Introduction: On 'Colonial Modernity.'" In *Formations of Colonial Modernity in East Asia,* edited by Tani E. Barlow, 1–20. Durham, NC: Duke University Press, 1997.

Beijing ribao [Beijing Daily]. "'Zhongguo zhizao' guanggao: zhuti jijing biandong, zhongding 'shijie hezuo'" ["'Made in China' Ad: Theme Underwent Several Changes before Being Finalized as 'Made with the World'"], December 4, 2009. http://www.chinanews.com/cul/news/2009/12-04/1999687.shtml.

Bejing Silk Street Market Ltd. "Xiushui shichang zhi wuda pinpai quanliren de gongkaixin (Open Letter from Silk Street Market to the Rights Holders of Five Brands)." *Judicial Protection of IPR in China,* February 10, 2009. http://www.chinaiprlaw.cn/file/20090212 14452.html.

Benjamin, Walter. "On the Concept of History" (1940). In *Theses on History.* Translated by Dennis Redmond. 2005. Available at http://www.marxists.org/reference/archive/benjamin/1940/history.htm.

Berry, Chris. "Cinema: From Foreign Import to Global Brand." In *The Cam-bridge Companion to Modern Chinese Culture,* edited by Kam Louie, 297–317. Cambridge: Cambridge University Press, 2008.

——. "If China Can Say No, Can China Make Movies? Or, Do Movies Make China? Rethinking National Cinema and National Agency." In *Modern Chinese Literary and Cultural Studies in the Age of Theory: Reimagining a Field,* edited by Rey Chow, 159–180. Durham, N.C.: Duke University Press, 2000.

——. *Perspectives on Chinese Cinema.* Ithaca, NY: Cornell East Asian Papers, no. 39, 1985.

——. "'What's Big about the Big Film?' 'De-Westernizing' the Blockbuster in Korean and China." In *Movie Blockbust-ers,* edited by Julian Stringer, 217–229. New York: Routledge, 2006.

Berry, Chris, and Mary Ann Farquhar. *China on Screen: Cinema and Nation.* New York: Columbia University Press, 2006.

Bhabha, Homi K. "DissemiNation: Time, Narrative, and the Margins of the Modern Nation." In *Nation and Narration,* edited by Homi K. Bhabha, 291–322. London: Routledge, 1990.

Bhattasali, Deepak, Shantong Li, and Will Martin, eds. *China and the wto: Accession, Policy Reform, and Poverty Reduction Strategies.* Trade and Development Series. Washington, DC: World Bank/Oxford University Press, 2004.

Biagioli, Mario, Peter Jaszi, and Martha Woodmansee. "Introduction." In *Making and Unmaking Intellectual Property : Creative Production in Legal and Cultural Perspective,* edited by Mario Biagioli, Peter Jaszi, and Martha Woodmansee, 1–22. Chicago: University of Chicago Press, 2011.

Bieger, Laura, Ramon Saldivar, and Johannes Voelz, eds. *The Imaginary and*

Its Worlds: American Studies After the Transnational Turn. Lebanon, NH: University Press of New England, 2013.

Bolter, J. David, and Richard Grusin. *Remediation: Understanding New Media*. Cambridge, MA: MIT Press, 1999.

Bongiorni, Sara. "A Year without 'Made in China.'" *Christian Science Monitor*. December 20, 2005. http://www.csmonitor.com/2005/1220/p09s01-coop.html.

——. *A Year without "Made in China": One Family's True Life Adventure in the Global Economy*. Hoboken, NJ: John Wiley & Sons, 2007.

Bosker, Bianca. *Original Copies*. Honolulu: University of Hawaii Press, 2013.

Cable News Network. "CNN Special: Made In China, Part 1," July 26, 2007.

Cable News Network. "CNN Special: Made in China, Part 2," July 26, 2007.

Caijing shibao [Business Times]. "Wangluo faxing + 'egao' quanqian zhuti: shitou rang quanguo fengkuang" ["Internet Distribution + 'E Gao' Baiting Themes: *Stone* Makes the Whole Country Crazy"], July 19, 2006. http.//net.chinabyte.com/131/2508631.shtml.

Calhoun, Craig J. *Nations Matter: Culture, History, and the Cosmopolitan Dream*. London: Routledge, 2007.

Callahan, William A. *China Dreams: 20 Visions of the Future*. Oxford: Oxford University Press, 2013.

Canaves, Sky. "A Makeover Attempt for 'Made in China.'" *Wall Street Journal*, November 27, 2009. http://blogs.wsj.com/chinarealtime/2009/11/27/a-makeover-attempt-for-made-in-china/tab/article/.

Canaves, Sky, and Juliet Ye. "Imitation Is the Sincerest Form of Rebellion in China." *Wall Street Journal*, January 22, 2009. http://online.wsj.com/article/SB123257138952903561.html.

Cartier, Carolyn L. *Globalizing South China*. RGS-IBG Book Series. Oxford: Blackwell Publishers, 2001.

Castells, Manuel, Mireia Fernández-Ardèvol, Jack Linchuan Qiu and Araba Sey. *Mobile Communication and Society: A Global Perspective*. Cambridge, MA: MIT Press, 2007.

Castoriadis, Cornelius. *The Imaginary Institution of Society*. Cambridge, MA: MIT Press, 1987.

CCTV. "Kuayue Zhongguo zhizao" ["Across Made in China"], August 6, 2009. http://jishi.cntv.cn/humhis/kuayuezhongguozhizao/videopage/index.shtml.

CCTV. *Shijie zhoukan* [World Weekly]. "Meiguoren meiyou zhongguo zhizao de yinian shenghuo" ["Americans' Year-Long Life without 'Made in China'"]. November 19, 2007.

CCTV. "'Xiangxin Zhongguo zhizao' – Zhongguo chanpin zhiliang guoying" ["Believe in 'Made in China' – Chinese Products Are of High Quality"], August 21, 2007. http://finance.cctv.com/special/C19197/20070821/102s8.shtml.

CCTV 4. "Xianxin Zhongguo Zhizao" ["Believe in 'Made in China'"]. *Jinri Guanzhu (Focus Today)*, August 27, 2007.

CCTV 13. "Xijinping zai canguan Fuxing Zhilu zhanlan shi qiangdiao chengqianqihou jiwangkailai jixu chaozhe zhonghua minzu weida fuxing mubiao fenyong qianjin" ["Xi Jinping emphasizes inheriting and carrying on the task to march toward the goal of the Chinese nation's great revival"]. *Xinwen lianbo* [Network News Broadcast], November 29, 2012. http://news.cntv.cn/program/xwlb/20121129/107673.shtml.

CCTV Chinese Finance and Economics Reports. *Shanzhai Laile* [Shanzhai is Coming]. Beijing: China Machine Press, 2009.

Cha, Ariana Eunjung. "Shopping on Silk Street with Bush Sr. And Other VIPS – Live Coverage." *Washington Post.* August 14, 2008. http://voices.wash ingtonpost.com/livecoverage/2008/08 /shopping_on_silk_street_with_b .html.

Chang'anjie (wu) dongjie gushi [Chang'An Avenue – Episode Five: Stories of East Avenue]. 2010. http://tv.cntv.cn/video /C15637/6b06bb5fb44a4a207fb928a9b 9a10e2c.

Chang, Hsiao-hung. "Fake logos, fake theory, fake globalization." *Inter-Asia Cultural Studies* 5, no. 2 (2004): 222–236.

Chatterjee, Partha. *The Nation and Its Fragments: Colonial and Postcolonial Histories.* Princeton, NJ: Princeton University Press, 1993.

———. "The nation in heterogeneous time." *Futures* 37, no. 9 (November 2005): 925–942.

Chen, Kuan-Hsing. *Asia as Method: Toward Deimperialization.* Durham, NC: Duke University Press, 2010.

Chen Peng. "Aosika qishi Zhongguo wenhua chanye" ["The Oscars Inspires China's Cultural Industry"]. *Liaowang* [Outlook], 2009.

Chen Taotao. "Yidong dianhua zhizaoye: waishang zhijie touzi yichu xiaoying anli yanjiu" ["Research on the Spillover Effect of Foreign Direct Investment: A Case Study of the Chinese Mobile Phone Manufacturing Sector"]. *Guoji jingji hezuo* [International Economic Cooperation] 1 (2005): 38–42.

Chen Yangyong. "Jiang Zemin 'zouchuqu' zhanlue de xingcheng ji qi zhongyao yiyi" ["The Formation and Significance of Jiang Zemin's 'Going Global' Strategy"]. *News of the Communist Party of China,* November 10, 2003. http:// theory.people.com.cn/GB/40557 /138172/138202/8311431.html.

Chen You. "Fengkuang de Shitou, mensao de Ning Hao" ["Crazy Stone, 'Secretly Sexy' Ning Hao"]. *Xibu guangbo dianshi* [West China Broadcasting TV] 7, no. 7 (2007): 40–41.

China Daily. "Silk Street Fake Goods Retailer Claims He Was Management's Puppet," January 20, 2010. http://www .chinadaily.com.cn/cndy/2010-01/20 /content_9346046.htm.

Choate, Pat. *Hot Property: The Stealing of Ideas in an Age of Globalization.* New York: Knopf, 2005.

ChongQiWaWa. "Haokan ge pi" ["Entertaining My Arse"]. *Douban.* July 24, 2006.

Chow, Rey. *Primitive passions: Visuality, Sexuality, Ethnography, and Contemporary Chinese Cinema.* New York: Columbia University Press, 1995.

Clark, Paul. *Chinese cinema: Culture and Politics Since 1949.* Cambridge: Cambridge University Press, 1987.

Coonan, Clifford. "China Bound to Tradition." *Variety,* January 15, 2007.

CRI *Online.* "Fengkuang de Shitou zhuchuang renyuan xiao tan 'Shitou'" ["Core Creative Team Lightheartedly Discusses *Crazy Stone*"]. August 2, 2006. http://gb.cri.cn/9964/2006 /08/02/1845@1158415.htm.

Cui Weiping. "Tianxia yingxiong shi guaren" ["The Hero of the World is the Emperor Myself"]. *Xuezhe shequ* [China Review], January 31, 2003. http:// www.china-review.com/sao.asp?id =1480.

De Kloet, Jeroen. "Crossing the Threshold: Chinese Cinema Studies in the Twenty-First Century." *Journal of Chinese Cinemas* 1, no. 1 (December 2006): 63–70.

Delanty, Gerard, and Krishan Kumar, eds. *The* SAGE *Handbook of Nations and Nationalism.* London: SAGE, 2006.

Deng Xiaoping. "Yao xishou guoji de jing-yan" ["We Must Learn from International Experiences"]. *Qiushi lilun wang* [Qiushi Theory], June 30, 2009. http://www.qstheory.cn/zl/llzz/dxpwjd3j/200906/t20090630_4731.htm.

Deng Xitao. "Xiushuijie zhi tong" ["The Grief of Xiushui Street"]. *Zhongguo xiaofeizhe bao* (Beijing) [China Consumer News], December 15, 2004.

Desai, Radhika. "Introduction: Nationalisms and Their Understandings in Historical Perspective." *Third World Quarterly* 29, no. 3 (2008): 397.

———. "The Inadvertence of Benedict Anderson: Engaging Imagined Communities." Japan Focus, March 16, 2009. japanfocus.org/data/Inadvertence.pics.pdf.

Dickie, Mure. "Beijing Market Fights Piracy Verdict." *Financial Times*, January 6, 2006.

Dirlik, Arif. "Markets, Culture, Power: The Making of a 'Second Cultural Revolution' in China." *Asian Studies Review* 25, no. 1 (March 2001): 1–33.

———. "Postsocialism? Reflections on 'Socialism with Chinese Characteristics.'" In *Marxism and the Chinese Experience: Issues in Contemporary Chinese Socialism*, edited by Arif Dirlik and Maurice J Meisner, 362–384. Armonk, NY: M. E. Sharpe, 1989.

Dirlik, Arif, and Xudong Zhang. "Introduction: Postmodernism and China." In *Postmodernism & China*, edited by Arif Dirlik and Xudong Zhang, 1–17. Durham, NC: Duke University Press, 2000.

Doane, Mary Ann. "Information, Crisis, Catastrophe." In *New Media, Old Media: A History and Theory Reader*, edited by Wendy Hui Kyong Chun and Thomas Keenan, 251–264. New York: Routledge, 2006.

Dong, ed. "Quanguo piaofang po 1600 wan, Ning Hao: 'Shitou' zan feng wo mei zan" ["With a Nationwide Box Office over 1.6 million, Ning Hao says: 'I am not making any money while the "stone" is, crazily'"]. Sohu.com, July 30, 2006. http://yule.sohu.com/20060730/n244523439.shtml.

Dou Hongmei. "Xiushuijie shanghu pingqing lushi gao shichang" ["Xiushui Street Traders Hire Lawyers to Sue the Market"]. *Beijing ribao* [Beijing Daily]. February 4, 2009.

Duara, Prasenjit. "The Legacy of Empires and Nations in East Asia." In *China Inside Out: Contemporary Chinese Nationalism and Transnationalism*, edited by Pál Nyíri and Joana Breidenbach, 35–54. Budapest: Central European University Press, 2005.

Dyer, Geoff. "CCTV Opens 'Believe in "Made in China."'" *Financial Times* (Shanghai), August 22, 2007.

Economist. Briefing. "Xi Jinping's Vision: Chasing the Chinese Dream," May 4, 2013. http://www.economist.com/news/briefing/21577063-chinas-new-leader-has-been-quick-consolidate-his-power-what-does-he-now-want-his.

Elley, Derek. "Crazy Stone." *Variety*. 2006.

ESWN Culture Blog. "Crazy Stone Is A Poisonous Weed," August 15, 2006. http://www.zonaeuropa.com/culture/c20060815_1.htm.

Farrar, Lara. "China's 'bandit phones' making big scores." CNN Digital Biz, August 3, 2009. http://edition.cnn.com/2009/TECH/07/29/china.fake.phones/index.html#cnnSTCText.

Feifeizhiyin. "Fengkuang de Shitou: chongman luoji meigan de chengshi dianying" ["*Crazy Stone*: An Urban Film Filled with the Beauty of Logic"]. *Nanqiangbeidiao – mingxing ban* [Star], 2006.

Feng He. "Baohu zhishi chanquan juefei jinxian koutou" ["Protecting IPR Is by No Means Just about Talks"]. *Guoji shangbao* (Beijing) [International Business Daily], January 14, 2006.

Fenghuang kuaipin [Phoenix Global Connection]. "Zhongguo zhengfu quanqiu da guanggao, zhongmei hupin ruanshili" ["Chinese Government Advertises Globally; China and America Compete in Soft Power"]. Phoenix Broadband Video, December 1, 2009. http://v.ifeng.com/news/world/200912/0f15d96b-a119-4ba9-8d70-114d07f87fce.shtml#b3a5ae4b-589b-4df8-b553-ea680711f328.

Fengkuang de shitou ba [*Crazy Stone* bar]. "Shitou li Beijing Tiananmen changjing faxian" ["An Observation regarding the Beijing Tiananmen Square Scene in *Stone*"], September 28, 2006. http://tieba.baidu.com/f?kz=136304385.

"Fengkuang de Shitou: heise de kuanghuan" ["*Crazy Stone:* The Carnival of Black Humor"]. *Dianying yishu* [Film Art] 5 (2006): 73–75.

"Fengkuang de Shitou zhuanlun" ["Special Comments on *Crazy Stone*"]. *Dianying wenxue* [Movie Literature] 9, no. 2 (August 2006): 10.

Fish, Stanley. *Is There a Text in This Class? The Authority of Interpretive Communities.* Cambridge, MA: Harvard University Press, 1980.

Fletcher, Keith, and Julia Wilkinson. "Giving a Whoop About the Olympics." *Fox sports.com,* n.d. (page no longer available)

Foucault, Michel. "Of Other Spaces, Heterotopias." Translated by Jay Miskowiec. *Architecture, Mouvement, Continuité* 5 (1984): 46–49. Available at http://foucault.info/documents/heteroTopia/foucault.heteroTopia.en.html.

Frank, Dana. *Buy American: The Untold Story of Economic Nationalism.* Boston: Beacon Press, 1999.

Freedman, David H. "Fakers' Paradise." *Forbes,* April 5, 1999.

Friedmann, Danny. "Lacoste vs. Silk Street Plaza: Litigation vs Contributory Liability." *Zhishi chanquan long* [IP Dragon], June 12, 2006. http://ipdragon.blogspot.com/2006/06/lacoste-vs-silk-street-plaza.html.

Friedman, Thomas L. "China Needs Its Own Dream." *New York Times,* October 2, 2012. http://www.nytimes.com/2012/10/03/opinion/friedman-china-needs-its-own-dream.html.

Gan Yang. "Bashi niandai wenhua taolun de jige wenti" ["Several Issues in the Cultural Discussions of the Eighties"]. In *Bashi Niandai Wenhua Yishi* [Cultural Consciousness of the Eighties], 3–33. Shanghai: Shanghai People's Press, 2006.

Gaonkar, Dilip Parameshwar. "Toward New Imaginaries: An Introduction." *Public Culture* 14, no. 1 (2002): 1–19.

Gao Suying and Fazhong Zhao. "Xiushuijie dengdai 'laozihao'" ["Silk Street Awaits 'Time-Honored Brands'"]. *Zhongguo jingying bao* (Beijing) [China Business], March 5, 2007.

Gao Yingming. "Pouxi Shanzhai shouji shichang xianxiang" ["Dissecting the Market Phenomenon of Shanzhai Cell Phones"]. *Dianzi yu diannao* [Compotech China], November 2008.

Geng Wen. "Beijing Xiushuijie rang laowai shu qi le muzhi" ["Beijing's Silk Street Got Thumbs Up from 'Lao Wai'"]. *Zhongguo luyou bao* (Beijing) [China Tourism News], February 5, 2007.

Geng Wen and Geqi Jiang. "20 nian de luyou pinpai gai bu gai chai?" ["Should a Twenty-Year-Old Tourism Brand be Demolished?"]. *Zhongguo luyou bao* (Beijing) [China Tourism News], October 10, 2003.

Gerth, Karl. *China Made: Consumer Culture and the Creation of the Nation.* Harvard East Asian Monographs 224. Cambridge, MA: Harvard University Asia Center, 2003.

Ge Shengjun and Xiangyu Piao. "Fengkuang de Shitou xiaofei jiegou fenxi" ["An Analysis of the Consumption Structure of *Crazy Stone*"]. *Dianying pingjie* [Movie Review] 24 (2007): 38–39.

Golden, Daniel. "U.S. College Test Prep in China Is": *Bloomberg Businessweek,* May 9, 2011.

Gong, Haomin, and Xin Yang. "Digitized parody: The politics of egao in contemporary China." *China Information* 24, no. 1 (March 1, 2010): 3–26.

Gong Jie. "Houxiandai yujing xia de kuanghuanhua xushu – jiedu dianying wenben Fengkuang de Shitou" ["A Carnivalesque Narrative in the Postmodern Context: Reading the Filmic Text *Crazy Stone*"]. *Dianying pingjie* [Movie Review] 4 (2007): 33–35.

Groening, Stephen Francis. "Connected Isolation: Screens, Mobility, and Globalized Media Culture." PhD diss., University of Minnesota, 2008.

Grossberg, Lawrence. "History, Imagination and the Politics of Belonging: Between the Death and the Fear of History." In *Without Guarantees: In Honour of Stuart Hall,* edited by Paul Gilroy, Lawrence Grossberg, and Angela McRobbie. London: Verso, 2000.

Guan Wen and Yuqing Zhu. "Fengkuang de Shitou 6 yue 30 ri qi dou ni mei shangliang" ["*Crazy Stone,* Starting June 30, Entertains Without Reservation"]. *Zhongguo dianying bao* (Beijing) [China Film], June 29, 2006.

Gui Jie. "Xiushuijie: aoyun chengjiu de 'shangye niaochao'" ["Silk Street: the Olympics-Made Merchant's Bird Nest"]. *Zhongguo qingnian bao* (Beijing) [China Youth Daily], August 24, 2008.

Gui Jie and Chenxi Liu. "Xiushuijie 'fengtan tingye zhengdun' fengbo" ["Silk Street 'Stall Closure for Reorganization' Disputes: Notary for Fake-Striking Rendered Suspect"]. *Zhongguo qingnian bao* (Beijing) [China Youth Daily], February 16, 2009. http://news.cctv.com /law/20090216/104644.shtml.

Guo Liang and Xiao Huang. *The Legend of Yu Minhong.* Beijing: China Machine Press, 2008.

Harvey, David. *A Brief History of Neoliberalism.* Oxford: Oxford University Press, 2005.

———. *The New Imperialism.* Oxford: Oxford University Press, 2005.

Hayden, Cori. "A Generic Solution? Pharmaceuticals and the Politics of the Similar in Mexico." *Current Anthropology,* no. 4 (2007): 475–495.

———. "No Patent, No Generic: Pharmaceutical Access and the Politics of the Copy." In *Making and Unmaking Intellectual Property: Creative Production in Legal and Cultural Perspective,* edited by Mario Biagioli, Peter Jaszi, and Martha Woodmansee, 285–303. Chicago: University of Chicago Press, 2011.

———. "The Proper Copy." *Journal of Cultural Economy* 3, no. 1 (March 2010): 85–102.

"'Hehuoren' shangying 10 tian po 3 yi, yi chaoxi 'Shejiao Wangluo'" ["'Partners' grossed over 300 million within 10 days, suspected of copying 'Social Network'"]. *Zhongguo wang* [China Net], May 27, 2013. http://www.china.com.cn/info /2013-05/27/content_28945564.htm.

He, Nan. "Xiushuijie, 'OK' jie" ["Silk Street, 'OK' Street"]. *Zhongguo jingying huabao* [China Business Pictorial], May 15, 1997.

Hengdian Group. "About Us." Hengdian Group, 2004. http://www.hengdian.com/site/en/en_com_history.htm.

Herzfeld, Michael. *Cultural Intimacy: Social Poetics in the Nation-State.* 2nd ed. New York: Routledge, 2005.

He, Wei. "Fengyu xiushuijie" ["Xiushui Alley in Wind and Rain"]. *Yingxiao xueyuan [Modern Marketing (Academy Edition)]* 3 (2005): 41.

He Yuan. "Nongmingong xinxihua shengcun baogao" ["Peasant Workers' Informational Survival Report"]. *Jisuanji shijie* [China Computer World], April 23, 2007.

Higson, Andrew. "The Concept of National Cinema." *Screen* 30, no. 4 (1989): 36–47.

———. "The limiting imagination of national cinema." In *Cinema and Nation,* edited by Mette Hjort and Scott MacKenzie, 63–74. London; New York: Routledge, 2000.

hkfilmart.com. "Crazy Stone's Chinese Box Office." *CRI English,* July 18, 2006. http://english.cri.cn/3086/2006/07/18/44@115534.htm.

Hohnen, Pernille. *A Market Out of Place? Remaking Economic, Social, and Symbolic Boundaries in Post-Communist Lithuania.* New York: Oxford University Press, 2003.

Ho, Josephine. "Shan-Zhai: Economic/Cultural Production through the Cracks of Globalization." Paper presented at the ACS (Association of Cultural Studies) Crossroads 2010, Hong Kong, June 18, 2010.

Hong Junhao, Yanmei Lu, and William Zou. "CCTV in the Reform Years: A New Model for China's Television?" In *TV China,* edited by Ying Zhu and Chris Berry, 40–55. Bloomington: Indiana University Press, 2009.

Hong, Shibin. "Shanzhai shouji shi 'minzu yingxiong'?" ["Shanzhai Cell Phones

are 'National Heroes'?"]. *Zhonghua pinpai guanli wang [China Brand Management Net],* February 3, 2009. http://www.cnbm.net.cn/article/vd168971363.html.

Hopkins, David. *Counterfeiting Exposed: Protecting Your Brand and Customers.* Hoboken, NJ: J. Wiley & Sons, 2003.

Hou Ge. "Caogen-shugen-jigen-wugen" ["Grassroots, Tree Roots, Thorny Roots, Rootless"]. *Mingzuo xinshang* [Appreciation of Famous Literary Works] 1 (2007): 133–135.

Huang Chaowu. "Xiushuijie zui shou 'laowai' zhuipeng" ["Silk Street Most Hounded by 'Lao Wai'"]. *Nongmin ribao* (Beijing) [Farmers' Daily], August 30, 2008.

Huang Ping. "Kuanghuanhua shixue xia de 'shitou' – jiedu Fengkuang de Shitou" ["Stone in Carnivalesque Poetics – Reading *Crazy Stone*"]. *Dianying pingjie* [Movie Review] 5 (2007): 28–29.

Huang Wei. "Banzhe zhitou zuo maoyi – zoufang beijing Xiushui shichang" ["Counting Fingers for Trade – A Visit to Beijing's Xiushui Market"]. *Renmin ribao* (Beijing) [People's Daily], June 21, 2004.

Hu Jintao. *Hu Jintao zai dang de shiqida shang de baogao* [Hu Jintao's Report at the Chinese Communist Party's Seventeenth National Congress]. Xinhua Net (Beijing), October 24, 2007. http://www.china.com.cn/chinese/news/1087527.htm.

Hu Man. "Beijing Xiushuijie jie aoyun tisheng pinpai meili" ["Beijing's Silk Street Relies on Olympics to Raise its Branding Charm"]. *Zhongguo zhishi chanquan bao* (Beijing) [China Intellectual Property News], August 22, 2008.

Hu Qing and Baotao Wei. "Cong yishixingtai chuanbo de jiaodu kan dianying Zhongguo Hehuoren dui

'Zhongguomeng' de jiangou" ["The construction of the 'Chinese Dream' in *American Dreams in China* from the perspective of ideological diffusion"]. *Wenxue pinglun* [Literary Review], n.d.

Hu Zuliu. "Cong 'Zhongguo zhizao' dao 'Zhongguo chuangzao'" ["From 'Made in China' to 'Created in China'"]. *Shichang bao* (Beijing) [Market News], March 3, 2006. http://www.tsinghua .edu.cn/publish/news/4205/2011/20110 225231719765674161/20110225231719765 674161_.html.

Internet Movie Database. "Reviews and Ratings for *Crazy Stone*." http://www .imdb.com/title/tt0843270/user comments.

Jameson, Fredric. "Notes on globalization as a philosophical issue." In *The Cultures of Globalization,* edited by Fredric Jameson and Masao Miyoshi, 54–77. Durham, NC: Duke University Press, 1998.

———. *The Geopolitical Aesthetic: Cinema and Space in the World System.* Bloomington: Indiana University Press, 1992.

———. *The Political Unconscious: Narrative as a Socially Symbolic Act.* Ithaca, NY: Cornell University Press, 1982.

———. "Third-World Literature in the Era of Multinational Capitalism." *Social Text,* no. 15 (Autumn 1986): 65–88.

Jenkins, Henry. *Convergence Culture: Where Old and New Media Collide.* New York: New York University Press, 2006.

———. "Quentin Tarantino's Star Wars? Digital Cinema, Media Convergence, and Participatory Culture." In *Rethinking Media Change: The Aesthetics of Transition,* edited by David Thorburn and Henry Jenkins, 281–312. Cambridge, MA: MIT Press, 2004.

Jiang, Xinjie. "Xiushuijie getihu: zai jingcheng bianyuan xingzou 19 nian" ["Independent Entrepreneurs at

Xiushui Street: Wandering on the Margins of the Capital City for Nineteen Years"]. *Zhongguo qingnian bao* (Beijing) [China Youth Daily], January 7, 2005.

Jiang, Zhipei. "Xiushui shichang zhi wuda pinpai quanliren de gongkaixin; Pinglun: Waiguo lushi zai guonei congye ying shenzhong 'yang Wanghai' xingwei huanxing" ["Open Letter from Silk Street Market to the Rights Holders of Five Brands; Comments: Foreign lawyer practicing in China should be more cautious and slow down 'foreign Wang Hai' behavior"]. Wangyou luntan [Net Friends Forum]. *Zhongguo zhishi chanquan sifa baohu* [China IPR Legal Protection], February 12, 2009.

Jinghua shibao [Beijing Times]. "Beijing Xiushuijie zouguo fengyu 20 nian" ["Beijing's Xiushui Street Went Through Twenty Years of Wind and Rain"]. January 6, 2005. http://news.sina.com.cn /c/2005-01-06/02584729708s.shtml.

———. "20 yu bu guochanpian jiang zhanying: Liang Wenli houhui mei yan Tian Gou" ["Over Twenty Domestic Films to Exhibit: Jiang Wenli Regrets Not Acting in *Heaven's Dog*"]. June 15, 2006.

Ji Yongqing. "Shanzhai zhongshengxiang: cong Shanzhai xianxiang kan zhongguoshi chuangxin" ["Panorama of Shanzhai: Chinese-style Innovation from the Perspective of the Shanzhai Phenomenon"]. *Sohu IT,* March 9, 2010. http://digi.it.sohu.com/20100309 /n270699087.shtml.

J. M. "The Chinese Dream: The Role of Thomas Friedman." *Analects* (blog) May 6, 2013. http://www.economist .com/blogs/analects/2013/05/chinese -dream-0.

jojo2046. "Zhongguo Hehuoren yu zhishi chanquan guansi *Chinese Partners* and Intellectual Property lawsuits." *Douban*

Dianying [Douban Movies], May 23, 2013. http://movie.douban.com/review /5986407/.

Kang Qinglian. "Fengkuang de Shitou weihe ruci fengkuang?" ["Why Is *Crazy Stone* So Crazy?"]. *Sichuan xiju* [Sichuan Drama] 1 (2007): 79–81.

Kaplan, Amy. "'Left Alone with America': The Absence of Empire in the Study of American Culture." In *Cultures of United States Imperialism,* edited by Amy Kaplan and Donald Pease, 3–21. Durham, NC: Duke University Press, 1993.

Keane, Michael. *Created in China: The Great New Leap Forward.* New York: Routledge, 2007.

kissinger. "Bao Shihong de laopo zhen biaozhi" ["Bao Shihong's Wife is So Beautiful"]. *Douban,* August 29, 2006. http:// movie.douban.com/review/1070051/.

Klein, Naomi. *No Logo: 10th Anniversary Edition.* New York: Picador USA, 2009.

Koopman, Robert, Zhi Wang, and Shang-Jin Wei. "The Myth of 'Made in China.'" *Foreign Policy* (June 10, 2009).

Kraidy, Marwan M. *Hybridity, or the Cultural Logic of Globalization.* Philadelphia: Temple University Press, 2007.

Lafraniere, Sharon. "Facing Counterfeiting Crackdown, Beijing Vendors Fight Back." *New York Times,* March 2, 2009. http://www.nytimes.com/2009/03/02 /world/asia/02piracy.html?_r=1&page wanted=all.

Lang Xianping. "Zhongguo zhizao zai haiwai" ["'Made in China' Overseas"]. *Caijing langyan* [Finance and Economics through Lang's Eyes]. Guangzhou: Guangdong Satellite, December 13, 2009. http://www.3a5a.com/caijing langyan/video_48.html.

Lao Meng. "Shanzhai chunwan jiemu zhengji" ["Shanzhai Gala Program Call"]. *Shanzhai chunwan guanfang*

Laomeng_xinlang boke [The Official Shanzhai Gala – Lao Meng's Blog on Sina.com], November 23, 2008. http:// blog.sina.com.cn/s/blog_045571650100 brs8.html.

Larson, Wendy. "Zhang Yimou's 'Hero': Dismantling the Myth of Cultural Power." *Journal of Chinese Cinemas* 2, no. 3 (2008): 181–196.

Lash, Scott, and Celia Lury. *Global Culture Industry: The Mediation of Things.* Cambridge: Polity, 2007.

Latour, Bruno. "Why Has Critique Run out of Steam? From Matters of Fact to Matters of Concern." *Critical Inquiry* 30 (Winter 2004): 225–248.

Leary, John, and Patrick Ma. "Luxury Brands Take on Landlords." *Financial Times,* January 25, 2006.

Lee, Benjamin, and Edward LiPuma. "Cultures of Circulation: The Imaginations of Modernity." *Public Culture* 14, no. 1 (2002): 191–213.

Lenin, Vladimir Ilyich. "Imperialism, the Highest Stage of Capitalism – A Popular Outline" (1916). Available at http:// www.marxists.org/archive/lenin /works/1916/imp-hsc/ch10.htm.

Leung, Helen Hok-Sze. "Unthinking: Chinese·Cinema·Criticism." *Journal of Chinese Cinemas* 1, no. 1 (December 2006): 71–73.

Leung, Helen Hok-Sze, and Audrey Yue. "Introduction: Chinese Cinemas as New Media." *Journal of Chinese Cinemas* 3, no. 1 (April 2009): 5–13.

Liang Jing. "Xiushui: hongsheng jingcheng yi tiao jie" ["Xiushui: A Street that Lights up the Capital City"]. *Jizhe guancha* [Reporters' Notes], February 15, 2000.

Liang, Lawrence. "Beyond Representation: The Figure of the Pirate." In *Making and Unmaking Intellectual Property: Creative Production in Legal and Cultural Perspective,* edited by Mario Biagioli,

Peter Jaszi, and Martha Woodmansee, 167–180. Chicago: University of Chicago Press, 2011.

Li Chun. "Toushi 'Xiushuijie' shangbiao jiufen" ["Probing the 'Silk Street' Trademark Dispute"]. *Zhongguo gongshang bao* (Beijing) [China Industry and Commerce News], July 1, 2004.

Li Dan. "Xiushuijie – Guojihua de gouwu zhi di" ["Silk Street – An Internationalized Shopping Destination"]. *Jingji ribao* (Beijing) [The Economic Daily], August 8, 2008.

Li Fang. "Xiushuijie: Gaige Kaifang de huohuashi" ["Xiushui Street: A Living Fossil for 'Reform and Opening Up'"]. *Diyi caijing ribao* (Beijing) [First Financial Daily], December 24, 2004. http://finance.sina.com.cn/review/20041224/04221247425.shtml.

Li, Henry Siling. "Popular Culture beyond the Fortress: Knock-Off Mobiles, Fake Celebrities and User-Created Videos." Paper presented at The Chinese Studies Association of Australia, Sydney, 2009.

Li, Hongmei. "Branding Chinese Products: Between Nationalism and Transnationalism." *International Journal of Communication* 2 (2008), 1125–1163. http://ijoc.org/ojs/index.php/ijoc/article/view/126/237.

Li Jiaoyan. "Zhongguo techan Xiushui 'xiu'" ["Chinese Special Goods 'Showing' at Silk Market"]. *Zhongguo zhiliang bao* (Beijing) [China Quality Daily], August 19, 2008.

Li Jinghua. "5 jia shijie zhuming pinpai gongsi zhuanggao Beijing Xiushuijie an zhong shen" ["Five Global Luxury Brands Filed a Lawsuit against Beijing's Silk Street and Won a Final Verdict"]. *Zhongguo guomen shibao* (Beijing) [China Gate Times], April 24, 2006.

Li Jing. "Xinshengdai nongmin gong qingku e shenghuo" ["New Generation of Peasant Workers' Simple and Austere E-Life"]. *Jisuanji shijie* [China Computer World], March 23, 2010.

Li, Jinying. "From D-Buffs to the D-Generation: Piracy, Cinema, and an Alternative Public Sphere in Urban China." *International Journal of Communication* 6 (2012): 542–563.

Li Junling, and Tao Yang. "Beijing Xiushuijie fengsha wuda jia mingpai" ["Beijing's Silk Street Bans Five Major Fake Brands"]. *Zhongguo shangbao* (Beijing) [China Business Herald], May 11, 2001.

Li Kun. "Xiushuijie: Cong jia mingpai dao zhen pinpai" ["Silk Street: From Fake Famous Brands to Real Quality Brands"]. *Beijing keji bao* [Beijing Sci-Tech Report]. August 25, 2008.

Li Lei. "Zhongguo dianying 'zhongguomeng' yao cong xianshi zuo qi" ["Chinese cinema's 'Chinese Dream' must start with reality"]. *Guangming ribao* [Guangming Daily]. Beijing, March 3, 2014.

——, ed. "Ruhe tisheng wenhua ruanshili" ["How to Enhance Cultural Soft Power"] *Renmin wang* [People Net], October 15, 2007. http://politics.people.com.cn/GB/30178/6486623.html.

Li Lingling. "Shanzhai wenhua: Web 2.0 shidai de caogen kuanghuan" ["Shanzhai Culture: Grass-Roots Carnival in the Age of Web 2.0"]. *Xinwenjie* [Press Circles] 1 (February 2009): 108–110.

Lim, Bliss Cua. *Translating Time: Cinema, the Fantastic, and Temporal Critique.* Durham, NC: Duke University Press, 2009.

Lin, Chun. *The Transformation of Chinese Socialism.* Durham, NC: Duke University Press, 2006.

Linden, Greg, Kenneth L. Kraemer, and Jason Dedrick. "Who Captures Value in a Global Innovation System? The case of Apple's iPod." Personal Computing Industry Center, University of California at Irvine, June 2007. http:// escholarship.org/uc/item/1770046n.

Lindsay, Greg. "China's Cell Phone Pirates Are Bringing Down Middle Eastern Governments." *Fast Company.* 2012. http://www.fastcoexist.com/1678136 /chinas-cell-phone-pirates-are-bringing -down-middle-eastern-governments.

Lindtner, Silvia. "Hackerspaces and the Internet of Things in China: How Makers are Reinventing Industrial Production, Innovation, and the Self." *China Information* 28, no. 2 (July 1, 2014): 145–167.

Lin, Yi-Chieh Jessica. *Fake Stuff: China and the Rise of Counterfeit Goods.* New York: Routledge, 2011.

——. "Knockoff: A Cultural Biography of Transnational Counterfeit Goods." PhD diss., Harvard University, 2009.

Liu Bo. "Waiguo pinpai Zhongguo dajia diyi'an, Beijing Xiushuijie baisu" ["First Case of Foreign Brands Cracking Down Fakes in China, Beijing's Silk Street Lost"]. *21 shiji jingji baodao* (Beijing) [21st Century Economic Report], April 21, 2006.

——. "Xiushuijie susong'an: weihu zhishi chanquan xin zhuzhang" ["The Silk Street Case: New Measures for Protecting IPR"]. *21 shiji jingji baodao* (Beijing) [21st Century Economic Report], January 16, 2006.

Liu Jia. "Guanzhong repeng Fengkuang de Shitou: youxiu guochanpian zhanying daidong guanying rechao" ["Audience Applauds *Crazy Stone*: 'Exhibition of Excellent Domestic Films' Stirred up Movie-Viewing Waves"]. *Zhongguo dianying bao* (Beijing) [China Film], July 6, 2006.

Liu Jing. "Jueqizhong de kunhuo: Shanzhai shouji jiang hequhecong?" ["Puzzle amid the Rise: What Course are Shanzhai Cell Phones to Follow?"]. *Guancha*

yu sikao [Observations and Thoughts] 17 (2008): 42–45.

Liu Jin. *Signifying the Local: Media Productions Rendered in Local Languages in Mainland China in the New Millennium.* Leiden: Brill, 2013.

Liu Min. "Xiushuijie shoujia an: shichang guanlizhe cheng dajia 'xin bazi'" ["Silk Street Fake-Selling Case: Market Management Became 'New Target' for Crackdowns"]. *Minying jingji bao* (Guangzhou) [Private Economy News], April 26, 2006.

Liu Qiang. "Yi 'xiao' bo 'da' chushou bufan" ["Use the 'Small' to Challenge the 'Big': A Skillful Opening Move"]. *Dianying pingjie* [Movie Review] 21 (2006): 28–30.

Liu Wanyong and Xinyu Zhou. "Xiushuijie miju" ["The Xiushui Street Conundrum"]. *Zhongguo qingnian bao* [China Youth Daily], July 14, 2004.

Li Xue. "Yingte puluo cangcu huiying Xiushui 'fengtan shijian'" ["IntellecPro Responds Hastily to Silk Street's 'Closure' Incident"]. *Renmin wang* [People Net], February 10, 2009. http://ip .people.com.cn/GB/8779125.html.

Li Yang. "Youxi: liudong de xiandaixing – cong Fengkuang de shitou dao Wo jiao Liu Yuejin" ["Game: the Liquidity of Modernity – From *Crazy Stone* to *I Am Liu Yuejin*"]. *Yishu pinglun* [Arts Criticism] 3 (2008): 54–56.

Li Yi. "Fengkuang de Shitou su qie zao" ["*Crazy Stone* Is Vulgar and Flippant"]. *Yishu pinglun* [Arts Criticism] 8 (2006): 27–29.

Lu, Hsiao-peng. "Historical Introduction: Chinese Cinemas (1896–1996) and Transnational Film Studies." In *Transnational Chinese Cinemas: Identity, Nationhood, Gender,* edited by Hsiao-peng Lu, 1–33. Honolulu: University of Hawaii Press, 1997.

Lull, James. *China Turned On: Television, Reform, and Resistance*. London: Routledge, 1991.

Lu Lu and Yang Xiang. "30 nian xiushui bianqian ji" ["The Thirty-Year Transformation of Xiushui"]. *Beijing jishi* [Beijing Document], 2009.

Luo De. "Zhongguo Hehuoren: Tujin de Shidai yu Fengkuang de Ziji" ["*American Dreams in China*: The Advancing Times and the Crazy Self"]. *Dongfang dianying* [Screen], 2013.

Luqiu Luwei. "Liaoliao Shanzhai" ["A Chat on Shanzhai"]. *Luqiu Luwei* (blog), January 4, 2009. http://blog .ifeng.com/article/1993312.html.

Lury, Celia. *Brands: The Logos of the Global Economy*. London: Routledge, 2004.

Lu Xinyu. "Ritual, Television, and State Ideology: Rereading CCTV's 2006 Spring Festival Gala." In *TV China*, edited by Ying Zhu and Chris Berry, 111–128. Bloomington: Indiana University Press, 2009.

Lu Xun. "Zhi Chen Yanqiao" ["To Chen Yanqiao"]. In *Lu Xun quanji* [Selected Works of Lu Xun], 12:390–392. Beijing: People's Literature Press, 1981.

MacFarquhar, Roderick. *Mao's Last Revolution*. Cambridge, MA: Belknap Press of Harvard University Press, 2006.

"Made in China Ads." YouTube video, 0:32. Posted by adamimg. December 1, 2009. http://www.youtube.com /watch?v=MINYux3mPUI&feature =youtube_gdata.

Ma Jie and Yilan Ding. "Fengkuang de Shitou: 'san wu' chanpin ruhe huoyi 300%" ["*Crazy Stone*: How Did a 'Three Nothing' Product Gain 300% Returns?"]. *Zhongguo dianying bao* (Beijing), [China Film], August 17, 2006.

Mao Zedong. "Mao Zedong: Wei Renmin Fuwu" ["Mao Zedong: Serve the People"]. September 8, 1944. Available at http://news.xinhuanet.com/ziliao /2004-06/24/content_1545077.htm.

Marquis, Chris, and Zoe Yang. "Chinese Dream? American Dream?" Danwei. com, June 28, 2013. http://www.danwei .com/a-tale-of-two-dreams/.

Martin, Randy. *Financialization of Daily Life*. Philadelphia: Temple University Press, 2002.

Marx, Karl. "Capital, Volume One." In *The Marx-Engels Reader*, edited by Robert C. Tucker, 294–438. 2nd ed. New York: W. W. Norton & Company, 1978.

Maskus, Keith E. *Intellectual Property Rights in the Global Economy*. Washington, DC: Institute for International Economics, 2000.

Ma Yan and Zhe Xue. "Cheshang chang shuanghuang shexia 'yilaguan' zhongjiang pianju" ["Con-Man Duo Set up 'Pull-Top Prize' Swindle on Bus"]. *Zhongguo shenzhen jingji wang* [China Shenzhen Economy Net], November 10, 2008. http://www.ceosz.cn/Area/lhsm /200811/Area_20081110110945_13201 .html.

May, Christopher. "The Denial of History: Reification, Intellectual Property Rights and the Lessons of the Past." *Capital & Class* 30, no. 1 (March 1, 2006): 33–56.

May, Christopher, and Susan K. Sell. *Intellectual Property Rights: A Critical History*. Boulder, CO: Lynne Rienners Publishers, 2006.

McGrath, Jason. *Postsocialist Modernity: Chinese Cinema, Literature, and Criticism in the Market Age*. Stanford, CA: Stanford University Press, 2008.

McIssac, Lee. "The City as Nation: Creating a Wartime Capital in Chongqing." In *Remaking the Chinese City: Modernity and National Identity, 1900–1950*, edited by Joseph Esherick, 174–191. Honolulu: University of Hawaii Press, 2000.

Meisner, Maurice J. *Mao's China and After: A History of the People's Republic.* 3rd ed. New York: Free Press, 1999.

Meng Bingchun. "Regulating egao: futile efforts of recentralization?" In *China's Information and Communications Technology Revolution: Social Changes and State Responses,* edited by Xiaoling Zhang and Yongnian Zheng, 52–67. London: Routledge, 2009.

Meng Yali. "Xiushui: Beijing aoyun de di 52 kuai jinpai – ji Xiushuijie de shangye yetai zhuanxing" ["Silk Street: The Fifty-Second Medal of the Beijing Olympics – On the Transformation of Silk Street's Business Model"]. *Zhongguo fangzhi* [China Textile & Apparel] 10 (2008): 76–78.

Metzger, Sean, and Olivia Khoo. "Introduction." In *Futures of Chinese Cinema: Technologies and Temporalities in Chinese Screen Cultures,* edited by Olivia Khoo and Sean Metzger, 11–34. Bristol, UK: Intellect, 2009.

Midler, Paul. *Poorly Made in China: An Insider's Account of the Tactics Behind China's Production Game.* Hoboken, NJ: Wiley, 2009.

Mignolo, Walter. *The Darker Side of Western Modernity: Global Futures, Decolonial Options.* Durham, NC: Duke University Press, 2011.

Miller, Toby, Nitin Govil, John McMurria, Richard Maxwell, and Ting Wang. *Global Hollywood 2.* London: BFI Publishing, 2005.

Morley, David. "Globalisation and Cultural Imperialism Reconsidered: Old Questions in New Guises." In *Media and Cultural Theory,* edited by James Curran and David Morley, 30–43. London: Routledge, 2006.

MuHe. "Fengkuang de Shitou de 'fengkuang' xianxiang" ["The 'Crazy' Phenomenon of *Crazy Stone*"]. *Zhongguo*

xinwen zhoukan [China Newsweek], July 18, 2006. http://yule.sohu.com /20060718/n244322608.shtml.

Naim, Moisés. *Illicit: How Smugglers, Traffickers, and Copycats Are Hijacking the Global Economy.* New York: Doubleday, 2005.

New Oriental Education and Technology Group. "Overview." 2009. http:// english.neworiental.org/Default.aspx ?tabid=3463.

Ning Hao. "Daoyan Ning Hao jiemi Fengkuang de Shitou" ["Director Ning Hao Decodes *Crazy Stone*"]. Netease.com. Made in China, August 23, 2009 http:// ent.163.com/09/0923/17/5JTPEQB 400033JON.html.

Ning Hao. "The Making of *Crazy Stone.*" n.d., DVD.

Niu Yanhong. "Wang Zili – Zhongguo diyi shewai shichang de 'yuhuo chongsheng'" ["Wang Zili – The Revival of China's No.1 Foreign-Directed Market"]. *Fangzhi fuzhuang zhoukan* [Textile Fashion Weekly], January 9, 2007.

Office of the United States Trade Representative. *Special 301 Report.* Office of the United States Trade Representative, 2009.

OlympicsOrBust: Silk Market Part 1. You Tube video, 9:56. Posted by Charleys Videos. September 10, 2008. http:// www.youtube.com/watch?v=fPj4e77 Enfc&feature=youtube_gdata.

Ong, Aihwa. *Flexible citizenship: The Cultural Logics of Transnationality.* Durham, NC: Duke University Press, 1999.

———. *Neoliberalism as Exception: Mutations in Citizenship and Sovereignty.* Durham, NC: Duke University Press, 2006.

"On the Brink." *Far Eastern Economic Review* 158, no. 7 (February 16, 1995): 54.

OpenV. "2005 nian chunjie lianhuan wanhui" ["The 2005 CCTV Gala"]. n.d.

http://t.openv.com/cctvspring/spring
_year_show_2005.html.

Organization for Economic Cooperation and Development. "Magnitude of Counterfeiting and Piracy of Tangible Products: An Update." Organization for Economic Cooperation and Development, November 2009.

Osnos, Evan. "The Long Shot." *The New Yorker,* May 11, 2009.

Palmer, Doug, and Melanie Lee. *Special Report: Faked in China; Inside the Pirates' Web.* Reuters.com, October 2010. http://www.reuters.com/article/2010/10/26/us-china counterfeit-idUSTRE 69P1AR20101026.

Palmer, Doug, and Rod Nickel. "U.S. to Appeal WTO Ruling against Meat Labels." *Reuters Canada,* March 23, 2012. http://ca.reuters.com/article/business News/idCABRE82M0NM20120323?pageNumber=2&virtualBrandChanne =0&sp=true.

Pang, Laikwan. "'China Who Makes and Fakes': A Semiotics of the Counterfeit." *Theory Culture Society* 25, no. 6 (2008): 117–140.

———. *Creativity and Its Discontents: China's Creative Industries and Intellectual Property Rights Offenses.* Durham, NC: Duke University Press, 2012.

———. *Cultural Control and Globalization in Asia: Copyright, Piracy, and Cinema.* London: Routledge, 2006.

———. "Piracy/Privacy: The Despair of Cinema and Collectivity in China." *boundary 2* 31, no. 3 (Fall 2004): 101–124.

———. "The Institutionalization of 'Chinese' Cinema as an Academic Discipline." *Journal of Chinese Cinemas* 1, no. 1 (December 2006): 55–61.

Panitchpakdi, Supachai, and Mark Clifford. *China and the WTO: Changing China, Changing World Trade.* Singapore: John Wiley & Sons (Asia), 2002.

Pan Qiwen. "Yiyuzhe yanzhong de zhongguo zhizao" ["'Made in China' in Foreigners' Eyes"]. *Zhongguo qingnian bao* (Beijing) [China Youth Daily], January 15, 2008.

Pease, Donald. "New Perspectives on U.S. Culture and Imperialism." In *Cultures of United States Imperialism,* edited by Amy Kaplan and Donald Pease, 22–37. Durham, NC: Duke University Press, 1993.

People's Daily. "Zhongguo Hehuoren – zhi women zhongjiang dida de zhongguomeng" [*"American Dreams in China – to Our Chinese Dream That Will Finally Arrive"*], May 24, 2013. http://news.xinhuanet.com/newmedia/2013 -05/24/c_124757652.htm.

People's Daily Online. "Silk Market Magnet for VIPs," August 12, 2008. http://english.people.com.cn/90001/6472727 .html.

Perkowski, Jack. "China Leads In Foreign Direct Investment." *Forbes,* November 5, 2012. http://www.forbes.com/sites/jackperkowski/2012/11/05/china-leads in foreign-direct-investment/.

Philip, Kavita. "What is a Technological Author? The Pirate Function and Intellectual Property." *Postcolonial Studies* 8, no. 2 (May 2005): 199–218.

Phillips, Tim. *Knockoff: The Deadly Trade in Counterfeit Goods; The True Story of the World's Fastest Growing Crime Wave.* London: Kogan Page, 2005.

Piao Haotian. "Fengkuang de Shitou zashang le Bannilu" ["Baleno Crushed by Crazy Stone"]. *Zhongguo pinpai* [China Brand], August 22, 2007.

Polidoro, Ronnie. "Apple CEO Tim Cook Announces Plans to Manufacture Mac Computers in USA." *Rock Center with Brian Williams,* December 6, 2012. http://rockcenter.nbcnews.com/_news /2012/12/06/15708290-apple-ceo-tim

-cook-announces-plans-to-manufacture
-mac-computers-in-usa?lite.

Pun, Ngai. *Made in China: Women Factory Workers in a Global Workplace.* Durham, NC: Duke University Press, 2005.

QiCaiZhiLang. "Tianna, shui shi xiongshou??? Qianshou guanyin de 21 min yanyuan zhong, juran you 18 ge shi yaowu zhilong de!!!" ["God, Who Is the Murderer? Eighteen Out of the Twenty-One Performers in 'Thousand-hand Kwan-Yin' Became Deaf Due to Medicines!!!"]. Tianya, August 15, 2006. http://www.tianya.cn/publicforum /content/free/1/774571.shtml.

Qi, Liuming. "Zhuazhu jiyu shixian Zhongguo chuangzao" ["Grasp the Opportunity to Achieve 'Created in China'"]. *Guangming ribao* (Beijing) [Guangming Daily], November 23, 2008. http://www.gmw.cn/01gmrb /2008-11/23/content_861805.htm.

Qiu, Jack Linchuan. *Working-Class Network Society: Communication Technology and the Information Have-Less in Urban China.* Cambridge, MA: MIT Press, 2009.

———. "Wangluo shidai de 'Shanzhai wen-hua'" ["Shanzhai Culture in the Network Age"]. *Ershiyi shiji* (Twenty-First Century) 112 (April 2009): 121–129.

Qu, Xuehun. "Daoge weishenme shibai yu hulianwang chuangye" ["The Reason Daoge Failed and Internet Entrepreneurship"]. *Qu Xuehun: Jinxing Zhixing* [Qu Xuehun: A Devoted Heart and An Intellectual Mind], 2006. http://blog .donews.com/azhai/archive/2006/09 /09/1033557.aspx.

Ren Hong. "Lizhi zongjingli jubao Xi-ushui taoshui 2 yi: Xiushui shichang lianye fouren" ["General Manager Who Resigned Discloses Silk Street's Tax Evasion, Market Denies Charges Over-night"]. *Beijing shangbao* [Beijing Business Today]. August 5, 2009. http:// business.sohu.com/20090805/n265 720667.shtml.

Renmin ribao [People's Daily]. "Aoyun guibin guang Xiushui" ["Distinguished Guests of the Olympics Stroll Down Silk Market"]. August 15, 2008. http://news .xinhuanet.com/world/2008-08/15 /content_9330465.htm.

Renmin wang [People Net]. "Fengkuang de Shitou zhaoliang Zhongguo dicheng-ben dianying shichang" ["*Crazy Stone* Lights up the Low-Budget Film Market of China"]. July 12, 2006.

———. "2008 Zhongguo 'Shanzhai' nian, meiti Shanzhai fengchao hen qiang hen badao" ["Two Thousand Eight, China's Year of 'Shanzhai': The Media Tide of Shanzhai Is Very Strong and Force-ful"]. January 19, 2009. http://media .people.com.cn/GB/40606/8693279 .html.

Rofel, Lisa. *Desiring China: Experiments in Neoliberalism, Sexuality, and Public Culture.* Durham, NC: Duke University Press, 2007.

Rosen, Philip. "Violence, State Theory, and Cinema Theory: Some Theses." Presented at the Society for Cinema and Media Studies Conference, New Orleans, March 11, 2011.

Rosen, Stanley. "The Wolf at the Door: Hollywood and the Film Market in China." In *Southern California and the World,* edited by Eric John Heikkila and Rafael Pizarro, 49–78. Westport, CT: Praeger, 2002.

Ross, Andrew. *Fast Boat to China: Ccor-porate Flight and the Consequences of Free Trade; Lessons from Shanghai.* New York: Pantheon Books, 2006.

Ryall, Tom. *Alfred Hitchcock & the British Cinema.* London: Croom Helm, 1986.

Schiller, Dan. "An Update on China in the Political Economy of Information and

Communications." *Chinese Journal of Communication* 1, no. 1 (January 2008): 109–116.

Schlesinger, Philip. "The Sociological Scope of 'National Cinema.'" In *Cinema and Nation*, 17–28. London: Routledge, 2000.

Seno, Alexandra A. "A Hong Kong Star Extends His Reach – Arts & Leisure – International Herald Tribune." *The New York Times*, October 12, 2006. http://www.nytimes.com/2006/10/12/arts/12iht-andylau.3139517.html?_r=0.

Shouji daigong wang [Mobile Phone Original Equipment Manufacturer Net]. "Shanzhaiji shinian fazhan licheng" ["A Ten-Year Developmental Path of Shanzhai Handsets"], March 13, 2009.

Shao, Xiaoli. "Dangnian Fengkuang de Shitou juben shencha yijian" ["Censors' Suggestions for the Script of *Crazy Stone* That Year"]. *Mtime*, December 26, 2009. http://group.mtime.com/shootinge/discussion/782985/.

shawnj. "Chaoxi nian – paoti mantan" ["The Year of Copying – An Off-Topic, Open-Ended Discussion"]. *Douban*, July 18, 2006. http://movie.douban.com/review/1058887/.

Shen, Jianli. "Duomian Xiushuijie – Getihu de mingyun bianqian" ["The Multi-Faceted Silk Street – Changing the Lives of Independent Entrepreneurs"]. *21 shiji jingji baodao* (Beijing) [Twenty-First Century Economic Report], December 16, 2008. http://news.qq.com/a/20081216/000667.htm.

Shen, Yanqi. "Mande'ersen Xiushui duzhan 'dajia'" ["Mandelson Oversees 'Fake Strikes' at Silk Street"]. *Beijing ribao* [Beijing Daily]. June 8, 2006.

Silk Street Market. "Silk Street Legends." Introduction to *Silk Street Market*, n.d.

Simone, Joseph. "Holding the Landlord Liable: New Tools for the Counterfeit Crackdown in China." *WIPO Magazine*, February 2008.

Simone, Joseph. "Silk Market Fakes – Light at the End of the Tunnel?" *China Business Review* 33, no. 1 (January 1, 2006).

Si Yu. "Ping Fengkuang de Shitou: yi xifang de mingyi chaoyue" ["On *Crazy Stone*: Transcendence in the Name of Parody"]. *Xin min zhoukan* [Xin Min Weekly], July 27, 2006.

Si Zhuang. "Cong Zhongguo zhizao dao Zhongguo chuangzao" ["From 'Made in China' to 'Created in China'"]. *Renmin ribao* (Beijing) [People's Daily], December 28, 2004. http://news.sina.com.cn/c/2004-12-28/04364644229s.shtml.

Smith, Neil. *American Empire: Roosevelt's Geographer and the Prelude to Globalization*. Berkeley: University of California Press, 2003.

Smith, Paul. *Clint Eastwood: A Cultural Production*. Minneapolis: University of Minnesota Press, 1993.

———. *Millennial Dreams: Contemporary Culture and Capital in the North*. London: Verso, 1997

———. *Primitive America: The Ideology of Capitalist Democracy*. Minneapolis: University of Minnesota Press, 2007.

Sohu.com. "Ning Hao Geren jianjie" ["Ning Hao Profile"]. August 22, 2008. http://yule.sohu.com/20080822/n259125342.shtml.

Sohu IT. "Most shocking Shanzhaiji." *Sohu IT*, 2008. http://it.sohu.com/s2008/3304/s260118816/.

Song Fagang. "Guozu rentong beihou de wenhua zifu – Zhongguo Hehuoren de jiazhi biaoda he xiuci liehen" ["The Cultural conceit behind National Identity: The Value Expression and Rhetorical Fissure in *American Dreams in China*"]. *Qingnian jizhe* [Youth Journalist] (January 2014).

Song Xiaobai. "Fengkuang de Shitaou: juyou Zhongguo tese de fuhe shehuizhuyi shichangjingji guilu de feichang shangye de leixing pian" ["*Crazy Stone:* A Very Commercialized Genre Film with Chinese Characteristics, Following the Rules of the Socialist Market Economy"]. *Sina,* April 18, 2006. http://club.ent.sina.com.cn/viewthread.php?tid=329287&highlight=%B7%E8%BF%F1%B5%C4%CA%AF%CD%B7.

Stemsel, George Stephen, ed. *Chinese Film: The State of the Art in the People's Republic.* New York: Praeger, 1987.

Su Juan. "Xiushuijie 'Ligui' zaoyu 'yang Likui'" ["'Li Gui' at Silk Street Meets 'foreign Li Kui'"]. *Zhongguo zhishi chanquan bao* (Beijing) [China Intellectual Property News], November 16, 2005.

Sun Chaoyang. "Bannilu, Pulada, A Huo B Huo" ["Baleno, Prada, luxury fantasy"]. *Sohu.com,* March 18, 2007. http://news.sohu.com/20070318/n248797283.shtml.

Sun Hui. "Guanzhu guochan shouji fazhan, tanqiu guochan shouji zouchuqu zhi lu" ["Concerning the Development of Domestic Handsets, in Search of Ways of Going Global"]. *Sina,* December 20, 2004.

Sun Ling. "Beijing Xiushui shichang: ruhe chongxian zuori huihuang" ["Beijing's Xiushui Market: How to Re-Create Yesterday's Glory?"]. *Zhongguo techan bao* (Beijing) [China Special Native Products], January 28, 2005.

Sun Liping. "Fengkuang de Shitou: guochan dianying cong shehua huigui pingmin" ["*Crazy Stone:* Domestic Cinema Returns from Luxury to the Common Folks"]. *Zhonghua xinwen bao* (Beijing) [China Press Journal], July 26, 2006.

Sun Shuyi. "Shida zhanlue: yinling Zhongguo zhizao zhuanxing Zhongguo chuangzao" ["Ten Major Strategies:

Leading the Transformation from 'Made in China' to 'Created in China'"]. *Zhongguo zhiliang wanlixing* [China Quality] (January 2008): 42–43.

Sun, Wanning. "Dancing with Chains: Significant Moments on China Central Television." *International Journal of Cultural Studies* 10, no. 2 (2007): 187–204.

Sun Wen. "Xiushuijie: xuxie chuanqi dongli hezai?" ["Xiushui Street: Where is the Motivation for Continuing the Legend?"]. *Huaxia shibao* (Beijing) [China Times], April 29, 2004.

Sun Yanbiao. "Shenzhen zaixian da heishouji fengbao, jingxiaoshang jinchan tuoke konggui yingdui" ["Shenzhen Re-Stirred the Storm of Black Cell Phone Crackdown, Dealers Responded with Empty Counters"]. *Diyi caijing ribao* [First Financial Daily], June 17, 2008.

Su Tong. "Cultural Resources, Creative Industries and the Long Economy." *International Journal of Cultural Studies* 9, no. 3 (2006): 307–316.

Tai Xing Xia Ke. "Shanzhai wenhua de minjian kuanghuan" ["The Popular Carnival of Shanzhai Culture"]. *Tai Xing Xia Ke* (blog), February 20, 2009. http://blog.sina.com.cn/s/blog_501ddf650100cc9m.html.

Tan Chee Beng. *Southern Fujian: Reproduction of Traditions in Post-Mao China.* Hong Kong: Chinese University Press, 2006.

Tang Min. "Renowned Market Faces Future Indoors, Big Move Planned for 'Silk Alley.'" *China Daily,* June 14, 1999.

Tan Mingyue. "Xiushuijie dajia bushi weile mingpai" ["Striking Fakes at Silk Street Not for Luxury Brands"]. *Jingji guancha bao* (Beijing) [Economic Observer News], April 24, 2006.

Tian Huiqun. "Zhongguo Hehuoren: Chuantong? Xiandai? Dongfang? Xifang?" ["*American Dreams in China:*

Tradition? Modernity? East? West?"].
Dangdai dianying [Contemporary Cinema] 7 (2013): 40–42.

TimeWarner. "China Film Group, Hengdian Group and Warner Bros. Pictures Partner to Create Warner China Film HG Corporation." TimeWarner Press Release, October 14, 2004.

Tomlinson, John. *Cultural Imperialism: A Critical Introduction.* Baltimore: Johns Hopkins University Press, 1991.

———. "Globalization and Cultural Identity." In *The Global Transformations Reader: An Introduction to the Globalization Debate,* edited by David Held and Anthony G. McGrew, 269–277. 2nd ed. Cambridge: Polity, 2003.

———. *Globalization and Culture.* Chicago: University of Chicago Press, 1999.

Tu Jianlu. "Mingjie tansuo: 'Xiushuijie' lu zai hefang" ["Exploring Famous Streets: Where is 'Xiushui Alley' Heading?"]. *Xinlang wang* [Sina.com], September 11, 2001. http://finance.sina.com .cn/b/20010911/106034.html.

United States Customs and Border Protection. *What Every Member of the Trade Community Should Know about: U. S. Rules of Origin – Preferential and Non-Preferential Rules of Origin.* Washington, DC, May 2004.

Virilio, Paul. *Speed and Politics: An Essay on Dromology.* Los Angeles: Semiotext(e), 2006.

Vukovich, Daniel. *China and Orientalism: Western Knowledge Production and the* PRC. New York: Routledge, 2012.

———. "Postcolonialism, Globalization, and the 'Asia Question.'" In *The Oxford Handbook of Postcolonial Studies,* edited by Graham Huggan, 587–604. Oxford: Oxford University Press, 2013.

Wallis, Cara. "'Immobile Mobility': Marginal Youth and Mobile Phones in Beijing." In *Mobile Communication: Bringing Us Together and Tearing Us Apart,* edited by Scott Campbell and Richard Seyler Ling, 61–81. New Brunswick, NJ: Transaction Publishers, 2011.

Wallis, Cara, and Jack Linchuan Qiu. "Shanzhaiji and the Transformation of the Local Mediascape in Shenzhen." In *Mapping Media in China: Region, Province, Locality,* edited by Wanning Sun and Jenny Chio, 109–125. London: Routledge, 2012.

Wall Street Journal. "Melamine Discovered in More Milk Products." October 2, 2008. http://online.wsj.com/article /SB122287248187494303.html.

Wang Chao. "Dianying shoufa de bentuhua – Fengkuang de Shitou yu Gai Liqi de yingpian bijiao fenxi" ["The Localization of Filmic Techniques – A Comparative Analysis of *Crazy Stone* and Guy Ritchie's Films"]. *Dianying pingjie* [Movie Review] 1 (2009): 51–52.

Wang Chunling. "Shanzhai wenhua de yousi" ["Troubled Thoughts on Shanzhai Culture"]. *Lingdao zhi you* [Friends of Leaders] 3 (2009): 39–40.

Wang Hui. *China's New Order: Society, Politics, and Economy in Transition.* Translated by Rebecca E. Karl. Cambridge, MA: Harvard University Press, 2003.

———. *Yazhou Shiye: Zhongguo Lishi de Xushu* [From An Asian Perspective: The Narrations of Chinese History]. Hong Kong: Oxford University Press, 2010.

Wang Jiamin and Mocang Han. "Bailing yong Fengkuang de Shitou duibai renao shangsi" ["White-Collar Employee's Use of *Crazy Stone* Dialogue Angered the Boss"]. *Shanghai qingnian bao* [Shanghai Youth Daily]. August 9, 2006.

Wang, Jing. *Brand new China: Advertising, Media, and Commercial Culture.* Cambridge, MA: Harvard University Press, 2007.

———. "Culture As Leisure and Culture As Capital." *positions: asia critique* 9, no. 1 (2001): 69–104.

———. "The Global Reach of a New Discourse: How Far Can 'Creative Industries' Travel?" *International Journal of Cultural Studies* 7, no. 1 (2004): 9–19.

Wang Naihua. "Fengkuang de Shitou yu xiju jingshen" ["*Crazy Stone* and the Spirit of Comedy"]. *Dianying wenxue* [Film Literature] 1 (2007): 13–15.

Wang Qian. "Lun changsuo tigongzhe goucheng shangbiao 'jianjie qinquan' de guize" ["On the Rules for 'Indirect Infringement' of Trademarks by Venue Providers"]. *Dianzhi zhishi chanquan* [Electronic Intellectual Property] 12 (2006): 47–51.

Wang Quan and Dongtian Xing, eds. "Shanzhai wenhua zongheng tan" ["An Open Discussion on Shanzhai Culture"]. *Shehui kexue luntan* [Tribune of Social Sciences] 2, no. 1 (2009): 56–90.

Wang, Shujen. "Big Shot's Funeral: China, Sony, and the WTO." *Asian Cinema* 14, no. 2 (Fall/Winter 2003): 145–154.

———. *Framing Piracy: Globalization and Film Distribution in Greater China*. Lanham, MD: Rowman & Littlefield, 2003.

Wang, Ting. "Global Hollywood and China's Filmed Entertainment Industry." PhD diss., Northwestern University, 2006.

———. "Understanding Local Reception of Globalized Cultural Products in the Context of The International Cultural Economy: A Case Study on the Reception of Hero and Daggers in China." *International Journal of Cultural Studies* 12, no. 4 (2009): 299–318.

Wang Wenzhong, Qiwen Liu, and Anqi Jiang. "Dianying Fengkuang de Shitou: yici chenggong de shangyepian tuwei" ["The Film *Crazy Stone*: A Successful Breakthrough by Commercial Films"]. *Dianying pingjie* [Movie Review] 22 (2006): 29–30.

Wangxiang dailiren [Agent of Delusion]. "Yangshi tuichu 'Zhongguo zhizao' xilie zao pengji" ["CCTV's 'Believe in Made in China' Series Attacked"]. *Guanjianzi zhadui'er* [Key Words Lumped Together], August 24, 2007. http://www.bullogger.com/blogs /judethefox/archives/93960.aspx.

Wang Xiaomei. "Tisheng 'Zhongguo chuangzao' yingdui jinrong weiji" ["Elevating 'Created in China' in Response to the Financial Crisis"]. *Zhongguo gongchandang xinwen wang* [China Communist Party News], March 23, 2009. http://cpc.people.com.cn/GB /64093/64103/9010385.html.

Wang Yan. "Houzhimin yujing xia de biaoshu jiaolu yu rentong weiji–jiedu dianying Zhongguo Hehuoren" ["The Expression of Anxiety and Identity Crisis in the Postcolonial Context: Interpreting the Film *American Dreams in China*"]. *Chuangzuo yu pinglun* [Creation and Criticism] 171 (August 2013): 84–88.

Wangyi. "Ninghao fouren Fengkuang de Shitou chaoxi Gai Ruiqi" ["Ning Hao Denies That *Crazy Stone* Copies Guy Ritchie"]. February 11, 2009. http://ent.163.com/09/0211/23/51TIPVV B000336A8.html.

Wang Yichuan. "Shidai jingshen de chouli yu bianxing" ["The Abstraction and Distortion of the Zeitgeist"]. *Dangdai dianying* [Contemporary Cinema] 7 (2013): 38–40.

Wang Ziye. "Chen Kexin tan Zhongguo Hehuoren" ["Chen Kexin on *American Dreams In China*"]. *Huohua* [Sparks] 7 (2013): 52.

Wan Xingya. "Xiushuijie baisu gei zhizao daguo de qishi" ["The Implication of Silk Street's Loss in Its Lawsuit for the Big Manufacturing Nation"]. *Zhonguo qingnian bao* (Beijing) [China Youth Daily], April 19, 2006.

Wark, McKenzie. *Virtual Geography: Living with Global Media Events.* Bloomington: Indiana University Press, 1994.

Watts, Jonathan. "Made in China: Tainted Food, Fake Drugs and Dodgy Paint." *The Guardian,* July 5, 2007. http://www.guardian.co.uk/business/2007/jul/05/china.internationalnews1.

Wei Xin and Dayong Zhu. "Fengkuang de Shitou piaofang tupo qianwan: yongduo guochanpian guanjun" ["*Crazy Stone* Box Office over Ten Million, Snatching the Championship for Domestic Films"]. *Chengdu ribao* [Chengdu Daily], July 16, 2006.

Wen Zhenhao. "Butong 'Xiushuijie' lunzhan shui qingquan" ["Different Versions of 'Xiushui Street': A Debate on Who Violates Rights"]. *Zhongguo zhishi chanquan bao* (Beijing) [China Intellectual Property News], July 29, 2005.

Williams, Holly. "Counterfeit China: Fake Goods Rife." *Sky News,* August 8, 2008. http://news.sky.com/story/625068/counterfeit-china-fake-goods-rife.

Williams, Linda. "Discipline and Fun: *Psycho* and Postmodern Cinema." In *Reinventing Film Studies,* edited by Linda Williams and Christine Gledhill, 351–378. London: Arnold, 2000.

Williams, Rosalind H. *Dream Worlds: Mass Consumption in Late Nineteenth-Century France.* Berkeley: University of California Press, 1982.

World Intellectual Property Organization. "Understanding Copyright and Related Rights," n.d. http://www.wipo.int/edocs/pubdocs/en/intproperty/909/wipo_pub_909.pdf.

World Trade Organization. "10 things the WTO can do." World Trade Organization, 2015. https://www.wto.org/english/res_e/publications_e/wtocan_e.pdf.

Wu Jing. "Fengkuang de Shitou daoyan shuo: Feng Xiaogang de youmo wo bugan bi" ["Director of *Crazy Stone,* Ning

Hao, says: I Can't Compete with Feng Xiaogang's Humor"]. *Huanqiu renwu* [Global People] (August 2006): 71–73.

Wu Kun. "Xianshi zhuyi de yulehua biaoda" ["The Expression of Realism through Entertainment – Is *Crazy Stone* 'Vulgar and Flippant'?"]. *Dianying wenxue* [Film Literature] 23 (2008): 113–115.

Wu Xiaogeng. "Toushi wenlu – guanyu yingpian Fengkuang de Shitou" ["Dropping a Stone for Directions: About the Film *Crazy Stone*"]. *Wenhua yishu bao* (Xi'an) [Culture and Arts News], September 20, 2006.

Wu Yue San Ren. "Shanzhai wenhua shi yizhong fanshi zhuanhuan" ["Shanzhai Culture is a Paradigm Shift"]. *Dongfang zaobao* (Shanghai) [Oriental Morning Post], December 25, 2008.

Xiao Dan. "Beijing Xiushuijie dongshizhang bei zhi taoshui 2 yi: shuiwuju cheng wei jie jubao" ["Chairman of Beijing's Silk Street Accused of CNY200 Million Tax Evasion, Taxation Affairs Claimed Report Never Received"]. *Beijing chenbao* [Beijing Morning Post], August 7, 2009. http://news.sohu.com/20090807/n265773325.shtml.

Xia Zhongmin. "'Shanzhai' wenhua de chuanboxue jiedu" ["A Decoding of Communication in 'Shanzhai' Culture"]. *Jin chuanmei* [Today's Mass Media] 4 (2009): 20–21.

Xie Lan. "Fengkuang de Shitou: yichang xianshi zhuyi de hongtangdaxiao" ["*Crazy Stone*: A Great Laugh of Neo-Realism"], *Xinwen chenbao* [Shanghai Morning Post]. Shanghai, July 16, 2006. http://old.jfdaily.com/gb/node2/node17/node33/node90102/node90113/userobject1ai1404145.html.

Xi Jinping. "Xi Jinping canguan Fuxing Zhilu zhanlan jianghua yuanwen" ["The Original Text for Xi Jinping's Speech at the Road to Revival Exhibition"].

Huainan City Science and Technology Bureau, December 4, 2012.

Xi Xiao Tang. "Wangyou ping 08 wei 'Shanzhai nian,' shida Shanzhai shijian chulu" ["Net Friends Designated Year 08 as 'The Year of Shanzhai,' Ten Shanzhai Events Revealed"]. *Xi Xiao Tang's Blog,* December 18, 2008. http://blog .sina.com.cn/s/blog_49f28d6d0100 b7uk.html.

Xinhua. "'Shanzhai': Faking it for money or fun?" *China Daily* (Beijing), December 9, 2008.

Xinwen lianbo [Network News Broadcast], "Shanzhai shouji jin xinwen lianbo le" ["Shanzhai Cell Phones Got into Network News Broadcast"], December 2, 2008.

Xiushui Shichang [Silk Street Pearl Market]. "Xiushuijie juxing baohu zhishi chanquan biaozhang dahui" ["Silk Street Holds Awards Ceremony for IPR Protection"], February 1, 2008.

Xiushuijie [Silk Street]. "Xiushuijie shichang chui xiang ying aoyun 'ji- jiehao'" ["Silk Street Market Blows the 'Assembly Bugle' to Welcome the Olympics"]. *Xinlang Boke* (blog), January 25, 2008.

Xiushui xinwen [Silk Street News]. "Guanyu Wang Zili jubao shijian de jingji shengming" ["Urgent Notice Regarding Wang Zili's Disclosure Incident"], August 6, 2009.

Xiushui xinwen [Silk Street News]. "Xiushui aoyun zhuanti baodao: Meiguo qian zongtong lao bushi zhixin Xiushuijie biaoshi ganxie" ["Silk Street Olympics Special Reports: Former U.S. President Bush Wrote a Letter to Silk Street Expressing Gratitude"], October 9, 2008.

Xu, Gary G. *Sinascape: Contemporary Chinese Cinema.* Lanham, MD: Rowman & Littlefield, 2007.

Xue Song. "Xinchanbu cheng bufa shouji xin paizhao, 3G shouji wu paizhao menkan" ["Ministry of Industry and Information Technology Claims It Will Issue No More New Mobile Phone Licenses, 3G Phones Have No More License Hurdles"]. *Netease,* June 24, 2004. http://mobile.163com /04/0624/16/0PLGHRCM0011179K .html.

Xun Jingjing. "Jingji weiji xia Zhongguo zhizao de weiji yu chulu" ["The Crisis and Resolution of 'Made in China' in the Economic Crisis"]. *Shengchanli yanjiu* [Study of Productivity] 3 (2009): 113–115.

Xu Xin. "Fengkuang de Shitou 'nishi' zouhong" ["*Crazy Stone* Becomes Popular Against All Odds"]. *Renmin ribao* (Beijing) [People's Daily], July 16, 2006.

Yang Yin. "Wo lai shoushuo Fengkuang de Shitou" ["My Comments on Crazy Stone"]. *Bu erduo de gushi* [Stories of Wooden Ears], August 11, 2006. http:// blog.sina.com.cn/s/blog_48d303 f10100051k.html.

Yajun. "Chaode! Gemen'er, fengkuang de shitou shi zui yunong ren de zuopin" ["Copied! Bro, Crazy Stone Is the Most Deceptive Work. One Can Never be So Shameless"]. *Sina Forum,* December 21, 2006.

Yang, Fan. "China's 'Fake' Apple Store: Branded Space, Intellectual Property and the Global Culture Industry." *Theory, Culture & Society* 31, no. 4 (July 2014): 71–96.

——. "The Politics of Exhibition: China's 'fake' in the 2008 Beijing Olympics." *antiTHESIS* 19 (June 2009): 56–70.

Yang, Guobin. "Power and Transgression in the Global Media Age: The Strange Case of Twitter in China." In *Communication and Power in the Global Era: Orders and Borders,* edited by Marwan M.

Kraidy, 166–183. London: Routledge, 2012.

———. *The Power of the Internet in China: Citizen Activism Online*. New York: Columbia University Press, 2009.

Yeh, Emilie Yueh-yu, and Darrell William Davis. "Re-nationalizing China's film industry: Case Study on the China Film Group and Film Marketization." *Journal of Chinese Cinemas* 2, no. 1 (2008): 37–51.

Yimin. "Yingping xinshang: Fengkuang de shitou" ["Film Review: An Appreciation of *Crazy Stone*"]. *Gotoart*, June 25, 2009.

Yin Xiaolin, and Shixiang Li. "Zhongguo zai quanqiu toufang xingxiang guanggao, zhanxian zhongguo zhizao shijie hezuo" ["China Projects Image Ad Globally, Displaying Made in China, Made with the World"]. *Renmin ribao* (Beijing) [People's Daily], December 1, 2009.

Yu Guoping. "Xiushuijie: bumai jiahuo xing bu xing" ["Xiushui Street: Is It Possible Not to Sell Fake Products?"]. *Zhongguo shangbao* (Beijing) [China Business Herald], February 11, 2003.

Yu, Haiqing. "From Active Audience to Media Citizenship: The Case of Post-Mao China." *Social Semiotics* 16, no. 2 (June 2006): 303–326.

Yu Hua. *China in Ten Words*. Translated by Allan Hepburn Barr. New York: Pantheon, 2011.

Yu Sui. "Fengkuang de Saiche: Shanzhai dianying guodu de shechi jingpin" ["*Crazy Racer*: Luxury Product of the Shanzhai Film Kingdom"]. *Yingping wang* [Film Review Net], December 28, 2008. http://yingpingwang.com/guo-nei-dianying-130.html.

Yuan Jiafang. "'Xiushui' yinggai shi shuide?" ["To Whom Should 'Xiushui' Belong?"]. *Zhonghua shangbao* [China Trademark] 1 (2000): 9.

Yuan Zhe. "Jingji banxiaoshi: Fengkuang de Shitou wei he fengkuang" ["Half-Hour Economy: Why Is '*Crazy Stone*' Crazy?"]. News. *Xinhua wang* [Xinhua Net], July 25, 2006.

Yuchen. "[Zhuanti] Fengkuang de Shitou huo fengkuang de chaoxi?" ["Repost: *Crazy Stone* or Crazy Copying?"]. *Gansu ribao* [Gansu Daily], July 17, 2006.

YunQingCheng. "Wo 'Shanzhai' gu wo zai" ["I Shanzhai, Therefore I Am"]. *Beijing qingnianbao* [Beijing Youth Daily]. November 6, 2008. http://blog.163.com/qq109083304@126/blog/static/731503722008109924117/.

Zeng Gaofei. "Tianyu: 'Shanzhaiji' moshi cheng diyu yangpinpai yitianjian?" ["Tianyu: Has the 'Shanzhaiji' Model Become the Weapon to Counter Foreign Brands?"]. *Zhongguo qiye bao* [China Enterprise News], July 18, 2008.

Zhang Bangsong and Huajun Ning. "Shanzhai shouji chanye diaocha" ["Shanzhai Cell Phone Industry Investigation"]. *Xinshiji zhoukan* [News Magazine, a.k.a. Century Weekly], July 20, 2008. http://business.sohu.com/20080721/n258273650.shtml.

Zhang Huiyu, ed. "Dangdai dazhong wenhua zhong de Meiguo xiangxiang" ["The 'American' Imaginary in Contemporary Popular Culture"]. *Wenyi lilun yu piping* [Literary Theory and Criticism] 5 (2013): 43–52.

———, ed. "Zai fansi 'Meiguomeng' zhong renshi Zhongguo" ["Understanding China by reflecting on the 'American Dream'"]. *Hongqi Wengao* [Red Flag Manuscript] 17 (2013): 8–13.

Zhang Jie. "Fengkuang de shitou: dianying yuyan de kuanghuan" ["*Crazy Stone*: The Carnival of Cinematic Language"]. *Dianying pingjie* [Movie Review] 8 (2007): 41.

Zhang Li. "Xiushuijie beipan qingquan 'Bei Mian' fushi shangbiao" ["Silk Street Held to Infringe 'North Face'

Apparel Trademark"]. *Zhongguo jingying bao* (Beijing) [China Trade News], November 1, 2007.

Zhang Qianqian. "Cong 'Zhongguo zhizao' dao 'Zhongguo chuangzao' haiyou duoyuan" ["How Far is it from 'Made in China' to 'Created in China'?"]. *Zuowen chenggong zhi lu* [The Path to Success in Essay Writing] (September 2008): 45.

Zhang, Rui. *The Cinema of Feng Xiaogang: Commercialization and Censorship in Chinese Cinema after 1989.* Hong Kong: Hong Kong University Press, 2008.

Zhang, Xudong. "Nationalism, Mass Culture, and Intellectual Strategies." In *Whither China: Intellectual Politics in Contemporary China*, 315–348. Durham, NC: Duke University Press, 2001.

——. "Zhang Xudong tan Zhongguomeng: zhongyu daole keyi tan mengxiang de shike" ["Zhang Xudong on the Chinese Dream: Finally It Is Time to Talk of Dreams"]. *Shehui guancha* [Social Outlook], 2013. http://www.guancha.cn /zhang-xu-dong/2013_07_11_156654 .shtml.

Zhang Xuemin. "Cong Fengkuang de Shitou shilun Zhongguo dianying de fazhan" ["A Discussion on the Development of Chinese Cinema, Drawing on *Crazy Stone*"]. *Dianying wenxue* [Film Literature] (October 2007): 64.

Zhang Yanguo. "'Zhongguo jueqi' de minzu yuyan: dianying Zhongguo Hehuoren de yishixinagtai jiangou celue" ["A National Allegory of 'China's rise': The Strategy of Ideological Construction in *American Dreams in China*"]. *Dianying wenxue* [Movie Literature] 24 (2013): 79–80.

Zhang, Yingjin. *Chinese National Cinema.* New York: Routledge, 2004.

——. *Cinema, Space, and Polylocality in a Globalizing China.* Honolulu: University of Hawaii Press, 2010.

——. "Playing with Intertextuality and Contextuality: Film Piracy on and off the Chinese Screen." In *Cinema, Law, and the State in Asia*, edited by Corey K. Creekmur and Mark Sidel, 213–230. New York: Palgrave Macmillan, 2007.

——. *Screening China: Critical Interventions, Cinematic Reconfigurations, and the Transnational Imaginary in Contemporary Chinese Cinema.* Ann Arbor, MI: Center for Chinese Studies, 2002.

Zhang Yiwu. "Yingxiong: xinshiji de yinyu" ["HERO: A Metaphor for the New Century"]. *Wenhua yanjiu* [Cultural Studies] 4 (July 25, 2003). http:// www.pkucn.com/redirect.php?tid =21635&goto=lastpost.

Zhang Zhen, ed. *The Urban Generation : Chinese Cinema and Society at the Turn of the Twenty-First Century.* Durham, NC: Duke University Press, 2007.

Zhao Ailing. "Xiushuijie yuanhe baisu?" ["Why did Silk Street lose?"]. *Zhongguo duiwai maoyi* [China's Foreign Trade] 6 (2006): 70–73.

Zhao, Juan, ed. "Fengkuang de Shitou" ["On *Crazy Stone*"]. *Dangdai dianying* [Contemporary Cinema] 5 (2006): 15–20.

Zhao Xia. "Xiushui shichang zai diaocha" ["Re-investigating the Silk Market"]. *Zhonghua gongshang shibao* (Beijing) [China Business Times], July 4, 2006.

Zhao, Yuezhi. "China's Quest for 'Soft Power': Imperatives, Impediments and Irreconcilable Tensions?" *Javnost – The Public* 20, no. 4 (2013): 17–30.

——. *Communication in China : Political Economy, Power, and Conflict.* Lanham, MD: Rowman & Littlefield, 2008.

——. "The Media Matrix: China's Integration into Global Capitalism." In *Socialist Register 2005: The Empire Reloaded*, edited by Leo Panitch and Colin Leys, 65–84. London: Merlin Press, 2004.

http://socialistregister.com/index.php
/srv/article/view/5831/2727#.VOzUxXb
MtNE.

——. "The Struggle for Socialism in
China: The Bo Xilai Saga and Beyond."
Monthly Review, October 2012. http://
monthlyreview.org/2012/10/01/the
-struggle-for-socialism-in-china/.

Zheng Junna. "Shanzhai shouji weihe
shou nongmingong xiongdi qinglai?"
["Why are Shanzhai Handsets Favored
by Peasant Workers?"]. *OK Shouji Wang*
[OK Cell Phone Net], January 8, 2011.

Zhi Qiu and Changchun Li. "Xiushuijie de
bian yu bubian" ["The Change and Continuity of Xiushui Street"]. *Zhongguo
guomen shibao* (Beijing) [China Inspection and Quarantine Times], November
26, 2004. http://info.yipu.com.cn/news
/focus/2004-11-30/20041130C203056
.html.

Zhongguo funu bao [China Woman]." Xiushuijie: nengfou chongfu zuotian de
gushi" ["Xiushui Street: Can Yesterday's
Story be Repeated?"], December 27,
2004.

Zhongguo fushi bao [China Fashion
Weekly]. "Beijing Xiushuijie deng
lingshou shichang yu Ouzhou mingpai
qianding dajia xieyi" ["Beijing's Silk
Street and Other Retail Markets Signed
'Fake Strike' Agreement with European
Luxury Brands"]." June 16, 2006.

Zhongguo guangbo wang [China Broadcasting Net]. "'Shouji zhong de zhandouji'
anran pojiang, bodao jiannan shengcun"
["'The Fighter Jet of Handsets' Forced
to Land, Bird Struggles to Survive"],
July 31, 2012. http://finance.cnr.cn/gs
/201207/t20120731_510417765.shtml.

Zhongguo xiaofeizhe bao [China Consumer News]. "Beijing Xiushuijie, zuotian
de chuanqi" ["Beijing's Xiushui Street:
Legends of Yesterday"]. January 8, 2005.
http://www.efu.com.cn/data/2005
/2005-01-08/79750.shtml.

Zhong Xiang. "Fengkuang de Shitou, feng-
kuang de yinyue" ["*Crazy Stone*, Crazy
Music"]. *Guangbo gexuan* [Broadcast
Music Choice], 2006.

Zhou Renjie, Xiaolin Zeng, and Tianzeng
Jing. "Jingji banxiaoshi: jiemi shouji
Shanzhaiji shichang" ["Economic Half-
Hour: Revealing the Cell Phone Shanzhaiji Market"], CCTV.com, June 10,
2008. http://money.163.com/08/0610
/05/4E282R3300252KFB.html.

Zhou Xinyu and Wanyong Liu. "Xiushui
miju zai diaocha" ["Re-investigating
the Xiushui Street Conundrum"].
Renmin wang [People Net], July 28,
2004. http://people.com.cn/BIG5
/shehui/8217/34282/34284/2670734
.html.

Zhuang Jun. "Xindushi lizhipian de xiandai tujing – yi Zhongguo Hehuoren
wei li" ["The Modern Vision of New
Urban Motivation Films – The Example
of *American Dreams in China*"]. *Changchun shifan daxue xuebao* [Journal of
Changchun Normal University] 33,
no. 2 (March 2013): 199–200.

Zhu, Ying. *Chinese Cinema during the Era
of Reform: The Ingenuity of the System.*
Westport, CT: Praeger, 2003.

Zhu Yuqing, and Ruoyi Wang. "Xiao
zhizuo bo da shichang" ["Small Production Plays Big Market"]. *Zhongguo
dianying bao* (Beijing) [China Film],
July 20, 2006.

Index

Beijing Planning Commission, 141
Beijing Yelusheng Commerce and Trade
 Ltd., 140
"Believe in Made in China" campaign,
 45, 53
belonging, 7, 8
Berry, Chris, 99
Bhabha, Homi, 40, 113, 117
Big Shot's Funeral (film, dir. Feng Xiao-
 gang, 2001), 230n124
bloggers, 53, 106, 121, 127
"Bloody Case that Started with a Steamed
 Bun, The" (video, dir. Hu Ge, 2006), 65,
 97, 222n6
Bo Xilai, 128, 129, 235n223, 243n139
Bolter, J. David, 81, 101
Bongiorni, Sara, 31–32, 35, 41, 43, 44–46,
 48, 57
Boss brand, 138
Bourdieu, Pierre, 233n188
bourgeoisie, national, 26, 59
brands, 15–16, 23; "brand" effect in Chinese
 cinema, 105; brand loyalty, 41, 51–52;
 capital accumulation and, 40, 170; fake
 luxury brands, 28; foreign versus local,
 124; "global brands versus Silk Street"
 lawsuit, 154–160; "Silk Street" brand,
 144, 149, 151; social imaginary and, 170;
 state support for national brands, 71;
 time-honored brands of Beijing (*Beijing
 laozhihao*), 148; "virtual," 60
Britain, colonial empire of, 173, 174
Burberry brand, 153
Bush, George H. W., 151, 152, 239n74
Bush, George W., 39
"Buy American" movement, 33, 36

Cai Guoqiang, 1
Calhoun, Craig, 49
Callahan, William, 189, 192
Cantonese dialect, 65, 228n89
capital movement, 2, 35, 58
capitalism, 21, 52, 75, 170, 190; in binary
 with socialism, 20; China's revolutionary past as challenge to, 25; film/video

piracy and, 99; "higher time" of, 60,
 222n107; imperialism and, 6; interests
 of capitalists and the nation, 58; People's Republic of China integrated into,
 92; postmodernism and, 127; print capitalism, 6, 40; reification of, 13; "virtual
 capitalism," 60
Castoriadis, Cornelius, 13, 48, 179
CCTV (China Central Television), 45, 46,
 48, 73, 175; *Annual Economic Figures*,
 61; changes during Reform years, 52,
 80; monopoly status, 52–53; national-
 developmentalism and, 89; Shanzhai
 discourse and, 66, 80–87, 199; Silk
 Street Market reports, 152; Spring Festival Gala, 232n166; as target of online
 parody and mockery, 53
Cell Phone (film, dir. Feng Xiaogang,
 2003), 231n148
cell phones, knockoff. *See* Shanzhaiji
 ("bandit cell phones")
censorship, 93
Chan, Peter, 181, 188, 190, 191
Chanel brand, 153
Chang'An Avenue (documentary on Silk
 Street), 152, 240n84
Chatterjee, Partha, 24
Chemise Lacoste company, 161
Chen Kaige, 92, 113, 222n6
China: "authoritarian" practices in, 32, 81–
 82; "century of humiliation" from imperialism, 175, 177; deterritorialization of,
 92, 167; economic restructuring of, 4;
 emerging middle class of, 176, 234n197;
 export industries, 50, 51; global reputation as thief, 3; imperial/dynastic, 174,
 243n14; newspaper reportage in, 110,
 229n120; peasant uprisings in history
 of, 70, 78; postsocialism and decolonial-
 ity, 20–25; Republican/Nationalist era
 (1911–1937), 47, 94, 239n69; rise as piracy
 and counterfeiting nation, 19; U.S. trade
 deficit with, 35, 38; as world's second
 largest economy, 2
China Bird (*Bo Dao*) mobile handset, 73

FAN YANG is Assistant Professor in the Department of Media and Communication Studies at the University of Maryland, Baltimore County.